THE
TOLKIEN
FAN'S
MEDIEVAL
READER

selected by
Turgon of TheOneRing.net

About the Author

Turgon has been reading and studying the writings of J. R. R. Tolkien since the 1960s. He is one of the founding members of the Green Books section at TheOneRing.net, the premier Tolkien website. His column, Turgon's Bookshelf, includes book news, reviews and interviews with leading Tolkien scholars. It has been a regular feature at Green Books since August 1999. Turgon is also a co-author of *The People's Guide to J. R. R. Tolkien* (Cold Spring Press, 2003). He lives with his family in Chicago, Illinois.

THE TOLKIEN FAN'S MEDIEVAL READER

selected by
Turgon of TheOneRing.net
(David E. Smith)

Cold Spring Press

𝕮old 𝕾pring 𝕻ress

P.O. Box 284, Cold Spring Harbor, NY 11724
E-mail: Jopenroad@aol.com

Acknowledgements

Thanks go to Jonathan Stein of Cold Spring Press, to Professor Verlyn Flieger for the Foreword, and to Douglas A. Anderson for supplying copies of two chapters from *The Story of Alexander*. I am also grateful to the Regenstein Library at the University of Chicago for the loan of some rare materials, and to the Newberry Library. Last a thanks for inspiration goes to Professors Tom Shippey and Jane Chance.

Contents

⊕ ⊕ ⊕

To all of my friends at TheOneRing.net:
Anwyn, Ostadan, Quickbeam, Tookish and WeeTanya, of Green Books
Calisuri, Corvar, Tehanu and Xoanon, the Founders
Balin, Jincey and the rest of the staff

And to Saxony:

"Loke, dame, to-morwe þatow be
Riȝt here vnder þis ympe-tre,
& þan þou schalt wiþ ous go,
& liue wiþ ous euer-mo."

"The squirrels, in their multifarious errands, had by way of the winds so
informed the Priest of Spiders, and the moon in turn, hurrying through
the night sky, beamed forth his benediction to the Queen of Oil."

FOREWORD

by Verlyn Flieger

Author of *Splintered Light: Logos and Language in Tolkien's World; A Question of Time: J.R.R. Tolkien's Road to Faerie;* and co-editor of *Tolkien's Legendarium: Essays on the History of Middle-earth*

When I first read *The Lord of the Rings* in the winter of 1957 I was, of course, overwhelmed by Tolkien's imaginative power, the beauty and terror of his world, and its capacity to convey a reality that was at once wonderfully strange and recognizably familiar — a reality that seemed more real than everyday life. I knew right away the book was unique; what I didn't at first recognize was that it was also firmly seated in a rich medieval tradition. However, when I got to Rohan, the medieval roots were unmistakeable. This was the culture of *Beowulf* and the early Anglo-Saxon period in English history and poetry. The Riders, their names, their poetry and customs, the Hall of Meduseld, the ageing Theoden — all were immediately recognizable, old friends I was delighted to meet again. "Wow," I thought. "This Tolkien knows what he's talking about."

It's then that, had there been one, I would have welcomed a volume like the present book, a gathering of the major medieval sources and exemplars that could have enlarged my burgeoning awareness of the breadth of Tolkien's knowledge and his ability to adapt his medieval sources and reform them to fit his own needs. Unfortunately, there wasn't then such a book. Now there is, and the overlapping worlds of Tolkien scholarship and fandom must be everlastingly grateful to Turgon for pulling together and presenting under one cover such a rich compendium of medieval narrative.

These are texts that Tolkien knew intimately, that he lived with, studied, taught, edited, translated, and absorbed into his imagination as a sponge absorbs water. That imagination transformed as well as taking in, so that the material, when it flowed out again onto the manuscript pages that became *The Lord of the Rings*, was no longer simply borrowings from medieval sources, but had been woven deep into the fabric of his own Middle-earth. It belonged there.

This book is a feast of medieval narrative from all over the Northern European and British worlds, cooked up by authors known and unknown out of the plentiful ingredients of myth and legend and folktale, and beautifully served for the pleasure and enlightenment of the contemporary reader.

Enjoy.

INTRODUCTION

Over the years Tolkien's fondness for and indebtedness to medieval literature has often been mentioned. His special devotion to older Germanic literature, including *Beowulf* and the *Eddas*, has long been known, for as a professor he taught these works in addition to teaching the languages in which they were written. But the number of Tolkien's general readers who are themselves familiar with classics such as these seems much smaller than it might be. This anthology has been compiled in the hope of sharing the pleasures of these —and other— classics of medieval literature that were part of Tolkien's professional life and inspirations to him in his creative work.

Tolkien taught at Leeds University in the north of England from 1920 through 1925, and at Oxford University from 1925 until his retirement in 1959. Over a teaching career spanning nearly forty years, he specialized in Old English, Middle English and Old Norse. This book presents selections in five major categories, the first three being the areas of Tolkien's professional expertise. The fourth section, Celtic, is a subject which Tolkien did not teach, but one in which he was certainly learned. So too with Finnish, the final category.

All of the translations included in this anthology were taken from the public domain. For many works there were multiple translations to select from, and in each case I have chosen one that seemed to me the best and most readable translation. For the most part, I have also preferred prose versions, though nearly all of the selections chosen for the Old English and Middle English sections were originally written as verse. To readers being introduced for the first time, say, to the story of *Sir Gawain and the Green Knight*, the intricate Middle English verse forms, unfamiliar to modern readers, may be seen as a stumbling block, even in the excellent verse translation by Tolkien himself. As with *Beowulf* when it was recited in mead-halls a thousand years ago, it helps to know the basic story to beforehand. Once the story itself is familiar, one can then better appreciate the way in which any particular poet chose to tell it.

Each section is headed with a short introduction that discusses Tolkien's relation to the subject and to the particular works included in that section. The translations have been very slightly edited—that is to say, while nothing has been cut out, some of the more excessive archaisms have smoothed over and replaced with more modern terms, and some of the names have been regularized according to current norms and standards.

This book is intended as an introduction to certain medieval works, not as an endpoint in itself. I encourage readers who appreciate these selections to seek out further translations, either ones more modern academically, or verse translations (like Tolkien's own) which reproduce the original form and meter. Recommendations for wider reading among medieval literature can be found in Tom Shippey's short essay "Tolkien's Sources: The True Tradition" (Appendix I, pp. 343-352) in his excellent study *The Road to Middle-earth*.

—Turgon

1. OLD ENGLISH

The Old English period ranges from around the fifth or sixth centuries, when the Germanic tribes known as the Angles, Saxons, and Jutes settled in the island of Britain, through roughly the twelfth century, with the demise of Anglo-Saxon culture brought about by Duke William of Normandy's defeat of Harold II at the Battle of Hastings in 1066, and the subsequent arrival of a Norman French aristocracy.

The Germanic tribes evidently had a rich poetic tradition, but it was all oral, and most Old English literature that survives today comes from manuscripts dating from late in the Old English period, around the year 1000. These manuscripts were mostly compiled by religious clerics in monasteries, as the people of the country were at that time being converted to Christianity. Hence much of the poetry shows a Christian influence mixed in with the heroic themes of pre-Christian times.

Tolkien knew Old English literature preeminently well, studying it very closely and teaching it for most of his life. The jewel of Old English literature is the poem *Beowulf*, the only extensive poem in Old English that survives, and that in a single manuscript. Tolkien spent much of his life working on various aspects of this poem about a hero named Beowulf who fights two monsters (Grendel and his mother) and, in old age, a dragon. Tom Shippey has appropriately singled out Beowulf as "the single work which influenced Tolkien most." (Shippey, *The Road to Middle-earth*, p. 344.) Tolkien's 1936 lecture to the British Academy, "Beowulf: The Monsters and the Critics," is considered a landmark in the criticism of the poem, for Tolkien's view of it as an artistic creation in its own right, rather than as a confused assemblage from different literary traditions, revolutionized the study of the poem. Tolkien's essay is most easily found collected in *The Monsters and the Critics and Other Essays* (1983), edited by Christopher Tolkien. This volume also includes Tolkien's essay "On Translating Beowulf," which originally appeared as prefatory remarks to a 1940 edition of John R. Clark Hall's prose translation of *Beowulf and the Finnesburg Fragment*, revised by Tolkien's colleague C. L. Wrenn.

Tolkien lectured for many years at Leeds and at Oxford on Old English literature, and some of his lecture materials have been published posthumously. These include *The Old English 'Exodus'* (1981), edited by Joan Turville-Petre, *Finn and Hengest: The Fragment and the Episode* (1982), edited by Alan Bliss, and *Beowulf and the Critics* (2002), edited by Michael D. C. Drout. The Old English poem "Exodus" is an incomplete epic about the Biblical crossing of the Red Sea by the Israelites— an original work and not merely an account lifted from the Old Testament. Tolkien's edition includes the text of the Old English poem, Tolkien's prose translation, and his commentary.

Finn and Hengest concerns two fifth-century figures, especially as to what we know of them through a section of *Beowulf* (the "Episode of King Finn" about one-third of the way through the poem), and through a short fragment of a poem usually referred to as "The Finnesburg Fragment." The references to Finn and Hengest are obscure and incomplete, and Tolkien's lecture notes reconstruct their stories with supporting material from a wide range of early Germanic histories and legends. Tolkien's editions (in Old English) of the fragment and the episode, and his prose translations of them, are also included in the book.

Beowulf and the Critics is the longer lecture series from which Tolkien redacted his essay "Beowulf: The Monsters and the Critics." Thus this longer work covers much of the same ground, but more expansively and in greater detail.

For this volume I have selected the original John R. Clark Hall prose translation of *Beowulf,* and I have also included his prose translation of "The Finnesburg Fragment." Of Old English "elegaic" poetry, I have included prose versions of "The Wanderer" and "The Seafarer." In the 1930s Tolkien worked closely with his friend E. V. Gordon to prepare editions of these poems, but they were never published (Chance. *Tolkien the Medievalist,* p.19). Both poems concern solitary wayfarers and contain rich imagery.

I have included a verse version of "The Battle of Maldon," another fragmentary poem. The battle described in the poem took place in August 991 between some Viking raiders and the local Anglo-Saxons of Essex led by their duke, Beorhtnoth, who was killed in the battle. The poem is considered by some to be one of the finest expressions of the Germanic heroic spirit. The verse version included herein attempts to reproduce in modern English the alliterative stresses of the original, wherein each poetic line consists of two half lines, each with two stresses (and with varying unstressed syllables). Tolkien was inspired by this poem to write a verse sequel, the drama "The Homecoming of Beorhtnoth, Beorhthelm's Son," first published in 1953 but most widely available in *The Tolkien Reader*. Tolkien's work can be viewed as a meditation on the faults of the heroic spirit.

In a few places, incomplete lines in the original texts have been rendered in this book with a series of ellipses."

There are many translations of *Beowulf*. Most recently, Seamus Heaney's *Beowulf: A New Verse Translation* (2000) won the prestigious Whitbread Book of the Year Award. The Penguin edition, published simply as *Beowulf* (1995) and edited by Michael Alexander, has the Old English text on one page with each word glossed on the facing page, which makes for an especially interesting reading experience. R. M. Liuzza's *Beowulf: A New Verse Translation* (2000) is a very accessible one, with much extra background material, including an appendix with samples from twenty different *Beowulf* translations showing how each one dealt with the same section of the poem. Tolkien's own translation of *Beowulf* remains unpublished.

There are also many worthy samplers of other Old English literature, including R. K. Gordon's *Anglo-Saxon Poetry* (rev. ed. 1954), which translates much of the verse as prose, and Charles W. Kennedy's *An Anthology of Old English Poetry* (1960), which translates the verse into a form suggestive of the original alliterative rhythms. Richard Hamer's *A Choice of Anglo-Saxon Verse* (1970) has the Anglo-Saxon verse on one page, with a facing page verse translation.

BEOWULF

translated by John R. Clark Hall (1911)

Lo! We have heard of the glory of the Spear-Danes' warrior-kings in days of yore – how the princes did valorous deeds!

Often Scyld of the Sheaf took mead-benches away from troops of foes, from many tribes. The noble inspired awe! After he was first found helpless he met with consolation for that, increased under the heavens and throve in honor, until each one of those who dwelt around, across the whale's road, had to serve him, and to pay him tribute. A noble king was he!

Later, a son was born to him, a young child in his castle, whom God had sent the people for their help; He knew of the profound distress which they, lacking a lord, long suffered in the past. To him, therefore, the Prince of Life, the glorious Ruler, granted worldly honor; Beowulf, the son of Scyld, had high repute, his fame spread widely in the Scedelands. So shall a young man compass in noble wise, by splendid money-gifts amongst his father's friends, that afterwards, in later years, willing companions may stand by him, – the folk may do him service when war comes. By commendable deeds a man may grow in power in any of the tribes!

Then, at the fated hour, Scyld, full of exploits, departed, to go into the keeping of the Lord; and they, his fast friends, carried him to the water's edge, as he himself had asked when he, protector of the Scyldings, still wielded his words. Dear prince of his country, for long he held sway. There, at the landing-place, the ring-prowed vessel lay, the prince's ship, sheeny and eager to start. They laid then the beloved chieftain, giver-out of rings, on the ship's bosom – the glorious hero by the mast. There were brought many treasures; ornaments from far-off lands. Never have I known a keel more fairly fitted out with war-weapons and battle-trappings, swords and coats of mail. Upon his breast lay many treasures, which were to travel far with him into the power of the flood. Certainly they furnished him with no less of gifts, of tribal-treasures, than those had done who, in his early days, started him over the sea alone, child as he was. Moreover, they set besides a gold-embroidered standard high above his head, and let the flood bear him, – gave him to the sea. Their soul was sad; their spirit sorrowful. Who received that load, men, chiefs of councils, heroes under heaven, cannot for certain tell!

Then in the strongholds was Beowulf of the Scyldings, dear king of the nation, long time renowned among peoples, – the prince his father had gone elsewhere from the earth, – until the noble Healfdene was born to him. While he lived, old and fierce in battle, he ruled the Scyldings graciously. To him awoke into the world four children in succession, Heorogar, captain of armies, and Hrothgar and Halga the Good. I have been told that . . . was Onela's queen, the cherished consort of the warrior-Scylfing.

Then was success in war granted to Hrothgar, glory in battle, so that his faithful tribesmen served him willingly, till the young warriors increased, a mighty troop of men.

It came into his mind that he would order men to build a hall-building, – a festive-chamber greater than the sons of men had ever heard of – and therewithin to give all things to young and old, whatever God had given him, except dominion and the lives of men.

Then on all sides I heard the work was being put on many a tribe throughout this middle-earth, – to adorn the people's hall. In time – quickly among men – it befell that the greatest of palace-halls was quite ready for him. He who by his word had empire far and wide, devised for it the name of Heorot. He did not break his promise, but gave out ornaments and treasure at the banquet.

The hall towered, lofty and wide-gabled, – it awaited the hostile surges of malignant fire. Nor was it long time after that the murderous vindictiveness twixt son-in-law and father-in-law was to arise, – the sequel to a deadly quarrel.

Then the mighty spirit who dwelt in darkness bore angrily the grievance, that he heard each day loud revelry in hall; there was the sound of the harp, the bright song of the minstrel.

He who could recount the origin of men from distant ages spoke, – he said that the Almighty made the earth, the beauteous plain which water belts around, and, triumphing in power, appointed the effulgence of the sun and moon as light for the land-dwellers, and decked the earth-regions with leaves and branches, and fashioned life for all the kinds that live and move.

So then brave men lived prosperously in joys, until a certain fiend of hell began to compass deeds of malice.

The grim stranger was called Grendel, the well-known border-haunter, who held the moors, the fen and fastness; the hapless being occupied a while the lair of monsters, after the Creator had banished them. On Cain's kindred did the everlasting Lord avenge the murder, for that he (Cain) had slain Abel. He (Cain) had no joy of that feud, but he, the Creator, drove him far from mankind for that misdeed. Thence all evil broods were born, monsters and elves and hell-devils, – giants also, who long time fought with God, for which he gave them their reward.

So, after night had come, he (Grendel) went to the lofty house, to find out in what sort the Ring-Danes had quartered in it after their beer-carouse. Then found he therewithin a band of noble warriors, sleeping after the banquet; they knew not sorrow, the sad lot of mortals.

Soon was the grim and greedy-demon of destruction, wild and furious, afoot, and seized thirty thanes in their resting-place. Thence started he off again, exulting in plunder, to go home, and to seek out his abode with that fill of slaughter.

Then in the morning light, at break of day, was Grendel's war-craft manifest to men; then was a wail, a mighty cry at morn, upraised after the meal. The famous prince, the long-distinguished chieftain, sat downcast, the strong man suffered, he endured sorrow for his lieges, when they surveyed the traces of the foe, the evil spirit; that anguish was too strong, too loathly and long-lasting.

There was no longer respite, but after one night he again contrived more deeds of murder, –had no regret for violence and outrage – he was too deep in them. Then was the man easy to find who sought elsewhere a more remote resting-place for himself, a bed among the out-buildings, when the hall-warder's hate had been declared to him, and truthfully made known by a clear token. He who escaped the fiend kept himself afterwards farther and more secure.

So then he (Grendel) was master, and strove, opposed to right, one against all; until the best of houses stood unoccupied.

It was a long while, twelve winters' space, the Scyldings' guardian endured distress – all sorts of woes, of ample sorrows – because it was then without concealment known to sons of men – sadly in song – that Grendel fought from time to time against Hrothgar, – kept up hate-begotten feuds, outrage and enmity for many years – continual strife, – and would not make peace with any man of Danish stock, avert the peril of death, or stay for tribute, – nor could any of the notables there expect a brilliant rescue from the murderer's hands.

But the demon, the dark death-shadow, kept pursuing young and old; laid wait for and entrapped them. Night after night he held the misty moors, – men know not where such sorcerers go in their wanderings.

So many outrages, severe afflictions, did the foe of man, the fearful solitary, achieve in quick succession. Heorot, he held, the gold-bespangled hall, on the dark nights. He (Hrothgar) could not visit that royal seat, that precious possession, because of the Creator, nor did he know His purpose.

That was great sorrow, breaking of heart, to the guardian of the Scyldings. Many a mighty one sat oft in council, pondered about help, – what it were best for men of courage to contrive against the sudden terrors. Sometimes they vowed sacrifices at idol-temples, – prayed aloud that the Destroyer of souls would provide them help against the national distress. Such was their custom, – the hope of the heathen, – they remembered hell in the thoughts of their hearts. They knew not the Creator, Judge of deeds; they knew not the Lord God, nor verily had they learned to worship the Protector of the heavens, the glorious Ruler.

Woe is his who is destined in dire distressful wise to thrust his soul into the fire's embrace, to hope for no comfort, in no way to change.

Weal is his, who may after his death-day stand before the Lord, and claim a refuge in the Father's arms!

Thus with the trouble of the times seethed ever and anon the son of Healfdene, the wise prince could not ward off the plague; the suffering which had befallen the people, the fiercely grim, enforced distress, greatest of night evils, was too severe, too loathly and long-lasting. This – the deeds of Grendel – a thane of Hygelac, excellent among the Geats, – he who was strongest of mankind in might in this life's-day, noble and stalwart, – heard of in his fatherland.

He bade make ready for himself a good wave-traverser, – said he would seek the warrior-king, the noted prince, over the swan's-road, since he (Hrothgar) was in need of men. Prudent folk did not blame him at all for that expedition, though he was dear to them; they egged on the stout-hearted one, and looked for favorable omens. The hero had chosen champions from the people of the Geats, from the keenest he could find; as one of fifteen he took ship; skilled in sea-craft, he himself pointed out the land-marks.

Time passed on; the bark was on the waves, the boat under the lee of the cliff. The warriors, equipped, stepped on to the prow; currents churned, sea against sand; men bore into the bosom of the ship bright armor, splendid war-gear; the heroes, the warriors on their willing adventure, shoved off the vessel of braced timbers. Then the foamy-necked floater, most bird-like, started off over the billowy sea, urged onwards by the wind, until in due time on the second day the curved prow had journeyed on so far that the voyagers saw the land, the sea-cliffs, glisten – the steep mountains, the bold promontories. Then was the sea traversed, the voyage at an end.

After that the people of the Weders went quickly up on to dry land, they made fast the ship; their corslets, their battle-dress, rattled; they thanked God that for them the sea-paths had been easy.

Then from the rampart the watchman of the Scyldings, who had to guard the sea-cliffs, saw them lift bright shields and trim war-harness over the gangway. In the thoughts of his mind he was bursting with curiosity as to who these men were. Then he, Hrothgar's officer, went off to ride on his horse to the shore; mightily he shook the strong spear-shaft in his hands, and asked in words of parley: "Who are ye, clad in the harness of such as bear arms, who have thus come and brought a towering ship over the water-ways, a ring-prowed bark hither over the seas? I have been acting as coast-guard, I kept watch over the shore, so that on Danish land no enemy might do us harm by naval harryings. No strangers have ever begun to land here more coolly with their shields, – nor did ye know at all the pass-word of men at arms, the permission of kinsmen. Never have I seen a mightier noble upon earth, a warrior in armor, than is one of you; that is no retainer dignified by weapons, unless his countenance, his peerless form, belies him.

"Now, I must know your origin, ere ye go further, as faithless spies, on Danish ground. Now, ye strangers from far, ye sea-traversers, hear my plain opinion; to make known whence your coming is, quickness is best!"

To him answered the chieftain; the leader of the troop unlocked his store of words: "We are people of the Geatish nation and hearth-companions of Hygelac. My father was renowned among the folk, a noble prince named Ecgtheow. He tarried many winters before he, an old man, passed away from his dwelling; each of the wise men far and wide throughout the earth recalls him readily. We have come to seek thy lord, the son of Healfdene, the protector of the people, with honorable intent; give us good counsel! We have a great errand to the famous Ruler of the Danes, nor shall aught of it be kept secret, as I think.

"Thou knowest if it is so, as verily we heard say, that among the Scyldings some foeman, some secret ravager, exhibits terribly in the dark nights malignity untold, carnage and crushing shame, I can give Hrothgar good counsel about this, with generous mind, – how he, the wise and good, may overcome the fiend; whether for him the torment of afflictions should ever cease, salvation come at last, and the seethings of care wax cooler; or he should ever hereafter endure a time of tribulation – crushing misery, long as the best of houses lasts there in its lofty place."

The watchman, bold retainer, answered where he sat on his horse: "The keen shield-warrior, who judges well, shall know the difference between the two – your words and deeds. I gather that this is a company friendly to the lord of the Scyldings. Pass forth, bearing your weapons and armor, I will guide you. Moreover, I will bid my comrades honorably guard against all enemies your ship, your fresh-tarred vessel, on the beach, until at last the wooden craft with twisted prow bears the beloved man back to the Weders' confines over the eddying seas. To such a well-intentioned man will it be granted that he shall get through the rush of battle whole."

They set out then to journey on; the vessel remained still, the roomy-breasted ship rode on the painter, held by its anchor. Above the cheek-guards shone the boar-images; covered with gold, gleaming and fire-hardened, the boar held ward. The men hastened; bent on the fray, they pushed along; they went together until they could descry the timbered hall, handsome and gold-adorned, which was for earth-dwellers the most pre-eminent of buildings under heaven; in which the Ruler dwelt, – its radiance gleamed o'er many lands. Then did the bold in battle point them out the radiant dwelling of brave men, that they might go straight thither. War hero as he was, he headed his horse round, and then he spake this word: "It is time for me to depart. May the Almighty Father keep you safe in your adventures by His grace. I will to the sea, to keep ward against hostile bands."

The road was paved, the path kept the men together. When they went thence to the Hall in their dread armor, each corslet, hard and hand-locked, glistened, each gleaming ring of iron chinked in their harness. Sea-weary, they put their broad shields, their trusty bucklers wondrous hard, against the palace wall; then seated they themselves upon the bench; the corslets, war-dress of the heroes, rang; the spears were piled together, the war-gear of the sea-men, – the ashen wood, gray at the tip. The iron-clad troop was well supplied with weapons.

There, then, a stately warrior asked the troopers of their race: "Whence have ye brought these plated shields, these hauberks gray and visored helmets, this pile of battle-shafts? I am Hrothgar's herald and officer. I have never seen so many foreigners more bold. I ween you have sought out Hrothgar, not from exile, but from valor and from loftiness of soul!"

Then the (hero) renowned in strength answered him; the proud leader of the Weders, hardy under his helmet, rejoined in speech: "We are Hygelac's table companions. Beowulf is my name. I wish to tell my errand to the son of Healfdene, the famous prince thy master, if he will grant us that we may speak with his gracious self."

Wulfgar replied (he was a chief of the Wendels; his nature, his prowess and wisdom were well known to many): "I will ask the Protector of the Danes, the Lord of the Scyldings and giver of rings, the illustrious prince, as thou makest request, concerning thy expedition, and will forthwith announce to thee the answer which the prince thinks fit to give me."

Then he returned quickly to where Hrothgar sat, old and hoary, with his suite of nobles; the valiant one went on until he stood before the shoulders of the Danish lord, – he knew the usages of court. Wulfgar outspoke to his beloved lord: "People of the Geats, come from far, over the seas, have voyaged hither; the warriors call their chief Beowulf. They make request that they may now exchange words with thee, my Ruler. Refuse them not thy conversation, gracious Hrothgar! In their war-trappings they seem worthy of the high esteem of nobles. Assuredly the chief is doughty who has led these battle-heroes hither."

Hrothgar, the Scyldings' shield, replied: "I knew him when he was a youth. His ancestor was called Ecgtheow; Hrethel the Geat gave him his only daughter into his household; his son has now come boldly here, and visited a trusty friend. Moreover, sea-farers, who carried thither costly presents for the goodwill of the Geats, used to say this –that he, the famed in battle, had in his grip of hand the force of thirty men. The holy God has of his mercy sent him to us West-Danes, as I hope, to meet the plague of Grendel. I shall proffer the chieftain treasures for his bravery. Do thou make haste; bid thou the banded brotherhood come in together for me to see. Tell them besides in words that they are welcome to the Danish people."

Then to the hall-door Wulfgar went, and brought the message from within: "My conquering lord, chief of the Eastern Danes, bade me inform you that he knows your noble blood, and that ye men of brave intent are welcome to him hither over the sea-billows. Now may ye go and see Hrothgar in your fighting raiment, under your war-masks; let your battle-shields and your wooden spear-shafts await here the issue of the parley."

Then the chieftain rose with many a warrior round him, — a picked band of followers; some waited there and guarded the accouterments, as the brave man directed them. Together they hastened them forward under the roof of Heorot, the warrior guiding them. The valiant one advanced, hardy under his helmet, until he stood within the chamber.

Beowulf spake, the corslet on him shone, the armor-net linked by the skill of the smith: "Hail to thee, Hrothgar! I am Hygelac's kinsman and warrior-thane. I have in my youth undertaken many deeds of daring. Grendel's doings became plainly known to me in my fatherland. Sea-farers say that this hall, this most noble building, stands empty and useless to every man after the evening sun has become hidden under the vault of heaven.

Then my people, the best folk, wise men, advised me thus, lord Hrothgar, —
that I should visit thee, because they knew the hugeness of my power; they had
themselves observed, when, battered by foes, I returned from the fight, where I
bound five, laid low a brood of giants and slew by night sea-monsters on the waves;
I suffered direful straits, and avenged the attacks upon the Weder Geats — they
courted trouble — I ground down the adversaries. And now I will decide the matter
alone against the wretch, the giant, Grendel!

"Now therefore I will beg of thee one boon, thou Ruler of the glorious Danes,
protector of the Scyldings. Do not refuse me this, defense of warriors, nation's
kindly Lord, now I am come thus far; — that I alone, with my band of noble
warriors, this troop of hardy men, may purge Heorot. Moreover, I have learnt that
in his rashness the monster recks not of weapons. Hence — so that Hygelac, my
prince, may be glad at heart on my account, I renounce this — that I should bear
a sword, or ample shield, or yellow buckler to the fray; but with the fiend I'll close
with grip of hand, and struggle about life, foe against foe.

"He whom death carries off shall resign himself to God's judgment. I doubt it
not that if he may prevail, he will eat fearlessly the Geatish folk in the war-hall, as
he has often done the flower of the Hrethmen.

"Thou wilt have no need to cover my head, for he will have me, blood-
bespattered, if death seizes me. He will bear off the bloody corpse, will set his mind
upon devouring it. The lonely one will feast unpityingly, and stain his swamp-lair;
— no longer wilt thou need to care about my body's sustenance. If battle takes me,
do thou send Hygelac this best of war-dresses, most excellent of corslets, which
protects my breast; it is Hrethel's legacy, the work of Weland. Wyrd goes ever as it
must!"

Then Hrothgar, protector of the Scyldings, spake: "My friend Beowulf, thou
hast sought us for defensive combat, and for kindly help. Thy father brought about
by fight the greatest of feuds; he was the hand-slayer of Heatholaf among the
Wylfings; then the people of the Weder Geats might not harbor him, from fear of
war. Thence went he to the South Danes' folk, the honored Scyldings, over the
surging of the waves, when I first ruled the people of the Danes, held in my younger
days the gem-decked treasure-burg of heroes, when Heorogar, my elder brother, the
son of Healfdene, was dead and lifeless. He was better than I! I settled afterwards the
feud with money. I sent old treasures over the sea's ridge to the Wylfings. He
(Egtheow) swore oaths to me.

"It is a grief to me in my soul to tell any man what Grendel with his thoughts
of hate has framed for me in Heorot of harm and sudden harassings. My chamber-
guard, my war-band is diminished. Fate (Wyrd) swept them off into the fearsome
toils of Grendel. Still, God can easily restrain the wild ravager from his deeds!

"Full often fighting men, elate with beer, pledged themselves over the ale-cup
that they would await in the beer-hall the combat with Grendel with terrible swords.
Then at morning-time, when day shone forth, was this mead-hall, this chamber for
retainers, stained with gore — all the bench-boards deluged with blood, the hall with

gore of swords. Through that I possessed the fewer trusty followers, dear warriors, for that death had taken them away. Sit now at the banquet and open thy mind, thy war-fame unto men, as inclination moves thee."

Then a bench was cleared in the beer-hall for the Geat-men, all together; thither went the bold ones to sit, exulting in strength. A servant did his office, who bare in his hands an overlaid ale-cup, and poured out the bright liquor. Now and again a minstrel sang, clear-voiced in Heorot. There was revelry among the heroes, — no small company of Danes and Weders.

Then Unferth, the son of Ecglaf, who sat at the feet of the lord of the Scyldings, spoke, and gave vent to secret thoughts of strife, — the journey of Beowulf, the brave sea-farer, was a great chagrin to him, for he grudged that any other man under heaven should ever obtain more glory on this middle-earth than he himself.

"Art thou that Beowulf who strove with Breca, contended with him on the open sea, in a swimming contest, when ye two for vainglory tried the floods, and ventured your lives in deep water for idle boasting? Nor could any man, friend or foe, dissuade you from your sorry enterprise when ye journeyed on the sea; when ye compassed the flowing stream with your arms, meted out the sea-paths, battled with your hands, and glided over the ocean; when the sea, the winter's flood, surged with waves. Ye two toiled in the water's realm seven nights; he overcame you at swimming, he had the greater strength. Then, at morning time, the ocean cast him up on the Heathoræmas' land. Thence, dear to his people, he sought his beloved fatherland, the land of the Brondings, his fair stronghold-city, where he had subjects and treasures and a borough. The son of Beanstan performed faithfully all that he had pledged himself to. So I expect for thee a worse adventure, — though thou hast everywhere prevailed in rush of battle, gruesome war, — if thou darest await Grendel at close quarters for the space of a night."

Beowulf, son of Ecgtheow, replied: "Well, my friend Unferth, thou hast talked a great deal, drunken with beer, concerning Breca, and hast said much about his adventure! In sooth I maintain that I had more strength in swimming, more battling with waves, than any other man.

"When, we were subalterns, we two agreed and pledged ourselves, — we were both then still in the time of youth — that we would venture our lives out on the sea, and that we did, accordingly. When we swam on the sea we had a naked sword, rigid in hand; we thought to guard ourselves against whales. He could not by any means float far from me on the flood-waves, swifter on the sea than I; I would not go from him. Thus we two were together on the sea for the space of five nights, till the flood, the tossing seas, the bitter-cold weather, the darkening night, drove us apart, and the fierce north wind turned on us, — rough were the waves. The wrath of the sea-fishes was aroused; then my corslet, hard and hand-locked, furnished me help against the foes; the woven shirt of mail, adorned with gold, covered my breast. A spotted deadly brute dragged me to the bottom, the grim beast had me fast in his grip; still, it was granted to me that I might strike the monster with my sword-point, with my fighting weapon; the force of battle carried off the sea beast by my hand.

"Thus did the miscreants press me hard and often. With my dear sword I served them out, as was befitting. The base destroyers did not have the pleasure of that feast, —that they might eat me, — sit round the banquet at the sea-bottom; but at morning they lay wounded by cutlasses, up along the foreshore — dispatched by swords — so that henceforth, they could not hinder sea-farers of their passage over the deep water-way. The sun, bright beacon of God, came from the east; the waters assuaged, so that I could descry sea-headlands, weather-beaten cliffs. Often Wyrd saves an undoomed earl, if his courage is good! Well, it was granted me to slay nine sea-monsters with my sword! Never have I been told of harder struggle at night under the vault of heaven, nor of a man in greater straits on ocean streams. Yet I endured the grip of the monsters with my life whole, weary of my enterprise. Then the sea bore me, the flood, by its current, the surging ocean, to the land of the Finns.

"I have never heard such contests, such peril of swords related about THEE. Never yet did Breca, at the battle play, nor either of you, perform so bold a deed with shining swords. . . . I do not boast much of that; though thou wast the slayer of thy brothers — thy blood relations; for that thou shalt bear punishment in hell, good though thy wit may be. In truth I tell thee, son of Ecglaf, that Grendel, the frightful demon, would never have done so many dread deeds to thy prince, such havoc in Heorot, if thy heart, thy spirit, were so warlike as thou sayest thyself. But he has found out that he need not too much dread the antagonism, the terrible sword-storm of your folk, the Victor-Scyldings. He takes pledges by force, spares none of the Danish people; but he fights for amusement, kills and feasts, and reeks not of the opposition of the Spear-Danes.

"Now, however, I shall quickly show him the strength and courage, the war-craft of the Geats. Afterwards — when the morning-light of another day, the ether-clad sun, shines from the South over the sons of men — let him who may go boldly to the mead-drinking!"

Then the giver of treasure, gray-haired and famed in battle, was in joyful mood; the prince of the Glorious Danes counted on help; the shepherd of the people heard from Beowulf his firm resolve.

There was laughter of warriors, song sounded forth, the words were joyous. Wealhtheow, Hrothgar's queen, went forth, mindful of court usage; gold-adorned, she greeted the men in hall, and then, as wife free-born, gave the cup first to the hereditary ruler of the East-Danes, and bade him be joyful at the beer-drinking, lovable to his people. He, the victorious king, partook in gladness of the feast and hall-cup.

Then the lady of the Helmings went round every part of the hall, to seniors and juniors; proffered the costly goblet; until occasion came that she, the diademed queen, ripe in judgment, bore the mead-cup to Beowulf. She greeted the prince of the Geats, and thanked God, discreet in speech, in that her desire had been fulfilled, that she might look to some warrior for help from these attacks.

He, death-dealing fighter, received the cup from Wealhtheow, and then discoursed, eager for the fray. Beowulf, son of Ecgtheow, said: "When I went on the sea and sat me in the sea-boat with my company of men, I purposed this: that I would once for all carry out the wish of your people, or fall in the field, fast in the clutches of the foe! I will show knightly courage, or in this mead-hall pass my latest day!"

These words the lady liked full well, — the Geat's defiant speech; the free-born folk-queen, gold-bedecked, went by her lord to sit.

Then again, as of yore, brave words were spoken in the hall, the people were in gladness, there was the clamor of a conquering tribe; until straightway the son of Healfdene wished to go to his evening-rest; he knew that an attack was purposed against the high Hall by the evil spirit, when they could not see the sun's light, and darkening night was over all, when shapes of dark envelopment came stalking, dusky beneath the clouds.

The whole company rose. Then Hrothgar saluted Beowulf — one hero the other — and wished him luck, power in the house of wine, and said these words: "Never yet have I entrusted the noble hall of the Danes to any man, since I could lift hand and shield, excepting now to thee. Take now and guard this best of houses, be mindful of thy fame, make known thy mighty valor, watch against the foe. No lack shall be to thee of what thou wilt, if thou dost get through this daring business with thy life."

Then Hrothgar, bulwark of the Scyldings, departed out of the Hall with his suite of warriors. The war-chief wished to join Wealhtheow, his queen, as consort. The King of Glory had, so men had heard, appointed a hall-guard against Grendel, who discharged a special office about the Lord of the Danes, — kept watch for monsters.

Verily the chief of the Geats trusted firmly in his fervid might, and in the favor of the Creator when he took off from himself the iron corslet, and the helmet from his head, and gave his figured sword, choicest of weapons, to his thane, and bade him guard the war-harness!

Then spake brave Beowulf of the Geats a boastful word, ere he lay down in bed: "I count myself no less in fighting power, in battle-deeds, than Grendel does himself, and therefore by the sword I will not kill him, — rid him of life, — though very well I might. He knows not of these noble arts — to strike back at me and hew my shield, brave though he be at feats of brutal force. But we at night shall not make use of swords, if he dare seek a combat without arms; and then may the wise God, the holy Lord, adjudge the victory to whichever side seems meet to him!"

Then the brave-in-battle laid him down, the pillow received the impress of the noble's face, and around him many a keen sea-warrior sank upon his chamber-couch. Not one of them supposed that thence he would ever revisit his sweet home, his folk and the castle in which he was brought up; nay, they had learned that in time past murderous death had taken off far too many of them, the Danish people, in the wine-hall. But to them, the people of the Weder-Geats, the Lord gave weavèd fortune of success in war, — help and support, so that they should all overcome their enemies through the power of one man, through his own strength. It is known for certain that the mighty God has always ruled over the race of men.

The shadow-goer came stalking in the dusky night. The liegemen who had to guard that pinnacled hall slept, — all except one. It was well-known to men that the worker of ill might not hurl them to the shades below when the Creator did not will it. Still, he, defiantly watching for the foe, awaited in swelling rage the ordeal of battle.

Then came Grendel, advancing from the moor under the misty slopes; God's anger rested on him. The deadly foe thought to entrap one of the human race in the high Hall; he strode beneath the clouds in such wise that he might best discern the wine-building, the gold-chamber of men, resplendent with adornments. Nor was that the first time that he had visited Hrothgar's home. Never in the days of his life, before or since, did he discover a braver warrior and hall-guards.

So this creature, deprived of joys, came journeying to the hall. The door, fastened by forged bands, opened straightway, when he touched it with his hands. Thus, bent on destruction, for he was swollen with rage, he tore away the entrance of the building.

Quickly, after that, the fiend stepped on to the fair-paved floor, — advanced in angry mood; out of his eyes there started a weird light, most like a flame. He saw many men in the hall, a troop of kinsmen, a band of warriors, sleeping all together. Then his spirit exulted; he, the cruel monster, resolved that he would sever the soul of every one of them from his body before day came; for the hope of feasting full had come to him. That was no longer his fortune, that he should devour more of human kind after that night. Hygelac's mighty kinsman kept watching how the murderous foe would set to work with his sudden snatchings. The monster was not minded to put it off, but quickly seized a sleeping warrior as a first start, rent him undisturbed, bit his sinews, drank the blood from his veins, swallowed bite after bite, and soon he had eaten up all of the dead man, (even) his feet and hands.

Forward and nearer he advanced, and then seized with his hands the doughty warrior on his bed — the fiend reached out towards him with his claw. He (Beowulf) at once took in his evil plans, and pressed heavily on his (Grendel's) arm. Instantly the master of crimes realized that never in this middle-world, these regions of earth, had he met with a mightier hand-grip in any other man. He became affrighted in soul and spirit, but he could get away no faster for all that. His mind was bent on getting off, — he wished to flee into the darkness and go back to the herd of devils. His case was unlike anything he had met with in his lifetime there before. Then Hygelac's brave kinsman was mindful of his evening speech; he stood erect and grasped him tight, — his fingers burst. The monster was moving out; the chief stepped forward too. The infamous creature thought to slip further off, wheresoever he could, and to flee away thence to his fen-refuge; he knew the power of his fingers was in the foeman's grip. That was a sorry journey which the baleful fiend had made to Heorot!

The warriors' hall resounded, there was panic among all the Danes, the castle-dwellers, the nobles and the heroes everyone. Both the raging wardens of the house were furious; the building rang again. Then was it a great wonder that the wine-hall was proof against the savage fighters, — that the fair earthly dwelling did not fall to the ground; yet it was (made) firm enough for it, inside and out, by means of iron clamps, forged with curious art. There, where the foemen fought, many a mead-bench adorned with gilding, started from the sill, as I have heard. Before that, veterans of the Scyldings never weened that any man could shatter it, splendid and horn-bedecked, in any wise, or ruin it by craft, although the embrace of fire might swallow it in smoke.

A sound arose, startling enough; a horrible fear clung to the North Danes, to everyone who heard the shrieking from the wall, — (heard) the adversary of God chant his grisly lay, his song of non-success, — the prisoner of hell wailing over his wound. He held him fast who was strongest of men in might in this life's day!

The defender of nobles would not by any means let the murderous visitor escape alive, — he did not count his (Grendel's) life(-days) of use to any of the peoples. There many a noble of Beowulf's company brandished an old ancestral weapon they wished to protect the life of their lord, of their famous chief, if so be they might. They did not know, brave-minded men of war, when they took part in the contest, and thought to hew at him on every side, and to hunt out his life, that no war-bill on earth, no best of sabres, could touch the cursèd foe for that he used enchantment against conquering weapons, every sort of blades.

In this life's day his breaking up was to be pitiable — the alien spirit was to journey far into the power of fiends. Then he who of yore had accomplished much of the joy of his heart, of crime against mankind, he, the rebel against God, discovered this — that his bodily frame was no help to him, but that the bold kinsman of Hygelac had him by the hands. While he lived, each was abhorrent to the other. The horrible wretch suffered deadly hurt, on his shoulder gaped a wound past remedy, the sinews sprang asunder — the tendons burst. Glory in fight was granted to Beowulf; Grendel, sick to death, must needs flee thence under the fen-fastnesses — seek out his joyless dwelling; he knew too well that the end of his life had come, the [daily-]number of his days. After that bloody contest, the desire of all the Danes had come to pass!

In such wise did he who first came from far, the wise and brave, purge Hrothgar's Hall, and free it from attack. He rejoiced in his night's work, in his heroic deeds. The chief of the Geatish men had made good his boast to the East Danes, and had removed besides all the trouble, the carking care, which erewhile they had endured, and had to undergo from dire compulsion, — no small humiliation. That was clear evidence, when the brave warrior deposited under the spacious roof the hand, the arm and shoulder —there was all of Grendel's clutching-limb complete!

Then, in the morning, as I have heard, there was many a warrior round the gift-hall, chiefs of the folk came from far and near along the highways to see the marvel, the traces of the monster. His parting from life did not seem a cause for sorrow to any of the men who saw the trail of the inglorious one, — how he, weary in spirit and vanquished in the fight, made tracks for his life, away from thence, fated and fugitive, to the lake of the water-demons. Then the water was boiling with blood, the frightful surge of the waves welled up, all mingled with hot gore, — with sword-blood; the death-doomed dyed it, and then, deprived of joys, he laid life down, — his heathen soul in the fen-refuge; there Hell received him!

Thence the older courtiers turned back, and many a young (man) from the joyous journey, to ride boldly from the mere on horses — warriors on steeds. Then Beowulf's exploit was proclaimed — many said that no other man, South or North, between the seas, the wide world over, was more excellent among shield-bearers under the expanse of heaven, (or) worthier of empire. Yet did they not at all decry their friend and lord, the gracious Hrothgar; he was their good king still.

Now and then the famous warriors let their bay horses gallop, — run on in races, where the country tracks seemed suitable, — excellent in repute.

Bit by bit a thane of the king, a vaunt-laden fellow exercised in lays, who recollected countless old traditions, framed a new story, founded upon fact; the man began to reproduce with skill the deed of Beowulf, and fluently to tell a well-told tale, — to weave a web of words.

[Episode of Sigemund the Volsung]

He related everything that he had heard men say of Sigemund, his deeds of valor, many untold things, the struggle of the son of Wæls, his wanderings far and wide, the feuds and treacheries — things that the sons of men knew nothing of save Fitela (who was) with him, when he, the uncle, would tell something of such a matter to his nephew, as they had always been friends in need in every struggle, and had felled with their swords large numbers of the race of monsters.

There arose no little fame to Sigemund after his death-day, since he, hardy in battle, had killed the dragon, keeper of the hoard. Under the gray rock he, son of a prince, ventured the perilous deed alone — Fitela was not with him.

Yet it befell him that the sword pierced through the wondrous snake, so that it, the sterling blade, stuck in the rock, — the dragon died a violent death. By valor had the warrior secured that he might enjoy the ring-hoard at his own will; the son of Wæls loaded a sea-boat, bare the shining treasures into the bosom of the ship. Fire consumed the dragon.

In deeds of bravery he was by far the most renowned of adventurers among the tribes of men, and hence he throve erewhile.

After Heremod's warring-time had slackened off, his might and daring, he among the Eotens was betrayed into the power of his enemies, hastily got rid of. Too long did the surgings of sorrow unhinge him; to his people, all the nobles, he was a heavy trouble. Besides, often in times gone by, many a wise vassal had bewailed the daring man's departure, (many a one) who hoped from him help out of misfortunes, — that that royal child might prosper, attain his father's rank, rule over people, citadel and treasure, the realm of heroes, the

Scyldings' fatherland. In that respect the kinsman of Hygelac was more popular with all mankind, and with his friends than he; him did treachery befall.

Now and again they covered the fallow streets, racing, with their horses. Then was the morning sun urged forth and hurried on. Many a retainer, valorous of mood, went to the lofty hall to see the curious wonder; the king, too, guardian of ring hoards, (went) from his bed-chamber; he, famed for sterling qualities, advanced majestically with a great company, and his queen with him passed over the path to the mead-hall with a retinue of maidens.

Hrothgar held forth, — went to the hall, stood on the threshold, looked on the lofty roof, adorned with gold, and Grendel's hand: "For this sight let thanksgiving rise at once to the Almighty! Many horrors and afflictions have I endured through Grendel, (yet) God, the King of Glory, can ever work wonder on wonder. It was but now that I despaired of ever seeing a remedy for any of my troubles, since the best of houses stood stained with the blood of battle, — besprent with gore, an all-embracing woe for every one of the counselors, of those who despaired of ever guarding the national monument of this people from foes, from monsters and hobgoblins. Now, through the might of the Lord, a subaltern has done a deed which up to now we all could not accomplish by our schemings. Lo! That selfsame woman who bare this child among the tribes of men may say, if she still lives, that the eternal God has been gracious to her in her child-bearing.

"Now, Beowulf, most noble hero, in my heart will I love thee as a son; henceforth observe thou well this new relationship. There shall be no lack to thee of any earthly objects of desire of which I have control. Full oft I have assigned a recompense for less, — honor by gifts, — and to a lesser hero, a weaker in the fray. Thou hast brought to pass for thyself by thy exploits, that thy fame shall live for ever and ever. May the Almighty requite thee with good, as he did just now!"

Spake Beowulf, son of Ecgtheow: "With right good will we brought that deed of daring, that onslaught, to fulfillment: boldly we grappled with mysterious powers. I heartily wish thou couldst thyself have seen him, the fiend ready to faint in his trappings. I thought to pin him down to his death-bed by tight grips, so that he might be struggling for life by reason of my hand-grasp, unless his body had escaped. I could not keep him from going, — the Creator did not will it. I did not stick to him, the deadly foe, well enough for that, — the fiend was too preëminently strong at going. However, he left behind his hand, his arm and shoulder, to save his life and show his track. Yet the wretched being bought himself no respite thus. None the longer will the evil doer live, tortured by sins; but pain has seized him tightly in its forceful grip, with deadly bonds. Thus shall the crime-stained mortal wait for the Great Assize; how the bright Deity will sentence him!"

Then was the son of Ecglaf a man more sparing of his boastful talk concerning warlike deeds, after the nobles had, through the chief's prowess, looked on the hand above the lofty roof, on the fingers of the foe; the tip of each one, each place of the nails, of the wild creature's claw, — the savage foe, — was most like steel. Everyone said that there was nothing harder which could bite them, (no) well-proved sword which would sever the bloody fighting-limb of the demon.

Forthwith it was ordered that Heorot should be adorned within by hand, Many There were of men and women who prepared that festive hall, that habitation for retainers. The tapestries shone gold-embroidered along the walls, many wondrous sights for those among men who have an eye for such things. That radiant house, all bound within with iron bands, was greatly shattered; the door-hinges were broken, the roof alone had kept entirely sound, when the demon, stained with guilty deeds, turned and fled, despairing of life.

That is not easy to escape from, let him try it who will; but he shall win the place prepared for soul-possessors, earth-dwelling sons of men, forced on him by fate, where his body, fast in its narrow bed, shall sleep after the banquet.

Then was the time and tide that Healfdene's son should go into the hall; the king himself would take part in the banquet. Never have I heard that that people bore themselves better round their treasure-giver, in a greater company. Then the prosperous. (band) turned them to bench; rejoiced in feasting. Hrothgar and Hrothulf, their stout-hearted kinsmen, drank in the lofty hall many a cup of mead in well-bred style. Heorot was filled within with friends, — the Scyldings folk never used treachery in those days.

Then the son of Healfdene bestowed on Beowulf as the reward of victory a gilded ensign, a decorated staff-banner, a helmet and a corslet; numbers saw the jeweled sword of honor borne before the hero. Beowulf drank of the cup in hall; no need had he to be ashamed of the costly gifts before the soldier throng. Not many men have I known to give more heartily four (such) treasures, decked with gold, to others on the ale-bench.

Around the helmet's crown, a projecting rim, beset with bands, guarded the head above, that the survivances of filing, hard in the storm of battle, might not sorely injure it, what time the shielded warrior must go forth against foes.

Then the protector of nobles bade eight horses, with gold-plated head-gear, be brought into the Hall, within the building; on one of them was placed a saddle cunningly inlaid, adorned with jewels, — that was the war-seat of the mighty king, when Healfdene's son would take part in the play of swords; never did courage fail the far-famed chieftain at the front, when men were falling dead.

And then the Ingwine's lord gave Beowulf ownership of both the two, of horses and of weapons, — bade him thoroughly enjoy them. In such manly wise did the renowned prince, treasure-warden of heroes, pay pluck in battle back with horses and with treasures, so that never man who wills to speak the truth in fairness can disparage them.

Besides that, the chief of the nobles bestowed something precious, an heir-loom, at the mead-bench, on each one of those who had traversed the ocean-way with Beowulf; and he bade recompense be made with gold for that one whom Grendel had lately killed in his wickedness, — as he would have (killed) more of them, had not the wise God and the courage of the man kept off that fate. The

Creator guided all the race of men, as he still does now. Wherefore understanding, forethought of mind, is best in every way. Much shall he experience of good and evil, who here, in these troublous times, long makes the earth his dwelling-place.

There was singing and music together in accompaniment in presence of Healfdene's warlike chieftain; the harp was played, and many a lay rehearsed, when Hrothgar's bard was to provide entertainment in hall along the mead-bench, — about the sons of Finn, and how the sudden attack came on them.

[Episode of King Finn]

"Hnæf of the Scyldings, a hero of the Half-Danes, was doomed to fall at the place of the Frisian slaughter. Hildeburh, however, had no cause to praise the good faith of the Eotens; innocent were the dear ones she lost at the shield-play, her son and brother; wounded by the spear, they fell as was fated; a sad princess was she! Not by any means did the daughter of Hoc mourn without reason over the decree of fate, when morning came — when she could see in the light of day the slaughter of her kinsfolk, where she once possessed the highest earthly pleasure. Warfare took off all Finn's officers save only a few, so that he might not in any way offer battle to Hengest on that meeting-place, nor save the sad survivors from the prince's general by fighting; but they (the Frisians) offered them (the Danes) terms, that they would give up to them entirely another hall, a chamber and a seat of honor, that they might share equal possession of it with the sons of the Eotens, and that at givings out of pay the son of Folcwalda (Finn) would each day bear in mind the Danes, — would gratify with rings the troop of Hengest, even with just so much costly treasure of plated gold as he would cheer the Frisian race with in the beer-hall.

"Then on both sides they ratified a treaty of fast friendship. Finn certified Hengest with oaths, absolutely and unreservedly, that he would treat the defeated remnant honorably according to the ordinance of his counselors; provided that no man there broke the covenant by word or deed, or although, being without a leader, they had followed the murderer of their ring-giver, ever mourn for it with false intent — for it was forced upon them thus; and (on the other hand) if any of the Frisians should call to mind the blood-feud by provoking words, then the edge of the sword should settle it. The oath was sworn, and treasure of gold was brought up from the hoard.

"The best of the War-Scyldings, the battle-heroes, was ready on the funeral pile. At the pyre the blood-stained corslet, the swine-image all-golden, the boar hard as iron, and many a noble killed by wounds, — for several had sunk in death — were visible to all. Then Hildeburh ordered her own offspring to be given over to the flames at Hnæf's funeral pile — his body to be burned and put upon the pyre. The unhappy woman sobbed on (his) shoulder, and lamented him in dirges. The war-hero ascended. The greatest of bale-fires curled (upwards) to the clouds, roared above the grave-mound; heads were consumed, gashes gaped open: then the blood sprang forth from the body, where the foe had wounded it. The fire, greediest of spirits, had consumed all of those whom war had carried off, of either nation — their flower had passed away.

"Then the warriors, deprived of their friends, went off to visit their dwellings, to see the Frisian land, their homes and head borough. Hengest still, however, stayed the dead, forbidding winter through with Finn, altogether without strife; his land was in his thoughts, albeit he might not guide over the sea a ring-prowed ship (the ocean heaved with storm, contended with the wind; winter locked the waves in its icy bond), until a new year came round to the homes of men, and the seasons gloriously bright, regularly observing their order, as they still do now.

"Then the winter was past, the bosom of the earth was fair, the stranger-guest hastened from his quarters, yet he (Hengest) thought rather about vengeance than sea-voyage, whether he could not bring about an altercation, in which he might remember (for evil) the sons of the Eotens. Hence he did not run counter to the way of the world, when the son of Hunlaf gave into his possession Hildeleoma, best of swords. Thus its, edges became well known among the Eotens. Moreover, cruel death by the sword afterwards befell the daring-minded Finn at his own home, when Guthlaf and Oslaf made sad complaint, after their sea-voyage, about the fierce attack, — blamed him for their share of woes. His flickering spirit could not keep its footing in his breast.

"Then was the hall reddened with corpses of the foes; Finn, the king, likewise was slain among his guard, and the queen taken. The bowmen of the Scyldings bore to the ship all the belongings of the country's king, — whatsoever they could find at Finn's homestead of necklaces and curious gems. They brought the noble lady over the sea-path to the Danes, and led her to her people."

The song was sung, the gleeman's lay. Then mirth rose high, the noise of revelry was clearly heard; cup-bearers proffered wine from curious vessels.

Then Wealhtheow came forth, and went, wearing a golden diadem, to where the two nobles sat, uncle and nephew; peace was between them still, each to the other true. Moreover, there sat spokesman Unferth at the Scylding chieftain's feet; all of them trusted in his spirit, that he had much courage, although he might not have been upright with his kinsfolk at the play of swords.

Then spake the Queen of the Scyldings: "Take this cup, my lord and master, giver out of treasure. Be thou of joyous mood, free-handed friend of men, and speak to the Geats with gracious words, (for) so one ought to do. Be affable towards the Geats, mindful of gifts. Now hast thou peace both far and near.

"It has been said to me that thou wouldst have this warrior as a son. The radiant ring-hall Heorot is cleansed; dispose, while thou mayst, of many gifts, and leave the people and the realm to thy descendants, when thou shalt pass away into the presence of death. I know my gracious Hrothulf, that he will honorably rule his juniors, if thou, lord of the Scyldings, leavest the world sooner than he. I trust that he will faithfully requite our offspring, if he is mindful of all that which in the past we both did for him in his childhood for his pleasure and advancement."

Then she turned to the bench where her boys were, — Hrethric and Hrothmund, — and the sons of the heroes, the younger warriors together, where the brave Beowulf of the Geats sat by the brothers twain.

To him the cup was borne, and friendly invitation was offered in words and twisted gold graciously presented, two armlets, a mantle and rings, and the finest of torques that I have ever known of in this world. Never under heaven have I heard of any better-hoarded gem of heroes since Hama carried off to the bright castle the necklace of the Brisings, the ornament and casket, — he fled the snares of Eormenric and chose eternal gain.

That circlet had Hygelac the Geat, the grandson of Swerting, on his last expedition, when under his banner he defended his treasure, — guarded the spoil of battle. Fate took him off when from reckless daring he brought trouble on himself, feud with the Frisians. He, the mighty chieftain, bore the jewels, the precious stones, across the basin of the waves; he died beneath his shield. Then the body of the king passed into the power of the Franks, — breast armor and torque as well; less able warriors plundered those slain by the chance of battle; people of the Geats occupied that place of corpses.

The Hall was filled with (merry) noise. Wealhtheow harangued; she said before the company: "Have joy of this circlet, Beowulf, beloved youth, with luck, and this mantle — a state treasure — and thrive well! Be known for valor, and be kind in counsel to these boys. For that will I be mindful of largess towards thee! Thou hast brought it to pass that men will magnify thee far and near, to all eternity, even as widely as the sea surrounds the windy coasts. Be prosperous, prince, so long as thou dost live. I wish thee store of costly treasures. Be friendly to my son in deeds, thou blessed one! Here is each noble true to other, in spirit mild, and faithful to his lord; the knights are well disposed, the people all alert, and warriors primed with wine perform my bidding."

Then went she to her seat. There was the pick of banquets; men drank wine; they knew not Wyrd, grim destiny, as it had gone forth for many of the nobles.

When even had come and Hrothgar had departed to his court, — the chieftain to his rest, — unnumbered nobles watched over the Hall, as they had often done before. They cleared the bench-boards, it [the Hall] was spread about with beds and bolsters. Among the feasters one sank on his hall-bed moribund and doomed. They set war-bucklers at their heads, the shining shield-wood. There on the bench, above each noble, was exposed the helmet, prominent in war, the ringèd habergeon, the proud spear-shaft. It was their practice to be ever ready for the fray at home and in the field, and each of them at just such times as need befell their lord and master. They were a doughty race!

[Beowulf and Grendel's Mother]

And so they fell asleep. One paid a heavy price for his night's rest, as had befallen them full oft since Grendel had inhabited the gold-hall, — practiced wrong, until the end came — death after his crimes.

It became manifest, — widely known to men, — that an avenger still lived after the monster — (lived) a long time after the troublous strife. Grendel's mother, a female harpy, brooded over her misery — she who must needs inhabit the dread waters, chilly streams, after that Cain was by weapon's edge slayer of his one brother, — of his father's son. He (Cain) then went forth outlawed, branded for murder, to flee social joy, — lodged in the wilderness. Thence arose numbers of doomed creatures, of whom Grendel was one, a hateful outcast-foe, who at Heorot found a watchful mortal waiting for the fray. The monster there laid hold of him; yet he bore in mind the power of his might, the lavish gift which God had granted him, and trusted himself to the Lord for grace, help and support; hence he overcame the foe, struck down the sprite of hell. Then he, the enemy of mankind, went off, abased, deprived of joy, to see his house of death.

And his mother, ravenous and gloomy, resolved in spite of it to go a sorry journey and avenge the death of her son. So she came to Heorot, where the Ring-Danes slept about the Hall.

Then forthwith there was a reaction among the nobles, when Grendel's mother thrust herself within. The terror was less by just so much as woman's strength, woman's war-terror, is (measured) by fighting-men, what time the ornamented, hammer-forgèd blade, the blood-stained sword, trusty of edge, cleaves off the boar-image prominent on the helmet.

Then in the hall, from above the benches, the hard-edged sword was taken down; many a broad shield (was) raised, firm in the hand. When the terror seized him none thought of helm or ample corslet.

She was in haste, — wished to be off from thence to save her life, when she had been discovered. Quickly she grasped one of the nobles tight, and then she went towards the fen. Of champions between the seas, he was to Hrothgar most beloved in point of fellowship, a mighty shield-warrior, a well-known hero, whom she killed in his resting-place.

Beowulf was not there, but before that, after the gift of treasure, another lodging-place had been allotted to the noble Geat.

There was clamor in Heorot. She took the well-known hand (reeking) in blood; sorrow was reinstalled — had come (back) to the building. That was no good exchange — that they should pay on both sides with the lives of friends.

Then the old king, the hoary warrior, was sad at heart, after he knew his dearest counselor was dead, — deprived of life.

Quickly was Beowulf, victory-blest hero, summoned to the bower. With break of day the noble champion went amongst his earls, himself with comrades, where the wise (king) waited, if haply the Almighty would ever bring about a change for him, after the spell of woe.

Then the war-worthy man walked up the flooring with his little band, — the hall-timbers resounded — that he might greet with words the wise lord of the Ingwines, — ask if he had had a quiet night, according to his wish.

Hrothgar, the Scyldings' shield, replied: "Ask not thou after joy! Sorrow has reappeared for Danish folk! Æschere's dead, Yrmenlaf's elder brother, my trusted counselor, my monitor and right-hand man, when we in battle looked after our heads, when foot-men fought, and hewed at boar-crests. As was Æschere, such should a noble be, a trusty peer. The wandering ogre has been his murderer by hand in Heorot. I know not whither the ghoul, proud of her carrion, took her backward way, manifest by her meal. She has avenged the quarrel, — that thou last night didst kill Grendel in fierce fashion by tight grips, because he had too long reduced and killed my people. He fell in battle, forfeit of his life, and now another mighty miscreant has come, and would avenge her son, and has carried the feud far; which may seem a hard heart-sorrow to many a thane who mourns his treasure-giver in his mind; now does the hand lie (dead) which helped your every will.

"I have heard dwellers in the country, subjects of mine, house-holders, say this: that they have seen two such-like huge border-haunters occupy the moors, alien spirits, of whom one was, so far as they could most clearly tell, the semblance of a woman. The other wretched (one) whom, in past days, peasants named Grendel, trod exile-paths in human form, howbeit he was greater than any other man. They have no knowledge of a father, whether any (such) had been begotten for them in times past among the obscure demons. They occupy a land unknown, wolf-slopes, windswept head-lands, perilous marsh-paths, where the mountain stream goes down under the mists of the cliffs, — a flood under the earth. It is not far hence, in measured miles, that the lake stands over which hang rimy groves: the wood fixed by its roots over-shadows the water.

"There may be seen each night a baleful wonder, — fire on the flood! Of the sons of men none lives so wise as to know the bottom. Although, pressed by the hounds, the ranger of the heath, the hart strong in its horns, may seek the forest, chased from far, he will give up his life, his being, on the brink, sooner than he will plunge in it to hide his head. That is no pleasant spot. Thence rises up the surging water darkly to the clouds, when the wind stirs up baleful storms, until the air is misty, the heavens weep.

"Now once more is counsel to be had from thee alone. Thou knowest not yet the haunt, the perilous place, where thou mayst find the sin-stained being. Seek it if thou darest! I will reward thee for the struggle with riches, with ancient treasures, as I did before, — with twisted gold, if thou dost come away."

Beowulf, son of Ecgtheow, answered: "Sorrow not, wise man. Better is it for each one of us that he should wreak his friend, than greatly mourn. Each of us must expect an end of living in this world; let him who may win glory before death, for that is best at last for the departed man of war.

"Rise, guardian of the realm! Come, let us go at once, and spy the track of Grendel's relative. I promise thee, he shall not escape to cover, neither to the lap of earth, nor into mountain wood, nor to the ocean's depth, go where he may! This day do thou have patience as to all thy woes, as I expect of thee!"

Then sprang the veteran up, — thanked God, the mighty Lord, for what the man had said. Then was a horse bridled for Hrothgar, a steed with plaited mane. The sapient prince advanced in stately wise: the foot force of shield-bearers went forth. Along the forest-paths footprints were freely visible — (her) course over the lands. She had gone forth over the dusky moors, and borne the best of vassals — of those who watched over the home with Hrothgar — lifeless! Then the sons of nobles went over the steep, rocky slopes, the narrow ways, the thin, lone paths — an unknown course, — the beetling crags, many homes of water-sprites. He with a few skilled men went on before to view the place, till suddenly he found mountain trees hanging over the gray rock — a dismal wood; the water stood below, blood-stained and turbid.

It was travail of soul for all the Danes, the Scyldings' friends, for many a knight to suffer, — pain for each of the nobles, when they found Æschere's head upon the sea cliff. The water surged with blood, with hot gore: the people gazed on it.

At times the horn sang out a ready battle-note. The warriors all sat down. Then they beheld about the water many of the race of reptiles, wondrous sea-dragons exercising in the deep: upon the cliff-slopes, too, they saw sea-monsters lie, who at morning time take their sad course over the sail-road, serpents and savage beasts. They rushed away, bitter and choleric, — they had heard the noise, the war-horn's note.

One the chief of the Geats severed from life, from his battling with the waters, by his shafted bow, so that the hard war-arrow stuck in his vitals, he was the slower at swimming in the mere, for that death carried him off. Quickly he was hard pressed upon the waves with sharp-barbed boar-spears, — subdued by force and dragged on to the cliff, a wondrous offspring of the waves. Men examined the horrible sprite.

Beowulf equipped himself with princely armor; no whit did he feel anxious for his life. His war-corslet, woven by hand, ample and deftly worked, was to make trial of the mere; the same was apt to shield his bone-girt chest, so that for him the battle-grasp, the fury's vengeful grip, might do no damage to his breast, his life! Thereto the shining helmet screened his head, which was to stir up the watery depths, to tempt the churning waves, adorned with gold, belted with lordly bands, as in past days the weapon-smith had wrought it, — formed it wondrously, and set it round with swine-figures, that after that no sword or battle-knife could ever bite it. That, too, was not the least of mighty aids, which Hrothgar's spokesman lent him in his need. Hrunting was the name of that hilted sword, which was one among the foremost of ancient heirlooms. The blade was iron, stained by poison-twigs, hardened with blood of battle; never had it failed any man in time of war, of those who grasped it with their hands, who durst approach the paths of terror, camping-place of foes: not the first time was that, that it had doughty work to do. When he lent the weapon to a braver swordsman, surely the son of Ecglaf, lusty in strength, did not remember what he said before, when drunk with wine. Himself he durst not risk his life beneath the tumult of the waves, — accomplish deeds of prowess; there he lost his fame, — renown for valor. Not thus was it with the other, when he had made ready for the fray.

Beowulf, son of Ecgtheow, spake: "Remember now, illustrious son of Healfdene, sapient chief, rewarding friend of men, now that I am at the point to start, what we two said a while ago: if I for thy necessity should cease from life, that thou wouldst always be in a father's place to me when I am gone. Be thou a guardian of my brother-thanes, my close companions, if combat takes me off; and send thou also unto Hygelac the treasures which thou gavest me, beloved Hrothgar. The Geatish lord may then appreciate from the gold, — the son of Hrethel see, when he looks on the treasure, that I found out a good ring-giver, high in excellence, — enjoyed (things) while I might.

"And let thou Unferth, widely famous man, have back the old heirloom, the curious wavy sword, hard of its edge. I will with Hrunting work me out renown, or death shall take me off!"

After these words the chief of the Weder Geats pressed bravely on, and would not even wait an answer. The water-flood received the warrior. It was a (good) part of the day before he could descry the solid bottom. Quickly she who, fiercely ravenous, had ranged the watery realm for fifty years, greedy and grim, found one of the human kind was there, examining from above the home of monsters.

Then she clutched at him, she seized the warrior with her horrid claws; for all that, she did not so soon wound his lusty frame, — outside the ring-mail hedged him round, so that she could not break the corslet through, the linkèd mail-shirt, with her loathly fingers.

Then the water-wolf, when she came to the bottom, bore the ring-clad lord to her own dwelling, so that, brave though he was, he could not wield his weapons; for so many of the monsters hampered him in swimming, many a sea-beast pressed with his warlike tusks upon his shirt of mail, — the monsters chased him.

Then the chief perceived that he was in some unfriendly hall or other, where no water harmed him in any way, nor might the sudden rush of the flood touch him, by reason of the vaulted chamber; a fiery light he saw, a glaring flame shine brightly. Then the brave man perceived the she-wolf of the deep, the mighty mere-wife; he gave a forceful impulse to his battle-sword; his hand did not hold back the blow, — so that the ringed blade sang out a greedy war-song on her head. Then the stranger found the shining weapon would not bite, could do no harm to life, in that the blade failed the chieftain in his need; it had stood many close encounters in times past, had often cleft the helmet, the corslet of the doomed; that was the first time for the precious treasure that its worth gave out.

Hygelac's kinsman was still resolute, by no means slack in courage, bent on daring deeds. Then the furious fighter cast aside the damasked sword, covered with ornament, so that on earth it lay, rigid and steely-edged; he trusted to his strength, the hand-grip of his might. So must a man do when he thinks to win enduring fame in war — he will have no care about his life.

The prince of the War-Geats then seized Grendel's mother by the shoulder — he reeked not of the struggle; the brave in combat, bursting as he was with rage, so flung the deadly foe that she fell upon the ground. She quickly yielded him a recompense again with fearful graspings, and clutched at him; sick at heart, she overthrew the strongest of warriors, of foot-combatants, so that he had a fall.

She sat then on her hall-visitor and drew her dagger, broad and brown of edge; she would avenge her child, her only offspring. The woven hauberk lay upon his shoulder, — that preserved his life, barred entry against point and edge. Then had the hero of the Geats perished under the wide earth, had not his war-corslet, his hardy battle-net, furnished him succor, and the holy God, the all-wise Lord, brought about victory in battle; without difficulty, the Ruler of the heavens decided it aright after he, (Beowulf) had got up again.

He saw then among the armor a victory-blest weapon, an old titanic sword, doughty of edge, a prize of fighters; choicest of weapons that, howbeit it was greater than any other man could carry to the battle-play, good and majestical, the work of giants. Then he, champion of the Scyldings, seized the belted hilt; swung the ringed sword, savage and battle-fierce; struck furiously, reckless of life, so that the sword clung hardly to her neck and broke her bone-rings; the blade cleft her doomed flesh-wrapping through and through; on the floor she fell. The sword was gory, in his work the man rejoiced. The gleam flashed forth, light was diffused within, as when the candle of the firmament shines brightly out of heaven.

He gazed about the chamber and then turned him by the wall; Hygelac's captain, incensed and resolute, grasped the weapon firmly by the hilt. The blade was not discarded by the hero, for he wished at once to pay back Grendel for the many raids which he had made upon the West-Danes, far oftener than at that one time when he slew Hrothgar's hearth-companions in their slumber, — ate fifteen men of Danish race while sleeping, and bore off as many more, a ghastly booty. He, wrathful warrior, paid him back that loan, to that degree that he saw Grendel lying in his resting-place, worn out with fighting, destitute of life, as he was maimed erewhile in fight at Heorot. The body gaped wide when it met the blow, the lusty sword-stroke after death, and he (Beowulf) cut off his head.

Soon, clear-sighted followers who looked upon the mere with Hrothgar noticed this — the wave-blendings were all churned up, the water stained with blood.

Together spake the gray-haired veterans about the hero, (saying) that they did not expect the noble chief again — that he would come, buoyant with victory, to seek their famous prince; for it seemed to many that the sea-wolf had dispatched him.

Then came the ninth hour of the day; the brave Scyldings deserted the headland; the generous friend of men gat him home from thence:

The foreigners sat down, sick at their heart, and gazed upon the mere; they wished, but did not expect that they should see their friend and lord again.

Then the sword, the war-blade, began to waste away in gory icicle, by reason of the foeman's blood. It was one of the marvels that it all melted, very like to ice, when as the Father — he who has mastery of times and tides, that is the real Ruler — loosens the bond of frost, unwinds the flood-ropes.

He, prince of the Weder Geats, did not take more of precious objects in the caves, — though he saw many there, — than the head, and the hilt besides, adorned with treasure; the sword was already melted, the damasked blade burnt up, — so hot had been the blood, the fiend so poisonous, who in that place had died.

Soon he was swimming who erewhile had in the fray survived the onslaught of the foes; he shot upwards through the water; the swirling eddies, the broad expanses were all purged, what time the stranger sprite let go his life-days and this passing world. Then came to land the sea-men's chief, sturdily swimming, and reveled in his lake-booty, the mighty burden that he had with him. Then went the trusty band of followers towards him; they thanked God, rejoiced about their lord, that they could see him safe-and-sound.

Then the helmet and the corslet were quickly loosened from the valiant one; the lake calmed down, the water overcast with clouds, stained with the blood of battle. Thence went they forth along the foot-worn tracks, glad at their hearts, the men of kingly pluck measured the country ways, the well-known roads; toilsomely for each one of those high heroes they bore the head from off the sea-girt cliff; four of them had much work to bear into the princely hall the head of Grendel on the murderous pole. So at last there came, suddenly advancing to the Hall, fourteen Geats, keen and warlike, and the lord of men among them, radiant in the multitude, trod the meadows by the mead-hall.

Then entered in the chief of the thanes, the man valiant in deeds, exalted with renown, the hero bold in battle, to greet Hrothgar. Then was Grendel's head borne by the hair on to the chamber-floor where people drank, a fearful thing before the nobles and the lady too; the men beheld a wondrous spectacle.

Beowulf, son of Ecgtheow, spoke. "Behold, we have brought thee with gladness, O son of Healfdene, ruler of the Scyldings, these sea-spoils which thou lookst on here, in token of success. I narrowly escaped it with my life in fight under the water; I achieved the work with difficulty; almost had (my) struggling ceased, if God had not protected me. I could do nothing in the fray with Hrunting, trusty though that weapon be, howbeit the Ruler of men granted me that I might see hanging in beauty on the wall a huge old sword (often and often has He guided those who are deprived of friends), so that I laid about me with that weapon. Then, — as occasion favored me, — I smote in fight the guardians of the dwelling. Then the war-blade, the chased sword, consumed when as the blood burst forth, hottest of battle-gore. The hilt I bore away thence from the foes; avenged the outrages — the slaughter of the Danes — as (it) was meet.

"I promise [it] thee, then, that thou-mayest sleep in Heorot free from care amid thy band of nobles and each chief among thy people, the older warriors and the younger — that thou, Lord of the Scyldings, needest not fear for them murderous attacks from that direction as thou didst aforetime."

Then was the golden hilt, the ancient work of giants, given into the hand of the old warrior, the hoary battle-chief; it came into the Danish lord's possession after the downfall of the demons, a work of cunning craftsmen; and what time the hostile-hearted being, God's adversary, doomed to a violent death, — his mother too — quitted this world, it passed into the power of the best earthly king between the seas, — of those who dealt out money gifts in Scandia. Hrothgar discoursed; he scrutinized the hilt, the ancient relic, upon which was writ the rise of the primeval strife; during which time the flood, the rushing deep, destroyed the brood of giants. They suffered terribly; that was a race alien from the eternal Lord, (and) for that the Sovereign Ruler gave them a final reward by water's surge. Also it was correctly marked in runic letters, on the sword-guards of pure gold noted down and said, for whom that sword, choicest of weapons, with twisted hilt and snake-adornment, had been made at first.

Then the wise son of Healfdene spoke, — silent was everyone! "Lo, this may he affirm who furthers truth and right among the folk, the aged chieftain (who) remembers all, far back — that this noble was born of the better (sort). Beowulf, my friend, thy fame is raised on high over each nation far and wide. Thou dost carry it all calmly, thy might with discreetness of spirit. I will fulfill my compact with thee, according as we two arranged before in talk. Thou shalt become the stay perpetual of thy people — a help of fighters.

"Not so did Heremod turn out to Ecgwela's progeny, the Glorious Scyldings. He did not flourish for the joy, but for the slaughter and the violent death of Danish folk. He killed his boon companions in his rage, his bosom friends, till he, notorious prince, turned him from human joys alone. Although the mighty God favored him above all men with the joys of power and strength and helped him on, still there grew up within his heart a savage spirit; never gave he presents to the Danes, after the custom, joyless he lived, in that he suffered misery for his violence, the long-continued trouble of his folk.

"Do thou instruct thyself by that, know thou what manly virtue is. I, wise from my many winters, have told this tale on thy account. It is a wondrous thing to say how mighty God deals out to mankind wisdom, lands and rank, by his vast spirit. He has control of all. Sometimes He allows the spirit of a man of famous stock to whirl in pleasure: gives him on his estate enjoyment of this world, a fenced city of men to hold; makes quarters of the world, a spacious empire subject to him in such wise that in his folly he himself thinks it will never end. He lives in plenty; nothing — sickness nor old age — stands in his way, no trouble clouds his soul, nor strife (nor) murderous hatred anywhere appears, but all the world moves to his will.

"He knows no worse estate until a measure of insolence waxes and rankles in him, when the warder, the soul's guardian, sleeps. That sleep is too sound, hedged in with sorrows: the murderer is very close, who from the winged bow shooteth with fell intent. Then he is struck at the heart, under his armor, by the piercing arrow,

— the crooked strange behests of the malignant Spirit. He cannot keep himself from them. What he had held for a long time seems to him too little. He covets, soured in mind; never gives, in proud rejoicing, circlets overlaid with gold, no thought has he about the world to come, and he disdains the share of honors God, the Lord of Glory, gave him in time past. It happens after, as the final act, that the precarious body droops and falls as fore-ordained; another, who gives out ornaments ungrudgingly, succeeds to the old possessions of the prince; he wrecks not of alarms.

"Against such baleful rancor guard thyself, dear Beowulf, best of men; choose thee that better part, thy lasting profit.

"Incline thee not to arrogance, famous warrior! Now shall the fullness of thy strength last for a while, but soon after it shall be, that malady or sword shall cut thee off from power, or the embrace of fire or welling of a flood, or onset with the knife, or arrow's flight, or hideous old age or glance of eyes will mar and darken all, and straightway it shall be that death shall overpower thee, noble chieftain!

"Thus have I ruled the Ring-Dancs fifty years under the heavens; and have protected them in war from many a tribe with spear and sword the whole world over, so that I did not deem that I had any foe under the breadth of heaven. And lo! A change from this came to me in my land, sorrow succeeding joy, since Grendel, ancient foe, became my visitant. By reason of this harrying I suffered constantly much grief of mind. And so, thanks be to the Creator, the eternal God, for what I have experienced while still alive, — that with mine eyes I gaze upon this bloody butchered head, the age-long struggling past!

"Go now to thy seat, take part in the joy of banqueting, honored for thy valor. Exceeding many treasures shall be shared between us, when tomorrow comes."

The Geat was glad of mood, and went straightway to seek his seat, as the sage (king) enjoined him. Then, as before, goodly provision was arranged afresh for the heroic banqueters. The shroud of night grew thicker — dark over the noble company. The whole band rose, the gray-haired patriarch Scylding would fain go to his bed. Exceeding much did the Geat, the brave shield-warrior, desire to rest. Straightway the chamberlain, who in courtesy looked after all the noble's needs — such (needs) as at that day seafarers used to have, guided him forth, weary with his adventure, come from far. Then the large-hearted man reposed, the chamber towered aloft, spacious and gold adorned; the stranger slept within, until the swarthy raven, blithe of heart, harbingered the radiance of heaven.

Then the bright sunshine came and glided o'er the plains. The warriors hastened, the nobles were eager to go back to their people, the high-souled visitor wished himself far from thence — wished to regain his ship. Then the brave son of Ecglaf bade Hrunting be brought in, — bade him (Beowulf) take his sword, his precious weapon; he (Beowulf) expressed his thanks to him for that gift, — said that he counted it a trusty friend in battle, doughty in war; no whit did he blame the sword's edge with his words. A chivalrous soul was he! And when the warriors ready in their mail were fit to start, the nobleman honored by the Danes went to the high seat where the other was. Hrothgar he greeted, hero bold in fight.

Beowulf, son of Ecgtheow, held forth: "Now we seafarers, come from far, desire to say that we intend to go to Hygelac. We have been treated here quite after our desires, — thou hast served us well. If then I can by any means gain on earth more of thy heart's affection, lord of men, than I have so far done, ready I'll be at once for warlike deeds. If I learn this across the circuit of the sea, — that those around thy borders threaten harm, as enemies have done in times gone by, I'll bring a thousand thanes and heroes to thy help. For Hygelac, lord of the Geats, I know, though he is young, that he, his people's shepherd, will further me by word and deed, so that I may support thee well, and to thy rescue bring my shafted spear, the succor of my might, when thou hast need of men.

And then if Hrethric, the king's son, decides (to come) to Geatish courts, he shall find friends in plenty there; for him who has good parts himself, far lands are visited with greater good."

Hrothgar addressed him in return: "The wise Lord put these speeches in thy mind. Never heard I a man talk more discreetly at so young an age; strong art thou in thy might and ripe in mind, wise in thy spoken words. I reckon there is chance, if this falls out, — that spear or combat fierce and grim, disease or knife, takes off the son of Hrethel, (takes) thy prince, the shepherd of thy people, and thou hast thy life, that the sea-roving Geats may have no better man to choose as king, as paymaster of warriors, than thyself, if thou dost will to rule the kingdom of thy kin. Thy disposition charms me more as time goes on, dear Beowulf.

"Thou hast effected that to both the folks — Spear-Danes and people of the Geats, — there shall be peace in common; wars shall cease, the vengeful enmities which erewhile they endured; that, while I govern this wide realm, there shall be interchange of treasure, many a man shall greet his fellow with good things across the gannet's bath; the ringèd ship shall bring over the seas gifts and love-tokens. I know the people are of steadfast build, both as to friend and foe, blameless in all respects, after old custom."

Then did the shield of nobles, Healfdene's son give him within twelve valuable gifts, and bade him go in health, visit his kindred people, quickly return again. Then the king, noble in lineage, the Scyldings' prince, kissed the best of thanes, and clasped him round the neck, — tears streamed adown him, grizzly-haired old man. For him, the aged patriarch, there was chance of either, but especially of this, that they might [not?] see each other more, brave men in council. The man was so beloved by him that he could not hold back his feelings, but in his bosom, rooted in his heart-strings, a sacred longing after the dear man burned in his blood.

Then Beowulf, champion brave with gold, flushed with his treasure, did the greensward tread; the sea-goer, which rode at anchor, waited its owning lord. Then, as they went, was Hrothgar's bountifulness often praised; that was an altogether blameless king, until old age deprived him of the joys of power, — he who had worsted many oftentimes.

Thus to the water came the troop of most courageous liegemen, — ring-mail they wore, limb-corslets interlocked. The land-guard spied the nobles coming back, as he had done before; not with contumely did he hail the visitors from off the headland's brow, but up towards them rode, and said to the Weder-folk, that they the bright-mailed warriors, I went with welcome to their ships.

Then was the spacious sea-boat on the beach laden with battle-gear, the ring-prowed ship with horses and valuables; the mast towered above Hrothgar's hoarded treasures.

To the boat-keeper he gave a sword bound round with gold, so that thenceforth he was more honored on the mead-bench for that treasure, — that heirloom of a gift.

Then gat he him off on ship, to ruffle the deep water; Danish land he left. Then to the mast a sail, one of the sea-cloths, was fastened by a sheet; the wave-borne timbers groaned, the wind over the billows did not throw out of her course the wave-floater; the sea-goer traveled, foamy-necked she sailed forth o'er the main, with wreathed prow over the sea-streams, so that they could descry the Geatish cliffs, the well-known headlands. The keel shot up, driven by the wind; it stuck upon the land.

The haven-ward was quickly ready at the water's edge, he who before upon the strand had long time gazed into the distance, longing for the dear men: he tethered to the beach the roomy ship, held fast with anchor-ropes, lest the waves' force should drive the winsome craft away from them.

Then he bade carry up the jewels and gold plate, treasure of noblemen; it was not far thence for him to seek out the distributor of wealth; Hygelac, son of Hrethel, sojourns there at home, himself and his retainers, hard by the sea-wall.

The building was magnificent, the chief a mighty ruler in the lofty hall; Hygd very youthful, wise, well-mannered, although she, the daughter of Hæreth, had dwelt but few winters within the castle walls; for all that she was not illiberal, nor too niggardly with gifts, with costly treasures, to the Geatish folk.

[Episode of Thryth]

She, high queen of the people, did not exhibit the pride, the terrible vindictiveness, of Thryth; no brave man among the court favorites, except her husband, durst gaze on her (Thryth) openly with his eyes, but he might count on deadly bonds being appointed for him, woven by hand; very soon. after his seizure was the knife brought into service, so that the damasked dirk might settle it, — proclaim the punishment of death. That is no queenly custom for a woman to practice, peerless though she may be, that a peace-weaver should assail the life of a valued liegeman, because of fancied insult. Howbeit the kinsman of Hemming detested all this.

Men at their ale-drinking said besides that she brought about less harm to the people, less spiteful vengeances, when once she had been given, gold-bedecked, to the young champion, dear and of high descent; when she, at her father's bidding, visited in a journey Offa's court over the dusky flood.

There, afterwards, she used her fortunes well upon the royal seat, famed for her goodness, while she was alive; held highest love towards the prince of heroes, who was of all mankind, as I have heard, the best between the seas of human kin. Wherefore Offa, spear-bold man, was noted far and wide for gifts and victories and ruled his native land with wisdom. Of him was born Eomær, stay of warriors, kinsman of Hemming, grandson of Garmund, mighty in the fray.

Then went the hero forth, himself and his companions, by the sand, treading the sea-beaches, the broad foreshores. The world's lamp shone, the sun hastening from the south; — they passed along their way, went quickly thither, where they heard say the prop of courtiers, the slayer of Ongentheow, the good young warrior-king, within the castle dealt out rings. Quickly was Beowulf's coming told to Hygelac, — that the warriors' shield, his mate in arms, had come alive into the precincts and was going on towards the court, whole from the tug of war.

Forthwith the chamber was prepared within for the warrior-band, as the great ruler ordered. Then he who had escaped in battle sat opposite (Hygelac) himself, kinsman facing kinsman, after the lord of men had greeted the faithful soul in courtly speech with forceful words. Round the hall Hæreth's daughter went with stoups of mead, cherished the folk, and bore the beaker to the warriors' hands.

Hygelac began courteously to ask his comrade in the lofty hall — tortured was he with thirst for news — as to what hap the sailor-Geats had had. "How went it with you on your journey, much-loved Beowulf, the while you suddenly resolved to seek a feud far off, across the briny water — battle at Heorot? Hast thou any whit lightened the well-known trouble of Hrothgar, famous prince? For that I seethed with gloomy care, surgings of sorrow; no faith had I in my loved liege's journey. Long time I begged thee, that on no account wouldst thou go near the murderous monster, but wouldst let the South Danes settle their feud with Grendel by themselves. I give thanks to God that I am suffered to see thee safe and sound."

Beowulf, son of Ecgtheow, spake forth: "It is well known, lord Hygelac, that great encounter, to many men, what a bout of fighting we had with Grendel upon that field, where he had wrought many and many a sorrow, age-long misery, for the Victor-Scyldings. I avenged it all, so that no kin of Grendel upon earth can boast about that uproar in the twilight, — not he who, hedged in by the fens, lives longest of the loathly race.

"Once there, I went first to the ring-hall to greet Hrothgar. Forewith the famous son of Healfdene, when he had learned my mind, allotted me a seat by his own son. The company was in high feather; never in my life have I seen greater joy at mead among sitters in hall, under the vault of heaven. From time to time the illustrious queen, the nations' pledge of peace, went up and down the hall, kept the young servers going, and often gave a circlet to some guest, ere she went back to her seat. Now and then, before the higher courtiers, Hrothgar's daughter bare the ale-cup to the nobles from end to end. I heard those sitting in hall call her Freawaru, as she presented the studded vessel to the heroes.

[Episode of Freawaru]

"Young and gold-adorned, she was betrothed to Froda's genial son. This had seemed good to the friend of the Scyldings, the protector of the kingdom, — he counts it good policy — that he should settle lots of deadly feuds, of quarrels, through that woman. Rare indeed, is it anywhere, however, that the murderous spear lies idle, even for a little while, after the downfall of a prince, capable though the bride may be.

"Then it may well displease the prince of the Heathobards and every thane of his nation, when he goes with the lady into hall, that his high lords should entertain a noble scion of the Danes. Upon him gleam the heirlooms of their ancestors, hard and ring-mailed, treasure of the Heathobards, so long as they might lord it with their weapons, until they led into the fatal play of shields their dear companions and their very lives.

"Then, at the beer-drinking, an aged spearman speaks, who eyes the treasure, recollects it all, the men's death by the spear. His heart is sore and he begins in gloomy wise to test the young campaigner's temper by the musings of his mind, to rouse accursèd strife, and says these words: 'Canst thou, my friend, discern the blade, the precious weapon, which thy father bore to battle when he was under fighting-mask for the last time, where the Danes slew him, the brave Scyldings took possession of the field, when Withergyld lay low after the fall of heroes? Now some offshoot or other of these cut-throats goes about here, in our hall, rejoicing in his trappings, — boasts of the carnage, wears the adornment you should have by right.'

"Thus he urges and prompts him time after time with bitter words, until the hour comes that on account of his father's deeds the lady's courtier sleeps bloodstained after sword-slash, forfeit of his life; the other gets him off from thence alive, — he knows the country well. Then is the oath of the chieftains broken on both sides, when savage spleen wells up in Ingeld, and his love for his wife grows cooler with the risings of care. Hence I count not the faith of the Heathobards, their share in the tribal peace, sincere towards the Danes, their friendship stable."

"Now I will proceed and tell again of Grendel, that thou, O Giver of treasure, mayst fully know what was the issue of the hand-to-hand struggle of the champions. After the gem of the heavens had glided over the earth, the furious spirit, the dread ogre of night, came to close with us where we, still whole, kept watch over the hall. There was battle brewing for Hondscio, violent death for the doomed man; he, belted champion, fell first; for him, my famous brother-thane, Grendel was a devouring murderer, — he gobbled up the beloved man's whole body. Howbeit the butcher bloody-toothed, intent on evil, would not after that leave the gold-hall again empty of hand, but first, lusty in strength, he ventured on me — gripped me with ready paw. His pouch hung, ample and strange, attached by curious clasps, — it was all cunningly contrived with fiendish skill and with the skins of dragons. Therein he wished, the dire deed-doer, to put, as one of many, unoffending me; thus he might not do, as soon as I stood upright in my wrath. It is too long to tell out how I paid this public scourge a recompense by hand for all his crimes; there, my prince; did I exalt thy nation by my works. He slipped away — enjoyed the sweets of life a little while, albeit his right hand kept trace of him at Heorot, and he, in doleful mood, fell miserably thence to the mere's bottom.

"The Scyldings' kindly ford repaid me richly for that deadly fight, with beaten gold, — with many treasures — when the morrow came and we had sat us down to the banquet. There was singing and merriment. The patriarch Scylding, asking many questions, told of bygone times; now and again a brave called forth enchantment from the harp, that wood of pastime; sometimes told a true and mournful tale; anon the generous king rehearsed aright a strange adventure; then again after that the veteran battle-chief, trammeled by his age, would make lament over his youthful days and strength in battle. His heart heaved within him, as he, old in years, brought much of the past to mind.

"Thus we took our pleasure therein the live-long day, until another night ensued for men. Then, after that, was Grendel's mother quickly ready for revenge; she journeyed full of care, death, — war-hate of the Weders — had cut off her son. The horrid hag avenged her child, boldly she laid a warrior low; there was the life parted from Æschere, the sage old counselor. Nor could they, the Danish folk, when morn had come, consume him, broken down and dead, with fire, nor lay the beloved man on the funeral pile. She bore away the body in her fiendish grasp, under the mountain stream. That was the bitterest of pangs for Hrothgar, out of all those which long had chanced the people's prince.

"Then in sad mood the sovereign begged me by thy life, that I would show prowess in the swirl of waters, risk my being, do heroic deeds; reward he promised me.

"Then, as is widely known, I found the grim and grisly guardian of the welling water's depths. There we were awhile, hand to hand; the water boiled with blood, and I with mighty blade cut off the head of Grendel's mother in the subterranean hall; thence with my life I hardly got away. I was not doomed as yet; but Healfdene's son, the shield of nobles, gave me thereafter many treasures.

"So lived the people's king, according to the customs; by no means did I lack the rewards, the meed of might, but he, the son of Healfdene, gave me treasures at my own discretion, which I will bring to thee, heroic king, and offer gladly. All of my favors still depend from thee; I have few blood-relatives save thee, O Hygelac!"

Then he bade them bear in the boar's-head banner, the helmet towering in battle, the gray corslet, the splendid war-sword, and thereto pronounced this speech:

"Hrothgar, the wise prince, gave this battle-gear to me, in language clear bade me that first of all I should acquaint thee of his friendly feeling. He said that King Hiorogar, Scylding lord, had it long time, yet would he not for all that give it — the breast armor — to his son, the valiant Heoroward, true as he might be to him. Enjoy it all well!"

I heard that four apple-fallow horses, perfectly alike, followed in the track of the armor, — he gave him possession of the steeds and treasures. So should a kinsman do, and never weave a cunning snare for other, or contrive death for his bosom friend by secret craft. His nephew was most true to Hygelac, the brave in battle, and each was mindful of the other's good.

I heard that he presented to Hygd the circlet, that curious, wondrous jewel, which Wealhtheow, the prince's daughter, had given him, and three horses as well, graceful and bright with saddlery; thenceforward was her breast adorned, after that gift of decorations.

Thus the son of Ecgtheow, the man renowned in war, showed himself doughty in brave deeds, he bore himself discreetly, never struck down his boon companions at the drinking; his was no brutal mind, but he, the brave in battle, guarded with the greatest human art the liberal gifts which God had granted him. For a long time he was contemned, as the children of the Geats knew him not to be brave, nor would the captain of war-hosts do him much honor at the mead-bench, they very much suspected he was slack, a feeble princeling; but rehabilitation as to every slight came for the brilliant man.

Then the protector of warriors, the king of martial glory, bade Hrethel's legacy be brought in, decked with gold; there was not at that time among the Geats a greater treasure in the shape of a sword. That he laid in Beowulf's lap, and gave him seven thousands, a mansion, and the rank of chief. To both of them alike had land descended in that country — an estate and hereditary right, but the other had more especially an ample realm, and was in that respect the more distinguished.

[Beowulf and the Dragon]

Afterwards, in later days, it fell out through frays of fighting thus; when Hygelac lay low and battle-blades were the death of Heardred, spite of sheltering shield, what time the martial Scyldings, hardy war-wolves, sought him out among his conquering people, and attacked the nephew of Hereric in force; then after that the spacious realm came into the hands of Beowulf. He ruled it well for fifty winters — that was an aged king, a veteran guardian of his people, — until in the dark nights a certain one began to have control, — a dragon, who on an upland heath kept watch over a hoard, a high stone-barrow; below there lay a path unknown to men.

Into that place went some man or other [Here follow six imperfect lines, apparently to the effect that the man took of the monster's hoard while he was asleep, and roused his ire].

By no means had he purposely, of his own accord, sought out the fullness of the dragon's hoards, — he who injured himself sorely, — but under stress of need the slave of some one or other of the sons of men fled from vengeful blows, lacking a home, and fell therein, a sin-perplexèd soul. Soon it happened that grisly horror rose up before the stranger [Three more lines imperfect]. While terror held him, he saw the treasure-chest. There in that earthy house were many of such old heirlooms as some man or other in days of yore had cautiously hid there, the vast leavings of a noble race, dear treasures. Death had carried them off in times now past, and then that one of the people's chieftains who was stirring longest became gloomy at the loss of friends, hoped to live on for this alone — that he might own for a little space the slowly gathered treasures. A barrow stood all ready to hand on open ground, near where the billows surged, hard by a cape, new made, secured by secret craft; into that place the keeper of the jewels bare a heavy portion of the princely wealth the plated gold; said these few words: "Now do thou, O Earth, hold fast what heroes might not, — property of nobles. Lo! Brave men won it at first from thee; death in war, horrid carnage, took away everyone of the men of my tribe who yielded up this life; they saw (the last of) festive joy. I have no one to bear sword, or to burnish the plated flagon, the precious drinking-cup; the noble warriors have departed to another place. Now will the hard helmet, bedight with gold, be deprived of its adornments; the cleaners sleep who had the battle-masks to furbish. The armor too, which stood the bite of swords in battle mid the crash of shields, molders as does the fighter; nor may the ringed mail take long journey with the captain, in partnership with heroes. There is no joy of harp, no pastime with the gladdening lute; no good hawk sweeping through the hall, nor does the swift steed paw the castle yard. The bale of death has banished hence many of the human race."

Thus with sad heart he mourned his troubles, alone after them all, and sorrowfully wept by day and night, until death's rising tide touched at his heart.

The long-lived twilight-foe found the delightful treasure standing open; he who fierily visits barrows, the naked vengeful dragon, wrapped in flame, who flies by night, — sorely the country yokels dread him. His was it to seek out the hoard under the earth, where he, old in winters, should keep watch over the heathen gold, — and not be one whit the better for it.

Thus this public scourge had for three hundred winters occupied on earth a mighty treasure-house, until a certain man enraged him in his heart; bore to his over-lord the plated goblet, and begged his master for conditions of peace. Then was the hoard ransacked, the hoard of jewels carried off, his boon was granted to the wretched man. For the first time the lord examined the ancient work of mortals.

Soon as the dragon woke, there sprang up strife; he sniffed the scent along the rock, the valiant-hearted beast descried the footprints of the foe — he had walked forwards and close to the head of the dragon with his stealthy craft. Thus may an undoomed man, — one who retains the favor of the Almighty, lightly pass through both woe and banishment. The hoard-keeper searched with care over the ground, he wished to find the man who had done him this injury in his sleep: glowing and fierce at heart he went completely round the barrow oftentimes; there was not any man there, in that deserted place. Still he had gleeful thoughts of fighting — of the work of battle; at times he turned back into the barrow, looked for the costly vessel.

Soon he discovered this, — that one of mortal kind had got wind of the gold, the splendid treasures.

The hoard-keeper waited impatiently till evening came; then was the guardian of the barrow bursting with rage, the evil beast meant to requite with fire the costly drinking-bowl. Then was the day departed, as the dragon wished, no longer would he watch upon the rampart, but he went forth with flame, furnished with fire! The outbreak was fearful for the country folk, and it had an end, speedily and sorely, in the person of their bounteous Lord.

Then the fiend began to vomit forth live coals, to burn the smiling homesteads; the gleam of fire blazed forth, a tenor to the sons of men; the loathly air-flyer would leave there no thing with life. The serpent's warfare was seen right and left, the vengeance of the devastator far and near — how the fighting pest hated and humbled the Geatic folk. He shot back to his hoard again, his dark head-quarters, ere the time of day; he had surrounded the land-folk with fire, with flame and burning; trusted in his barrow, his fighting powers and wall, — and his trust played him false! Then was the horror made known to Beowulf, quickly and credibly, that his own home, best of buildings, the princely seat of the Geats, was being swallowed by the waves of fire. That was a trial for the brave man's soul, greatest of heart-sorrows; the wise chief supposed that he had sorely angered the Almighty, the everlasting Lord, contrary to the eternal law; within him heaved his breast with gloomy thoughts, which was not wonted for him.

The flaming dragon had wasted with fire the national stronghold, the maritime land, all that region of earth; for that the warlike king, the Weders' prince, contrived vengeance against him. The warriors' protector, chief of earls, then bade a curious shield, all iron, be made for him; he knew full well that forest-wood — a linden shield — could not avail him against flame. The venerable prince was doomed to meet with the end of his loan of days — of this world's life, — and the serpent as well, though he had held the hoarded treasure long.

Then did the lord of rings disdain to seek out the wide-flier with a host, an ample army. He did not fear the battle for himself, nor did he count for anything the serpent's fighting powers, his strength and courage; for that he, bold in extremity erewhile, had passed through many contests, — battle-crashes — after he, the man of victories, had purged Hrothgar's hall, and seized in combat Grendel's kin, of hated race.

Not least was that of hand-to-hand encounters, in which Hygelac was slain, when the Geatic king, the gracious lord of peoples, son of Hrethel, died a bloody death in Friesland, by the sword struck down. Thence Beowulf got away by his own strength, used his power of swimming — alone he on his arm had thirty battle-dresses, when in the sea he plunged. The Hetwaras, who, bearing their shields, went forth against him, had no cause to boast about their fight on foot; few got them back again from that war-wolf to see their homes.

Thus did the son of Ecgtheow swim back to his people over the sea's expanse, a wretched solitary. There Hygd offered him wealth and a kingdom, treasure and a royal throne; she trusted not her child, that he could hold the royal seats as against foreign armies, now that Hygelac was dead. But none the more could the bereaved people bring the noble chief on any conditions to be Heardred's lord, or to be willing to accept the kingly dignity. Still he upheld him with the folk by friendly counsel, kindly but with respect, until he grew older, — ruled the Weder-Geats.

Banished men, sons of Ohthere, sought him out from over sea, — they had rebelled against the protector of the Scylfings, the best of the sea-kings who in Sweden gave out treasure — a famous prince. That made an end of him (Heardred), he, son of Hygelac, in return for his hospitality, had as his lot a deadly wound by thrustings of the sword, and Ongentheow's son went back again to visit his home when Heardred lay low, and suffered Beowulf to occupy the throne and rule the Geats. He was a noble king!

He took care to requite the national calamity in later days; the friend of lonely Eadgils he became, he supported the son of Ohthere over the wide sea with an army, with warriors and weapons; avenged him afterwards by means of cold and bitter marches; he (Eadgils) deprived the king of life.

So he, the son of Ecgtheow, got safely through each one of the attacks, the savage feuds, the desperate encounters, until that day on which he had to try conclusions with the Reptile. Then, lord of the Geats, he went, one among twelve, bursting with rage, to look upon the Dragon. He had learnt then from whence the feud arose, the hate baleful to men, — the famous treasure-vessel had come into his possession by the hand of the finder. He (the latter) who had brought about the beginning of the quarrel was the thirteenth man of the company, a sad-souled thrall; thither he had humbly to show the way. Against his will he went to the point where he knew of a certain earthy chamber, a vault under the ground, hard by the surgings of the sea, the strife of waters, which was full within of gems and filigrees. The hideous warder, a spirited fighter long time under the earth, guarded the golden treasures; property not easy for any man to get possession of.

So the king hardy in war sat on the headland, and from that place the Geats' gold-giving friend spake words of greeting to his hearth-companions. His spirit was sad, restless and ready to depart, the Fate immeasurably near which was to wait upon the aged man, to seek the treasure of his soul, to part asunder life from body; not long after that was the spirit of the prince enwrapped in flesh.

Beowulf, son of Ecgtheow spake: "In my youth I passed through many battle-charges, times of war; I recollect it all. I was seven winters old when the lord of treasures, the gracious ruler of nations, received me from my father. King Hrethel had and kept me, gave me pay and food, bore in mind our kinship. Never through life was I a whit less liked by him as page within the castle than were any of his sons — Herebeald and Hæthcyn or my own Hygelac. For the eldest a bed of death was undeservedly prepared by the action of his kinsman, for Hæthcyn struck him down, — his lord and friend — by an arrow from his horn-tipped bow; he missed the mark and shot his relative — one brother the other — with his bloody shaft. That was an onset beyond compensation, sorely sinful, sickening to the heart; and yet for all that the prince had to quit life unavenged.

"So it is painful to an old man to experience that his son should swing upon the gallows in his youth; that he may utter then a dirge, a doleful song; when his son hangs as a sport for the raven, and he, old, stricken in years, can frame no help for him. Unceasingly, at every morn, he is reminded of the passing of his son; he cares not to wait for another son and heir within his quarters, when one has had his experience of deeds in the shape of a violent death. With anxious care he sees in his son's dwelling the festive hall abandoned, a lodgment for the winds, its merriment all gone; the rider sleeps, the champion, in his grave, there is no sound of harp, no merrymaking in the courts, as once there was.

"So he goes to his couch and sings alone a sorrowful lay for the other; everything seems too spacious for him, both fields and dwelling-place. In like manner the protector of the Weders bore with heaving breast his heart's sorrow about Here-beald; he could not in any wise avenge that feud upon the murderer; none the sooner could he pursue the man of war with hostile acts, though he was not beloved by him. Thus he gave up the joys of men, from that sorrow which the mishap had brought him: he chose God's light. He left to his sons, when he withdrew from life, the land and castle, as a wealthy man does.

"Then was there conflict and strife between the Swedes and Geats, a common feud across the broad water, harsh enmity, after Hrethel was dead; and the sons of Ongentheow were vigorous and keen on fighting, — no wish had they to hold the peace across the lakes, but near Hreosnabeorh planned oftentimes a dire and treacherous trap.

"That — the feud and outrage — did my friendly relatives avenge, as was well known, though one of them paid for it with his life, — a hard bargain; to Hæthcyn, lord of the Geats, the fight was fatal. Then, at morn, as I have been told, one brother avenged the other on the murderer with the edge of the sword, where Ongentheow met with Eofor; the helm of battle split asunder, faint from a sword-stroke fell the aged Scylfing, his hand remembered feuds enough, it kept not back the fatal blow.

"I requited him the treasures which he had given me, by fighting, by my gleaming sword, as was permitted me; he gave me land, a dwelling-place, a glad possession. There was no need for him that he should have to seek among the Gepidæ or Spear-Danes, or in the Swedish realm, a second-rate campaigner, — to purchase him with treasure. For him I would always be to the fore in the host, — by myself at the front, and so through life shall do battle, while this sword lasts, which has often done me service, early and late, since by valor I became the slayer of Dæghrefn, champion of the Hugas, by hand. He could not bring the adornments, the breast-decoration, to the Frisian king, but he, the standard-bearer, sank in battle, a noble in prowess; nor was the sword his slayer, but my unfriendly hug finished his bony frame, the surgings of his heart.

"Now shall weapon's edge, hand and hard sword, do battle for the hoard"

Beowulf discoursed, — spoke a last time with words of boasting: "I ventured on many battles in my younger days; once more will I, the aged warden of the people, seek a combat and acquire renown, if the destructive miscreant will encounter me outside his earthly vault." Then he addressed all of the men, the brave helmet-wearers, his close companions, for the last time. "I would not bear a sword or weapon against the Reptile, if I knew how else I might stick to my boast against the monster, as I did aforetime against Grendel. But there I look for hot destructive fire, for blast and venom; therefore I have upon me shield and corslet. I will not flee the space of a foot from the keeper of the mound, but at the rampart it shall be to us as Wyrd, the portion-giver of every man, decides. I am eager in spirit, so that I can forbear from boasting against the winged fighter.

"Watch on the barrow, ye corslet-clad warriors, in your accouterments, which of us two can stand the hacking best, after the desperate onslaught. That is not your affair, nor a possibility for any man, save for me alone, to put forth his power against the monster, and do knightly deeds. By my valor I will win gold; or war, the dread bane of life, shall carry off your lord!"

Then rose the doughty champion by his shield, hardy under his helmet, he went clad in his war-corslet to beneath the rocky cliffs, and trusted to his individual strength — not such is the coward's way. Then he, who, preëminent in virtues, had lived through many wars, — shocks of battle, when armies dash together, — saw by the rampart a rocky arch erect, whence burst a stream out from the mound; hot was the welling of the flood with deadly fire. He could not any while endure unscorched the hollow near the hoard, by reason of the dragon's flame.

Then did the chieftain of the Weder-Geats, puffed up with rage, let sally forth a word out of his breast, stout-heartedly he stormed, his voice, distinct in battle, went ringing under the gray rock. Hate was enkindled, — the hoard-keeper discerned the voice of man. No time was left to beg for peace.

First came from out the rock the monster's breath, the hot vapor of battle; the earth resounded. Under the mound the hero, Geatish lord, raised his shield's disc against the gruesome stranger; then was the coiled creature's heart impelled to seek the contest. The doughty war-prince had-just drawn his sword, an ancient relic, quick of edge; in each one of the bloody-minded pair was terror at the other. Stout-heartedly the paramount of friends stood by his upright shield, what time the serpent quickly coiled itself together; he waited in his armor. The fiery one then framed to advance upon him twisting — hastened to his fate. The shield gave its good shelter to the famous chief in life and limb a shorter time than had his longing looked for, if he on that occasion, that first day, was to command victory in the contest, but Fate did not thus ordain for him. The Lord of the Geats swung his hands upwards, struck the grisly monster with Ing's heirloom, so that the brown blade gave way on his bone, and bit less firmly than the warrior-king, driven to straits, required of it.

Then was the warder of the barrow mad in spirit after the battle stroke, and threw out murderous fire; his hostile flames flew far and wide. The Geat's free-handed friend crowed not in pride of victory; the bare war-weapon, the blade trusty in former times, had failed him in the fray, as it should not have done. That was no pleasant journey, that the famous son of Ecgtheow should have to leave the surface of this earth and occupy against his will a dwelling otherwhere; for so must every man let go his loan of days.

Not long was it before the champions charged each other again. The hoard-possessor nerved himself, his breast heaved with his breathing once again; and he who used to rule a nation suffered anguish, hedged about with flame. Never a whit did his right-hand-men, those sons of nobles, stand round him in a body, doing deeds of warlike prowess, but they shrank back into the wood and took care of their lives. The heart of one of them alone surged with regrets, — in him who is right thinking nothing can ever set aside the claims of kinship!

He was called Wiglaf, son of Weohstan, a much loved shield-warrior, a Scylfing prince, kinsman of Ælfhere. He perceived that his lord and master was tortured by the heat under his battle-mask. Then he called to mind the favors which he had bestowed upon him in time past, the rich dwelling place of the Wægmundings, and all power over the people, just as his father had it; and then he could not forbear; his hand seized the disc, the yellow linden-shield, and drew his ancient sword.

This last was known by mortals as the relic of Eanmund, the son of Ohthere, of whom, when a friendless exile, Weohstan was slayer in fight by edge of sword, and bore off to his kin the brown-hued helmet, the ring-mail corslet and the old gigantic sword, which Onela had given him — his kinsman's war-harness, a battle-outfit ready to his hand. He (Onela) did not speak about the feud, although he (Weohstan) had laid low his (Onela's) brother's son. He kept these treasures — sword and corslet — many years, until his son could compass doughty deeds, like his old father did. Then when he passed away from life, full of years, on his journey hence, he gave to him among the Geats a countless number of habiliments of war of every kind.

This was the first occasion on which the young champion was to go through the storm of battle with his ruling lord; his courage did not melt within him, nor did his kinsman's heirloom fail him in the contest; the serpent found that out, when they had come together.

Wiglaf spoke many fitting words (sad was his soul) and said to his companions: "I recollect that time at which we drank the mead, how in the beer-hall we pledged ourselves to our lord, who gave us the rings, that we would repay him for the war-equipments, the helmets and hard swords, if any need like this befell him. He who of his own will chose us among the host for this adventure, reminded us of honor, and gave to me these treasures, because he counted us distinguished spear-men, gallant helmet-bearers, although he, our lord, the shepherd of his people, purposed to achieve this deed of bravery by himself, because he among men had done the greatest acts of heroism, daring deeds. Now has the day arrived, when our liege lord needs the main force of noble fighting men. Come! let us go to him, and help our captain, so long as heat, grim fire-horror may be. As for myself, God knows, far liefer had I that the flame should swallow up my body with my gold-giver. To me it does not seem befitting that we should carry back our bucklers to our home, unless we may first fell the foe, and shield the Weder-Geat Lord's life.

"Full well I know that this is not what he deserves for his past deeds, that he alone of Geatic rank should suffer this hard fortune, — break down in the fray. To us shall be in common sword and helmet, corslet and coat of mail."

Then plunged he through the deadly reek; went helmeted to help his lord; spoke in few words: "Dear Beowulf, do thy best all round, just as thou saidst in youthful days, of yore, that thou wouldst never in thy life cause thy repute to fail; now must thou, resolute chief, protect thy life with all thy might, and I will help thee."

After these words, the serpent, the fell spiteful spirit, came angrily a second time, bright with belched fire, and fell upon his foes, the loathed mankind. His shield was burnt up to the boss by waves of flame, his corslet could afford the youthful spear-warrior no help; but the young man did valorously under his kinsman's shield after his own was burnt up by the gleeds. Then once more the battle-prince was mindful of his reputation, by main force he struck with his battle-sword so that it stuck in the head, driven in by the onslaught. Nægling had snapped! Beowulf's old, gray-hued sword had failed him in the fray. That was not granted him, — that iron blades should help him in the fight. The hand was too strong which, so I have heard, by its stroke overstrained every sword, — it was no better for him when he bare so wondrous hard a weapon to the fray.

Then a third time the public scourge, the dreadful salamander, was intent on fighting; he rushed upon the hero, when occasion favored him, hot and fierce in battle, and enclosed his whole neck between his cutting jaws; he was bathed in lifeblood — the gore gushed out in streams.

I am told that then in the (dire) need of the nation's king, the earl upstood and showed his pluck, his skill and daring, as his nature was; he reeked not about the head, but the brave man's hand was scorched the while he helped his kinsman, so that he, the man in armor, struck the vengeful stranger a little lower down, in such wise that the sword, gleaming and overlaid, plunged in, and the fire began thenceforth to abate.

Then the king himself once more gained sway over his senses, drew the keen battle-sharp death-dirk he wore upon his corslet, and he, protector of the Storm-Geats, cut through the reptile in the middle. They had felled the foe, daring had driven out his life, and thus they, the kindred nobles, had put an end to him. So should a man and captain be in time of need! That was for the prince the last of triumph-days by his own deeds, — of working in the world.

Then the wound which erewhile the dragon had inflicted on him began to burn and swell; quickly he found out this — that deadly venom seethed within his breast, — internal poison.

Then the chieftain went on until he sat, still clear in mind, on a seat by the rampart, and gazed on the work of giants — how the primeval earth-dwelling contained within it rocky arches, firm on columns. Then the thane, preëminently good, laved with his hands the famous prince, bloody from battling, his friend and lord, exhausted by the fight, with water, and undid his helmet.

Beowulf discoursed: spite of his hurt, his grievous deadly wound, he spoke, — he knew full well that he had spent his measured while of earthly joy, — then was his count of days all passed away, and death incalculably near: "Now should I have wished to give my son my war accouterments, if it had been so ordained that any heir, issuing from my body, should come after me. I have ruled over this people fifty winters; there was not one of the neighboring kings who dared encounter me with weapons, or could weigh me down with fear. In my own home I awaited what the times destined for me, kept my own well, did not pick treacherous quarrels, nor have I sworn unjustly any oaths. In all this may I, sick with deadly wounds, have solace; because the Governor of men may never charge me with the murder of kinsfolk, when my life parts from my body.

"Now quickly do thou go, beloved Wiglaf, and view the hoard under the hoary rock, now that the snake lies dead, — sleeps sorely wounded and bereft of treasure. Haste now, that I may see the ancient wealth, the golden store, may well survey the bright artistic gems, so that by reason of my wealth of treasure I may leave life more calmly and the nation which I ruled over so long."

Then, I was told, after these words, the son of Weohstan quickly obeyed his wounded lord, the maimed in fight, and went in his chain-mail, his woven battle-sark, under the barrow's vault. There, proud in triumph, the brave kinsman-thane beheld, when he went by the seat, many a costly ornament — glittering gold lying on the ground, marvels on the wall, and the lair of the reptile, the old twilight-flier, — drinking-cups standing, vessels of bygone races, dingy and of their overlayings shorn. There was many a helmet, old and rusty, many an armlet, twisted with cunning. Treasure, gold in the earth, may easily turn the head of any man, conceal it who will!

Moreover, he saw, towering above the hoard a standard all of gold, greatest of marvels wrought by hand, woven by human skill. From this a light shone forth, so that he could discern the surface of the ground, and scrutinize the treasures. There was no vestige of the reptile, for the sword had done away with him.

Thus I learnt how in the caverned hill one man rifled the hoard, the old-time work of giants, and at his own will loaded his lap with drinking-cups and dishes; also he took the banner, brightest of beacons. The sword of the aged prince (its blade was iron) had before that scotched him who had long been keeper of the treasures, who had for the hoard put forth his burning awe of flame, at midnight fierily welling out, till by a violent death he died.

The emissary hastened, eager for return, impelled by the valuables; anxiety tortured him as to whether he, the brave-minded one, would find the Storm-Geats' lord alive in the open place where he had left him, shorn of his strength, erewhile. At last he, bearing the treasures, found the famous prince, his lord, bleeding at the last gasp of life. Once more he began to sprinkle him with water, until the beginning of a speech broke forth from the store-house of his mind, — in pain the aged Beowulf spake, and looked upon the gold.

"I utter in words my thanks to the Ruler of all, the King of Glory, the everlasting Lord, for the treasures which I here gaze upon, in that I have been allowed to win such things for my people before my day of death! Now that I have given my old life in barter for the hoard of treasure, do ye henceforth supply the people's needs, — I may stay here no longer.

"Bid ye war-veterans raise a conspicuous barrow after the funeral fire, on a projection by the sea, which shall tower high on Hronesness as a memorial for my people, so that seafarers who urge their tall ships over the spray of ocean shall thereafter call it Beowulf's barrow."

The brave-souled prince undid from off his neck the golden collar, gave it to the thane, the young spear-warrior, and his gold-mounted helmet, ring and corslet, — bade him use them well. "Thou art the last of our race, the Wægmundings. Fate has swept all my kinsfolk off, undaunted nobles, to their doom. I must go after them."

That was the veteran's last expression of his spirit's thoughts before the bale-fire was his lot, — the hot destructive flames. His soul departed from his body to journey to the doom of righteous men.

So it went hardly with the younger man, that he beheld the most beloved on the ground, suffering miserably at the end of life. His destroyer, the terrible cave-dragon, lay also, bereft of being, overwhelmed by bale. No longer might the curling snake control the hoard of treasures, but iron blades, the hard, battle-dinted result of forging, took him off, so that the far-flier fell motionless from his wounds upon the ground, hard by his treasure-house. Never more did he whirl through the air in sport at midnight, and show his form, proud of his rich belongings, but on the earth he fell by the war-prince's power of hand.

So far as I have heard, indeed, no man of might, daring though he might be in every sort of deed, could prevail to rush against the venomous foe's blast or ransack with his hands the hall of rings, if on the mount he found the keeper standing guard.

In Beowulf's case the share of the splendid treasures was paid for with death; (but) both had traveled to the end of fitful life.

Not long after was it that the laggards in battle left the wood, ten timorous troth-breakers together, who had just shrunk from wielding their spears in their lord's great need; but in shame they bore their shields, their war-harness, to where the old chief lay, and gazed on Wiglaf. He, the foot-warrior, sat exhausted by the shoulders of his lord, and tried to rally him with water, — but it availed him nothing. He could not keep on earth the chieftain's spirit, much though he wished it, nor alter the will of the Almighty. For men of all degrees God's judgment had to issue in performance, just as it still does now.

Then a severe retort came promptly from the youthful hero for such as had erewhile lacked nerve. Wiglaf, the son of Weohstan, spoke out, the youth, sick at heart, looked on the unloved (crew): "Lo! this can he say who wills to speak the truth;

that the Lord of men who gave you those costly things, the war-harness that you stand there in, when he, the chieftain, gave many a time, on his ale-bench, helmets and corslets, the trustiest he could find far or near, to sitters in hall, his thanes — (that he) completely threw away those battle dresses, — woefully, when war befell him. No reason had the king — not he — to boast about his comrades in the field; albeit God, master of victories, accorded him that single-handed he might avenge himself with the sword, when prowess was required of him. Poorly was I able to act as body-guard for him in the fight, and yet I made a start beyond my power to help my relative; when with the sword I struck the deadly foe, he ever was the weaker, — the fire welled forth less strongly from his head. Too few defenders thronged around the prince, what time the crisis came for him.

"Now shall all loot-sharing and gifts of swords, all joy, all rights of ownership, be wanting to your breed; each mortal of your family will have to wander, shorn of his citizen-rights, as soon as nobles far and wide hear of your flight, your despicable act! Better is death to everyone of noble birth than an inglorious life."

Then he bade the battle-deed be told in the entrenchment, up over the sea-cliff, where, depressed in spirit, the band of noble warriors remained, the shield-bearers, in suspense about two things — his death-day and the return of the dear man.

Little did he who rode up to the headland keep back of the latest tidings, — he told it faithfully among all; "Now lies the joy-giver of the Weder-Folk, the Geatish Lord, still on his death-bed, — lies by the dragon's deeds in slaughterous rest. Lies side by side with him the taker of his life, prostrate from knife-gashes, — he could not with a sword inflict a wound in any way upon the monster. Wiglaf, the son of Weohstan, sits by Beowulf, the living noble by the dead; he stands guard over the head of friend and foe with reverent mien.

"Now there is likelihood for the folk of times of warfare, soon as the king's fall becomes widely known among the Franks and Frisians. Hard fighting was purposed against the Hugs, when Hygelac came journeying with his floating troop to Frisian land, where the Hetwaras vanquished him in battle, and bravely brought to pass by their superior strength that he, the armored chieftain, had to yield; he fell among his followers, — not an ornament did that prince give to his captains. Ever since that, the favor of the Merovingian (king) has been denied to us.

[Episode of the Battle of Ravenswood and Death of Ongentheow]

"Nor do I in the least expect peace or fair dealing from the Swedish nation; for it is widely known that Ongentheow deprived Hæthcyn, the son of Hrethel, of his life near Ravenswood, when the warlike Scylfings first attacked the Geatish people from vainglory. Quickly did the veteran father of Ohthere, old and terrible, give him a return-blow, killed the sea-king (Hæthcyn) and, though an old man, got him back his wife, the mother of Onela and Ohthere, though bereft of her gold adornments; and then he followed his deadly enemies until they escaped, hardly and without a chief, to Ravenswood. Then with a mighty army be encompassed those whom the sword had not dispatched, faint from their wounds, and through the livelong night he often vowed the wretched band a punishing — said he would get at them by morn with edge of sword — (hang) some on gallow-trees as sport for birds. Once more came help to the sad-hearted ones with early dawn, when they became aware of Hygelac's horn, his trumpet blast, — when the hero came, bearing down on their track with a picked body of his troops.

"The bloody track of Swedes and Geats, the murderous strife of men, was noticeable far and wide, — how these nations fostered the feud between themselves. Then the brave (king), the care-worn veteran, went with his tribesmen to his fastness, the lord Ongentheow moved further off. He had had experience of Hygelac's fighting powers, of the proud one's skill in war, and trusted not in resistance, that he might withstand the sea-folk and defend his treasures, children and wife from the ocean-farers, and so after that the aged man retreated from thence once more behind an earth-wall. Then was chase given to the Swedish folk, the banners of Hygelac overran the fastness until the Hrethlings pressed on the serried ranks.

"There was the gray-haired Ongentheow brought to bay by the edges of swords, so that the nation's king had to submit to his end at the hands of Eofor alone. Angrily did Wulf the son of Wonred strike at him with his weapon, so that at the stroke the blood spurted from the veins forth under his hair. Yet was the veteran Scylfing not affrighted, but quickly paid the deadly blow back with a harder counter-stroke, as soon as he, the nation's king, had turned on him. The active son of Wonred could not give the return blow to the older man, but he (Ongentheow) first clave his (Wulf's) helmet on his head, so that he had to budge, beflecked with gore. He fell to earth; and still he was not doomed, but he came round, though the wound punished him.

"Hygelac's sturdy follower (Eofor) let his broad blade, his old titanic sword, break, over the wall of shields, the massive helmet, the while his brother lay (prostrate); and then the king bowed down, — the shepherd of his folk was wounded mortally.

"Then were there many who bandaged up his brother (Wulf) and raised him up quickly, when power over the battle-field had been allowed them. Meanwhile one warrior stripped the other, and took from Ongentheow his iron corslet, his strong and hilted sword and also his helmet, — bare to Hygelac the veteran's harness. And he received the spoils and honorably promised him (Eofor) rewards before his men; and he performed it too, — he, lord of the Geats and son of Hrethel, recompensed Wulf and Eofor for the charge with copious treasure when he had got back home, and gave to each of them a hundred thousand in land and clustered rings; no man on earth could blame him for the gifts, since they (Eofor and Wulf) had earned the honors by fighting, — and to Eofor he gave his only daughter as a pledge of favor, and to grace his home."

"Such is the feud and enmity, the deadly hatred of the men, the Swedish folk, the valorous Scylfings, who will attack us, as I have no doubt, after the fall of their champions, when they have learned our lord is gone from life, who in the past guarded our wealth and nation against enemies, advanced the people's welfare, and furthermore did deeds of valor.

"Now speed is best, that we should look upon the people's king there, and bring him who gave us circlets on his way to the funeral pyre. No solitary object shall be consumed with the man of mettle; for there is a hoard of treasures, unnumbered gold, acquired at terrible cost, and now at last rings bought with his own life; these shall the fire eat up, the flames consume. No earl shall wear an ornament in his memory, nor shall fair maiden have a torque-adornment round her neck, but sad of mood and stripped of jewelry shall tread the land of exile — often, not merely once, — now that the army-leader has laid aside laughter, joy and mirth. Therefore shall many a spear, chill at morn, be grasped with fingers, lifted by the hand: no sound of harp shall wake the warriors, but the ashy raven, busy after doomed men, shall chatter much, and tell the eagle how it sped him at the feast, when he contending with the wolf laid bare the slain."

Thus the brave youth was a teller of grievous tales, nor was he much amiss in facts or words.

The whole band rose; they went sadly, with welling tears, by Earnanæs to see the wondrous sight. There they found on the sand, lifeless, keeping his helpless bed, him who in times past gave them rings; there had the hero's last day gone, in which the warrior-king, the Storm-Geats' prince, had died his wondrous death. But first they saw a stranger being there, — the odious reptile, lying on the plain there opposite. The fiery dragon, a grisly horror, was with glowing embers scorched. Fifty measured feet long was it as it lay; sometimes by night it used to occupy the gladsome air; then it came down again to seek its den; and there it was, rigid in death; it had inhabited the last of its earth-caves. Goblets and flagons by it stood, dishes there lay and precious swords, rusty and eaten through, as if they had lodged there a thousand winters in earth's bosom. At that time the mighty heritage, the gold store of men of old, was hedged round with a spell, that no man might touch the treasure-chamber, had not God himself, true king of victories, (he is the shield of men) granted to whom he would to open the hoard, even to such a man as seemèd meet to him.

Then it was manifest that the way of him who had unrighteously concealed the treasure under the rock-wall had not prospered. The keeper had at first killed off some few; and then the feud was savagely avenged. It is ever a mystery in what place a noble of brave repute may have to meet his fortunes' end, — when the man may occupy no longer the mead-hall with his kinsmen. With Beowulf thus it was, when he sought out the keeper of the mound, and deadly conflicts — he knew not on what account his parting from the world should happen. So the great chiefs who put that (treasure) there had laid on it a deep curse until doomsday, that the man who should plunder that place should be guilty of sin, be shut up in devils' haunts, bound in hell-bonds and visited with plagues. Yet he (Beowulf) was not eager after gold, foremost and first for the Lord's favor had he looked.

Wiglaf, son of Weohstan, spoke: "Often must many a noble suffer misery through the will of one, as it has happened to us. We could not instill any advice into the dear prince, the guardian of his kingdom, — that he should not attack the keeper of the gold, but let him lie where he had long time been, — rest in his quarters till the world's end. We have received the fate appointed from on high! The hoard is open to view, (but) terribly acquired, — too cruel was the fate the nation's king there tempted. I was within, and scanned it all, — the treasures of the chamber, — when it was granted me; not by any means was the journey under the earth-wall allowed me in friendly wise. I grasped hastily with my hands a great o'erwhelming load of hoarded treasures, — bore it out hither to my king: he was then still alive, conscious and sound in mind; the old man said many things in his distress, — told me to greet you, bade you form, appropriately to your champion's deeds, a lofty barrow at the bale-fire spot, great and magnificent, for that he was of men on the wide earth the worthiest warrior so long as he was suffered to enjoy the riches of his castle.

"Come now and let us haste to see once more and scan the heap of cunning treasures, a wondrous sight under the (rocky) wall! I will direct you, that you may see the rings and thick gold near enough. Let the bier be quickly made ready when we come out, and then let us carry our lord, the beloved man, to where he shall wait long in the keeping of the Almighty."

Then Weohstan's son, the hero bold in battle, bade orders be given to many castle-owning notables, that they, having retainers, should fetch firing-wood from far to place by the brave chief: "Now shall hot coals consume, the lurid flame tower round the strong support of warriors, who often braved the shower of darts, when a storm of arrows, forced from the strings, quivered above the wall of shields; when the shaft did its office, and urged forth the barb, sped by its feather-gear."

And so the wise son of Weohstan called from out the band the picked thanes, seven all told, of the king, — and they eight went under the foeman's vault; one warrior who went in front, bore in his hand a flaming torch. Who should then spoil the hoard was not arranged by lot, as soon as the warriors saw any part of it remain unguarded in the chamber and lie perishing; little did any reck that hurriedly they carried off the costly treasures. Also they shoved the dragon, that reptile, over the cliff-wall, — let the waves take the treasure-warder, the flood enfathom him. There was an altogether countless store of twisted gold, loaded upon a wagon; and the prince, the hoary warrior, was borne away to Hronesness.

The people of the Geats then made ready for him on the ground a firm-built funeral pyre, hung round with helmets, battle-shields, bright corslets, as he had begged them to. Then the sad men-at-arms laid in its midst the famous prince, their much-loved lord. The warriors then began to kindle on the mount the greatest of bale-fires; the swarthy wood-smoke towered above the blazing mass; the roaring flame mixed with the noise of weeping — the raging of the winds was stilled — till it had crumbled up the bony frame, hot to its core. Depressed in soul, they uttered forth their misery, [and mourned] their lord's decease. Moreover, the aged woman, with hair bound up, [sang] a doleful dirge [and said] repeatedly that she [greatly feared] evil days for herself, much carnage, the dread of [warriors, humiliation and captivity.]

Heaven swallowed up the smoke.

Then people of the Storm Geats raised a mound upon the cliff, the which was high and broad and visible from far by voyagers on sea, and in ten days they built the veteran's beacon.

The remnant of the burning they begirt with a wall in such sort as skilled men could plan most worthy of him. In the barrow they placed collars and fibulæ — all such adornments as brave-minded men had previously taken from the hoard. They left the wealth of nobles to the earth to keep, — (left) the gold in the ground, where it still exists, as unprofitable to men as it had been before.

Then the brave in battle, sons of nobles, twelve in all, rode round the barrow; they would lament their loss, mourn for their king, utter a dirge, and speak about their hero. They reverenced his manliness, extolled his noble deed with all their might; so it is meet that man should praise his friend and lord in words, and cherish him in heart when he must needs be fleeting from the body and go forth.

Thus did the people of the Geats, his hearth-companions, mourn the downfall of their lord, and said that he had been a mighty king, the mildest and the gentlest of men, the kindest to his people and the keenest after praise.

THE FINNESBURG FRAGMENT

translated by John R. Clark Hall (1911)

"... [T hese] are never gables burning!" Then spake the king young in war—
"This is no dawning from the east, nor here does any dragon fly, nor here do this
hall's gables burn, but hither forth they (the enemy) fare, the birds (of battle) sing,
the gray-coat howls, there is din of spear, shield answers to shaft. Now shines the
errant moon beneath the clouds. Now begin evil deeds, which will bring trouble on
this folk. But wake ye now: my men of war, hold fast your shields, think of brave
deeds, show courage at the front, be stout of heart!"

Then arose many a thane, bedight with gold, and girded on his sword. Then
to the doors two noble warriors went, Sigeferth and Eawa, and drew their swords,
and at the other doors Ordlaf and Guthlaf; and Hengest himself turned him upon
their track. Moreover, Garulf exhorted Guthhere, that he would not lead so noble
a life at the first onset to the chamber doors in armor, now that the man hardy in
battle purposed to take it; forasmuch as he, the valiant warrior, asked clearly over all,
WHO HELD THE DOOR?

"Sigeferth is my name," quoth he, "I am prince of the Secgs, a well-known
rover. Many troubles, hard conflicts, have I passed through; here is ordained for thee
whatever thou thyself dost try on me."

Then at the wall was sound of carnage; the keel-shaped shield, screen of man's
bony frame, was like to come apart in heroes' hands. The house-floor dinned, till in
the fight Garulf lay prone, Guthlaf's son, of all the landsmen first, and by him many
heroes. A crowd of foemen fell; the raven hovered, swarthy and sallow-brown; a sword-
gleam shone, as if all Finnesburg were on fire. Never have I heard tell in mortal strife
of sixty conquering fighters bearing themselves better and more worthily, nor ever
swains pay better for the luscious mead than did his liegemen yield return to Hnæf. Five
days they fought, and of their followers fell not one, although they held the doors. Then
did the wounded chief retire and went away, —said that his coat of mail was broken
through, his armor unavailing and his helmet pierced, as well.

Then straightway the shepherd of the people asked him how the warriors got
over their wounds, or which of the youths. . . .

THE WANDERER

translated by Nora Kershaw (1922)

The solitary man is constantly looking for mercy and God's compassion, though over the watery ways with gloomy heart he has long had to stir with his arms the icy sea, treading the paths of exile. Fate is absolutely fixed!

These are the words of a wanderer whose memory was full of troubles and cruel carnage, wherein his dear kinsmen had fallen:

"Ever it has been my lot to bewail my sorrows in solitude in the twilight of each morning. There is now no-one left alive to whom I dare tell frankly the feelings of my heart. I know truly that it is a mark of nobility in a knight that he should fasten securely and keep to himself the treasury in which his thoughts are stored – think what he will! For all his grief of heart a man cannot resist Fate, nor can his troubled spirit give him any help. And so those who are eager to be of good report generally keep their sorrow imprisoned in the secret chamber of the heart.

"I myself too, in my misery and distress, have constantly had to bind my feelings in fetters – exiled from home and far from my kinsmen – ever since the day when the dark earth closed over my generous lord, and I wandered away over the expanse of waters, destitute and distraught with the dangers of winter, looking in sorrow for the abode of a generous prince – if far or near I could find one who would feel regard for me in his banqueting hall, or comfort me in my friendlessness and entertain me with good cheer."

It will be realized by him who experiences it what a cruel companion anxiety is to one who has no kind protector. His thoughts are full of homeless wanderings – not of gold rings; of his shivering breast – not of the good things of the earth. He calls to mind the men of the hall and the giving of treasure, and how when he was young he was entertained to his heart's content by his generous lord. But now all his happiness has passed away!

It will be realized, assuredly, by him who will have to forego for all time the instructions of his dear lord and friend. Ever when distress and sleep together lay hold on the poor solitary, he dreams that he is greeting and kissing his liege-lord, and laying his hands and head on his knee – just as he used to do when he enjoyed the bounty of the throne in days of old. Then the friendless man awakes again and sees before him the gray waves – sees the sea-birds bathing and spreading their wings, and rime falling, and snow mingled with hail. The grievous wounds, which the loss of his lord has made in his heart, are all the harder to bear, and his sorrow comes back to him when the memory of his kinsmen passes through his mind. He greets them in glad strains and scans them all eagerly. His warrior comrades again melt away, and as they vanish their spirits bring no familiar greetings to his ear. His sorrow comes back to him as on and on he must urge his aching heart over the expanse of waters.

Assuredly I cannot think of any reason in the world why my spirit should not be clouded, when I reflect upon the whole life of noblemen – how halls have suddenly been left destitute of proud warrior squires – just as mankind here droops and perishes day by day.

Assuredly no man can acquire wisdom until he has spent many years in the world. A man of authority must be patient, – not too impetuous, or too hasty of speech, or too slack or reckless in combat, or too timid, or jubilant, or covetous, or too ready to boast ere he knows full well the issue. When an impetuous warrior is making a vow, he ought to pause until he knows full well the issue – whither the impulse of his heart will lead. A wise man must perceive how mysterious will be the time when the wealth of all this age will lie waste – just as now in diverse places throughout this earth walls are standing beaten by the wind and covered with rime. The bulwarks are dismantled, the banqueting halls are ruinous; their rulers lie bereft of joy and all their proud chivalry has fallen by the wall. Some have been cut off by battle, borne on their last journey. One was carried by birds over the deep sea; one was given over to death by the gray wolf; one was buried in a hole in the earth by a knight of sad countenance. Thus did the Creator of men lay waste this place of habitation until the clamor of its occupants all ceased, and the buildings raised of old by giants stood empty. He then who in a spirit of meditation has pondered over this ruin, and who with an understanding heart probes the mystery of our life down to its depths, will call to mind many slaughters of long ago and give voice to such words as these:

"What has become of the steed? What has become of the squire? What has become of the giver of treasure? What has become of the banqueting houses? Where are the joys of the hall? O shining goblet! O mailed warrior! O glory of the prince! How has that time passed away, grown shadowy under the canopy of night as though it had never been! There remains now of the beloved knights no trace save the wall wondrously high, decorated with serpent forms. The nobles have been carried off by the violence of spears, by weapons greedy for slaughter and by mighty Fate, and these ramparts of stone are battered by tempests. Winter's blast, the driving snow-storm enwraps the earth when the shades of night come darkly lowering, and sends from the North a cruel hail-storm in wrath against mankind.

"All the realm of earth is full of tribulation. The life of mankind in the world is shattered by the handiwork of the Fates. Here wealth and friends, liegemen and kinsfolk pass away. Desolation will hold sway throughout the wide world."

Thus spake the man wise of understanding as he sat communing with himself in solitude. Good is he who keeps his faith. A warrior must never be too precipitate in giving vent to the grief in his heart, unless he has learnt zealously to apply the remedy. Well will it be for him who seeks mercy and comfort from the Father in Heaven, upon whom all our security rests.

THE SEAFARER

translated by Nora Kershaw (1922)

I will recite a lay about my own history and recount my adventures – how in days of stress I have constantly suffered times of hardship. I have endured bitter anguish of heart and experienced many anxious moments in my bark through the terrible rolling of the waves. A distressing vigil has often been my lot at the stern of the ship, when it was dashing against the rocks. My feet have been numbed with cold, bound with chill fetters of frost, while my heart was beset with passionate sighs of distress and my spirit within me was torn by hunger – exhausted as I was by my struggle with the waves. A man whose blissful lot is cast on land cannot realize how I have passed the winter in paths of exile on the icy sea, miserable and distraught, deprived of my dear kinsmen and hung about with icicles, while the hail flew in showers. There I heard nothing but the roaring of the sea, the icy waves. Sometimes I had the song of the swan for my entertainment, the cry of the gannet and the shriek of the godwit for the laughter of men, the calling of the mew instead of mead-drinking. Storms buffeted the rocky cliffs, and the tern with icy plumage gave them answer, and again and again the eagle with dripping feathers took up the cry. I had no protecting kinsman who could comfort my desolate soul. Assuredly one who has spent a happy life in luxury and feasting in a great house, free from perilous adventures, can hardly believe what exhaustion I have repeatedly suffered on my sea-voyages. The shades of night came lowering, snow fell from the North, frost bound the land, and hail, coldest of grains, fell on the earth.

But assuredly even now my thoughts are making my heart to throb, until of my own accord I shall venture on the deep waters, the tossing of the salt waves. At every opportunity a yearning impulse incites my heart to set forth and seek the land of strangers far away. Assuredly there is no man on earth so high-hearted, or so generous, or so full of youthful vigor, or so bold in his deeds, or so high in his lord's favor, that he can ever be free from anxiety as to what is the Lord's purpose with regard to him, when he has to travel across the sea.

His thoughts are not on the harp or the giving of rings, he has no pleasure in womankind, nor joy in life, nor thought of anything whatever save the tossing waves: for there is never any peace of mind for him who goes to sea. The houses of the great are beautified by blossoming groves, the fields begin to look bright, mankind begins to stir itself; all these things urge the heart of a high-spirited man towards travel, if he has any inclination thereto. – They set out on long journeys over the paths of the sea. – The cuckoo too, summer's herald, incites him, calling with plaintive note, and cruelly foretells troubles to his heart. A nobleman who lives in luxury cannot realize what is endured by many of those who travel far and wide on paths of exile.

Assuredly my thoughts are now soaring beyond my breast; along the course of the sea my spirit soars, over the home of the whale and throughout the great expanse of earth. Again it comes back to me, eager and hungry, screaming on its solitary flight. Resistlessly it impels my heart to the road of the whale, over the expanse of waters. Assuredly I feel more passion for the joys of the Lord than for this lifeless and transient existence on land. I do not believe that earth's blessings will endure for ever. Always and under all circumstances it is matter for uncertainty until the time of its occurrence which of these three – sickness or old age or violence – will cut off the life of a man when the fated hour of his departure comes upon him.

Assuredly the best of records for every man is the praise of those who will live on and speak of him in after days – that before he has to depart he should succeed in prevailing on earth against the hostility of fiends, encountering the devil with daring deeds, so that the children of men may praise him in after days, and his fame may endure henceforth with the angels for ever and ever – the glory of eternal life, bliss among the righteous.

All the days of splendor of earth's realm are departed. There are now no kings or emperors or generous princes such as once there were, when they surpassed all their peers in glory, and lived in the most lordly splendor. All this chivalry has perished. Its joys are departed. A weaker race lingers on and possesses this world, living by toil. Glory lies in the dust. All that is noble on earth grows aged and fades away – just as every man now does throughout the world. Old age comes upon him, his face grows pallid; gray-haired he grieves in the knowledge that his friends of old days, the scions of princes, have been committed to the earth. While his spirit is ebbing his bodily frame cannot relish delicacies, nor suffer pain, nor raise the hand, nor think with the brain. Though he will spread with gold the grave of his own brother, and bury with the dead in treasures of various kinds what he wishes to have with him, yet gold, which he has hidden while he is still alive here, will not be able to help a soul which is sinful, in place of the fear of God.

Great is the terror of God, for the earth will be transformed. He fixed the immovable depths, the surface of the earth and the Heavens above.

Foolish is he who fears not his Lord: death will come to him when he is unprepared. Blessed is he who lives in humility: mercy will come to him from Heaven. God will stablish his heart for him, because he has faith in his might. A man must control a fierce temper and keep it within bounds. He must be true to his pledges, unblemished in his life. Every man should use moderation in cherishing love towards his friend and hatred towards his foe .... Fate is stronger, and God mightier than any man can imagine. Let us consider where our home lies and meditate further as to how we may reach it; and let us also further strive that we may attain to eternal bliss, where life is to be found in the love of the Lord, and joy in Heaven. Thanks be to the holy Prince of glory, the everlasting Lord, that he has shown us favor for all time! Amen.

THE BATTLE OF MALDON

translated by Cosette Faust and Stith Thompson (1918)

.... was broken;
He bade the young barons   abandon their horses,
To drive them afar   and dash quickly forth,
In their hands and brave heart   to put all hope of success.
The kinsman of Offa   discovered then first
That the earl would not brook   dishonorable bearing.
He held in his hand   the hawk that he loved,
Let him fly to the fields;   to the fight then he stepped;
By this one could know   that the knight was unwilling.
To weaken in war,   when his weapons he seized.
Edric wished also   to aid his chief,
His folk-lord in fight;   forward he bore
His brand to the battle;   a brave heart he had
So long as he held   locked in his hand
His board and his broad sword;   his boast he made good,
Fearless to fight   before his lord.
        Then Beorhtnoth began   to embolden the warriors;
He rode and counseled them,   his comrades he taught
How they should stand   in the stronghold's defense,
Bade them to bear   their bucklers correctly,
Fast by their hands   without fear in their hearts.
When the folk by fair words   he had fired with zeal,
He alighted in a crowd   of his loyal comrades,
Where he felt that his friends   were most faithful and true.
Then he stood on the strand;   sternly the messenger
Of the Vikings called   in vaunting words,
Brought him the boast   of the bloody seamen,
The errand to the earl,   at the edge of the water:
        "I am sent to thee   by seamen bold;
They bade me summon thee   to send them quickly

69

Rings for a ransom,   and rather than fight
It is better for you   to bargain with gold
Than that we should fiercely   fight you in battle.
It is futile to fight   if you fill our demands;
If you give us gold   we will grant you a truce.
If commands thou wilt make,   who art mightiest of warriors,
That thy folk shall be free   from the foemen's attack,
Shall give of their wealth   at the will of the seamen,
A treasure for tribute,   with a truce in return,
We will go with the gold   again to our ships,
We will sail to the sea   and vouchsafe to you peace."
Beorhtnoth burst forth,   his buckler he grasped,
His spear he seized,   and spoke in words
Full of anger and ire,   and answer he gave:
        "Dost thou hear, oh seamen,   what our heroes say?
Spears they will send   to the sailors as tribute,
Poisoned points   and powerful swords,
And such weapons of war   as shall win you no battles.
Envoy of Vikings,   your vauntings return,
Fare to thy folk   with a far sterner message,
That here staunchly stands   with his steadfast troops,
The lord that will fight   for the land of his fathers,
For the realm of Æthelred,   my royal chief,
For his folk and his fold;   fallen shall lie
The heathen at shield-play;   shameful I deem it
With our treasure as tribute   that you take to your ships,
Without facing a fight,   since thus far hither
You have come and encroached   on our king's domain.
You shall not so easily   earn our treasure;
You must prove your power   with point and sword edge,
With grim war grip   ere we grant you tribute."
        He bade then his band   to bear forth their shields,
Until they arrived   at the river bank.
The waters prevented   the warriors' encounter;
The tide flowed in,   the flood after the ebb,
Locked up the land;   too long it seemed
Until they could meet   and mingle their spears.
By Panta's stream   they stood in array,
The East Saxon army   and the eager shield-warriors ;
Each troop was helpless   to work harm on the other,
Save the few who were felled   by a flight of arrows.
The flood receded;   the sailors stood ready,
All of the Vikings   eager for victory.

Beorhtnoth bade the   bridge to be defended,
The brave-hearted warrior,   by Wulfstan the bold
With his crowd of kinsmen;   he was Ceola's son,
And he felled the first   of the foemen who stepped
On the bridge, the boldest   of the band of men.
There waited with Wulfstan   the warriors undaunted,
Ælfhere and Maccus,   men of courage;
At the ford not a foot   would they flee the encounter,
But close in conflict   they clashed with the foe,
As long as they wielded   their weapons with strength.
As soon as they saw   and perceived it clearly,
How fiercely fought   was the defense of the bridge,
The treacherous tribe   in trickery asked
That they be allowed   to lead their hosts
For a closer conflict,   to cross over the ford.
Then the earl, too eager   to enter the fight,
Allowed too much land   to the loathed pirates.
Clearly then called   over the cold water
Beorhthelm's son;   the soldiers listened:
        "Room is now made for you;   rush quickly here
Forward to the fray;   fate will decide
Into whose power shall pass this place of battle."
Went then the battle-wolves—   of water they recked not—
The pirate warriors   west over Panta;
Over the bright waves   they bore their shields;
The seamen stepped   to the strand with their lindens.
        In ready array   against the raging hosts
Stood Beorhtnoth's band;   he bade them with shields
To form a phalanx,   and to defend themselves stoutly,
Fast holding the foe.   The fight was near,
The triumph at conflict;   the time had come
When fated men   should fall in battle.
        Then arose an alarm;   the ravens soared,
The eagle eager for prey;   on earth was commotion.
Then sped from their hands   the hardened spears,
Flew in fury   file-sharpened darts;
Bows were busy,   boards met javelins,
Cruel was the conflict;   in companies they fell;
On every hand   lay heaps of youths.
Wulfmær was woefully   wounded to death,
Slaughtered the sister's   son of Beorhtnoth;
With swords he was strongly   stricken to earth.

To the vikings quickly   requital was given;
I learned that Edward   alone attacked
Stoutly with his sword,   not stinting his blows,
So that fell at his feet   many fated invaders;
For his prowess the prince   gave praise and thanks
To his chamberlain brave,   when chance would permit.
So firm of purpose   they fought in their turn,
Young men in battle;   they yearned especially
To lead their line   with the least delay
To fight their foes   in fatal conflict,
Warriors with weapons.   The world seethed with slaughter.
Steadfast they stood,   stirred up by Beorhtnoth;
He bade his thanes   to think on battle,
And fight for fame   with the foemen Danes.
The fierce warrior went,   his weapon he raised,
His shield for a shelter;   to the soldier he came;
The chief to the churl   a challenge addressed;
Each to the other   had evil intent.
The seamen then sent   from the south a spear,
So that wounded lay   the lord of the warriors;
He shoved with his shield   till the shaft was broken,
And burst the spear   till back it sprang.
Enraged was the daring one;   he rushed with his dart
On the wicked warrior   who had wounded him sore.
Sage was the soldier;   he sent his javelin
Through the grim youth's neck;   he guided his hand
And furiously felled   his foeman dead.
Straightway another   he strongly attacked.
And burst his byrnie;   in his breast he wounded him.
Through his hard coat-of-mail;   in his heart there stood
The poisoned point.   Pleased was the earl,
Loudly he laughed,   to the Lord he gave thanks
For the deeds of the day   the Redeemer had granted.
A hostile youth hurled   from his hand a dart;
The spear in flight   then sped too far,
And the honorable earl   of Æthelred fell.
By his side there stood   a stripling youth,
A boy in battle   who boldly drew
The bloody brand   from the breast of his chief.
The young Wulfmær,   Wulfstan's son,
Gave back again   the gory war-lance;
The point pierced home,   so that prostrate lay
The Viking whose valor   had vanquished the earl.

To the earl then went   an armed warrior;
He sought to snatch   and seize his rings,
His booty and bracelets,   his bright shining sword.
Beorhtnoth snatched forth   the brown-edged weapon
From his sheath, and sharply   shook the attacker;
Certain of the seamen   too soon joined against him,
As he checked the arm   of the charging enemy;
Now sank to the ground   his golden brand;
He might not hold   the hilt of his mace,
Nor wield his weapons.   These words still he spoke,
To embolden the youths;   the battle-scarred hero
Called on his comrades   to conquer their foes;
He no longer had strength   to stand on his feet,
....   he looked to heaven:
"Ruler of realms,   I render thee thanks
For all of the honors   that on earth I have had;
Now, gracious God,   have I greatest of need
That thou save my soul   through thy sovereign mercy,
That my spirit speed   to its splendid home
And pass into thy power,   O Prince of angels,
And depart in peace;   this prayer I make,
That the hated hell-fiends   may harass me not."
     Then the heathen dogs   hewed down the noble one,
And both the barons   that by him stood
Ælfnoth and Wulfmær   each lay slaughtered;
They lost their lives   in their lord's defense.
Then fled from the fray   those who feared to remain.
First in the frantic   flight was Godric,
The son of Odda;   he forsook his, chief
Who had granted him gifts   of goodly horses;
Lightly he leapt   on his lord's own steed,
In its royal array —   no right had he to it;
His brothers also   the battle forsook.
Godwin and Godwy   made good their escape,
And went to the wood,   for the war they disliked;
They fled to the fastnesses   in fear of their lives.
And many more   of the men than was fitting,
Had they freshly in mind   remembered the favors,
The good deeds he had done them   in days of old.
Wise were the words   spoken once by Offa
As he sat with his comrades   assembled in council:
     "There are many who boast   in the mead-hall of bravery
Who turn in terror   when trouble comes."

The chief of the folk   now fell to his death,
Æthelred's earl;   all his companions
Looked on their lord   as he lay on the field.
Now there approached   some proud retainers;
The hardy heroes   hastened madly,
All of them eager   either to die
Or valiantly avenge   their vanquished lord.
They were eagerly urged   by Ælfric's son,
A warrior young in winters;   these words he spoke
Ælfwine then spoke,   an honorable speech:
     "Remember how we made   in the mead-hall our vaunts,
From the benches our boasts   of bravery we raised,
Heroes in the hall,   of hard-fought battles;
The time has now come   for the test of your courage.
Now I make known   my noble descent;
I come from Mercia,   of mighty kinsmen;
My noble grandsire's   name was Ealdhelm,
Wise in the ways   of the world this elder.
Among my proud people   no reproach shall be made
That in fear I fled   afar from the battle,
To leave for home   with my leader hewn down,
Broken in battle;   that brings me most grief;
He was not only my earl   but also my kinsman."
Then harboring hatred   he hastened forth,
And with the point of spear   he pierced and slew
A seaman grim   who sank to the ground
Under weight of the weapon.   To war he incited
His friends and fellows,   in the fray to join.
     Offa shouted;   his ash-spear shook:
"Thou exhortest, O Ælfwine,   in the hour of need,
When our lord is lying   full low before us,
The earl on the earth;   we all have a duty
That each one of us   should urge on the rest
Of the warriors to war,   while his weapons in hand
He may have and hold,   his hard-wrought mace,
His dart and good sword.   The deed of Godric,
The wicked son of Offa,   has weakened us all;
Many of the men thought   when he mounted the steed,
Rode on the proud palfry,   that our prince led us forth;
Therefore on the field   the folk were divided,
The shield-wall was shattered.   May shame curse the man
Who deceived our folk   and sent them in flight. "

Leofsunu spoke   and his linden-shield raised,
His board to defend him   and embolden his fellows:
     "I promise you now   from this place I will never
Flee a foot-space,   but forward will rush,
Where I vow to revenge   my vanquished lord.
The stalwart warriors   round Sturmere shall never
Taunt me and twit me   for traitorous conduct,
That lordless I fled   when my leader had fallen,
Ran from the war;   rather may weapons,
The iron points slay me."   Full ireful he went;
Fiercely he fought;   flight he disdained.
     Dunhere burst forth;   his dart he brandished,
Over them all;   the aged churl cried,
Called the brave ones to battle   in Beorhtnoth's avenging:
"Let no hero now hesitate   who hopes to avenge
His lord on the foemen,   nor fear for his life. "
Then forward they fared   and feared not for their lives;
The clansman with courage   the conflict began;
Grasped their spears grimly,   to God made their prayer
That they might dearly repay   the death of their lord,
And deal defeat   to their dastardly foes.
A hostage took hold now   and helped them with courage;
He came from Northumbria   of a noble kindred,
The son of Ecglaf,   Æscferth his name;
He paused not a whit   at the play of weapons,
But unerringly aimed   his arrows uncounted;
Now he shot on the shield,   now he shattered a Viking;
With the point of his arrow   he pierced to the marrow
While he wielded his weapons   of war unsubdued.
     Still in the front   stood the stalwart Edward,
Burning for battle;   his boasts he spoke:
He never would flee   a foot-pace of land,
Or leave his lord   where he lay on the field;
He shattered the shield-wall;   with the shipmen he fought,
Till on the treacherous tribesmen   his treasure-giver's death
He valiantly avenged   ere his violent end.
     Such daring deeds   did the doughty Æthric,
Brother of Sibyrht   and bravest of soldiers;
He eagerly fought   and the others followed;
They cleft the curvèd shields;   keenly they battled;
Then burst the buckler's rim,   and the byrnies sang.
A song of slaughter.   Then was slain in battle,
The seaman by Offa;   and the earth received him;

Soon Offa himself   was slain in battle;
He had laid down his life   for his lord as he promised
In return for his treasure,   when he took his vow
That they both alive   from battle should come,
Hale to their homes   or lie hewn down in battle,
Fallen on the field   with their fatal wounds;
He lay by his lord   like a loyal thane.
    Then shivered the shields;   the shipmen advanced,
Raving with rage;   they ran their spears
Through their fated foes.   Forth went Wistan,
Thurstan's son then,   to the thick of the conflict.
In the throng he slew   three of the sailors,
Ere the son of Wigeline   sent him to death.
The fight was stiff;   and fast they stood;
In the cruel conflict   they were killed by scores,
Weary with wounds;   woeful was the slaughter.
    Oswald and Eadwold   all of the while,
Both the brothers,   emboldened the warriors,
Encouraged their comrades   with keen spoken words,
Besought them to strive   in their sore distress,
To wield their weapons   and not weaken in battle.
Byrhtwold then spoke;   his buckler he lifted,
The old companion,   his ash-spear shook
And boldly encouraged   his comrades to battle:
    "Your courage be the harder,   your hearts be the keener,
And sterner the strife   as your strength grows less.
Here lies our leader   low on the earth,
Struck down in the dust;   doleful forever
Be the traitor who tries   to turn from the war-play.
I am old of years,   but yet I flee not;
Staunch and steadfast   I stand by my lord,
And I long to be   by my loved chief."
    So the son of Æthelgar   said to them all.
Godric emboldened them;   oft he brandished his lance,
Violently threw   at the Vikings his war-spear,
So that first among the folk   he fought to the end;
Hewed down and hacked,   till the hated ones killed him—
Not that Godric who fled   in disgrace from the fight.

2. MIDDLE ENGLISH

The period of Middle English literature runs sometime roughly after the Norman Conquest (1066) on through about the next four centuries. Tolkien's major interests in this period lay in the works of two poets and in the language of one dialect of Middle English, that of the West Midlands, where, far away from the courts of London and the Norman aristocracy, the language and poetry retained many Anglo-Saxon features and characteristics for much longer than it did anywhere else.

We do not know for certain the name of the first poet to whom Tolkien devoted much of his attention. This poet wrote in the West Midlands dialect of Middle English, and is remembered especially for four poems that survive in a single manuscript, *Sir Gawain and the Green Knight*, *Pearl*, *Cleanness* (sometimes called *Purity*), and *Patience*. Another work found in a different manuscript, *Saint Erkenwald*, is sometimes attributed to the same poet, who is now generally referred to as the Gawain-Poet or the Pearl-Poet. *Sir Gawain and the Green Knight* is written in a complex poetical stanza, using alliteration (or head-rhyme) and end-rhyme. It is, as Tolkien himself observed, a fairy tale for adults, in which a knight from Arthur's court is tested through a pact with a large otherworldly green man. *Pearl*, also written in a complex poetical stanza (very different from that used in *Gawain*), is an example of a popular genre of the Middle Ages, the medieval dream-vision. In *Pearl* a man laments the loss of his young daughter, but is granted a vision of her in paradise.

With his colleague E. V. Gordon, Tolkien co-edited the standard edition of *Sir Gawain and the Green Knight* (1925), and though they also worked together on an edition of *Pearl*, it eventually came out in 1953 under Gordon's name alone, edited by Gordon's widow. Tolkien worked on his own translations of these two poems for many years, but they were published only posthumously, edited by Christopher Tolkien, in the volume titled *Sir Gawain and the Green Knight, Pearl, and Sir Orfeo* (1975). Tolkien's primary object in these translations was to attempt to reproduce the complex Middle English poetical forms in modern English versions.

Tolkien's critical views on the *Gawain* poem were given as the W. P. Ker Memorial Lecture at the University of Glasgow in April 1953. This lecture was finally published, under the title "Sir Gawain and the Green Knight," in *The Monsters and the Critics and Other Essays*, edited by Christopher Tolkien.

The second poet to whom Tolkien devoted much attention is Geoffrey Chaucer, who was born around 1340 and who died in 1400. Chaucer is best remembered for *The Canterbury Tales*, a remarkably diverse collection of tales shared by pilgrims amongst themselves while on a journey to Canterbury. Chaucer's other major works include *The Book of the Duchess*, *The House of Fame*, *The Parliament of Fowls*, *Troilus and Criseyde*, and *The Legend of Good Women*.

One of Tolkien's major pieces of scholarship was his article "Chaucer as a Philologist: *The Reeves' Tale*," in which he shows how Chaucer, for humorous purposes, used a northern dialect of Middle English in the speech of the two students in *The Reeve's Tale*.

Tolkien's other publications with regard to Middle English include his first book, *A Middle English Vocabulary*, which is basically a glossary that was designed to accompany Kenneth Sisam's anthology *Fourteenth Century Verse and Prose* (1921). In 1944, Tolkien prepared an edition of the poem *Sir Orfeo*, a reworking on the Orpheus legend in the manner of a Breton lay, for use of the students in a naval cadet's course. Tolkien's own translation of it, collected in *Sir Gawain and the Green Knight, Pearl, and Sir Orfeo*, is a superb rendering of an excellent poem. It is simply so good on its own that no prose version could do it justice, and I refer readers immediately to Tolkien's translation.

In 1962, Tolkien published an edition of *The Ancrene Wisse*, a work of devotional literature for anchorites—women who have withdrawn into religious seclusion and committed themselves to living in the solitary enclosure of a single small place, usually a cell attached to a church, where their main activities include prayer, meditation and devotional reading. This work is written in the West Midlands dialect of Middle English, and Tolkien's interest in it seems to have been largely to do with its language. One of Tolkien's students, M.B. Salu, published a translation of it, as *The Ancrene Riwle* (1955), with a short preface by Tolkien.

For this anthology I have included prose versions of the two best-known works of the Gawain-poet, *Sir Gawain and the Green Knight*, translated by Jessie L. Weston, and *Pearl*, translated by Charles G. Osgood, Jr. To represent Chaucer, I have selected three very different stories from *The Canterbury Tales*, translated into prose by John S. P. Tatlock and Percy MacKaye. *The Reeve's Tale* (a "reeve" was a kind of local official) is a variation on French *fabliaux*, bawdy and scurrilous popular tales which are usually situation comedies that burlesque the weaknesses of human nature. The Tatlock and MacKaye translation interestingly reproduces the speech of the two students in a kind of northern dialect (following Chaucer's original intent), but otherwise their version was significantly bowdlerlized. I have silently restored the missing sections to present the tale as Chaucer original told it. *The Nun's Priest's Tale* is an animal fable, using an episode from the popular stories of Reynard the Fox. I selected for inclusion here both *The Reeve's Tale* and *The Nun's Priest's Tale* owing to the fact that Tolkien impersonated Chaucer and recited these two tales from memory at the "Summer Diversions" in Oxford in 1938 and 1939. (Anderson, *The Annotated Hobbit*, pp. 70-71.) *The Franklin's Tale* is in the style of a Breton lay. Thus while it was written in Middle English, its content is actually Celtic. Tolkien himself wrote a variation on a Breton lay in his poem "The Lay of Aotrou and Itroun."

The final item in this section is not strictly a translation, but a retelling from the various medieval legends of Alexander—particularly from some Middle English accounts. In the introduction to his anthology *Tales before Tolkien*, Douglas A. Anderson noted that Tolkien's Two Trees in Valinor were inspired by the medieval legends of Alexander the Great, who had discovered the Trees of the Sun and Moon in the Far East. (Anderson, *Tales before Tolkien*, p. 1.)

For my September 2003 column for Green Books at TheOneRing.net, I did a question and answer session with Anderson, and specifically asked him about this reference to a possible source of inspiration for the Two Trees. In his answer, he stated:

"There is as large a tradition of medieval literature about Alexander the Great, much of which is forgotten today. Some of these legends are very fanciful, and in at least one Middle English version Alexander travels to the Far East where he encounters the Trees of the Sun and Moon, which he consults like oracles and they foretell his future. Tolkien himself is the authority for this comment. An interviewer asked

79

him in 1965 if his Two Trees were in any way a reflection of the World Tree in Old Norse mythology, and Tolkien responded: "No, no, they're not like it; they're much more like the Trees of the Sun and Moon discovered in the Far East, in the great Alexander stories." ("Q&A with Douglas A. Anderson," http://greenbooks.theonering.net/turgon/files/ 091503_01.html)

Most of the medieval Alexander stories remain untranslated, but Richard Steele used many of them as a basis for his retelling of *The Story of Alexander*. Two chapters are here reprinted from his retelling. Steele's source for the section about the Trees of the Sun and Moon is apparently a Middle English version called *The Wars of Alexander*, printed by the Early English Text Society.

For verse translations of *Sir Gawain and the Green Knight* and *Pearl*, most Tolkien readers will no doubt turn to Tolkien's own excellent translations. Those by Marie Borroff, *Sir Gawain and the Green Knight: A New Verse Translation* (1967) and *Pearl: A New Verse Translation* (1977), are worthy and recommended. Also notable are the translations by John Gardner published as *The Complete Works of the Gawain Poet* (1965), which includes both *Sir Gawain and the Green Knight* and *Pearl*, as well as *Purity*, *Patience*, and *Saint Erkenwald*.

For a complete version of *The Canterbury Tales*, among the many translations I would recommend the verse translation by Tolkien's friend and fellow Inkling Nevill Coghill, first published by Penguin in 1952. Chaucer's other major works are available in various translations.

There are many other works of Middle English literature available in modern translations. To name only a few, I might single out William Langland's poem *Piers Plowman* (look for the 1996 translation by George Economou), Sir John Mandeville's *Travels*, or a personal favorite, the anonymous verse debate *The Owl and the Nightingale*. John Gardner included a translation of the latter, with other very interesting works, in his anthology *The Alliterative Morte Arthure, The Owl and the Nightingale, and Five Other Middle English Poems* (1971). Lastly, there are several other Breton lays written in Middle English beyond *Sir Orfeo*.

SIR GAWAIN AND THE GREEN KNIGHT

translated by Jessie L. Weston (1898)

After the siege and the assault of Troy; when that burg was destroyed and burnt to ashes, and the traitor tried for his treason, the noble Aeneas and his kin sailed forth to become princes and patrons of well-nigh all the Western Isles. Thus Romulus built Rome (and gave to the city his own name, which it bears even to this day); and Ticius turned him to Tuscany; and Langobard raised him up dwellings in Lombardy; and Felix Brutus sailed far over the French flood, and founded the kingdom of Britain, wherein have been war and waste and wonder, and bliss and bale, oft-times since.

And in that kingdom of Britain have been wrought more gallant deeds than in any other; but of all British kings Arthur was the most valiant, as I have heard tell, therefore will I set forth a wondrous adventure that fell out in his time. And if ye will listen to me, but for a little while, I will tell it even as it stands in story stiff and strong, fixed in the letter, as it hath long been known in the land.

King Arthur lay, at Camelot upon a Christmas-tide, with many a gallant lord and lovely lady, and all the noble brotherhood of the Round Table. There they held rich revels with gay talk and jest; one while they would ride forth to joust and tourney, and again back to the court I to make carols; for there was the feast holden fifteen days with all the mirth that men could devise, song and glee, glorious to hear, in the daytime, and dancing at night. Halls and chambers were crowded with noble guests, the bravest of knights and the loveliest of ladies, and Arthur himself was the comeliest king that ever held a court. For all this fair folk were in their youth, the fairest and most fortunate under heaven, and the king himself of such fame that it were hard now to name so valiant a hero.

Now the New Year had but newly come in, and on that day a double portion was served on the high table to all the noble guests, and thither came the king with all his knights, when the service in the chapel had been sung to an end. And they greeted each other for the New Year, and gave rich gifts, the one to the other (and they that received them were not wroth, that may ye well believe!), and the maidens

81

laughed and made mirth till it was time to get them to meat. Then they washed and sat them down to the feast in fitting rank and order, and Guinevere the queen, gaily clad, sat on the high dais. Silken was her seat, with a fair canopy over her head, of rich tapestries of Tars, embroidered, and studded with costly gems; fair she was to look upon, with her shining gray eyes, a fairer woman might no man boast himself of having seen.

But Arthur would not eat till all were served, so full of joy and gladness was he, even as a child; he liked not either to lie long, or to sit long at meat, so worked upon him his young blood and his wild brain. And another custom he had also, that came of his nobility, that he would never eat upon an high day till he had been advised of some knightly deed, or some strange and marvelous tale, of his ancestors, or of arms, or of other ventures. Or till some stranger knight should seek of him leave to joust with one of the Round Table, that they might set their lives in jeopardy, one against another, as fortune might favor them. Such was the king's custom when he sat in hall at each high feast with his noble knights, therefore on that New Year tide, he abode, fair of face, on the throne, and made much mirth withal.

Thus the king sat before the high tables, and spake of many things; and there good Sir Gawain was seated by Guinevere the queen, and on her other side sat Agravain, *à la dure main* ; both were the king's sister's sons and full gallant knights. And at the end of the table was Bishop Bawdewyn, and Ywain, King Urien's son, sat at the other side alone. These were worthily served on the dais, and at the lower tables sat many valiant knights. Then they bare the first course with the blast of trumpets and waving of banners, with the sound of drums and pipes, of song and lute, that many a heart was uplifted at the melody. Many were the dainties, and rare the meats, so great was the plenty they might scarce find room on the board to set on the dishes. Each helped himself as he liked best, and to each two were twelve dishes, with great plenty of beer and wine.

Now I will say no more of the service, but that ye may know there was no lack, for there drew near a venture that the folk might well have left their labor to gaze upon. As the sound of the music ceased, and the first course had been fitly served, there came in at the hall door one terrible to behold, of stature greater than any on earth; from neck to loin so strong and thickly made, and with limbs so long and so great that he seemed even as a giant. And yet he was but a man, only the mightiest that might mount a steed; broad of chest and shoulders and slender of waist, and all his features of like fashion; but men marveled much at his color, for he rode even as a knight, yet was green all over.

For he was clad all in green, with a straight coat, and a mantle above; all decked and lined with fur was the cloth and the hood that was thrown back from his locks and lay on his shoulders. Hose had he of the same green, and spurs of bright gold with silken fastenings richly worked; and all his vesture was verily green. Around his waist and his saddle were bands with fair stones set upon silken work,' twere too long to tell of all the trifles that were embroidered thereon – birds and insects in gay gauds of green and gold.

All the trappings of his steed were of metal of like enamel, even the stirrups that he stood in stained of the same, and stirrups and saddle-bow alike gleamed and shone with green stones. Even the steed on which he rode was of the same hue, a green horse, great and strong, and hard to hold, with broidered bridle, meet for the rider.

The knight was thus gaily dressed in green, his hair falling around his shoulders, on his breast hung a beard, as thick and green as a bush, and the beard and the hair of his head were clipped all round above his elbows. The lower part of his sleeves were fastened with clasps in the same wise as a king's mantle. The horse's mane was crisp and plaited with many a knot folded in with gold thread about the fair green, here a twist of the hair, here another of gold. The tail was twined in like manner, and both were bound about with a band of bright green set with many a precious stone; then they were tied aloft in a cunning knot, whereon rang many bells of burnished gold. Such a steed might no other ride, nor had such ever been looked upon in that hall ere that time; and all who saw that knight spake and said that a man might scarce abide his stroke.

The knight bore no helm nor hauberk, neither gorget nor breast-plate, neither shaft nor buckler to smite nor to shield, but in one hand he had a holly-bough, that is greenest when the groves are bare, and in his other an axe, huge and uncomely, a cruel weapon in fashion, if one would picture it. The head was an ell-yard long, the metal all of green steel and gold, the blade burnished bright, with a broad edge, as well shapen to shear as a sharp razor. The steel was set into a strong staff, all bound round with iron, even to the end, and engraved with green in cunning work. A lace was twined about it, that looped at the head, and all adown the handle it was clasped with tassels on buttons of bright green richly broidered.

The knight rideth through the entrance of the hall, driving straight to the high dais, and greeted no man, but looked ever upwards; and the first words he spake were, "Where is the ruler of this folk? I would gladly look upon that hero, and have speech with him." He cast his eyes on the knights, and mustered them up and down, striving ever to see who of them was of most renown.

Then was there great gazing to behold that chief, for each man marveled what it might mean that a knight and his steed should have even such a hue as the green grass; and that seemed even greener than green enamel on bright gold. All looked on him as he stood, and drew near unto him wondering greatly what he might be; for many marvels had they seen, but none such as this, and phantasm and faerie did the folk deem it. Therefore were the gallant. knights slow to answer, and gazed astounded, and sat stone still in a deep silence through that goodly hall, as if a slumber were fallen upon them. I deem it was not all for doubt, but some for courtesy that they might give ear unto his errand.

Then Arthur beheld this adventurer before his high dais, and knightly he greeted him, for fearful was he never. "Sir," he said, "thou art welcome to this place – lord of this hall am I, and men call me Arthur. Light thee down, and tarry awhile, and what thy will is, that shall we learn after."

"Nay," quoth the stranger, "so help me He that sitteth on high, 'twas not mine errand to tarry any while in this dwelling; but the praise of this thy folk and thy city is lifted up on high, and thy warriors are holden for the best and the most valiant of those who ride mail-clad to the fight. The wisest and the worthiest of this world are they, and well proven in all knightly sports. And here, as I have heard tell, is fairest courtesy, therefore have I come hither as at this time. Ye may be sure by the branch that I bear here that I come in peace, seeking no strife. For had I willed to journey in warlike guise I have at home both hauberk and helm, shield and shining spear, and other weapons to mine hand, but since I seek no war my raiment is that of peace. But if thou be as bold as all men tell thou wilt freely grant me the boon I ask."

And Arthur answered, "Sir Knight, if thou cravest battle here thou shalt not fail for lack of a foe."

And the knight answered, "Nay, I ask no fight, in faith here on the benches are but beardless children, were I clad in armor on my steed there is no man here might match me. Therefore I ask in this court but a Christmas jest, for that it is Yule-tide, and New Year, and there are here many fain for sport. If anyone in this hall holds himself so hardy, so bold both of blood and brain, as to dare strike me one stroke for another, I will give him as a gift this axe, which is heavy enough, in sooth, to handle as he may list, and I will abide the first blow, unarmed as I sit. If any knight be so bold as to prove my words let him come swiftly to me here, and take this weapon, I quit claim to it, he may keep it as his own, and I will abide his stroke, firm on the floor. Then shalt thou give me the right to deal him another, the respite of a year and a day shall he have. Now haste, and let see whether any here dare say aught."

Now if the knights had been astounded at the first, yet stiller were they all, high and low, when they had heard his words. The knight on his steed straightened himself in the saddle, and rolled his eyes fiercely round the hall, red they gleamed under his green and bushy brows. He frowned and twisted his beard, waiting to see who should rise, and when none answered he cried aloud in mockery, "What, is this Arthur's hall, and these the knights whose renown hath run through many realms? Where are now your pride and your conquests, your wrath, and anger, and mighty words? Now are the praise and the renown of the Round Table overthrown by one man's speech, since all keep silence for dread ere ever they have seen a blow!"

With that he laughed so loudly that the blood rushed to the king's fair face for very shame; he waxed wroth, as did all his knights, and sprang to his feet, and drew near to the stranger and said, "Now by heaven foolish is thy asking, and thy folly shall find its fitting answer. I know no man aghast at thy great words. Give me here thine axe and I shall grant thee the boon thou hast asked." Lightly he sprang to him and caught at his hand, and the knight, fierce of aspect, lighted down from his charger.

Then Arthur took the axe and gripped the haft, and swung it round, ready to strike. And the knight stood before him, taller by the head than any in the hall; he stood, and stroked his beard, and drew down his coat, no more dismayed for the king's threats than if one had brought him a drink of wine.

Then Gawain, who sat by the queen, leaned forward to the king and spake, "I beseech ye, my lord, let this venture be mine. Would ye but bid me rise from this seat, and stand by your side, so that my liege lady thought it not ill, then would I come to your counsel before this goodly court. For I think it not seemly when such challenges be made in your hall that ye yourself should undertake it, while there are many bold knights who sit beside ye, none are there, methinks, of readier will under heaven, or more valiant in open field. I am the weakest, I know, and the feeblest of wit, and it will be the less loss of my life if ye seek sooth. For save that ye are mine uncle naught is there in me to praise, no virtue is there in my body save your blood, and since this challenge is such folly that it beseems ye not to take it, and I have asked it from ye first, let it fall to me, and if I bear myself ungallantly then let all this court blame me."

Then they all spake with one voice that the king should leave this venture and grant it to Gawain.

Then Arthur commanded the knight to rise, and he rose up quickly and knelt down before the king, and caught hold of the weapon; and the king loosed his hold of it, and lifted up his hand, and gave him his blessing, and bade him be strong both of heart and hand. "Keep thee well, nephew," quoth Arthur; "that thou give him but the one blow, and if thou redest him rightly I trust thou shalt well abide the stroke he may give thee after."

Gawain stepped to the stranger, axe in hand, and he, never fearing, awaited his coming. Then the Green Knight spake to Sir Gawain, "Make we our covenant ere we go further. First, I ask thee, knight, what is thy name? Tell me truly, that I may know thee."

"In faith," quoth the good knight, "Gawain am I, who give thee this buffet, let what may come of it; and at this time twelvemonth will I take another at thine hand with whatsoever weapon thou wilt, and none other."

Then the other answered again, "Sir Gawain, so may I thrive as I am fain to take this buffet at thine hand," and he quoth further, "Sir Gawain, it liketh me well that I shall take at thy fist that which I have asked here, and thou hast readily and truly rehearsed all the covenant that I asked of the king, save that thou shalt swear me, by thy troth, to seek me thyself wherever thou hopest that I may be found, and win thee such reward as thou dealest me today, before this folk."

"Where shall I seek thee?" quoth Gawain. "Where is thy place? By Him that made me, I know never where thou dwellest, nor know I thee, knight, thy court, nor thy name. But teach me truly all that pertaineth thereto, and tell me thy name, and I shall use all my wit to win my way thither, and that I swear thee for sooth, and by my sure troth."

"That is enough in the New Year, it needs no more," quoth the Green Knight to the gallant Gawain, "if I tell thee truly when I have taken the blow, and thou hast smitten me; then will I teach thee of my house and home, and mine own name, then mayest thou ask thy road and keep covenant. And if I waste no words then farest thou the better, for thou canst dwell in thy land, and seek no further. But take now thy toll, and let see how thy strikest."

"Gladly will I," quoth Gawain, handling his axe.

Then the Green Knight swiftly made him ready, he bowed down his head, and laid his long locks on the crown that his bare neck might be seen. Gawain gripped his axe and raised it on high, the left foot he set forward on the floor, and let the blow fall lightly on the bare neck. The sharp edge of the blade sundered the bones, smote through the neck, and clave it in two, so that the edge of the steel bit on the ground, and the fair head fell to the earth that many struck it with their feet as it rolled forth. The blood spurted forth, and glistened on the green raiment, but the knight neither faltered nor fell; he started forward with out-stretched hand, and caught the head, and lifted it up; then he turned to his steed, and took hold of the bride, set his foot in the stirrup, and mounted. His head he held by the hair, in his hand. Then he seated himself in his saddle as if naught ailed him, and he were not headless. He turned his steed about, the grim corpse bleeding freely the while, and they who looked upon him doubted them much for the covenant.

For he held up the head in his hand, and turned the face towards them that sat on the high dais, and it lifted tip the eyelids and looked upon them and spake as ye shall hear. "Look, Gawain, that thou art ready to go as thou hast promised, and seek loyally till thou find me even as thou hast sworn in this hall in the hearing of these knights. Come thou, I charge thee, to the Green Chapel, such a stroke as thou hast dealt thou hast deserved, and it shall be promptly paid thee on New Year's morn. Many men know me as the knight of the Green Chapel, and if thou askest, thou shalt not fail to find me. Therefore it behoves thee to come, or to yield thee as recreant."

With that he turned his bridle, and galloped out at the hall door, his head in his hands, so that the sparks flew from beneath his horse's hoofs. Whither he went none knew, no more than they knew whence he had come; and the king and Gawain they gazed and laughed, for in sooth this had proved a greater marvel than any they had known aforetime.

Though Arthur the king was astonished at his heart, yet he let no sign of it be seen, but spake in courteous wise to the fair queen: "Dear lady, be not dismayed, such craft is well suited to Christmas-tide when we seek jesting, laughter and song, and fair carols of knights and ladies. But now I may well get me to meat, for I have seen a marvel I may not forget." Then he looked on Sir Gawain, and said gaily, "Now, fair nephew, hang up thine axe, since It has hewn enough," and they hung it on the dossal above the dais, where all men might look on it for a marvel, and by its true token tell of the wonder. Then the twain sat them down together, the king and the good knight, and men served them with a double portion, as was the share of the noblest, with all manner of meat and of minstrelsy. And they spent that day in gladness, but Sir Gawain must well bethink him of the heavy venture to which he had set his hand.

This beginning of adventures had Arthur at the New Year; for he yearned to hear gallant tales, though his words were few when he sat at the feast. But now had they stern work on hand. Gawain was glad to begin the jest in the hall, but ye need have no marvel if the end be heavy. For though a man be merry in mind when he has well drunk, yet a year runs full swiftly, and the beginning but rarely matches the end.

For Yule was now over-past, and the year after, each season in its turn following the other. For after Christmas comes crabbed Lent, that will have fish for flesh and simpler cheer. But then the weather of the world chides with winter; the cold withdraws itself, the clouds uplift, and the rain falls in warm showers on the fair plains. Then the flowers come forth, meadows and grove are clad in green, the birds make ready to build, and sing sweetly for solace of the soft summer that follows thereafter. The blossoms bud and blow in the hedgerows rich and rank, and noble notes enough are heard in the fair woods.

After the season of summer, with the soft winds, when zephyr breathes lightly on seeds and herbs, joyous indeed is the growth that waxes thereout when the dew drips from the leaves, beneath the blissful glance of the bright sun. But then comes harvest and hardens the grain, warning it to wax ripe ere the winter. The drought drives the dust on high, flying over the face of the land; the angry wind of the welkin wrestles with the sun; the leaves fall from the trees and light upon the ground, and all brown are the groves that but now were green, and ripe is the fruit that once was flower. So the year passes into many yesterdays, and winter comes again, as it needs no sage to tell us.

When the Michaelmas moon was come in with warnings of winter, Sir Gawain bethought him full oft of his perilous journey. Yet till All Hallows Day he lingered with Arthur, and on that day they made a great feast for the hero's sake, with much revel and richness of the Round Table. Courteous knights and comely ladies, all were in sorrow for the love of that knight, and though they spake no word of it, many were joyless for his sake.

And after meat, sadly Sir Gawain turned to his uncle, and spake of his journey, and said, "Liege lord of my life, leave from you I crave. Ye know well how the matter stands without more words, tomorrow am I bound to set forth in search of the Green Knight."

Then came together all the noblest knights, Ywain and Erec, and many another. Sir Dodinel le Sauvage, the Duke of Clarence, Launcelot and Lionel, and Lucan the Good, Sir Bors and Sir Bedivere, valiant knights both, and many another hero, with Sir Mador de la Porte, and they all drew near, heavy at heart, to take counsel with Sir Gawain. Much sorrow and weeping was there in the hall to think that so worthy a knight as Gawain should wend his way to seek a deadly blow, and should no more wield his sword in fight. But the knight made ever good cheer, and said, "Nay, wherefore should I shrink? What may a man do but prove his fate?"

He dwelt there all that day, and on the morn he arose and asked betimes for his armor; and they brought it unto him on this wise: first, a rich carpet was stretched on the floor (and brightly did the gold gear glitter upon it), then the knight stepped on to it, and handled the steel; clad he was, in a doublet of silk, with a close hood, lined fairly throughout. Then they set the steel shoes upon his feet, and wrapped his legs with greaves, with polished knee-caps, fastened with knots of gold. Then they cased his thighs in cuisses closed with thongs, and brought him the byrnie of bright steel rings sewn upon a fair stuff. Well-burnished braces they set on each arm with good elbow-pieces, and gloves of mail, and all the goodly gear that should shield him in his need. And they cast over all a rich surcoat, and set the golden spurs on his heels, and girt him with a trusty sword fastened with a silken bawdrick. When he was thus clad his harness was costly, for the least loop or latchet gleamed with gold. So armed as he was he hearkened Mass and made his offering at the high altar. Then he came to the king, and the knights of his court, and courteously took leave of lords and ladies, and they kissed him, and commended him to Christ.

With that was Gringalet ready, girt with a saddle that gleamed gaily with many golden fringes, enriched and decked anew for the venture. The bridle was all barred about with bright gold buttons, and all the covertures and trappings of the steed, the crupper and the rich skirts, accorded with the saddle; spread fair with the rich red gold that glittered and gleamed in the rays of the sun.

Then the knight called for his helmet, which was well lined throughout, and set it high on his head, and hasped it behind. He wore a light kerchief over the vintail, that was broidered and studded with fair gems on a broad silken ribbon, with birds of gay color, and many a turtle and true lovers knot interlaced thickly, even as many a maiden had wrought diligently for seven winter long. But the circlet which crowned his helmet was yet more precious, being adorned with a device in diamonds. Then they brought him his shield, which was of bright red, with the pentangle painted thereon in gleaming gold. And why that noble prince bare the pentangle I am minded to tell you, though my tale tarry thereby. It is a sign that Solomon set ere-while, as betokening truth; for it is a figure with five points and each line overlaps the other, and nowhere hath it beginning or end, so that in English it is called "the endless knot." And therefore was it well suiting to this knight and to his arms, since Gawain was faithful in five and five-fold, for pure was he as gold, void of all villainy and endowed with all virtues. Therefore he bare the pentangle on shield and surcoat as truest of heroes and gentlest of knights.

For first he was faultless in his five senses; and his five fingers never failed him; and all his trust upon earth was in the five wounds that Christ bare on the cross, as the Creed tells. And wherever this knight found himself in stress of battle he deemed well that he drew his strength from the five joys which the Queen of Heaven had of her Child. And for this cause did he bear an image of Our Lady on the one half of his shield, that whenever he looked upon it he might not lack for aid. And the fifth five that the hero used were frankness and fellowship above all, purity and courtesy that never failed him, and compassion that surpasses all; and in these five virtues was that hero wrapped and clothed. And all these, five-fold, were linked one in the other, so that they had no end, and were fixed on five points that never failed, neither at any side were they joined or sundered, nor could ye find beginning or end. And therefore on his shield was the knot shapen, red-gold upon red, which is the pure pentangle. Now was Sir Gawain ready, and he took his lance in hand, and bade them all *Farewell,* he deemed it had been for ever.

Then he smote the steed with his spurs, and sprang on his way, so that sparks flew from the stones after him. All that saw him were grieved at heart, and said one to the other, "By Christ, 'tis great pity that one of such noble life should be lost! In faith, 'twere not easy to find his equal upon earth. The king had done better to have wrought more warily. Yonder knight should have been made a duke; a gallant leader of men is he, and such a fate had beseemed him better than to be hewn in pieces at the will of an elfish man, for mere pride. Who ever knew a king to take such counsel as to risk his knights on a Christmas jest?" Many were the tears that flowed from their eyes when that goodly knight rode from the hall. He made no delaying, but went his way swiftly, and rode many a wild road, as I heard say in the book.

So rode Sir Gawain through the realm of Logres, on an errand that he held for no jest. Often he lay companionless at night, and must lack the fare that he liked. No comrade had he save his steed, and none save God with whom to take counsel. At length he drew nigh to North Wales, and left the isles of Anglesey on his left hand, crossing over the fords by the foreland over at Holyhead, till he came into the wilderness of Wirral, where but few dwell who love God and man of true heart. And ever he asked, as he fared, of all whom he met, if they had heard any tidings of a Green Knight in the country thereabout, or of a Green Chapel? And all answered him, Nay, never in their lives had they seen any man of such a hue. And the knight wended his way by many a strange road and many a rugged path, and the fashion of his countenance changed full often ere he saw the Green Chapel.

Many a cliff did he climb in that unknown land, where afar from his friends he rode as a stranger. Never did he come to a stream or a ford but he found a foe before him, and that one so marvelous, so foul and fell, that it behoved him to fight. So many wonders did I that knight behold, that it were too long to tell the tenth part of them. Sometimes he fought with dragons and wolves; sometimes with wild men that dwelt in the rocks; another while with bulls, and bears, and wild boars, or with giants of the high moorland that drew near to him. Had he not been a doughty knight, enduring, and of well-proved valor, and a servant of God, doubtless he had been slain, for he was oft in danger of death. Yet he cared not so much for the strife, what he deemed worse was when the cold dear water was shed from the clouds, and froze ere it fell on the fallow ground. More nights than enough he slept in his harness on the bare rocks, near slain with the sleet, while the stream leapt bubbling from the crest of the hills, and hung in hard icicles over his head.

Thus in peril and pain, and many a hardship, the knight rode alone till Christmas Eve, and in that tide he made his prayer to the Blessed Virgin that she would guide his steps and lead him to some dwelling. On that morning he rode by a hill, and came into a thick forest, wild and drear; on each side were high hills, and thick woods below them of great hoar oaks, a hundred together, of hazel and hawthorn with their trailing boughs intertwined, and rough ragged moss spreading everywhere. On the bare twigs the birds chirped piteously, for pain of the cold. The knight upon Gringalet rode lonely beneath them, through marsh and mire, much troubled at heart lest he should fail to see the service of the Lord, who on that self-same night was born of a maiden for the cure of our grief; and therefore he said, sighing, "I beseech Thee, Lord, and Mary Thy gentle Mother, for some shelter where I may hear Mass, and Thy mattins at morn. This I ask meekly, and thereto I pray my Paternoster, Ave, and Credo." Thus he rode praying, and lamenting his misdeeds, and he crossed himself, and said, "May the Cross of Christ speed me."

Now that knight had crossed himself but thrice ere he was aware in the wood of a dwelling within a moat, above a lawn, on a mound surrounded by many mighty trees that stood round the moat. 'Twas the fairest castle that ever a knight owned; built in a meadow with a park all about it, and a spiked palisade, closely driven, that enclosed the trees for more than two miles. The knight was ware of the hold from the side, as it shone through the oaks. Then he lifted off his helmet, and thanked Christ and St. Julian that they had courteously granted his prayer, and hearkened to his cry. "Now," quoth the knight, "I beseech ye, grant me fair hostel." Then he pricked Gringalet with his golden spurs, and rode gaily towards the great gate, and came swiftly to the bridge end.

The bridge was drawn up and the gates close shut; the walls were strong and thick, so that they might fear no tempest. The knight on his charger abode on the bank of the deep double ditch that surrounded the castle. The walls were set deep in the water, and rose aloft to a wondrous height; they were of hard hewn stone up to the corbels, which were adorned beneath the battlements with fair carvings, and turrets set in between with many a loophole; a better barbican Sir Gawain had never looked upon. And within he beheld the high hall, with its tower and many windows with carven cornices, and chalk-white chimneys on the turreted roofs that shone fair in the sun. And everywhere, thickly scattered on the castle battlements, were pinnacles, so many that it seemed as if it were all wrought out of paper, so white was it.

The knight on his steed deemed it fair enough, if he might come to be sheltered within it to lodge there while that the Holy-day lasted. He called aloud, and soon there came a porter of kindly countenance, who stood on the wall and greeted this knight and asked his errand.

"Good sir," quoth Gawain, "wilt thou go mine errand to the nigh lord of the castle, and crave for me lodging?"

"Yea, by St. Peter," quoth the porter. "In sooth I trust that ye be welcome to dwell here so long as it may like ye."

Then he went, and came again swiftly, and many folk with him to receive the knight. They let down the great drawbridge, and came forth and knelt on their knees on the cold earth to give him worthy welcome. They held wide open the great gates, and courteously he bid them rise, and rode over the bridge. Then men came to him and held his stirrup while he dismounted, and took and stabled his steed. There came down knights and squires to bring the guest with joy to the hall. When he raised his helmet there were many to take it from his hand, fain to serve him, and they took from him sword and shield.

Sir Gawain gave good greeting to the noble and the mighty men who came to do him honor. Clad in his shining armor they led him to the hall, where a great fire burnt brightly on the floor; and the lord of the household came forth from his chamber to meet the hero fitly. He spake to the knight, and said: "Ye are welcome to do here as it likes ye. All that is here is your own to have at your will and disposal."

"Gramercy!" quote Gawain, "may Christ requite ye."

As friends that were fain each embraced the other; and Gawain looked on the knight who greeted him so kindly, and thought 'twas a bold warrior that owned that burg.

Of mighty stature he was, and of high age; broad and flowing was his beard, and of a bright hue. He was stalwart of limb, and strong in his stride, his face fiery red, and his speech free: in sooth he seemed one well fitted to be a leader of valiant men.

Then the lord led Sir Gawain to a chamber, and commanded folk to wait upon him, and at his bidding there came men enough who brought the guest to a fair bower. The bedding was noble, with curtains of pure silk wrought with gold, and wondrous coverings of fair cloth all embroidered. The curtains ran on ropes with rings of red gold, and the walls were hung with carpets of Orient, and the same spread on the floor. Therewith mirthful speeches they took from the guest his byrnie and all his shining armor, and brought him rich robes of the choicest in its stead. They were long and flowing, and became him well, and when he was clad in them all who looked on the hero thought that surely God had never made a fairer knight: he seemed as if he might be a prince without peer in the field where men strive in battle.

Then before the hearth-place, whereon the fire burned, they made ready a chair for Gawain, hung about with cloth and fair cushions; and there they cast around him a mantle of brown samite, richly embroidered and furred within with costly skins of ermine, with a hood of the same, and he seated himself in that rich seat, and warmed himself at the fire, and was cheered at heart. And while he sat thus the serving men set up a table on trestles, and covered it with a fair white cloth, and set thereon salt-cellar, and napkin, and silver spoons; and the knight washed at his will, and set him down to meat.

The folk served him courteously with many dishes seasoned of the best, a double portion. All kinds of fish were there, some baked in bread, some broiled on the embers, some sodden, some stewed and savored with spices, with all sorts of cunning devices to his taste. And often he called it a feast when they spake gaily to him all together, and said, "Now take ye this penance, and it shall be for your amendment." Much mirth thereof did Sir Gawain make.

Then they questioned that prince courteously of whence he came; and he told them that he was of the court of Arthur, who is the rich royal King of the Round Table, and that it was Gawain himself who was within their walls, and would keep Christmas with them, as the chance had fallen out. And when the lord of the castle heard those tidings he laughed aloud for gladness, and all men in that keep were joyful that they should be in the company of him to whom belonged all fame, and valor, and courtesy, and whose honor was praised above that of all men on earth. Each said softly to his fellow, "Now shall we see courteous bearing, and the manner of speech befitting courts. What charm lieth in gentle speech shall we learn without asking, since here we have welcomed the fine father of courtesy. God has surely shown us His grace since He sends us such a guest as Gawain! When men shall sit and sing, blithe for Christ's birth, this knight shall bring us to the knowledge of fair manners, and it may be that hearing him we may learn the cunning speech of love."

By the time the knight had risen from dinner it was near nightfall. Then chaplains took their way to the chapel, and rang loudly, even as they should, for the solemn evensong of the high feast. Thither went the lord, and the lady also, and entered with her maidens into a comely closet, and thither also went Gawain. Then the lord took him by the sleeve and led him to a seat, and called him by his name, and told him he was of all men in the world the most welcome. And Sir Gawain thanked him truly, and each kissed the other, and they sat gravely together throughout the service.

Then was the lady fain to look upon that knight; and she came forth from her closet with many fair maidens. The fairest of ladies was she in face, and figure, and coloring, fairer even than Guinevere, so the knight thought. She came through the chancel to greet the hero, another lady held her by the left hand, older than she, and seemingly of high estate, with many nobles about her. But unlike to look upon were those ladies, for if the younger were fair, the elder was yellow. Rich red were the cheeks of the one, rough and wrinkled those of the other; the kerchiefs of the one were broidered with many glistening pearls, her throat and neck bare, and whiter than the snow that lies on the hills; the neck of the other was swathed in a gorget, with a. white wimple over her black chin. Her forehead was wrapped in silk with many folds, worked with knots, so that naught of her was seen save her black brows, her eyes, her nose, and her lips, and those were bleared, and ill to look upon. A worshipful lady in sooth one might call her! In figure was she short and broad, and thickly made – far fairer to behold was she whom she led by the hand.

When Gawain beheld that fair lady, who looked at him graciously, with leave of the lord he went towards them, and, bowing low, he greeted the elder, but the younger and fairer he took lightly in his arms, and kissed her courteously, and greeted her in knightly wise. Then she hailed him as friend, and he quickly prayed to be counted as her servant, if she so willed. Then they took him between them, and talking, led him to the chamber, to the hearth, and bade them bring spices, and they brought them in plenty with the good wine that was wont to be drunk at such seasons. Then the lord sprang to his feet and bade them make merry, and took off his hood, and hung it on a spear, and bade him win the worship thereof who should make most mirth that Christmas-tide. "And I shall try, by my faith, to fool it with the best, by the help of my friends, ere I lose my raiment." Thus with gay words the lord made trial to gladden Gawain with jests that night, till it was time to bid them light the tapers, and Sir Gawain took leave of them and gat him to rest.

In the morn when all men call to mind I how Christ our Lord was born on earth to die for us, there is joy, for His sake, in all dwellings of the world; and so was there here on that day. For high feast was held, with many dainties and cunningly cooked messes. On the dais sat gallant men, clad in their best. The ancient dame sat on the high seat, with the lord of the castle beside her. Gawain and the fair lady sat together, even in the midst of the board, when the feast was served; and so throughout all the hall each sat in his degree, and was served in order. There was meat, there was mirth, there was much joy, so that to tell thereof would take me too long, though peradventure I might strive to declare it. But Gawain and that fair lady had much joy of each other's company through her sweet words and courteous converse. And there was music made before each prince, trumpets and drums, and merry piping; each man hearkened his minstrel, and they too hearkened theirs.

So they held high feast that day and the next, and the third day thereafter, and the joy on St. John's Day was fair to hearken, for 'twas the last of the feast and the guests would depart in the gray of the morning. Therefore they awoke early, and drank wine, and danced fair carols, and at last, when it was late, each man took his leave to wend early on his way. Gawain would bid his host farewell, but the lord took him by the hand, and led him to his own chamber beside the hearth, and there, he thanked him for the favor he had shown him in honoring his dwelling at that high season, and gladdening his castle with his fair countenance. "I think, sir, that while I live I shall be held the worthier that Gawain has been my guest at God's own feast."

"Gramercy, sir," quoth Gawain, "in good faith, all the honor is yours, may the High King give it you, and I am but at your will to work your behest, inasmuch as I am beholden to you in great and small by rights."

Then the lord did his best to persuade the knight to tarry with him, but Gawain answered that he might in no wise do so. Then the host asked him courteously what stern behest had driven him at the holy season from the king's court, to fare all alone, ere yet the feast was ended?

"Forsooth," quoth the knight, "ye say but the truth: 'tis a high quest and a pressing that hath brought me afield, for I am summoned myself to a certain place, and I know not whither in the world I may wend to find it; so help me Christ, I would give all the kingdom of Logres an I might find it by New Year's morn. Therefore, sir, I make request of you that ye tell me truly if ye ever heard word of the Green Chapel, where it may be found, and the Green Knight that keeps it. For I am pledged by solemn compact sworn between us to meet that knight at the New Year if so I were on life; and of that same New Year it wants but little – in faith, I would look on that hero more joyfully than on any other fair sight! Therefore, by your will, it behoves me to leave you, for I have but barely three days, and I would as fain fall dead as fail of mine errand."

Then the lord quoth, laughing, "Now must ye needs stay, for I will show you your goal, the Green Chapel, ere your term be at an end, have ye no fear! But ye can take your ease, friend, in your bed, till the fourth day, and go forth on the first of the year and come to that place at midmorn to do as ye will. Dwell here till New Year's Day, and then rise and set forth, and ye shall be set in the way; 'tis not two miles hence."

Then was Gawain glad, and he laughed gaily. "Now I thank you for this above all else. Now my quest is achieved I will dwell here at your will, and otherwise do as ye shall ask."

Then the lord took him, and set him beside him, and bade the ladies be fetched for their greater pleasure, though between themselves they had solace. The lord, for gladness, made merry jest, even as one who knew not what to do for joy; and he cried aloud to the knight, "Ye have promised to do the thing I bid ye: will ye hold to this behest, here, at once?"

"Yea, forsooth," said that true knight, "while I abide in your burg I am bound by your behest."

"Ye have traveled from far," said the host, "and since then ye have waked with me, ye are not well refreshed by rest and sleep, as I know. Ye shall therefore abide in your chamber, and lie at your ease tomorrow at Mass-tide, and go to meat when ye will with my wife, who shall sit with you, and comfort you with her company till I return; and I shall rise early and go forth to the chase." And Gawain agreed to all this courteously.

"Sir knight," quoth the host, "we will make a covenant. Whatsoever I win in the wood shall be yours, and whatever may fall to your share, that shall ye exchange for it. Let us swear, friend, to make this exchange, however our hap may be, for worse or for better."

"I grant ye your will," quoth Gawain the good; "If ye list so to do, it liketh me well."

"Bring hither the wine-cup, the bargain is made," so said the lord of that castle. They laughed each one, and drank of the wine, and made merry, these lords and ladies, as it pleased them. Then with gay talk and merry jest they arose, and stood, and spoke softly, and kissed courteously, and took leave of each other. With burning torches, and many a serving-man, was each led to his couch; yet ere they gat them to bed the old lord oft repeated their covenant, for he knew well how to make sport.

Full early, ere daylight, the folk rose up; the guests who would depart called their grooms, and they made them ready, and saddled the steeds, tightened up the girths, and trussed up their mails. The knights, all arrayed for riding, leapt up lightly, and took their bridles, and each rode his way as pleased him best.

The lord of the land was not the last. Ready for the chase, with many of his men, he ate a sop hastily when he had heard Mass, and then with blast of the bugle fared forth to the field. He and his nobles were to horse ere daylight glimmered upon the earth.

Then the huntsmen coupled their hounds, unclosed the kennel door, and called them out. They blew three blasts gaily on the bugles, the hounds bayed fiercely, and they that would go a-hunting checked and chastised them. A hundred hunters there were of the best, so I have heard tell. Then the trackers gat them to the trysting-place and uncoupled the hounds, and the forest rang again with their gay blasts.

At the first sound of the hunt the game quaked for fear, and fled, trembling, along the vale. They betook them to the heights, but the liers in wait turned them back with loud cries; the harts they let pass them, and the stags with their spreading antlers, for the lord had forbidden that they should be slain, but the hinds and the does they turned back, and drave down into the valleys. Then might ye see much shooting of arrows. As the deer fled under the boughs a broad whistling shaft smote and wounded each sorely, so that, wounded and bleeding, they fell dying on the banks. The hounds followed swiftly on their tracks, and hunters, blowing the horn, sped after them with ringing shouts as if the cliffs burst asunder. What game escaped those that shot was run down at the outer ring. Thus were they driven on the hills, and harassed at the waters, so well did the men know their work, and the greyhounds were so great and swift that they ran them down as fast as the hunters could slay them. Thus the lord passed the day in mirth and joyfulness, even to nightfall.

So the lord roamed the woods, and Gawain, that good night, lay ever a-bed, curtained about, under the costly coverlet, while the daylight gleamed on the walls. And as he lay half slumbering, he heard a little sound at the door, and he raised his head, and caught back a corner of the curtain, and waited to see what it might be. It was the lovely lady, the lord's wife; she shut the door softly behind her, and turned towards the bed; and Gawain was shamed, laid him down softly and made as if he slept. And she came lightly to the bedside, within the curtain, and sat herself down beside him, to wait till he wakened. The knight lay there awhile, and marveled within himself what her coming might betoken; and he said to himself, "'Twere more seemly if I asked her what hath brought her hither." Then he made feint to waken, and turned towards her, and opened his eyes as one astonished, and crossed himself; and she looked on him laughing, with her cheeks red and white, lovely to behold, and small smiling lips.

"Good morrow, Sir Gawain," said that fair lady; "ye are but a careless sleeper, since one can enter thus. Now are ye taken unawares, and lest ye escape me I shall bind you in your bed; of that be ye assured!" Laughing, she spake these words.

"Good morrow, fair lady," quoth Gawain blithely. "I will do your will, as it likes me well. For I yield me readily, and pray your grace, and that is best, by my faith, since I needs must do so." Thus he jested again, laughing. "But an ye would, fair lady, grant me this grace that ye pray your prisoner to rise. I would get me from bed, and array me better, then could I talk with ye in more comfort."

"Nay, forsooth, fair sir," quoth the lady," ye shall not rise, I will advise ye better. I shall keep ye here, since ye can do no other, and talk with my knight whom I have captured. For I know well that ye are Sir Gawain, whom all the world worships, wheresoever ye may ride. Your honor and your courtesy are praised by lords and ladies, by all who live. Now ye are here and we are alone, my lord and his men are afield; the serving men in their beds, and my maidens also, and the door shut upon us. And since in this hour I have him that all men love, I shall use my time well with speech, while it lasts. Ye are welcome to my company, for it behoves me in sooth to be your servant."

"In good faith," quoth Gawain, "I think me that I am not him of whom ye speak, for unworthy am I of such service as ye here proffer. In sooth, I were glad if I might set myself by word or service to your pleasure; a pure joy would it be to me!"

"In good faith, Sir Gawain," quoth the gay lady, "the praise and the prowess that pleases all ladies I lack them not, nor hold them light; yet are there ladies enough who would liever now have the knight in their hold, as I have ye here, to dally with your courteous words, to bring them comfort and to ease their cares, than much of the treasure and the gold that are theirs. And now, through the grace of Him who upholds the heavens, I have wholly in my power that which they all desire!"

Thus the lady, fair to look upon, made him great cheer, and Sir Gawain, with modest words, answered her again: "Madam," he quoth, "may Mary requite ye, for in good faith I have found in ye a noble frankness. Much courtesy have other folk shown me, but the honor they have done me is naught to the worship of yourself, who knoweth but good."

"By Mary," quoth the lady, "I think otherwise; for were I worth all the women alive, and had I the wealth of the world in my hand, and might choose me a lord to my liking, then, for all that I have seen in ye, Sir Knight, of beauty and courtesy and blithe semblance, and for all that I have hearkened and hold for true, there should be no knight on earth to be chosen before ye!"

"Well I know," quoth Sir Gawain, "that ye have chosen a better; but I am proud that ye should so prize me, and as your servant do I hold ye my sovereign, and your knight am I, and may Christ reward ye."

So they talked of many matters till mid-morn was past, and ever the lady made as though she loved him, and the knight turned her speech aside. For though she were the brightest of maidens, yet had he forborne to show her love for the danger that awaited him, and the blow that must be given without delay.

Then the lady prayed her leave from him, and he granted it readily. And she have him good-day, with laughing glance, but he must needs marvel at her words:

"Now He that speeds fair speech reward ye this disport; but that ye be Gawain my mind misdoubts me greatly."

"Wherefore?" quoth the knight quickly, fearing lest he had lacked in some courtesy.

And the lady spake: "So true a knight as Gawain is holden, and one so perfect in courtesy, would never have tarried so long with a lady but he would of his courtesy have craved a kiss at parting."

Then quoth Gawain, "I know I will do even as it may please ye, and kiss at your commandment, as a true knight should who forbears to ask for fear of displeasure."

At that she came near and bent down and kissed the knight, and each commended the other to Christ, and she went forth from the chamber softly.

Then Sir Gawain arose and called his chamberlain and chose his garments, and when he was ready he gat him forth to Mass, and then went to meat, and made merry all day till the rising of the moon, and never had a knight fairer lodging than had he with those two noble ladies, the elder and the younger.

And even the lord of the land chased the hinds through holt and heath till eventide, and then with much blowing of bugles and baying of hounds they bore the game homeward; and by the time daylight was done all the folk had returned to that fair castle. And when the lord and Sir Gawain met together, then were they both well pleased. The lord commanded them all to assemble in the great hall, and the ladies to descend with their maidens, and there, before them all, he bade the men fetch in the spoil of the day's hunting, and he called unto Gawain, and counted the tale of the beasts, and showed them unto him, and said, "What think ye of this game, Sir Knight? Have I deserved of ye thanks for my woodcraft?"

"Yea, I think," quoth the other, "here is the fairest spoil I have seen this seven year in the winter season."

"And all this do I give ye, Gawain," quoth the host, "for by accord of covenant ye may claim it as your own."

"That is sooth," quoth the other, "I grant you that same; and I have fairly won this within walls, and with as good will do I yield it to ye." With that he clasped his hands round the lord's neck and kissed him as courteously as he might. "Take ye here my spoils, no more have I won; ye should have it freely, though it were greater than this."

" 'Tis good," said the host, "gramercy thereof. Yet were I fain to know where ye won this same favor, and if it were by your own wit?"

"Nay," answered Gawain, "that was not in the bond. Ask me no more: ye have taken what was yours by right, be content with that."

They laughed and jested together, and sat them down to supper, where they were served with many dainties; and after supper they sat by the hearth, and wine was served out to them; and oft in their jesting they promised to observe on the morrow the same covenant that they had made before, and whatever chance might betide to exchange their spoil, be it much or little, when they met at night. Thus they renewed their bargain before the whole court, and then the night-drink was served, and each courteously took leave of the other and gat him to bed.

By the time the cock had crowed thrice the lord of the castle had left his bed; Mass was sung and meat fitly served. The folk were forth to the wood ere the day broke, with hound and horn they rode over the plain, and uncoupled their dogs among the thorns. Soon they struck on the scent, and the hunt cheered on the hounds who were first to seize it, urging them with shouts. The others hastened to the cry, forty at once, and there rose such a clamor from the pack that the rocks rang again. The huntsmen spurred them on with shouting and blasts of the horn; and the hounds drew together to a thicket betwixt the water and a high crag in the cliff beneath the hillside. There where the rough rock fell ruggedly they, the huntsmen, fared to the finding, and cast about round the hill and the thicket behind them. The knights knew well what beast was within, and would drive him forth with the bloodhounds. And as they beat the bushes, suddenly over the beaters there rushed forth a wondrous great and fierce boar, long since had he left the herd to roam by himself. Grunting, he cast many to the ground, and fled forth at his best speed, without more mischief. The men hallooed loudly and cried, *"Hay! Hay!"* and blew the horns to urge on the hounds, and rode swiftly after the boar. Many a time did he turn to bay and tare the hounds, and they yelped, and howled shrilly. Then the men made ready their arrows and shot at him, but the points were turned on his thick hide, and the barbs would not bite upon him, for the shafts shivered in pieces, and the head but leapt again wherever it hit.

But when the boar felt the stroke of the arrows he waxed mad with rage, and turned on the hunters and tare many, so that, affrightened, they fled before him. But the lord on a swift steed pursued him, blowing his bugle; as a gallant knight he rode through the woodland chasing the boar till the sun grew low.

So did the hunters this day, while Sir Gawain lay in his bed lapped in rich gear; and the lady forgat not to salute him, for early was she at his side, to cheer his mood.

She came to the bedside and looked on the knight, and Gawain gave her fit greeting, and she greeted him again with ready words, and sat her by his side and laughed, and with a sweet look she spoke to him:

"Sir, if ye be Gawain, I think it a wonder that ye be so stern and cold, and care not for the courtesies of friendship, but if one teach ye to know them ye cast the lesson out of your mind. Ye have soon forgotten what I taught ye yesterday, by all the truest tokens that I knew!"

"What is that?" quoth the knight. "I believe I know not. If it be sooth that ye say, then is the blame mine own."

"But I taught ye of kissing," quoth the fair lady. "Wherever a fair countenance is shown him, it behoves a courteous knight quickly to claim a kiss."

"Nay, my dear," said Sir Gawain, "cease that speech; that durst I not do lest I were denied, for if I were forbidden I know I were wrong did I further entreat."

"In faith," quoth the lady merrily; "ye may not be forbid, ye are strong enough to constrain by strength an ye will, were any so discourteous as to give ye denial."

"Yea, by Heaven" said Gawain, "Ye speak well; but threats profit little in the land where I dwell, and so with a gift that is given not of good will! I am at your commandment to kiss when ye like, to take or to leave as ye list."

Then the lady bent her down and kissed him courteously.

And as they spake together she said, "I would learn somewhat from ye, an ye would not be wroth, for young ye bare and fair, and so courteous and knightly as ye are known to be, the head of all chivalry, and versed in all wisdom of love and war — 'tis ever told of true knights how they adventured their lives for their true love, and endured hardships for her favors, and avenged her with valor, and eased her sorrows, and brought joy to her bower; and ye are the fairest knight of your time, and your fame and your honor are everywhere, yet I have sat by ye here twice, and never a word have I heard of love! Ye who are so courteous and skilled in such love ought surely to teach one so young and unskilled some little craft of true love! Why are ye so unlearned who art otherwise so famous? Or is it that ye deemed me unworthy to hearken to your teaching? For shame, Sir Knight! I come hither alone and sit at your side to learn of ye some skill; teach me of your wit, while my lord is from home."

"In good faith," quoth Gawain, "great is my joy and my profit that so fair a lady as ye are should deign to come hither, and trouble ye with so poor a man, and make sport with your knight with kindly countenance, it pleaseth me much. But that I, in my turn, should take it upon me to tell of love and such like matters to ye who know more by half, or a hundred fold, of such craft than I do, or ever shall in all my lifetime, by my troth 'twere folly indeed! I will work your will to the best of my might as I am bounden, and evermore will I be your servant, so help me Christ!"

Then often with guile she questioned that knight that she might win him to woo her, but he defended himself so fairly that none might, in any wise blame him, and naught but bliss and harmless jesting was there between them. They laughed and talked together till at last she kissed him, and craved her leave of him, and went her way.

Then the knight arose and went forth to Mass, and afterward dinner was served and he sat and spake with the ladies all day. But the lord of the castle rode ever over the land chasing the wild boar, that fled through the thickets, slaying the best of his hounds and breaking their backs in sunder; till at last he was so weary he might run no longer, but made for a hole in a mound by a rock. He got the mound at his back and faced the hounds, whetting his white tusks and foaming at the mouth. The huntsmen stood aloof, fearing to draw nigh him; so many of them had been already wounded that they were loth to be torn with his tusks, so fierce he was and mad with rage. At length the lord himself came up, and saw the beast at bay, and the men standing aloof. Then quickly he sprang to the ground and drew out a bright blade, and waded through the stream to the boar.

When the beast was aware of the knight with weapon in hand, he set up his bristles and snorted loudly, and many feared for their lord lest he should be slain. Then the boar leapt upon the knight so that beast and man were one atop of the other in the water; but the boar had the worst of it, for the man had marked, even as he sprang, and set the point of his brand to the beast's chest, and drove it up to the hilt, so that the heart was split in twain, and the boar fell snarling, and was swept down by the water to where a hundred hounds seized on him, and the men drew him to shore for the dogs to slay.

Then was there loud blowing of horns and baying of hounds, the huntsmen smote off the boar's head, and hung the carcass by the four feet to a stout pole, and so went on their way homewards. The head they bore before the lord himself, who had slain the beast at the ford by force of his strong hand.

It seemed him o'er long ere he saw Sir Gawain in the hall, and he called, and the guest came to take that which fell to his share. And when he saw Gawain the lord laughed aloud, and bade them call the ladies and the household together, and he showed them the game, and told them the tale, how they hunted the wild boar through the woods, and of his length and breadth and height; and Sir Gawain commended his deeds and praised him for his valor, well proven, for so mighty a beast had he never seen before.

Then they handled the huge head, and the lord said aloud, "Now, Gawain, this game is your own by sure covenant, as ye right well know!"

" 'Tis sooth," quoth the knight, "and as truly will I give ye all I have gained." He took the host round the neck, and kissed him courteously twice. "Now are we quits," he said, "this eventide, of all the covenants that we made since I came hither."

And the lord answered, "By St. Giles, ye are the best I know; ye will be rich in a short space if ye drive such bargains!"

Then they set up the tables on trestles, and covered them with fair cloths, and lit waxen tapers on the walls. The knights sat and were served in the hall, and much game and glee was there round the hearth, with many songs, both at supper and after; song of Christmas, and new carols, with all the mirth one may think of. And ever that lovely lady sat by the knight, and with still stolen looks made such feint of pleasing him, that Gawain marveled much, and was wroth with himself, but he could not for his courtesy return her fair glances, but dealt with her cunningly, however she might strive to wrest the thing.

When they had tarried in the hall so long as it seemed them good, they turned to the inner chamber and the wide hearth-place, and there they drank wine, and the host proffered to renew the covenant for New Year's Eve; but the knight craved leave to depart on the morrow, for it was nigh to the term when he must fulfill his pledge. But the lord would withhold him from so doing, and prayed him to tarry, and said:

"As I am a true knight I swear my troth that ye shall come to the Green Chapel to achieve your task on New Year's morn, long before prime. Therefore abide ye in your bed, and I will hunt in this wood, and hold ye to the covenant to exchange with me against all the spoil I may bring hither. For twice have I tried ye, and found ye true, and the morrow shall be the third time and the best. Make we merry now while we may, and think on joy, for misfortune may take a man whensoever it wills."

Then Gawain granted his request, and they brought them drink, and they gat them with lights to bed.

Sir Gawain lay and slept softly, but the lord, who was keen on woodcraft, was afoot early. After Mass he and his men ate a morsel, and he asked for his steed; all the knights who should ride with him were already mounted before the hall gates.

'Twas a fair frosty morning, for the sun rose red in ruddy vapor, and the welkin was clear of clouds. The hunters scattered them by a forest side, and the rocks rang again with the blast of their horns. Some came on the scent of a fox, and a hound gave tongue; the huntsmen shouted, and the pack followed in a crowd on the trail. The fox ran before them, and when they saw him they pursued him with noise and much shouting, and he wound and turned through many a thick grove, often cowering and hearkening in a hedge. At last by a little ditch he leapt out of a spinney, stole away slyly by a copse path, and so out of the wood and away from the hounds.

But he went, ere he knew, to a chosen tryst, and three started forth on him at once, so he must needs double back, and betake him to the wood again.

Then was it joyful to hearken to the hounds; when all the pack had met together and had sight of their game they made as loud a din as if all the lofty cliffs had fallen clattering together. The huntsmen shouted and threatened, and followed close upon him so that he might scarce escape, but Reynard was wily, and he turned and doubled upon them, and led the lord and his men over the hills, now on the slopes, now in the vales, while the knight at home slept through the cold morning beneath his costly curtains.

But the fair lady of the castle rose betimes, and clad herself in a rich mantle that reached even to the ground, left her throat and her fair neck bare, and was I bordered and lined with costly furs. On her head she wore no golden circlet, but a network of precious stones, that gleamed and shone through her tresses in clusters of twenty together. Thus she came into the chamber, closed the door after her, and set open a window, and called to him gaily, "Sir Knight, how may ye sleep? The morning is so fair."

Sir Gawain was deep in slumber, and in his dream he vexed him much for the destiny that should befall him on the morrow, when he should meet the knight at the Green Chapel, and abide his blow; but when the lady spake he heard her, and came to himself, and roused from his dream and answered swiftly. The lady came laughing, and kissed him courteously, and he welcomed her fittingly with a cheerful countenance. He saw her so glorious and gaily dressed, so faultless of features and complexion, that it warmed his heart to look upon her.

They spake to each other smiling, and all was bliss and good cheer between them. They exchanged fair words, and much happiness was therein, yet was there a gulf between them, and she might win no more of her knight, for that gallant prince watched well his words he would neither take her love, nor frankly refuse it. He cared for his courtesy, lest he be deemed churlish, and yet more for his honor lest he be traitor to his host. "God forbid," quoth he to himself, "that it should so befall." Thus with courteous words did he set aside all the special speeches that came from her lips.

Then spake the lady to the knight, "Ye deserve blame if ye hold not that lady who sits beside ye above all else in the world, if ye have not already a love whom ye hold dearer, and like better, and have sworn such firm faith to that lady that ye care not to loose it – and that am I now fain to believe. And now I pray ye straitly that ye tell me that in truth, and hide it not."

And the knight answered, "By St. John" (and he smiled as he spake) "no such love have I, nor do I think to have yet awhile."

"That is the worst word I may hear," quoth the lady, "but in sooth I have mine answer; kiss me now courteously, and I will go hence; I can but mourn as a maiden that loves much."

Sighing, she stooped down and kissed him, and then she rose up and spake as she stood, "Now, dear, at our parting do me this grace: give me some gift, if it were but thy glove, that I may bethink me of my knight, and lessen my mourning."

"Now I think," quoth the knight, "I would that I had here the most precious thing that I possess on earth that I might leave ye as love-token, great or small for ye have deserved forsooth more reward than I might give ye. But it is not to your honor to have at this time a glove for reward as gift from Gawain, and I am here on a strange errand, and have no man with me, nor mails with goodly things – that mislikes me much, lady, at this time; but each man must fare as he is taken, if for sorrow and ill."

"Nay, knight highly honored," quoth that lovesome lady, "though I have naught of yours, yet shall ye have somewhat of mine." With that she reached him a ring of red gold with a sparkling stone therein, that shone even as the sun (wit ye well, it was worth many marks); but the knight refused it, and spake readily:

"I will take no gift, lady, at this time. I have none to give, and none will I take."

She prayed him to take it, but he refused her prayer, and sware in sooth that he would not have it.

The lady was sorely vexed, and said, "If ye refuse my ring as too costly, that ye will not be so highly beholden to me, I will give you my girdle as a lesser gift. With that she loosened a lace that was fastened at her side, knit upon her kirtle under her mantle. It was wrought of green silk, and gold, only braided by the fingers, and that she offered to the knight, and besought him though it were of little worth that he would take it, and he said nay, he would touch neither gold nor gear ere God give him grace to achieve the adventure for which he had come hither. "And therefore, I pray ye, displease ye not, and ask me no longer, for I may not grant it. I am dearly beholden to ye for the favor ye have shown me, and ever, in heat and cold, will I be your true servant."

"Now," said the lady, "ye refuse this silk, for it is simple in itself, and so it seems, indeed; lo, it is small to look upon and less in cost, but whoso knew the virtue that is knit therein he would, peradventure, value it more highly. For whatever knight is girded with this green lace, while he bears it knotted about him there is no man under heaven can overcome him, for, he may not be slain for any magic on earth."

Then Gawain bethought him, and it came into his heart that this were a jewel for the jeopardy that awaited him when he came to the Green Chapel to seek the return blow – could he so order it that he should escape unslain, 'twere a craft worth trying. Then he bare with her chiding, and let her say her say, and she pressed the girdle on him and prayed him to take it, and he granted her prayer, and she gave it him with good will, and besought him for her sake never to reveal it but to hide it loyally from her lord; and the knight agreed that never should any man know it, save they two alone. He thanked her often and heartily, and she kissed him for the third time.

Then she took her leave of him, and when she was gone Sir Gawain arose, and clad him in rich attire, and took the girdle, and knotted it round him, and hid it beneath his robes. Then he took his way to the chapel, and sought out a priest privily and prayed him to teach him better how his soul might be saved when he should go hence; and there he shrived him, and showed his misdeeds, both great and small, and

102

besought mercy and craved absolution; and the priest assoiled him, and set him as clean as if Doomsday had been on the morrow. And afterwards Sir Gawain made him merry with the ladies, with carols, and all kinds of joy, as never he did but that one day, even to nightfall; and all the men marveled at him, and said that never since he came thither had he been so merry.

Meanwhile the lord of the castle was abroad chasing the fox; awhile he lost him, and as he rode through a spinny he heard the hounds near at hand, and Reynard came creeping through a thick grove, with all the pack at his heels. Then the lord drew out his shining brand, and cast it at the beast, and the fox swerved aside for the sharp edge, and would have doubled back, but a hound was on him ere he might turn, and right before the horse's feet they all fell on him, and worried him fiercely, snarling the while.

Then the lord leapt from his saddle, and caught the fox from the jaws, and held it aloft over his head, and hallooed loudly, and many brave hounds bayed as they beheld it; and the hunters hastened them thither, blowing their horns; all that bare bugles blew them at once, and all the others shouted. 'Twas the merriest meeting that ever men heard, the clamor that was raised at the death of the fox. They rewarded the hounds, stroking them and rubbing their heads, and took Reynard and stripped him of his coat; then blowing their horns, they turned them homewards, for it was nigh nightfall.

The lord was gladsome at his return, and found a bright fire on the hearth, and the knight beside it, the good Sir Gawain, who was in joyous mood for the pleasure he had had with the ladies. He wore a robe of blue, that reached even to the ground, and a surcoat richly furred, that became him well. A hood like to the surcoat fell on his shoulders, and all alike were done about with fur. He met the host in the midst of the floor, and jesting, he greeted him, and said, "Now shall I be first to fulfil our covenant which we made together when there was no lack of wine." Then he embraced the knight, and kissed him thrice, as solemnly as he might.

"Of a sooth," quoth the other, "ye have good luck in the matter of this covenant, if ye made a good exchange!"

"Yea, it matters naught of the exchange," quoth Gawain, "since what I owe is swiftly paid. "

"Marry" said the other, "mine is behind, for I have hunted all this day, and naught have I got but this foul fox-skin, and that is but poor payment for three such kisses as ye have here given me."

"Enough," quoth Sir Gawain, "I thank ye, by the Rood."

Then the lord told them of his hunting, and how the fox had been slain.

With mirth and minstrelsy, and dainties at their will, they made them as merry as a folk well might till 'twas time for them to sever, for at last they must needs betake them to their beds. Then the knight took his leave of the lord, and thanked him fairly.

"For the fair sojourn that I have had here at this high feast may the High King give ye honor. I give ye myself, as one of your servants, if ye so like; for I must needs, as you know, go hence with the morn, and ye will give me, as ye promised, a guide to show me the way to the Green Chapel, an God will suffer me on New Year's Day to deal the doom of my weird."

"By my faith," quoth the host, "all that ever I promised, that shall I keep with good will." Then he gave him a servant to set him in the way, and lead him by the downs, that he should have no need to ford the stream, and should fare by the shortest road through the groves; and Gawain thanked the lord for the honor done him. Then he would take leave of the ladies; and courteously he kissed them, and spake, praying them to receive his thanks, and they made like reply; then with many sighs they commended him to Christ, and he departed courteously from that folk. Each man that he met he thanked him for his service and his solace, and the pains he had been at to do his will; and each found it as hard to part from the knight as if he had ever dwelt with him.

Then they led him with torches to his chamber, and brought him to his bed to rest. That he slept soundly I may not say, for the morrow gave him much to think on. Let him rest awhile, for he was near that which he sought, and if ye will but listen to me I will tell ye how it fared with him thereafter.

Now the New Year drew nigh, and the night passed, and the day chased the darkness, as is God's will; but wild weather wakened therewith. The clouds cast the cold to the earth, with enough of the north to slay them that lacked clothing. The snow drave smartly, and the whistling wind blew from the heights, and made great drifts in the valleys. The knight, lying in his bed, listened, for though his eyes were shut, he might sleep but little, and hearkened every cock that crew.

He arose ere the day broke, by the light of a lamp that burned in his chamber, and called to his chamberlain, bidding him bring his armor and saddle his steed. The other gat him up, and fetched his garments, and robed Sir Gawain.

First he clad him in his clothes to keep off the cold, and then in his harness, which was well and fairly kept. Both hauberk and plates were well burnished, the rings of the rich byrnie freed from rust, and all as fresh as at first, so that the knight was fain to thank them. Then he did on each piece, and bade them bring his steed, while he put the fairest raiment on himself; his coat with its fair cognizance, adorned with precious stones upon velvet, with broidered seams, and all furred within with costly skins. And he left not the lace, the lady's gift, that Gawain forgot not, for his own good. When he had girded on his sword he wrapped the gift twice about him, swathed around his waist. The girdle of green silk set gaily and well upon the royal red cloth, rich to behold, but the knight ware it not for pride of the pendants, polished though they were with fair gold that gleamed brightly on the ends, but to save himself from sword and knife, when it behoved him to abide his hurt without question. With that the hero went forth, and thanked that kindly folk full often.

Then was Gringalet ready, that was great and strong, and had been well cared for and tended in every wise; in fair condition was that proud steed, and fit for a journey. Then Gawain went to him, and looked on his coat, and said by his sooth, "There is a folk in this place that thinketh on honor; much joy may they have, and the lord who maintains them, and may all good betide that lovely lady all her life long. Since they for charity cherish a guest, and hold honor in their hands, may He who holds the heaven on high requite them, and also ye all. And if I might live any while on earth, I would give ye full reward, readily, if so I might." Then he set foot in the stirrup and bestrode his steed, and his squire gave him his shield, which he laid on his shoulder. Then he smote Gringalet with his golden spurs, and the steed pranced on the stones and would stand no longer.

By that his man was mounted, who bare his spear and lance, and Gawain quoth, "I commend this castle to Christ, may He give it ever good fortune." Then the drawbridge was let down, and the broad gates unbarred and opened on both sides; the knight crossed himself, and passed through the gateway, and praised the porter, who knelt before the prince, and gave him good-day, and commended him to God. Thus the knight went on his way with the one man who should guide him to that dread place where he should receive rueful payment.

The two went by hedges where the boughs were bare, and climbed the cliffs where the cold clings. Naught fell from the heavens, but 'twas ill beneath them; mist brooded over the moor and hung on the mountains; each hill had a cap, a great cloak, of mist. The streams foamed and bubbled between their banks, dashing sparkling on the shores where they shelved downwards. Rugged and dangerous was the way through the woods, till it was time for the sun-rising. Then were they on a high hill; the snow lay white beside them, and the man who rode with Gawain drew rein by his master.

"Sir" he said "I have brought ye hither, and now ye are not far from the place that ye have sought so specially. But I will tell ye for sooth, since I know ye well, and ye are such a knight as I well love, would ye follow my counsel ye would fare the better. The place whither ye go is accounted full perilous, for he who liveth in that waste is the worst on earth, for he is strong and fierce, and loveth to deal mighty blows; taller is he than any man on earth, and greater of frame than any four in Arthur's court, or in any other. And this is his custom at the Green Chapel; there may no man pass by that place, however proud his arms, but he does him to death by force of his hand, for he is a discourteous knight, and shows no mercy. Be he churl or chaplain who rides by that chapel, monk or mass priest, or any man else, he thinks it as pleasant to slay them as to pass alive himself. Therefore, I tell ye, as sooth as ye sit in saddle, if ye come there and that knight know it, ye shall be slain, though ye had twenty lives; trust me that truly! He has dwelt here full long and seen many a combat; ye may not defend ye against his blows. Therefore, good Sir Gawain, let the man be, and get ye away some other road; for God's sake seek ye another land, and there may Christ speed ye! And I will hasten me home again, and I promise ye further that I will swear by God and the saints, or any other oath ye please, that I will keep counsel faithfully, and never let any wit the tale that ye fled for fear of any man."

"Gramercy," quoth Gawain, but ill-pleased. "Good fortune be his who wishes me good, and that thou wouldst keep faith with me I will believe; but didst thou keep it never so truly, an I passed here and fled for fear as thou sayest, then were I a coward knight, and might not be held guiltless. So I will to the chapel let chance what may, and talk with that man, even as I may list, whether for weal or for woe as fate may have it. Fierce though he may be in fight, yet God knoweth well how to save His servants."

"Well," quoth the other, "now that ye have said so much that ye will take your own harm on yourself, and ye be pleased to lose your life, I will neither let nor keep ye. Have here your helm and the spear in your hand, and ride down this same road beside the rock till ye come to the bottom of the valley, and there look a little to the left hand, and ye shall see in that vale the chapel, and the grim man who keeps it. Now fare ye well, noble Gawain; for all the gold on earth I would not go with ye nor bear ye fellowship one step further." With that the man turned his bridle into the wood, smote the horse with his spurs as hard as he could, and galloped off, leaving the knight alone.

Quoth Gawain, "I will neither greet nor groan, but commend myself to God, and yield me to His will."

Then the knight spurred Gringalet, and rode adown the path close in by a bank beside a grove. So he rode through the rough thicket, right into the dale, and there he halted, for it seemed him wild enough. No sign of a chapel could he see, but high and burnt banks on either side and rough rugged crags with great stones above. An ill-looking place he thought it.

Then he drew in his horse and looked around to seek the chapel, but he saw none and thought it strange. Then he saw as it were a mound on a level space of land by a bank beside the stream where it ran swiftly, the water bubbled within as if boiling. The knight turned his steed to the mound, and lighted down and tied the rein to the branch of a linden; and he turned to the mound and walked round it, questioning with himself what it might be. It had a hole at the end and at either side, and was overgrown with clumps of grass, and it was hollow within as an old cave or the crevice of a crag; he knew not what it might be.

"Ah," quoth Gawain, "can this be the Green Chapel? Here might the devil say his mattins at midnight! Now I think there is wizardry here. 'Tis an ugly oratory, all overgrown with grass, and 'twould well beseem that fellow in green to say his devotions on devil's wise. Now feel I in five wits, 'tis the foul fiend himself who hath set me this tryst, to destroy me here! This is a chapel of mischance: ill-luck betide it, 'tis the cursedest kirk that ever I came in!"

Helmet on head and lance in hand, he came up to the rough dwelling, when he heard over the high hill beyond the brook, as it were in a bank, a wondrous fierce noise, that rang in the cliff as if it would cleave asunder. 'Twas as if one ground a scythe on a grindstone, it whirred and whetted like water on a mill-wheel and rushed and rang, terrible to hear.

"By God," quoth Gawain, "I trust that gear is preparing for the knight who will meet me here. Alas! naught may help me, yet should my life be forfeit, I fear not a jot!" With that he called aloud. "Who waiteth in this place to give me tryst? Now is Gawain come hither: if any man will aught of him let him hasten hither now or never."

"Stay," quoth one on the bank above his head, "and ye shall speedily have that which I promised ye." Yet for a while the noise of whetting went on ere he appeared, and then he came forth from a cave in the crag with a fell weapon, a Danish axe newly prepared, wherewith to deal the blow. An evil head it had, four feet large, no less, sharply ground, and bound to the handle by the lace that gleamed brightly. And the knight himself was all green as before, face and foot, locks and beard, but now he was afoot. When he came to the water he would not wade it, but sprang over with the pole of his axe, and strode boldly over the field that was white with snow.

Sir Gawain went to meet him, but he made no low bow. The other said, "Now, fair sir, one may trust thee to keep tryst. Thou art welcome, Gawain, to my place. Thou hast timed thy coming as befits a true man. Thou knowest the covenant set between us: at this time twelve months agone thou didst take that which fell to thee, and I at this New Year will readily, requite thee. We are in this valley, verily alone, here are no knights to sever us, do what we will. Have off thy helm from thine head, and have here thy pay; make me no more talking than I did then when thou didst strike off my head with one blow."

"Nay," quoth Gawain, "by God that gave me life, I shall make no moan whatever befall me, but make thou ready for the blow and I shall stand still and say never a word to thee, do as thou wilt."

With that he bent his head and showed his neck all bare, and made as if he had no fear, for he would not be thought a-dread.

Then the Green Knight made him ready, and grasped his grim weapon to smite Gawain. With all his force he bore it aloft with a mighty feint of slaying him: had it fallen as straight as he aimed he who was ever doughty of deed had been slain by the blow. But Gawain swerved aside as the axe came gliding down to slay him as he stood, and shrank a little with the shoulders, for the sharp iron. The other heaved up the blade and rebuked the prince with many proud words:

"Thou art not Gawain," he said, "who is held so valiant, that never feared he man by hill or vale, but thou shrinkest for fear ere thou feelest hurt. Such cowardice did I never hear of Gawain! Neither did I flinch from thy blow, or make strife in King Arthur's hall. My head fell to my feet, and yet I fled not; but thou didst wax faint of heart ere any harm befell. Wherefore must I be deemed the braver knight."

Quoth Gawain, "I shrank once, but so will I no more, though an my head fall on the stones I cannot replace it. But haste, Sir Knight, by thy faith, and bring me to the point, deal me my destiny, and do it out of hand, for I will stand thee a stroke and move no more till thine axe have hit me – my troth on it."

"Have at thee, then," quoth the other, and heaved aloft the axe with fierce mien, as is he were mad. He struck at him fiercely but wounded him not, withholding his hand ere it might strike him.

Gawain abode the stroke, and flinched in no limb, but stood still as a stone or the stump of a tree that is fast rooted in the rocky ground with a hundred roots. Then spake gaily the man in green, "So now thou hast thine heart whole it behoves me to smite. Hold aside thy hood that Arthur gave thee, and keep thy neck thus bent lest it cover it again."

Then Gawain said angrily, "Why talk on thus? Thou dost threaten too long. I hope thy heart misgives thee."

"Forsooth," quoth the other, "so fiercely thou speakest I will no longer let thine errand wait its reward." Then he braced himself to strike, frowning with lips and brow, 'twas no marvel that it pleased but ill him who hoped for no rescue. He lifted the axe lightly and let it fall with the edge of the blade on the bare neck. Though he struck swiftly it hurt him no more than on the one side where it severed the skin. The sharp blade cut into the flesh so that the blood ran over his shoulder to the ground. And when the knight saw the blood staining the snow, he sprang forth, swift-foot, more than a spear's length, seized his helmet and set it on his head, cast his shield over his shoulder, drew out his bright sword, and spake boldly (never since he was born was he half so blithe), "Stop, Sir Knight, bid me no more blows. I have stood a stroke here without flinching, and if thou give me another, I shall requite thee, and give thee as good again. By the covenant made betwixt us in Arthur's hall but one blow falls to me here. Halt, therefore."

Then the Green Knight drew off from him and leaned on his axe, setting the shaft on the ground, and looked on Gawain as he stood all armed and faced him fearlessly – at heart it pleased him well. Then he spake merrily in a loud voice, and said to the knight, "Bold sir, be not so fierce, no man here hath done thee wrong, nor will do, save by covenant, as we made at Arthur's court. I promised thee a blow and thou hast it – hold thyself well paid! I release thee of all other claims. If I had been so minded I might perchance have given thee a rougher buffet. First I menaced thee with a feigned one, and hurt thee not for the covenant that we made in the first night, and which thou didst hold truly. All the gain didst thou give me as a true man should. The other feint proffered thee for the morrow: my fair wife kissed thee, and thou didst give me her kisses – for both those days I gave thee two blows without scathe – true man, true return. But the third time thou didst fail, and therefore hadst thou that blow. For 'tis *my* weed thou wearest, that same woven girdle, my own wife wrought it, that do I know for sooth. Now know I well thy kisses, and thy conversation, and the wooing of my wife, for 'twas mine own doing. I sent her to try thee, and in sooth I think thou art the most faultless knight that ever trod earth. As a pearl among white peas is of more worth than they, so is Gawain, in faith, by other knights. But thou didst lack a little, Sir Knight, and wast wanting in loyalty, yet that was for no evil work, nor for wooing neither, but because thou lovedst thy life – therefore I blame thee the less."

Then the other stood a great while, still sorely angered and vexed within himself; all the blood flew to his face, and be shrank for shame as the Green Knight spake; and the first words he said were, "Cursed be ye, cowardice and covetousness, for in ye is the destruction of virtue." Then he loosed the girdle, and gave it to the knight. "Lo, take there the falsity, may foul befall it! For fear of thy blow cowardice bade me make friends with covetousness and forsake the customs of largess and loyalty, which befit all knights. Now am I faulty and false and have been afeared: from treachery and untruth come sorrow and care. I avow to thee, Sir Knight, that I have ill done; do then thy will. I shall be more wary hereafter."

Then the other laughed and said gaily, "I know I am whole of the hurt I had, and thou hast made such free confession of thy misdeeds, and hast so borne the penance of mine axe edge, that I hold thee absolved from that sin, and purged as clean as if thou hadst never sinned since thou wast born. And this girdle that is wrought with gold and green, like my raiment, do I give thee, Sir Gawain, that thou mayest think upon this chance when thou goest forth among princes of renown, and keep this for a token of the adventure of the Green Chapel, as it chanced between chivalrous knights. And thou shalt come again with me to my dwelling and pass the rest of this feast in gladness." Then the lord laid hold of him, and said, "I know we shall soon make peace with my wife, who was thy bitter enemy."

"Nay, forsooth," said Sir Gawain, and seized his helmet and took it off swiftly, and thanked the knight: "I have fared ill, may bliss betide thee, and may He who rules all things reward thee swiftly. Commend me to that courteous lady, thy fair wife, and to the other my honored ladies, who have beguiled their knight with skilful craft. But 'tis no marvel if one be made a fool and brought to sorrow by women's wiles, for so was Adam beguiled by one, and Solomon by many, and Samson all too soon, for Delilah dealt him his doom; and David thereafter was wedded with Bathsheba, which brought him much sorrow — if one might love a woman and believe her not, 'twere great gain! And since all they were beguiled by women, methinks 'tis the less blame to me that I was misled! But as for thy girdle, that will I take with good will, not for gain of the gold, nor for samite, nor silk, nor the costly pendants, neither for weal nor for worship, but in sign of my frailty. I shall look upon it when I ride in renown and remind myself of the fault and faintness of the flesh; and so when pride uplifts me for prowess of arms, the sight of this lace shall humble my heart. But one thing would I pray, if it displease thee not: since thou art lord of yonder land wherein I have dwelt, tell me what thy rightful name may be, and I will ask no more."

"That will I truly," quoth the other. "Bernlak de Hautdesert am I called in this land. Morgain le Fay dwelleth in mine house, and through knowledge of clerkly craft hath she taken many. For long time was she the mistress of Merlin, who knew well all you knights of the court. Morgain the goddess is she called therefore, and there is none so haughty but she can bring him low. She sent me in this guise to yon fair hall to test the truth of the renown that is spread abroad of the valor of the Round Table. She taught me this marvel to betray your wits, to vex Guinevere and fright her to death by the man who spake with his head in his hand at the high table. That is she who is at home, that ancient lady, she is even thine aunt, Arthur's half-sister, the daughter of the Duchess of Tintagel, who afterward married King Uther. Therefore I bid thee, knight, come to thine aunt, and make merry in thine house; my folk love thee, and I wish thee as well as any man on earth, by my faith, for thy true dealing."

But Sir Gawain said nay, he would in no wise do so; so they embraced and kissed, and commended each other to the Prince of Paradise, and parted right there, on the cold ground. Gawain on his steed rode swiftly to the king's hall, and the Green Knight got him whithersoever he would.

Sir Gawain who had thus won grace of his life, rode through wild ways on Gringalet; oft he lodged in a house, and oft without, and many adventures did he have and came off victor full often, as at this time I cannot relate in tale. The hurt that he had in his neck was healed, he bare the shining girdle as a baldric bound by his side, and made fast with a knot 'neath his left arm, in token that he was taken in a fault – and thus he came in safety again to the court.

Then joy awakened in that dwelling when the king knew that the good Sir Gawain was come, for he deemed it gain. King Arthur kissed the knight, and the queen also, and many valiant knights sought to embrace him. They asked him how he had fared, and he told them all that had chanced to him – the adventure of the chapel, the fashion of the knight, the love of the lady – at last of the lace. He showed them the wound in the neck which he won for his disloyalty at the hand of the knight, the blood flew to his face for shame as he told the tale.

"Lo, lady," he quoth, and handled the lace, "this is the bond of the blame that I bear in my neck, this is the harm and the loss I have suffered, the cowardice and covetousness in which I was caught, the token of my covenant in which I was taken. And I must needs wear it so long as I live, for none may hide his harm, but undone it may not be, for if it hath clung to thee once, it may never be severed."

Then the king comforted the knight, and the court laughed loudly at the tale, and all made accord that the lords and the ladies who belonged to the Round Table, each hero among them, should wear bound about him a baldric of bright green for the sake of Sir Gawain. And to this was agreed all the honor of the Round Table, and he who ware it was honored the more thereafter, as it is testified in the best book of romance. That in Arthur's days this adventure befell, the book of Brutus bears witness. For since that bold knight came hither first, and the siege and the assault were ceased at Troy, I think

Many a venture herebefore
Hath fallen such as this:
May He that bare the crown of thorn
Bring us unto His bliss.
Amen.

PEARL

translated by Charles G. Osgood, Jr. (1907)

O Pearl, delight of Christ the Prince; now safe, afar, in his clear regions of pure shining gold!

Truly no pearl of the Orient have I ever found her peer in price – so round and radiant and unchanging, so tender and slight of form. At all times when I have appraised bright gems, her I have set apart and alone. But alas, one day I lost her; in an arbor it was that she slipped from me, and fell through the grass into the ground; and now, as with a death-wound, I pine away in the thrall of longing for the spotless Pearl that was mine. Often, since there she sprang from my reach, I have lingered in that place, yearning for the happiness that erstwhile was wont to banish my troubles and exalt my blessed lot; her absence pierces my heart continually, and makes my breast ever swell and burn in wretchedness.

But never seemed to me any song so sweet as that which, on a day, in a quiet season, came stealing upon me. Truly, one after another, sad feelings welled up in my heart, as I sat thinking of her bright color now clad in clay. O earth, thou marrest a lovely jewel – the Pearl that was spotless, and mine own!

Many a plant of spice must needs spring and spread its leaves where such riches have fallen to decay; flowers, yellow, and blue, and red, there turn their faces all bright and shining towards the sun; no flower or fruit can wither in that place, since my Pearl there sank into the dark of the mold. Each spear of grass springs from a lifeless seed, or else there were no wheat to be gathered into barns; of good ever each good cometh. Surely then from so fair a seed sweet spices cannot fail to spring and grow – from that precious Pearl so pure.

Into this place of which I speak – this arbor green – I had gone one day, after my wont. It was a high season in August, when corn is cut with sickles keen. There was a mound in the place where the Pearl had fallen and rolled away from me; upon it fell shadows of flowers bright and sheen – gilliflower, ginger, and gromwell, with peonies scattered all about. And if the sight was fair to behold, sweet too was the fragrance which rose thence, where dwells, as I think, that adorable one, my precious, spotless Pearl.

Before that place I wrung my hands in the clutches of cold care. A desolate grief lay deep in my heart, though reason tried to make peace therein. Wild forebodings warred fiercely within my soul, and I wailed aloud for my Pearl that was fast imprisoned in that place: and, though Christ in his true compassion comforted me, yet my wretched will toiled on in woe. At last I fell upon the flowery turf, when suddenly such sweet fragrance entered and filled my brain that I sank into deep slumber, and dreamed of my precious Pearl so pure.

Thence sprang my soul aloft while my body lay at the grave-mound in dreams. For in God's grace my soul set forth on a strange journey to behold marvels. I knew not where in the world it was; I only saw that I was brought into a place where great cliffs stood cleaving together. Toward a forest I took my way, where were seen rocks of richest hue. The light – the gleaming glory that flashed from them might no man believe; no fabric woven by men was ever half so bright and rare. All the hillsides thereabout were adorned with cliffs of clearest crystal, and among them were shining groves with boles as blue as indigo. Like burnished silver were the shifting leaves, quivering unnumbered on every branch, as gleams fell upon them from the sky; with splendid shimmer all bright they shone. The gravel under foot was precious orient pearl. Ah, dim and dark are the very sun's beams beside all that splendor!

The glory of those fair hills made my spirit forget all its woe; so fresh were the odors from the fruits growing there that they fully satisfied me, as it had been sweet food; Birds of flaming colors, large and small, flew about in the woodland there; but string of citole, or cithern-player, could ill counterfeit their lively notes, as with fluttering wings they sang together in sweet accord. Such joyous rapture could no man attain as to hear their lovely song, and see their bright array.

In like glory shone all that woodland whithersoever fortune led me; no man that beareth tongue is worthy to tell the glory thereof. I walked on and on with untroubled mind; no hillside was so steep and high as to threaten me with harm. The farther I went through this woodland, the fairer grew meadows and plants, spice-trees and pear-trees, hedges and borders of brooks, and bright rivers whose steep banks were as fine threads of gold.

At length I came to a stream which ran swiftly by its shore. Ah God, how rare its beauty. Those fair depths lay between radiant banks of bright beryl, and, flowing sweetly, the water ran forth on its way with a murmuring sound as of many voices. At the bottom were glittering stones that shimmered and glowed like a flash of light through glass; they were as stars in streaming splendor that shine in the sky all a winter's night, while men of this earth lie fast asleep. For each pebble in those depths was either emerald, or sapphire, or other precious gem, so that the deep pools were all agleam of light, so rare was their beauty. The fair glory of hill and vale, of wood and water and sweet meadows, caused bliss to spring anew within me, and, quieting my grief, undid my anguish and healed my pain. Down along that stream, as it flowed on in its might, I sped in ecstasy that filled my mind brimful; and the farther I followed that watery vale, the mightier the joy that urged my heart. For though fortune fareth whithersoever she will, whether she send solace or sorrow, yet the man to whom she inclines her favor strives hard to win more and more. Happier then my lot than I could ever tell, even in much space; for no mortal heart could hold a tenth part of the glad rapture of that place. Wherefore I thought Paradise lay over against those broad-sloping shores, and that the waters were but divisions between its pleasant places. Over the river, somewhere by hill or dale, must stand, I thought, that heavenly city. But the water was deep, and I dared not wade; yet ever the more I longed to behold it. Yes, more and more I yearned to see what lay beyond the stream; for if the place where I walked was fair, how much lovelier that farther shore! All about I stumbled and looked, and tried hard to find a fording-place, but the farther I went picking my way along the shore, the more the dangers there about me; and yet it seemed that I could not pause in dismay where joys were so alluring.

Then a strange thing befell me, that stirred my mind more deeply still. For greater wonder than ever seized me, as I saw beyond that pleasant stream a cliff of gleaming crystal, that shot forth many a dazzling ray. At its base there sat a child, a gentle maiden full debonaire, in raiment all gleaming white. I knew her well, for I had seen her aforetime. Like glistening gold which men cut into fine threads, so shone that radiant one at the cliff's base. From my distance I gazed at her, and the longer I looked, the more came I to know her; and still as I searched her fair face, and scanned her lovely form, such transporting glory fell upon my sense as I had never known. A glad desire to call her pursued me – but confusion dealt my heart a sudden blow; so strange it was to see her in that place, that my sense was stricken and well-nigh stunned at the sight.

Then lifted she her fair brow, her face white as smooth ivory, and it stung my heart with wild dismay ever deeper and deeper the longer I gazed. Great fear rose within me in spite of myself. I stood utterly still, and dared not cry out; with eyes wide open and mouth fast shut, I was as quiet as hawk in hall. I thought this apparition something spectral, and feared what might come of it – that she whom I there descried might escape before I could call aloud and stop her. Then she, the sweetly radiant, pure and unspotted, so soft, so slight, so fair and winsomely slender – that precious one all adorned in pearls – arose in her royal array. Pearls of kingly price might one then have seen by God's grace, when, fresh as a fleur-de-lis, she stepped forth down the shore. All gleaming white was her robe of fine linen, open at the sides, and purfled with the loveliest margery-pearls, as I guess, that I ever beheld; long were her sleeve-laps, I know, and adorned round about with pearls in double border. Her kirtle showed beneath of the same bright stuff, all set about with precious pearls. A rich crown of margery-pearls unmingled with gems of any other kind this maiden wore; high-pinnacled it was, all of clear white pearls wrought in figures of flowers. No fillet nor braid she wore besides, but the folds of her hair fell loose about her. Sober and demure was her face – fit for duke or earl; her hue was paler than ivory. Her hair glistened like bright shorn gold, as it lay loose and light upon her shoulders. Yet her color was deep, wanting not the adornment of the precious pearls in broidery all about. Every hem – at the wrists, the sides, and the openings – was edged and pointed with white pearls only, and all her vesture was lustrous white. One marvelous pearl without blemish was set secure in the midst of her breast; a man's mind would be sadly baffled ere he could measure the full beauty of that gem. No tongue, I think, could utter the sweet tale of that vision – so fair, so bright, so pure was the precious pearl there set.

All thus adorned in pearls that dear one beyond the stream came down the opposite shore. From here to Greece there was no happier man than I when she had reached the brink; nearer was she to me than aunt or niece, wherefore my joy was greater than ever. Then this peerless one made as if to speak, for, bowing low in sweet womanly grace, she lightly caught off her crown of rich treasure, and blithely greeted me. Happy was I that was born to speak with that fair one in her array of pearls!

"O Pearl, all adorned in pearls," said I, "art thou mine own, my Pearl, that I have bewailed and mourned in night and solitude? Great yearning have I suffered for thee in secret since thou didst slip away from me into the grass. Gloomy, wasted, nigh spent with pain am I, while thou, unracked with strife, hast fallen upon a pleasant life in the homeland of Paradise. What fortune has brought my jewel hither, and cast me into grief and bondage? For, since we were separated and torn asunder, I have been but a wretched jeweler."

Then that jewel, all arrayed in precious gems, lifted her face, raised to me her gray eyes, set on again her crown of orient pearl, and at length said gravely: "Sir, ill have you heeded your own words when you say that your Pearl is utterly lost, which is now so fair enclosed here in a coffer – I mean this garden bright and lovely – here to dwell for ever and make merry, where sin and mourning draw not nigh. This place were indeed a treasury for thee, if thou were truly a noble jeweler. But, gentle sir, if thou must willfully lose thy joy for a mere gem that was dear, methinks thou art given over to mad intent, and troublest thyself about a trifle. What thou hast lost was only a rose that flowered and faded according to its kind; but now by nature of the chest that secureth it, it proveth a pearl of price. If thou hast called thy good fortune a thief, which manifestly hath made for thee something out of thy nothing; then dost thou reproach the very remedy of thine ill; thou art no grateful jeweler."

A very jewel was then this visitant to me, and jewels were her gentle words.

"Indeed," said I, "my dear, blest child, now dost thou unravel all my woe. I beseech thee, pardon me, for I thought my Pearl was gone forth from life. But, now that I have found it, I shall make merry, and dwell with it in woodlands sheen, praising my Lord and his ways, who hath brought me hither near unto such bliss. Now, were I only at your side, beyond this water, so indeed were my joy complete!"

Then answered this pure gem: "Ah, jeweler! Why must thou, and all men, be for ever mad? Three words in a breath hast thou spoken, and all three of them ill-considered; thou knowest not in the least what one of them does mean, and thy tongue doth outrun thy wit. Thou sayest that thou dost think that I dwell here in this vale, because forsooth thou canst see me here with thine own eyes; and again, thou sayest that in this country thou art to dwell with me, yea, in this very place; and again, that thou shalt pass over this water unhindered – a thing that no man may lightly do. I hold him undeserving who believes only what he sees with his eyes; and he indeed is much to blame, and wants true courtesy, who thinks our Lord falsely uttered his loyal promise to raise you up unto life, albeit fate hath committed your body unto death. Ye men turn his words all awry, and believe nothing unless ye see it; it is a trait of pride ill-becoming every good, man, to believe no tale trustworthy unless his own poor reason can prove it so. Rather judge for thyself whether thou hast spoken wisely, considering what words man ought to offer God. Thou sayest thou art to dwell in this domain. Methinks it first behooves thee to ask leave; yet withal thou mightest fail to gain it. Thou desirest to cross this stream, but, ere that, thou must change thy purpose; thy body shall first sink all cold into the ground, since it was forfeit in the garden of Paradise, in the ill-keeping of our father Adam. Through dreary death must each man be brought, ere God will appoint him to cross this stream."

"Alas, then," said I, "if thou dost condemn me to sorrow again, my sweet, I shall pine away. Now that, I have found what I had lost, must I forego it again, even until I die? Why must I find it, if only to lose it straightway? My precious Pearl doth me great pain! What profiteth treasure but to make a man weep, if forthwith he must lose it with bitter pangs? Nay, then, I care not whether I return to earth, nor how far thence I am banished, if I am to have no part in my Pearl. Ah, what may man expect on earth but unceasing sorrow!"

Then said the maiden: "So thou lookest for naught but agony of grief? Why dost thou so? By the clamor of his grief at trifling losses, many a man oft foregoes the greater benefits. It behooves thee better to look after thine own welfare, and ever to praise God, come weal, come woe; for resentment profiteth thee not a straw. Let him who must needs endure be not so impatient. For though thou plunge like a wild doe, and toss thy limbs about in frenzy, and utter thy rage in shrieks, yet, when thou canst make way no farther, to or fro, then must thou still abide what he shall decree. The Lord shall ordain and dispose all things, for he will never turn one foot aside from the way. Though thou in thy sorrow be never glad again, it availeth thee naught. Have done, then, with thy strife, cease to contend, and seek his compassion with all speed; haply thy prayer will lay hold on his pity, and mercy will then show thee her power; his comfort may soothe thy suffering, and drive thy lowering looks lightly away. For, in failure or in fortune, in grief remembered or forgotten, all things abide in him to decree and ordain."

Then said I to the maiden: "O let not my Lord be angry, though in my haste I rave, and rush headlong in my talk! My heart was all stricken and melted with my loss, like water welling up and running forth from a spring. But now I give myself up unto his tender mercy. Chide me no longer with thy dreadful words, my dearly beloved, though I speak idly, but tender me lovingly thy comfort, thinking in pity of this – that thou hast made reconciliation between me and care – thou who wast erstwhile the root of all my joy. My joy, and my grief too, hast thou been, wherefore so much the louder was my lament. For after thou wast withdrawn from every danger of earthly life, I knew not whither my Pearl was gone; and now that I see it again, my trouble has ceased. If, when we parted, we were of one mind, God forbid that we be at odds now, since we meet so seldom by stock or stone. And though you speak on full courteously, I am but dust, and undone with sin. But the mercy of Christ and Mary and John – these shall be the root of all my joy.

"I behold thee now entered into the life of bliss, while I am all dejected and downcast. Perhaps of this you take little heed, or of the burning wrongs that often fall to my lot. But now that I am here in your very presence, I would cease from dispute, and beseech you to tell me willingly and earnestly what sort of life ye lead early and late. For I am full glad that your estate is indeed changed to one of worship and good fortune; it is the highroad of all my joy, the root of all my peace."

"Now joy betide thee, sir," then said she so fair of face and form; "and welcome here both to rest and roam, for now are thy words precious to me. Masterful heart and overweening pride, I assure thee, are bitterly hated here; yet my Lord loveth not to chide in anger, for meek are all they that dwell near him. And when thou shalt appear in his holy place, be thou deep-devout in all humility; for my Lord the Lamb still loveth such demeanor, and he is the root of all my joy.

"A joyous life I lead, thou sayest true, and wouldst learn the station thereof. Thou knowest well that when thy Pearl fell away from thee I was yet very young and of tender years. Yet my Lord the Lamb by his divine nature took me in marriage, and crowned me his queen, to dwell in bliss throughout the length of all days to come. Moreover I am his love, established in his full heritage, and am his and his alone. His worth, his excellence, his high lineage, are root and ground of all my joy."

"Ah blessed," said I, "if this be true, be not angry, though the question I ask thee be foolish and wrong. Art thou that queen of blue heaven to whom all this world shall do honor? We believe in Mary, Author of Grace, who in maiden innocence bore a child. What queen could take away her crown from her, unless she passed her in goodliness? Nay, for that her sweetness is beyond all compare, we call her Phoenix of Araby, that bird of blameless fashion, like the Queen of Courtesy."

Then knelt the radiant one upon the ground, and covered her face with the folds of her garment, and prayed, saying: "Hail gracious Queen peerless Mother, all-glorious Maiden, blessed Well-spring of every grace!"

Then she arose, and paused, and, after a space, said to me : "Sir, many there are who gain possessions here, and hold them fast, but usurpers are there none in this place; the Empress Mary holdeth all heaven and earth and hell in her dominion, yet no one doth she drive forth from his heritage, for she is the Queen of Courtesy. The court of the kingdom of the ever-living God hath of its very essence this property: each one that entereth therein is king or queen of the whole realm, nor shall any other dispossess such an one, but each rejoiceth in the other's possession, and would that her comrade's crown were fivefold as rich, if such increase were possible. But my Lady, of whom Jesus was born, beareth rule full high above us all; yet that offendeth none of our company, for she is the Queen of Courtesy. By the Spirit of true courtesy, saith Saint Paul, we are all members of Jesus Christ; as head, and leg, and arm, and nail, are all attached to their proper body, faithful and true, so in like manner is every Christian soul a proper limb of the Master of Might. Therefore see whether rancor or bitterness is fixed or seated between thy members; thy head harboreth not anger and resentment, though arm or finger wear a ring; and with like courtesy do we all bear ourselves in love and joy towards king and queen among us."

"Yea," said I, "I believe that courtesy and all charitableness prevail among you; but, lest my words grieve you. . . . If thou exaltest thyself to heaven to become a queen – thou who wert so young – what greater honor can he achieve who has continued faithful and strong in the world, and lived in lifelong penance to purchase heavenly bliss with torment of the flesh? What greater worship could such an one attain than to be crowned a king by courtesy? This courtesy of which you speak is too large of deed, if that be true which thou hast said. Thou livedst not two years among our folk on earth. Thou never knewest then how to please God by deed or prayer, by Pater Noster or Creed. And crowned a queen on the first day after! God help me, but I cannot believe that he would turn aside so far from the right. Indeed, dear maiden, the estate of a countess you might fairly hold in heaven, or at least of a lady of less array; but a queen – nay, that is too much!"

Then said to me that adorable one: "Of his goodness there is no end. For all is justice which he ordereth, and he can do naught but right, as saith Saint Matthew in the Mass, in the true Gospel of Almighty God. In a parable he frameth an image true and exact, and likens it to bright heaven. 'My kingdom on high,' he saith, 'is like unto a lord who had a vineyard. The end of the year was at hand, and it was hard upon the time to prepare the vineyard for winter. Now all laborers know full well that time of year. The lord rose early to hire laborers into his vineyard, and among them found some suited to his purpose. They enter into agreement for a penny a day, and go forth, and bend to their work, and travail sore; they prune, and bind, and make everything snug.

" 'About the third hour the lord goeth into the market, and findeth idle men standing there, and saith unto them: 'Why stand ye idle? Know ye not that this day must end?'

" 'And they answered with one accord, murmuring: 'Ere the dawn came we hither, here have we stood since the sun rose, and yet no man hath commanded us to work.'

" ' 'Go into my vineyard, and do what ye can,' said the lord, and made good his command, saying, 'Whatsoever reasonable hire be earned by nightfall I will pay you in good faith.'

" ' 'They went into his vineyard and wrought, and all day the lord went his way, bringing new men thither. At length this long-awaited day of toil was far spent. The time of evensong was come, an hour before sunset, and still he found strong men yet idle; and he said to them gravely: 'Why stand ye idle this whole day long?'

" 'They said that wages nowhere awaited their toil.

" ' 'Then go into my vineyard, young yeomen; there labor and do what ye can.'

" 'Soon all the world grew brown and dark; the sun had gone down and it waxed late. Then bade he summon the workmen, for the day was past. The lord was mindful of the eventide, and called to his reeve, saying: 'Sirrah, now pay the servants; give them the wages I owe them. And further, that none may complain, set them all in a row, and give to all alike a penny. Begin with the last and lowest, until thou come to the first.'

" 'Then the first began to murmur, and say that they had travailed sore. 'These,' said they, 'toiled but an hour; it seems right, then, that we should receive more. We think that we who have borne the heat of the day have done greater service than those who wrought not even two hours, and yet thou dost make them equal unto us.'

" 'Then said the lord to one of them: 'Friend, I would not have thee lose aught by me. Take what is thine, and go thy way. If I hired thee at a penny for the whole day's work, why dost thou begin now to complain? Was not thy covenant made for a penny? Thou mayest plead for nothing beyond the covenant. Then why wilt thou ask for more? Is it not my lawful privilege to do whatsoever I will with mine own? Else is thine eye bent on evil, but I am good and defraud no man.'

"And Christ saith: 'So will I appoint each man his portion – he that is last shall be the first to enter, and the first shall be last, be he never so swift of foot. Many are called, though few be chosen unto the high places. Thus each poor man beareth away his just portion, though he hath come late, and is of low degree.' And, though his labor cease with little done, yet far more than his labor availeth the mercy of God. Wherefore I have here more joy and bliss and ladyship and abundance of life than all men in the world could win, if they sought payment according to their works. Yet I have hardly begun my labor, and it was already eventide when I entered into the vineyard; nevertheless my Lord at once took thought of my hire, and I was forthwith paid in full. But there were others who had labored longer, who toiled and sweat long ere I began, but who have not yet got a tithe of their hire, nor will they perhaps for a year to come."

Then in all frankness I said: "To me thy tale seems unreasonable. God's justice is ever ready and alert, else Holy Writ is but a fable. In the Psalter is a versicle that clearly and openly declareth this truth: 'Thou renderest to every man according to his desert, O high and all-disposing King.' But if thou, my child, come to thy reward before him who abode steadfast the whole day long, then he who hath done the less work may win the greater reward, which means that the less work a man does, the greater his pay."

Then answered that gentle one: "Of less and more in God's kingdom there is no hazard, for there every man is paid alike, whether little or much seem his reward. Our gentle Liege is no churl. Whether his dealings be harsh or tender, he poureth out gifts as lavishly as water runs from a moat, or streams from a deep and never-failing pool. Large is that man's exemption who hath ever continued in fear before him that giveth succor in the hour of temptation and sin; no joy shall be withheld from such an one, for the grace of God is sufficient there unto.

"But now thou wilt checkmate me by urging that I have here received my penny unjustly. Thou sayest that I am come too late, and am not worthy of so great a reward. Where hast thou ever known a man who abode at all times so holy in his prayer, that he forfeited not in some way, at some time, the guerdon of bright heaven? And still the older such men grew, the oftener did they forsake the right, and do wrong. Then are mercy and grace become their only guides, for the grace of God is sufficient thereunto. But grace enough, without works, have the innocent. As soon as they are born, they descend at once into the water of baptism, and then are led into the vineyard. Anon the day, shot through with darkness, boweth before the power of Death. The gentle Lord then payeth his laborers who did no wrong ere they went forth from his vineyard. Long have they abode there, and done his bidding; why should he not give them their labor's due, and grant them their pay in the very hour of their passing? For his grace is sufficient thereunto. We know full well that all mankind was first fashioned for a life of perfect bliss, but our forefather forfeited it by the apple of which he ate, and in that eating we were condemned to die in wretchedness and banishment from bliss, and at length to pass into the heat of hell, there to abide without respite. But straightway there interposed a healing remedy, for in that plight fair streams of blood and water ran plenteously down the rough cross, and God's grace was sufficient. Abounding rose the tide of blood and water from out the well of that great wound; the blood redeemed us from the bale of hell, and delivered us from the second death; and truly the water which followed the sword with cruel edge is baptism, and washeth away the fell guilt that Adam brought upon us when he drowned us in death. Now between us and bliss there is no barrier in the round world which he hath not withdrawn, and no access thereunto which he hath not restored in blessed hour; whereunto God's grace is sufficient. He who hath sinned again may find grace enough, if he truly repent, but he must crave such grace with sorrow and contrition, and suffer the penalty that goeth with true remorse. But he that is wholly innocent shall be saved by the justice of God that never can err. It was never God's decree that the guiltless should perish. The guilty man may indeed attain contrition, and through mercy be brought speedily unto grace; but he who never turned aside unto wickedness, and is in all things innocent – he is justly saved.

"This one thing in truth I know of this matter – it is meet and right that both orders of men be saved: the penitent-righteous man shall see his face, and the innocent also shall come unto him. Thus saith the Psalter in one place: 'Lord, who shall ascend into thy high hill, or stand in thy holy place?' Nor is God slow to answer: 'He that worketh not evil with his hands, that is both pure and clean of heart, there shall his foot be established for ever.' In justice shall the innocent be saved.

"But the righteous penitent shall also draw near unto that fair mansion – he that taketh not his life in vain, nor flattereth his neighbor deceitfully. Of the man who is thus righteous Solomon speaketh plainly, declaring how gently our King received him, and led his feet in the ways that are straight, and showed him the kingdom of God for a little space, as who would say: 'Lo yon fair realm! Thou mayest win it for thine own, if thou be brave.' But without fear or danger of falsehood I say, in justice ever shall the innocent be saved.

"Of righteous men speaketh yet another – David in the Psalter, if haply ye have seen his words: 'Lord, draw not thy servant unto judgment, for in thy sight shall no man living be justified.' Wherefore, when thou shalt come before that bar where all our causes shall be tried, urge in thy defense thy right of being received by these very words that I have cited. But he that died the bloody death on the cross, with hands grievously pierced, grant that, when thou come to trial, thou be acquitted by innocence, and not by pleading.

"Let him who can read aright consider the Holy Book, and learn how Jesus walked among people of old, and how men eagerly brought their little ones unto him. With fair words they besought him to touch their children for the health and happiness that went forth from him. Impatiently his disciples charged them to let him be, and many were kept back with their chiding. Then Jesus said sweetly: 'Nay, suffer the children to come unto me, since for such is prepared the Kingdom of Heaven.' Thus ever in justice shall the innocent be saved. Then Jesus called unto him a gentle child, and said no man could win his kingdom unless he should come thither as such an one; else let him never enter therein. Innocent, true, undefiled, without spot or stain of polluting sin – when such knock at the door, quickly shall the bolt be drawn. Therein is bliss that shall never end – such as the merchant sought among goodly pearls, when he sold all that he had, both wool and linen, to buy himself a pearl without spot. 'This spotless pearl which the merchant bought with a great price – nay, with all his goods – is like unto the Kingdom of bright Heaven' – so spake the Father of earth and sea; for it is stainless pure and bright, and one perfect round, and glad of heart, and common to all the righteous. Lo, even in the center of my breast it abideth! My Lord, the Lamb, who spent his blood, hath put it there in token of peace. I advise thee, forsake the mad world, and get for thyself this spotless pearl."

"Ah Pearl so pure," said I, "arrayed in fair pearls, wearing the pearl of great price, who fashioned thy fair figure? Full skilful was he that wrought thy vesture. Thy beauty is not the mere gift of Nature; from Pygmalion came not thy bright color, nor did Aristotle in all his books describe the true quality of these thy attributes. Thy color passes the fleur-de-lis; thy demeanor as of angels is so pure and gracious – ah, tell me, bright creature, what station is held by Pearl so rare?"

Then said she: "My Lamb without blemish, who excelleth all others, he, my dear Destiny, chose me for his mate, unworthy as I was; a fitting time was set for that union –the day when I departed from your world of tears. He called me to share his gentle condition, saying: 'Come unto me, my sweet love, for in thee is neither spot nor stain.' Then he clothed me in strength and beauty, and washed my robes in his blood, setting me in the place of honor, and crowned me in pure virginity, and arrayed me in spotless pearls."

"Nay," said I, "thou spotless bride flaming with light, clothed in royalty so rich and free, of what nature is the Lamb that he would take thee to his wife? Hast thou in truth mounted so high above all the rest to live with him a life of such ladyship? So many a fair one there is, the world over, that hath endured long struggle for Christ; and if thou didst thrust out all those dear ones, and put down all others from that marriage, save only thyself so strong and firm, then art thou not immaculate only, but matchless."

Then said that lovely queen: "Immaculate, unblemished, and unspotted am I indeed, and so may I aver in all seemliness; but I said not 'matchless queen.' We in bliss are brides of the Lamb – one hundred and forty and four thousand in all, as it is written in the Apocalypse. Saint John saw them all in a company on the Mount of Sion, that fair height; the Apostle beheld them in ghostly vision arrayed unto the marriage, upon that hill which is the new city of Jerusalem. Of this Jerusalem I now come to speak. If thou wilt know his true nature – my Lamb, my Lord, my precious Jewel, my Joy, my Bliss, my fair Loved One – hear what the prophet Isaiah spake of him, in pity at his sweet submission: 'This glorious Innocent that was slain of men, without taint of sin, was brought as a sheep to the slaughter; and, as a lamb which the shearer taketh in the field, so closed he his mouth at every question, when the Jews tried him in Jerusalem.'

"In Jerusalem was my Love slain and torn by shameless ruffians. Full willing was he to bear our sorrows, and he hath taken upon himself our bitter griefs. With buffets was his face all flayed, that had been so fair to look upon. For our sin he set himself at naught – he who had no sin that he could call his own. For us he suffered himself to be flayed, and bowed down, and stretched upon the brutal cross, as meek as a lamb that uttereth no plaint. For us he died in Jerusalem. And when the good Saint John was baptizing at Jerusalem, in Jordan, and in Galilee, his words accorded with Isaiah; for when Jesus drew near unto him he spake of him this prophecy: 'Behold the Lamb of God, unchanging as the rock, that taketh away the burden of sins which all men have heaped upon themselves. As for him, not one hath he wrought, yet upon himself he hath taken them all. Who shall declare his generation that died for us in Jerusalem?'

"Thus at Jerusalem, by true witness of either prophet, my sweet Loved One was twice likened to a Lamb in lowliness of mind and manner. The third time also is duly set down full clear in the Apocalypse. In the midst of the throne, where the saints were sitting, the Apostle John beheld him all unveiled, opening the book with great square leaves, where the seven seals were set in order; and at that sight every creature in heaven, in earth, and in hell, trembled with fear. This Lamb of Jerusalem was without sin or blemish; his only hue was shining white, admitting neither spot nor stain, and he was clothed in white wool rich and flowing.

"Wherefore each soul that never knew the taint of sin is an adorable wife unto the Lamb. And though each day he fetcheth hither a great number, yet there entereth among us no rivalry nor strife, except that we would that each one of our comrades were five; the more the merrier, by the blessing of God. Our love is one that doth thrive in a great company, where honor grows from more to more. Decrease of joy can no one bring upon us who wear this pearl upon our breasts, for they that bear the device of spotless pearls can utter no impure thing. Though our bodies shrivel among clods of clay, and though ye without rest cry out for sorrow, yet we have perfect knowledge in all things. Our dread of the bodily death hath been realized; the Lamb now maketh us to rejoice, our care is done away, he ever filleth our hearts with mirth at the heavenly mass, each one's joy is perfect to the uttermost, and no one's honor shall ever grow less.

"But lest thou find my tale unseemly, thus is it written in a place in the Apocalypse: 'I saw,' saith John, 'the Lamb standing on Mount Sion in the fullness of his strength, and with him were one hundred and forty and four thousand virgins. And in their foreheads I beheld written the name of the Lamb, and of his Father. And I heard then a voice from heaven like the voice of many waters rushing in a mighty torrent; and, as thunder leaps among the darkened hills, such, I fancied, was this sound of mingled voices. And though the sound was sharp and loud, yet could I hear them singing a melody new and strange, and deliciously sweet it was to hearken thereto. As the voice of harpers harping with their harps, full clear was the new song that they sang; a sweet discourse of sounding notes it was, as they took up the strains, singing together in pure concert of voices. Right before the throne of God, and the four beasts that bow down unto him, and the elders so grave of mien, they sang their song unceasingly. Yet there was never a man of such skill, for all the arts that he ever knew, that could sing one note of that song, except this company that followeth the Lamb. For they are redeemed and far removed from the earth, being the first fruits appointed unto the gentle Lamb, and like unto him in the light of their countenances; since naught that they have suffered hath defiled their tongues with falsehood or deceit.' Nor can that pure company be removed from its immaculate Lord even for ever."

Then said I: "Bear with my inquiry yet a little while. Though I confront thee with many questions, I ought not to tempt thy true understanding who art elect unto Christ's bridechamber. I am the while but dust and muck, and thou a rose all fresh and fair, dwelling here by this blessed hill where the joy of life is unfailing. Yet, gracious maiden, in whom simplicity abideth, I would expressly ask of thee one thing; and, though I be as hasty as fire, nevertheless let my prayer avail; bold and sincere is my appeal, if haply thou seest a way to grant what I ask; and, as thou art filled with glory and free from corruption, withhold not this boon from me in my sorrow. Have ye no dwellings enclosed in castle-walls, no manor where ye may assemble, and live together? Thou tellest me of Jerusalem rich and royal, where David, the beloved one, was upon his throne; yet not among these woods may that fair city stand, but in Judea. And since ye are in all things pure, so must your dwelling-places be likewise without taint. This spotless company of which thou hast spoken, this throng of thousands, is so vast a multitude that ye must needs possess a large city, for great is your number. Evil it were if so fair a crowd of bright jewels must lodge without its walls. If I see no building hereabouts, as I tarry among these hills, then I think ye must dwell alone and apart, as ye gaze upon the glory of this lovely stream. But if elsewhere thou hast strong mansions, bring me now to that bright citadel."

Then said this precious creature unto me: "That city of Judea that thou hast in mind is the city that the Lamb did seek wherein to suffer for man's sake. It is the old Jerusalem, for there the old guilt was done away. But the new city that hath come down to us of God's own sending – that is the theme of the Apostle in the Apocalypse. The Lamb, pure from every defiling spot, hath conveyed thither his fair company. And, as his flock needeth not earthly pinfold, so his city is without confine of earthly moat. To speak exactly of these two cities, if both are alike called Jerusalem, that name should mean to you no more than City of God, or Vision of Peace. In the one our peace was made perfect, for there the lamb chose to suffer in penal agony for us. In the other, peace, and peace alone, is to be found, which shall endure unbroken for ever. That is the city to which we press forward from the day that our flesh is laid down to decay. There shall glory and bliss increase ever for the company of them that are without stain."

Then said I to that lovely flower: "Ah, maiden pure, so meek and mild, bring me now to that pleasant abode."

But she, so radiant, replied: "Nay, for God will not suffer it. Thou mayest not enter into his stronghold; but from the Lamb, through his great loving-kindness, I have won for thee a glimpse thereof. Thou mayest behold that fair enclosure from without, but not one foot within its walls mayest thou go. Nay, thou couldst not walk in its streets, unless thou were wholly pure. If I am to reveal to thee this city, take now thy way up toward this river's head, and I shall follow along with thee on this side, till thou gain a certain hill."

Then would I tarry no longer, but stole away among leafy, pleasant boughs, till I spied a hill, and, as I hurried on, looked out upon the city beyond the river, revealed at a distance, shining with rays brighter than the sun. In the Apocalypse is shown its fashion, as there described by John the Apostle. And as John beheld it with his own eyes, in like manner saw I that city of renown – Jerusalem so new, so royally arrayed, as it was descended out of heaven.

The city was all of fine gold, bright, burnished, and radiant, like clear shining glass, and garnished beneath with precious gems. In twelve steps up from the lowest base rose twelve foundations of rich jointure, and each tier was a separate stone. Thus splendidly doth John the Apostle describe this very city in the book of his Vision. As he there doth name these stones, so knew I their names after his tale: jasper was the name of the first that I discerned on the first stage; it shone all green along the lowest course; sapphire filled the second step; then chalcedony without blemish shone pure and pale in the third; the fourth was emerald all green; the fifth, sardonyx; then the ruby hath the Apostle named sixth in order. Thereto he added the chrysolite as the seventh in the foundation; and the eighth, beryl, clear and white; the ninth, topaz of twofold hue inlaid; tenth in order, the chrysoprase; the eleventh is the precious jacinth; the twelfth, the most precious of all, is the purple amethyst blent with indigo. Above these courses overhung the wall of jasper clear as glass; I knew it by John's story in the Apocalypse.

Still more did I see, as he hath set it forth. These twelve steps were broad yet steep, and above them stood the city, a perfect square – in length, breadth, and height, all fair and equal. The streets of gold were as transparent glass; the jasper walls gleamed like glair [the white of an egg]; the houses within were adorned with all kinds of precious stones that could be brought together. And each side of this city stretched the space of twelve furlongs ere it ended, in height, and length, and breadth, just equal, for the Apostle saw it measured.

Yet more did I see of what John hath written. Each side of the city had three gates, and thus I beheld twelve in order, the portals overlaid with rich plates; and each gate of a single margery-pearl that fadeth never. Each one bore a name in writing, which are the names of the children of Israel in the order of their birth, beginning with oldest.

Such light shone in all the streets that they had no need of the sun, neither of the moon. Sun nor moon wanted they; for surely the very God was their bright lamp, and the Lamb was their lantern, and through him the whole city was filled with brightness. Over wall and dwelling ran my eyes, for air so subtle and clear could bar no light. The high throne one might there behold surrounded with all the array declared in the words of John; and the high God himself was seated thereon. Forth out of the throne there ran a river brighter than sun or moon. Neither of these ever shone with light so sweet as did that abounding flood, where it gushed forth from the ground. Swift did it run on through every street, without any mingling of filth, or pollution, or slime. Church, nor chapel, nor temple was ever set in that place, but the Almighty was their proper sanctuary, the Lamb, the sacrifice, was there as refreshment. The gates of the city were never shut, but stood always open toward every quarter. Therein entereth none to take refuge who beareth any taint whatsoever. The moon could never share that glory; too spotty is her globe, too grim her favor; and since there is no night there, what need that the moon climb thither in her course, or try to equal that supernal light that shineth upon the river's brink? The planets are in too poor a plight, and the very sun himself is far too dim. On either side of the water are trees all bright that bear the twelve fruits of life full early; and twelve times a year do they bring forth in their vigor, and renew their fruit each month.

No heart of mortal man beneath the moon could endure so great a marvel as I beheld when I gazed upon that city, so wondrous was its fashion. I stood as still as a frightened quail at that strange and radiant apparition; of neither rest nor toil was I aware, so ravished was I with its pure gleam. For I dare say in all surety that, if one in the body had met that boon, though all the learned men in the world had him in cure, his life had been lost for ever.

And as the moon doth rise in mighty splendor, ere the last day-gleam hath sunk with the sun, so in wondrous manner I was suddenly aware of a procession. This noble city of glory and splendor was presently filled with virgins all unsummoned, in the same guise as was my blessed one that wore the crown; so crowned were they all alike and appareled in pearls and robes of white; and each one's breast was delightfully adorned with the blessed pearl. Joyfully they walked together on the golden streets that shone as glass; hundreds of thousands I thought there were, and all alike in their liveries. Hard was it to find the gladdest face among them. Before them walked the Lamb in state, having seven horns of bright red gold; like pearls of great price was his raiment. Toward the throne they took their way. And, though great was their number, there was no crowding among them, but mild as gentle maidens at mass, so walked they forth in perfect joy.

The joy that awoke at the Lamb's forthcoming was too great to tell. The elders, as he drew near, fell prostrate at his feet. Legions of angels, assembled there, scattered incense of sweet savor. Then the sounds of praise and joy burst forth anew: all sang together in honor of that bright Jewel; and the sound of voices which the angels of heaven then uttered in their joy could have struck down through earth into hell. Then in sooth I conceived a great and glad desire to praise the Lamb there in the midst of his train, and delight filled my heart to tell of him and his marvelous guise. Best was he, and blithest, and worthiest of all that ever I heard praised – so adorably white his raiment, so simple his look, himself so gentle. But a wound full wide and wet with blood appeared close against his heart, torn through his skin; and from his fair side gushed his blood. Alas! thought I, who did that outrage? Any breast ought to have burned up for sorrow, ere one found delight in that deed. Yet could no one doubt the Lamb's joy. For though he was hurt and wounded, it appeared not in his countenance, so full of light and gladness and glory were his eyes.

I looked among his bright company, and saw how abounding and filled they were with eternal life. Then I found there my little queen that I thought had stood near me in the valley. Ah God, with many a sweet sound did she make merry, so white among her peers! The sight of her made me think in my ecstasy of wading the stream for my love's desire. Delight filled eye and ear, and my mortal mind dissolved in madness. When I saw my wondrous child, I yearned to be there with her, though she was withheld from me beyond the water. I thought nothing could hurt me by striking me a blow and laming me. If no one could prevent my plunging into the stream, I hoped to swim the interval in safety, though I should die for it at last.

But from that sudden purpose I was shaken, for when in my perversity, I would have started forward into the water, back was I called from my intent – it was not my Prince's will. It pleased him not that I rushed headlong over these wondrous marches in so mad a plight. Though I was rash and rude in my haste, yet quickly was I stayed therein; for, as I hurried to the brink, the start roused me suddenly from my dream.

Then I awoke in that pleasant arbor, and my head was still laid upon the very hillock where my Pearl had slipped from me into the ground. And, as I stretched myself, I became dazed with a great fear; and anon with a deep sigh I said: "Now let all things be according to the Prince's pleasure." I was ill pleased to be thrust out so suddenly from that beauteous region, with all its sights vivid and fair; a heavy longing struck me down into a swoon; and thereafter I cried out ruefully: "O Pearl of rich renown, dear to me is all that thou hast told in this true vision. If it be a right and true report that thou farest thus in a bright garland, then it is well with me also here in this dungeon of sorrow to know that thou art dwelling in the Prince's favor."

Had I always yielded to the Prince's pleasure, and yearned for no more than was given me, and kept myself in true intent as the Pearl besought me, she that is now so happy – had I been rather drawn to God's presence than forced my way – then into more of his mysteries I should have been led. But a man would always seize greater fortune than rightfully belongeth to him. Wherefore my joy was soon torn asunder, and I was cast out from that country that endureth for ever. Ah God, mad are they that strive against thee, or try to resist thy will!

To please the Prince and be at peace with him is full easy for the good Christian. I have found him, day and night, a God, a Lord, a true Friend. Such as I have now told was the fortune that befell me at this mound, bowed in grief for my Pearl; and straightway I gave her up unto God in Christ's dear blessing and mine own – he whom in the form of bread and wine the priest showeth unto us each day. And now may Christ our Prince grant that we become servants of his own household, and precious pearls to delight him ever. Amen.

THE REEVE'S TALE

from *The Canterbury Tales* by Geoffrey Chaucer
translated by John S. P. Tatlock and Percy MacKaye (1912)

When folks had laughed at this plight of Absalom and of gentle Nicholas [as told in "The Miller's Tale"], sundry folk said sundry things, but for the most part they laughed and made merry over the tale, nor saw I any man take it ill except only Oswald the Reeve. Because he was of his trade a carpenter, a little ire was yet lingering in his heart, and he began to grumble and to censure it a little.

"By my soul, I could pay 'ee back full well," quoth he, "with a tale about the hoodwinking of a bold miller, if I would speak of ribaldry. But I be old, I choose not make sport; grass-time is over, all my fodder now is hay; this white pate writes me down an old man, and my heart is as dried up as my hair, — if I be not like a medlar tree, that ever grows softer and worse till it lie rotten amongst muck or straw. We old men, I doubt, we fare even so, we cannot ripen till we be rotten. We dance ever whilst the world will pipe to us, for ever it sticks in our desire to have a hoar head and a green tail, as has a leek. Though our might be gone, ever alike our will hankers after folly, for when we cannot do it yet will we talk of it. Still is the fire there, raked over in our old ashes. We have four burning coals, — boasting, lying, anger and covetousness; these four sparks belong to age. In very deed, for all that our old limbs may be feeble, our desire fails us not. Ever I have kept my colt's-tooth, many a year as is passed since my tap of life began to run. Verily, when I was born, Death drew out the tap of life and let it run, and ever since has it so run till now the cask is well-nigh empty. The stream of life now trickles in upon the rim. The poor old tongue may well chime and ring of wretchedness long past; with old folk naught is left save dotage."

When our Host had heard this homily, he began to speak as lordly as a king. "Why all this wisdom?" he said. " Are we to talk all day of Holy Writ? Dally not with the time; the Devil made a shipman or a doctor out of a cobbler, and the Devil made a reeve to preach. Tell forth your tale. Lo Deptford, and it is half-way prime; lo Greenwich, where is many a rascal! It were fully time to begin your tale."

"Now, sirs, I pray you all not to take it ill," quoth this Oswald the Reeve, "though I answer this Miller with a gibe or flout. For it is lawful for a man to shove off force with force. This drunken Miller has told us here how a carpenter was beguiled, peradventure in mockery, because I am one. And by your leave I shall forthwith requite him, even in his own churl's language. I pray God, may his neck break! He can well see a stick in mine eye, but cannot see a beam in his own."

Here beginneth the Reeve's Tale.

At Trumpington, not far from Cambridge, there goes a brook over which stand a bridge and a mill; and this is very truth that I tell you. Long time there dwelt there a miller, as proud and gay as any peacock. He could fish and mend nets and turn cups on a lathe, pipe and wrestle well and shoot; he wore by his belt a full sharp-bladed sword, and a long cutlass, and in his pouch he carried a jolly dagger. There was no man who dared touch him for the peril! And also in his hose he carried a Sheffield knife. His skull was as bald as an ape's, round was his face and his nose a pug. He was a notable swaggerer at markets; there no person dared lay hand on him but he swore he should pay dear for it. He was a thief of corn and meal, and that a sly and unwearying, in very sooth. His name was called Bully Simkin.

He had a wife, of gentle blood; the parson of the town was her father, who gave as her dowry many a brazen pan, that Simkin might marry into his kin. She had been brought up in a nunnery; Simkin would have no wife, he affirmed, but she were well nurtured and a maiden, for the sake of his honor as a yeoman. And she was proud and pert as a magpie. A full fair sight were the two together on holy days; he would walk before her with the tail of his hood wound about his head, and she came after in a scarlet petticoat, and Simkin wore hose of the like. No one dared call her aught but "dame;" no man so bold walked by the way that once trifled or dallied with her, unless he would be slain by Simkin with cutlass or knife or dagger. For jealous folk are evermore perilous; leastways they would have their wives believe so. And likewise, because she was somewhat smirched in her name, she was as repellent as water in a ditch, and full of disdain and of insolence. She thought ladies should treat her with respect, what with her gentle kin and her elegance that she had learned in the nunnery.

They had betwixt them a daughter twenty years old, and no other children save one of six months; it lay in a cradle, and was a proper lad. This wench was stout and well grown, with broad hips and round high breast, and a pug-nose and eyes gray as glass. Right pretty was her hair, I will not deny it. Because she was comely, the parson of the town purposed to make her his heir, both of his movable property and his house, and full nice and captious he was about her marriage; his purpose was to bestow her well, into some family of exalted lineage and blood. For Holy Church's goods must be spent on the blood that is descended from Holy Church; therefore he meant to dignify his holy blood, though to do so he should devour Holy Church.

A great toll, of a surety, did this miller collect on the wheat and malt from all the land round about. And chiefest there was a great college that men call King's Hall at Cambridge, all the wheat and malt for which were ground by him. It happened on a day that the manciple of the college fell sick of some malady; men deemed that surely he could never recover. Wherefore this miller stole of the meal and corn a hundred times more than aforetime; of old he stole but courteously, but now he was an outrageous plunderer. Thereat the warden chided and made much ado but the miller recked not a straw, and blustered and said it was not so.

Now there dwelt in this Hall that I tell of two young poor clerks; bold and headstrong they were, and lusty in sport, and only for the frolic of it they begged eagerly of the warden to grant them a leave for but a little while to go to the mill and see their corn ground; and verily they would wager their heads the miller should not steal half a peck of corn from them by cunning, nor plunder from them by force. And at last the warden gave them leave. John one of them was named, and the second Alan. They were born in the same town, that was called Strother, far in the north, I cannot tell where.

This Alan, the clerk, made ready all that he must take, cast the sack of corn over a horse, and forth he went with John, and good swords and bucklers by their thighs. John knew the way, they needed no guide, and at the mill door he laid down the sack. Alan spoke first: "All hail, Simon, in faith! How fares your wife, and your fair daughter?"

"Alan, welcome, by my head!" quoth Simkin. "And John too! How now, what do you at Trumpington?"

"Simon," replied John, "by God, need has na peer. It behooves him serve himself that has na swain, as clerks say, or else he is a fool. I trust our manciple will die anon, so the jaws waggle in his head. And therefore I is come with Alan to grind our corn and carry it home. I pray you speed us hence as fast as you may."

"In faith it shall be done," quoth Simkin. "What will you do whilst it is in hand?"

"By God, I will be here right by the hopper," quoth John, "and see how that the corn gaes in. By my father's soul, I never yet saw how that the hopper wags till and fra."

"And will you swa? " answered Alan. "Then by my pate I will be beneath, and see how that the meal falls down into the trough; that shall be my disport. In faith, John, I must be of your class, I is as ill a miller as you."

This miller smiled at their simplicity. "All this is but done for a fetch," he thought; "they deem no man can beguile them. But I vow by my trade, for all the craft in their philosophy, I shall blear their eyes yet. The more cunning wiles they put on, the more I will take when I steal. I shall yet give them bran in the place of flour.

"The greatest clerks be not the wisest men,"

as the mare once said to the wolf. I care not a bean for their art!"

Out at the door he privily went when he saw his time. He looked up and down till he found the clerks' horse where he stood tied under an arbor behind the mill;

and went softly to the horse and soon stripped off the bridle. And when the horse was loose, forth he started with a "Wehee!" through thick and thin toward the fen, where wild mares were running.

This miller went back; not a word he said, but did his business and chaffed with the clerks till their corn was ground all fair and well. And when the meal was sacked and fastened, this John went out and found his horse gone, and began to cry, "Help! Alackaday, our horse is lost! Alan, for God's sake, man, step on your feet, come out at once! Alas, our warden has lost his palfrey!"

This Alan forgot all his thrifty mood; clean out of his mind went meal and corn and all, and he began to cry, "What! whilk way is he gane?"

The goodwife came leaping in with a run. "Alas!" she said, "your horse is going to the fen with wild mares, as fast as he can gallop. Bad luck on his hand that bound him so ill, and should have knit the rein better."

"Alas!" quoth John. "By the rood, Alan, lay down your sword, and I will mind alswa. I is full nimble, God knows, as a deer. By God! he shall not escape us baith. Why had you not pit the nag in the barn? Ill luck to thee, Alan, thou is a fool."

These poor clerks ran full hard toward the fen, both Alan and John. And when the miller saw they were off, he took half a bushel of their flour, and bade his wife go and knead it in a loaf. "I believe the clerks were afeared what I might do. Yet can a miller," he said, "trim a clerk's beard for all his art; now let them go where they will. Lo where they go! By my pate, they get him not so lightly. Yea, let the children play!"

These poor clerks ran up and down, with "Whoa, whoa! Gee! Stop, stop! Ha! Look out behind! Gae whistle you whilst I head him off here!" But in brief, till it was dark night, with all their power they could not catch their nag, he ran alway so fast, till at length they caught him in a ditch.

Wet and weary, like a beast in the rain, came poor John and Alan with him. "Alack the day I was born!" quoth John. "Now we are brought till mockery and derision. Our corn is stolen; men will call us fools, baith the warden and all our friends, and chiefest the miller. Alack the day!" Thus John lamented as he walked along the road toward the mill, leading Bayard by the bridle. He found the miller sitting by the fire, for it was night. They could go no further then, but besought him for the love of God to give them lodging and entertainment, for their pence.

"If there be any," the miller replied, "such as it is, you shall have your part in it. My house is strait; but you have studied book-learning, you know how to make twenty foot of space a mile broad by arguments. Let see now if this house may suffice, or make it bigger by talking, as you clerks do."

"Now, Simon," said John, "thou is ever merry, by Saint Cuthbert, and that was fairly answered. I have heard say a man shall take ane of the twa, such-like as he finds or such-like as he brings. But specially I pray thee, dear host, get us some meat and drink and make us some cheer, and we will pay faithfully and fully. Men lure no hawks with empty hand; lo here our silver all ready to spend!"

This miller dispatched his daughter into town for ale and bread, and roasted a goose for them, and secured their horse so that it should go astray no more. He made them a bed in his own chamber, fairly adorned with sheets and blankets, only eight foot or ten from his own bed. His daughter had a bed to herself right in the same chamber and full near; it could be no other way, and reason why, because there was no more room in the place. They supped and talked and disported them, and drank ever deeper of the strong ale, and about midnight went to rest.

Well had this miller varnished his head with the beer, and had drunk himself all pale when he went to bed. He hiccoughed and spoke through his nose as if he had a rheum or a hoarseness. To bed went his wife also, as light and frisky as any jay, so well had she wet her jolly whistle. The cradle was put at her bed's foot, that she might rock it and nurse the child. And when all that was in the crock had been drunk, soon the daughter went to bed; and to bed went Alan and John. None of them took aught else, they needed no opiate! Verily, so had the miller bibbed his ale that he snorted in his sleep as a horse. His wife bore him the bass, a full strong one; men might have heard their snoring two furlongs away. The wench snored also, *par compagnie.*

Alan the clerk, hearing all this tunefulness, poked John and said, "Sleeps thou? Heard thou ever such a sang ere this? Lo, whilk a compline they are singing amongst them, Saint Antony's fire fall on their bodies! Wha hearkened ever to such a marvelous thing? Yea, may they come to the worst of bad ends! This lang night I shall get na sleep; yet na matter, all shall be for the best. For, John, swa may I ever thrive, some easement the law allows us. For, John, there is a law says that gif a man be harmed in ane point, he shall be relieved in another. Our corn is stolen, without a doubt, and all day we have had an ill fit; and since all that cannot be remedied, I shall have some easement to countervail my loss. By my sawl, it shall be nane otherwise!"

"Have a care, Alan," John answered. "The miller is a perilous man, and gif he started out of his sleep he might do us baith a shrewd turn."

"I count him not a fly," Alan replied, and up he rose, and to the girl's bed he crept. This wench lay on her back, and soundly slept, until he was so near, ere she might spy him, that was too late to struggle or cry; and to be brief, these two were soon at one. Now play, Alan! For I will speak of John.

This John lay still a brief time, and to himself lamented and wept for all his woe. "Alas," said he, "this is a wicked jest! Now I see that I am but an ape. Yet has my fellow there something for his troubles. He has the miller's daughter in his arms. He risked it, and his needs are now fulfilled, while I lie like a sack of chaff in bed. And when this joke is told, another day, I shall be held a fool! I will arise and chance it, by my faith! 'Unhardy is unhappy,' as men say."

And up he rose, and softly then he went to find the cradle, and bore it over to the foot of his own bed.

Soon after this the wife stopped snoring and woke. She rose and went outside to piss, and on returning missed the cradle. She groped round, here and there, but found nothing. "Alas!" thought she, "I had almost misgone. I nearly found myself in the clerk's bed. Eh, *ben'cite*, that were wrong!" And on she went until she found the cradle. And groping a bit farther with her hand, she found the bed, and thought of nought because the cradle by it stood. And she knew not where she was, for it was dark; but fair and well she crept in by the clerk, and lay right still, and would have gone to sleep. But presently this John the clerk did leap up, and over on this good wife did he lie. No such merry time had she known in years. He pricked her hard and deep, as if he were mad. And so a jolly life had these two clerks, till the third cock began to sing.

Alan grew weary in the gray dawning, for he had toiled all the long night; and said: "Farewell, now, sweet ane! The day is come, I may na longer bide; but evermore, whether I walk or ride I am your own clerk, so have I bliss."

"Now, sweetheart," said she, "god save and keep thee! But ere you go, there's one thing I must tell you. When you pass the mill going homeward, even at the entrance behind the door you will find a loaf that was made of half a bushel of your own meal, which I helped my father to steal. And now, good friend, God save and keep you!" And with that word she well nigh wept.

Alan rose up and thought, "Ere it be day I will go creep in by my fellow;" and soon his hand touched the cradle. "By God," he thought, "I have misgone all wrangly; my head is all giddy to-night, and therefore I walk not straight. I know well by the cradle, here lie the miller and his wife, and I have misgone."

And with the Devil's own luck, forth he went to the bed where the miller lay. He thought to have crept in by his fellow John, and he crept in by the miller and caught him by the neck, and said softly, "Thou John, thou swine's-head, awake, for Christ's soul, and hear a noble sport! For by the lord that is called Saint James, I have three times this night swived the miller's daughter on her back, while thou like a coward were aghast."

"Ye, false knave!" quoth the miller. "Ah, false traitor, false clerk! You shall die, by God's dignity! Who dares be so bold to disparage my daughter, that is come of such lineage?" And he caught Alan by the throat. Alan caught him in turn furiously, and smote him on the nose with his fist. Down ran the bloody stream on the miller's breast, and on the floor they wallowed like two pigs in a poke, with nose and mouth crushed and bleeding. Up they got, and down again, till the miller stumbled against a stone and fell down backward upon his wife, who knew naught of this ridiculous fight. With the shock she started up, and cried, "Help, holy cross of Bromholm! Lord, I call to thee! *In manus tuas*! Awake, Simon, the fiend has dropped on us. My heart is crushed; help, I am but dead! Some one lies on my head and body; help, Simon! The false clerks fight!"

John started up as fast as ever he could, and groped to and fro by the wall to find a staff. She started up also, and knew the room better than did John, and soon found a staff by the wall. She saw a little shimmer of light where the moon shone in by a hole, and by it she saw the two on the floor, but in truth knew not which was which. When she caught a sight of a white thing, she thought one of the clerks had worn a night-cap, and drew nearer with the staff and thought to smite this Alan a shrewd rap, but smote the miller on the bald pate. Down he went, crying, "Help, I die!" These clerks beat him well, and let him lie, and they clothed themselves, and soon

132

took their horse and also their meal and went their way. And at the mill they took their loaf also, full well baked, of half a bushel of flour.

Thus is the proud miller well beaten, and has lost his toll for grinding their corn, and paid every penny for the supper of Alan and John who beat him. His wife is swived, and his daughter also. Lo, such a thing it is for a miller to be false! And therefore this proverb is full sooth,

"Look not for good and do iniquity,
The guileful shall himself beguiled be."

And God That sits on high in glory save all this company, high and low. Thus have I requited the Miller in my tale.

Here is ended the Reeve's Tale.

THE NUN'S PRIEST'S TALE

from *The Canterbury Tales* by Geoffrey Chaucer
translated by John S. P. Tatlock and Percy MacKaye (1912)

Then our Host, with rude and bold speech, said forthwith to the Nun's Priest, "Come nearer, thou priest, thou Sir John, come hither and tell of somewhat to gladden our hearts. Be blithe, though you ride upon a nag. What though your horse be foul and lean! If he serve you, reck not a bean. Look that your heart be evermore merry."

"Yea, sir," quoth he, "yea, Host, in faith if I be not merry, you may chide me well." And forthwith he broached his tale and spoke thus to us all, this goodly man, this sweet priest, Sir John.

Explicit.

Here beginneth the Nun's Priest's Tale of the Cock and the Hen, Chanticleer and Partlet.

A widow, poor and somewhat on in years, dwelt whilom in a little cottage that stood in a dale beside a grove. Since the day she was last a wife, this widow of whom I tell this tale had lived full patiently and simply; for her goods and earnings were but small. By husbanding what God sent, she kept herself and her two daughters; she had three large sows and no more, three cows and a sheep named Molly. Her bower and hall were full sooty, where she ate many a slender meal; she needed never a bit of pungent sauce, nor did dainty morsel ever pass her throat; her diet matched her gown. Surfeiting never made her sick, her only physic was a temperate diet, with exercise and heart's content. It was not the gout kept her from dancing, nor did the apoplexy molest her head. Neither red wine nor white drank she; her board was served for the most with white and black, of which she found no want, milk and brown bread, with broiled bacon and at times an egg or two, for she was a kind of dairy-woman.

She had a yard enclosed all about with sticks and a dry ditch, and herein she had a cock, Chanticleer. In all the land was not his match for crowing; his voice was merrier than the merry organ, that goes in church on mass-days. More trusty was his, crowing in his yard than a clock or an abbey horologe; he knew by nature each revolution of the equinoctial in that longitude, for when each fifteen degrees were ascended, then he crew, that it could not be bettered. His comb was redder than fine coral, and indented like a castle-wall. His black bill shone like jet; like azure were his legs and toes, his nails whiter than the lily-flower, and his hue like burnished gold. This noble cock had in his governance seven hens, to do all his pleasure, his sisters and paramours, and wondrous like him in looks; of which the fairest hued on her throat was named fair Demoiselle Partlet. She was courteous, discreet, debonair and companionable, and bore herself so fairly since she was seven nights old that truly she held the heart of Chanticleer all locked, and herself bore the key; he loved her so that well was him. But such a joy as it was to hear them sing in sweet accord when the bright sun began to rise,

"My love is far from land!"

For at that time, as I have made out, beasts and birds could sing and speak.

Now it so befell, one dawning, as Chanticleer sat on his perch amongst his wives in the hall, and next him this fair Partlet, that he began to groan in his throat as a man grievously troubled in his dream. When Partlet heard him thus roar, she was aghast, and said: "Oh dear heart, what ails you to groan thus? A fine sleeper you are; fie, for shame!"

And he answered, "Madame, take it not amiss, I pray you; 'tis God's truth, I dreamed right now that I was in such mishap that my heart is yet sore affrighted. Now God bring my dream to good, and keep my body from foul prison! I dreamed how I roamed up and down within our yard, and saw there a beast like a hound, who would have made arrest upon my body and killed me. He was betwixt yellow and red in color, his tail and ears tipped with black, unlike the rest of his coat; his snout was slender and his two eyes glowing. For fear of his looks I almost die even now. This caused my groaning, doubtless."

"Avaunt!" quoth she; "fie upon you, faint heart! Alas! for by that God in heaven you have now lost my heart and love. In faith, certainly, I cannot love a coward. Whatsoever any woman will say, all of us desire to have husbands bold, wise, and liberal, trusty with secrets, not a niggard nor a fool, nor aghast at every weapon, nor yet a boaster, by the heaven above us! How durst you, for shame, say to your dear that aught could make you afraid? Have you not a man's heart, yet have a beard! Alas, can you be aghast at dreams? There is naught in dreams but vanity, God knows. Dreams are engendered of surfeit and often of fumes and of folks' temperaments, when his humors are too abundant in a person. Truly this dream which you have dreamed comes from a superfluity of your red choler. This causes folk in their dreams to have dread of arrows and of fire with red blazes, of huge beasts, that they will bite them, of fighting, and great and small whelps; even as the melancholy humor causes full many a man to cry out in sleep for fear of black bears or black bull, or likewise black devils will catch him. I could tell also of other humors that work woe to many a man in sleep. But I will pass on as lightly as I may. Lo Cato, who was so wise! said he not thus, 'Take no heed of dreams'? Now sir," quoth she, "for the love of heaven, when we fly down from these rafters, do take some laxative. On peril of my life and soul, I lie not and counsel you for the best, that you purge you both of choler and of melancholy; and, that you delay not, though there be no apothecary in this town, I will myself direct you to herbs that shall be for your health and weal; and I shall find the herbs in our yard which have the natural property to purge you beneath and also above. Forget not this, for God's sake! You are full bilious of temperament. Beware lest the sun as he climbs up find you replete with hot humors. And if he do, I dare lay a groat that you will have a tertian fever, or an ague that may be the death of you. For a day or two, you shall have a light diet of worms ere you take your laxatives, — your spurge-laurel, centaury, and fumitory or else hellebore, that grows there, your caper-spurge or buck-thorn berries, or herb-ivy growing in our yard, and pleasant to take. Peck them right up growing and eat them in. By your father's soul, husband, be merry and dread no dreams. I can say naught else."

"Gramercy for your lore, madame! But nevertheless," quoth he, "as to Sir Cato, who has such a name for wisdom, though he bade fear no dreams, by God, men may read in old books of many a man of more authority than ever Cato had, who says all the reverse of his opinion, and has well found by experience that dreams are significant as well of joy as of tribulations that folk endure in this present life. There needs no argument for this; very experience shows it.

"It is told by one of the greatest authors that men read that once two companions went in full pious mood an a pilgrimage, and it so happed they came into a town so full of people and so scant of lodgings that they found not so much as one cottage where they could both be lodged. Wherefore they needs must part company far that night, and each went to his quarters as chance assigned them. One was lodged in a stall far off in a yard, with plow-oxen; the other was well enough housed, as was his chance or his fortune, that governs all of us. It so befell that long ere dawn this man dreamed, as he lay in his bed, that his friend began to call upon him, saying, "Alas! for I shall be murdered in an ox's stall this night. Now help me, brother dear, ere I die; come to me in all haste." This man started out of his sleep for fear, but when he had waked he turned over and took no heed of this, thinking his dream but vanity. Thus he dreamed twice in his sleep. And at the third time his fellow seemed to come to him and say, "I am now slain. Behold my wounds, deep, wide and bloody. Arise early in the morn, and at the west gate of the town thou shalt see a dung-cart in which my body is privily hid; stay that cart boldly. In sooth, my gold caused my murder." And he told him every point, how he was slain, with a pale pitiful face. And trust well, his fellow found the dream full true, for on the morrow, at earliest day, he betook him to his fellow's lodging, and when he reached the ox-stall, he began to shout after him. The inn-keeper answered forthwith, "Sir, your fellow is gone. At daybreak he left the town." This man began to fall into suspicion, remembering his dream, and forth he went without tarrying to the west gate of the town, and found a dung-cart, ready to dung a field, and in such shape as you have heard the dead man say. And with a bold heart he began to call far vengeance and justice upon this felony. "My fellow is murdered this very night and lies gaping in this cart on his back. I cry out upon the magistrates who should rule and keep the city. Help! alas! here my fellow lies slain!" Why more of this tale? The people rushed out, cast the dung-cart over, and in the middle of the dung they found the dead man, all freshly murdered. O blessed God, faithful and just! Lo, how Thou ever revealest murder! Murder will out, that we see daily. Murder is so horrible and abominable to the God of justice and reason that He will not suffer it be covered up. Though it lie hid for years, murder will out, this is my conclusion. And right anon the magistrates seized the carter and tortured him so sore, and also the inn-keeper, on the rack, that they soon acknowledged their wickedness and were hanged by the neck-bone.

"By this may men see that dreams are to be feared. And verily I read in the same book in the very next chapter following (I lie not, as I hope to be saved), of two men that for a certain cause would have passed over the sea into a distant land, if the wind had not been adverse, and made them to tarry in a city standing pleasantly on a haven-side. But on a day, at evening, the wind changed and blew even as they would. Merry and glad they went to rest, and planned to sail early. But a great marvel befell one man as he lay asleep, who dreamed toward day a wondrous dream. He thought a man stood beside his bed and bade him tarry; "if thou go tomorrow, thou shalt be drowned; my tale is done." He woke and told his fellow his dream, and prayed him to give up his journey. His fellow, who lay by his bed's side, began to laugh and sore mocked him." No dream can so affright my heart that I will stay my business; I set not a straw by thy dreamings, for dreams are but vanity and humbug. Men are ever dreaming of owls or apes and likewise of many a bewildering thing; they dream of things that never were nor shall be. But since I see that you intend to tarry here and thus of your free will lose your chance by sloth, God knows it grieves me, but have good-day." Thus he took his leave and departed. But ere he had voyaged over half his course, I know not why, nor what mischance ailed it, but by some mishap the ship's bottom was rent, and ship and man went down in sight of other ships hard by, that had sailed at the same time. Therefore, fair Partlet so dear, you may learn by such old ensamples that no man should reck too lightly of dreams, for I tell you that without doubt many a dream is to be dreaded full sore.

"Lo, I read in the life of St. Kenelm, the son of Kenulph, the noble king of Mercia, how he dreamed a dream; on a day a little before he was murdered, he saw his murder in a vision. His nurse expounded all his dream and bade him beware of treason; but he was no more than seven years old, and paid little heed to any dream, so holy he was of spirit. By heaven, I would give my shirt that you had read his legend as I have! I tell you truly, Dame Partlet, that Macrobius, who wrote the vision of the noble Scipio in Africa, affirms dreams to be forewarnings of things that men see afterward.

"Furthermore, I pray you look well in the Old Testament and see if Daniel held dreams to be a vanity. Read of Joseph also, and there you will find whether dreams be sometimes (I say not always), warnings of future things. Look at the king of Egypt, Sir Pharaoh, and at his baker and his butler, whether they felt no virtue in dreams! Whoso will turn to the chronicles of sundry realms may read many a wondrous thing about them. Lo Croesus, once king of Lydia! Dreamed he not that he sat upon a tree, which signified that he should be hanged? Lo Andromache, Hector's wife! She dreamed the very night before that the life of Hector should be lost if he went that day to battle; she warned him, but it availed not, for he went none the less to fight, and anon was slain by Achilles. But that tale would be all too long to tell, and I must not tarry, for it is high day. In short, I conclude that I shall have adversity after this vision; and I say, moreover, I set no store by laxatives. They are poison, I know it well; I defy them, I like them not a bit.

"Now let us speak of mirth, and stint all this. In one thing, Madame Partlet, as I hope for joy, God has greatly blessed me; for when I see how scarlet-red you are about your eyes, and the beauty of your face, all my fear dies away. For as true as the Gospel, *Mulier est hominis confusio*," madame, the meaning of this Latin is that woman is man's whole bliss and joy! For when I feel your soft side at night, though I cannot draw closer, because our perch is so narrow, alas!, I am so full of joy and comfort that I defy all dreams and visions."

And with that, down he flew from the rafter, and with him all his hens, for it was day. He began to call them all with a *chuck*, for he had found a grain of corn lying in the yard. He was royal, he was afraid no longer; twenty times ere prime he clasped Partlet; he looked as it were a grim lion, and roamed up and down on his toes, he deigned not to set his foot to ground. He chucked when he came upon a grain of corn, and his wives ran to him. Thus royal, like a prince in his hall, I will leave this Chanticleer in his feeding-ground, and afterward I will say what befell him.

The month in which the world was made, March, when God first created man, was complete, and there had passed two and thirty days more. It befell that Chanticleer in all his glory, with his seven wives walking beside him, cast his eyes to the bright sun, which had sped through one-and-twenty degrees and somewhat more in the sign of Taurus; and by nature and not education he knew that it was prime, and he crew with joyous voice. "The sun," he said, "is climbed up the heavens one-and-forty degrees and more. Madame Partlet, my world's bliss, hearken to the happy birds how they sing, and see the fresh flowers springing up; mine heart is full of comfort and revelry." But suddenly a sorrowful case befell. For the latter end of joy is ever woe, God knows; joy of this world is soon gone, and an orator that could indite fairly might safely put it in a chronicle for a profound truth. Now let every wise man hearken; this story is every bit as true, I dare be bound, as the book of Lancelot of the Lake, which women hold in great reverence. Now will I return to my text.

A coal-fox, sly and unrighteous, who had dwelt three years in the grove, by decree of almighty Providence burst through the hedges that same night into the yard whither stately Chanticleer was wont to repair with his wives, and there lay quietly in a bed of herbs till it was past eleven of the clock, awaiting his time to fall upon Chanticleer, as all these homicides are fain to do that lie in wait to murder men. False murderer, lurking in thy lair! Thou new Iscariot, new Ganelon, false dissimulator, even as the Greekish Sinon that brought Troy utterly to woe! Accursed be that morn, O Chanticleer, on which thou flewest from thy rafter into the yard! Well thou was warned by thy dreams that this day was perilous to thee. But what God foresees must needs come to pass, according to certain clerks; as witness any perfect clerk that there is great altercation in the schools and great disputing about this matter, and ever has been amongst an hundred thousand men. But I cannot sift it to the chaff, as can the holy doctor Augustine or Boethius or Bishop Bradwardine; whether God's glorious foreknowing compels me of necessity to do a thing, (by necessity I mean absolute necessity), or else whether I am granted free choice to do or not that same thing, though God foreknew it long before; or whether His knowing constrains not at all except by a conditional necessity. With such matters I will not have to do. My tale is all of a cock, as you may hear, who took his wife's counsel (out upon it!) to walk in the yard that morning, after he had dreamed his dream of which I told you. Women's counsels are oft baneful. Woman's counsel brought us first to woe and made Adam depart from Paradise where he was at ease and fun merry. But because I know not whom I might vex if I should upbraid women's counsel, let us pass it over, for I said it but in sport. Read what authors, who treat of such matters, say of women. These be the cock's words and not mine; I cannot imagine harm of any woman.

Fairly lay Partlet in the sunshine with all her sisters by, to bathe her merrily in the sand, and the gallant Chanticleer sang merrier than the mermaid in the sea; for Physiologus in truth says that they sing merrily and well. And it so befell, as he cast his eye upon a butterfly amongst the herbs, that he was ware of this fox who lay hidden. He had no mind then to crow, but cried anon, "cok cok!" and started up like a man affrighted in his heart. For by instinct a beast is fain to flee from his natural enemy if he see it, though he had never cast eye upon it before.

This Chanticleer, when he first espied him, would have fled, but that the fox straightway spoke, "Alas, gentle sir, where will you go? Are you afeard of me, your own friend? Now certainly I were worse than a fiend if I desired harm or indignity to you. I am not come to spy upon your privacy, but in truth, only to hearken how you sing. For truly you have as merry a voice as any angel in heaven, and more feeling in music than Boethius had, or any singer. My lord your father (God rest his soul!), and your mother too, of her courtesy, have been in my house, to my great content; and you, sir, I would fain please, verily. And speaking of singing, I must say, — may I be struck blind if I ever heard man, save you, sing as did your father in the morning. In truth, all that he sung was from the heart. And to make his voice the stronger he took such pains that he must needs shut both his eyes, so loud he cried, standing on

139

tip-toe withal and stretching forth his long, slender neck. And also he was of such discretion that there was no man in any land who could pass him in song or wisdom. I have indeed read in the life of Burnel the Ass, amongst the verses, about a cock, who, because a priest's son, when he was young and foolish, gave him a rap on his leg, in after years made him to lose his benefice. But certainly there is no comparison betwixt his wisdom and subtlety and discretion and your father's. Now sing, sir, for sweet charity's sake. Let see, can you imitate your father?"

This Chanticleer began to flap his wings; he could not espy the cozenage, so ravished he was by the flattery. Alas! ye lords, many a false flatterer and parasite is in your courts, who please you more, in faith, than he who says you sooth. Read of flattery in *Ecclesiasticus*, and beware their treachery.

This Chanticleer stood high on his toes, stretching his neck and shutting his eyes, and began to crow loudly for the nonce. Up started Sir Russel the fox forthwith, seized Chanticleer by the throat and bore him on his back away toward the wood, for as yet no man gave chase.

O destiny that mayst not be eluded! Alas that Chanticleer flew down from the rafters and that his wife recked not of dreams! And all this mischance fell on a Friday! O Venus, goddess of pleasance, why wouldst suffer Chanticleer to die upon thy day, who was thy servant and did all within his might in thy service, more for delight than to multiply the world? O Geoffrey de Vinsauf, dear sovereign master, that when thy noble king Richard was slain by shot, didst mourn his death so sore, why have I not now thy learning and thy pen to chide the Friday as thou didst! (For truly it was on a Friday he was slain.) Then I would show you how I could mourn Chanticleer's dread and torment. Not when Ilium was won and Pyrrhus had seized King Priam by the beard and slain him with his naked sword, as *Aeneid* says, was ever such cry and lamentation made by ladies as by the hens in the yard, when they saw this sight of Chanticleer. Above all Dame Partlet shrieked louder than Hasdrubal's wife when her husband perished and the

Romans had burned Carthage; who was so full of torment and frenzy that she leapt into the fire and burned herself with a steadfast heart. O woeful hens, even so ye cried as the senators' wives when Nero burned the city of Rome and their husbands all perished, slain guiltless by this Nero.

But now I return to my tale once more. This poor widow and her two daughters heard these hens cry and lament, and started out at the door forthwith and saw the fox make toward the wood, bearing the cock away on his back. "Out! alas! help!" they cried. "Ho! ho! the fox!" and after him they ran, and many another persons with cudgels. Ran Colle, our dog, and Garland and Talbot, and Malkin with her distaff in hand; ran cow and calf and the very hogs, so afeared they were for the barking of the hounds and the shouting of the men and women. They ran till they thought their hearts would burst, they yelled like fiends in hell, the ducks quacked as if they were being slaughtered, the geese in fear flew over the tree-tops, a swarm of bees came out of the hive; so hideous was the noise, ah *benedicite!*, certainly Jack Straw and his rabble never made shouts half so shrill when they were slaughtering a Fleming, as

140

were made this day after the fox. They brought horns of brass, of wood, of horn and bone, and blew and bellowed in them, and so shrieked and whooped withal till it seemed as if the heavens would drop. Now, good men, I pray you all hearken.

Lo, how Fortune suddenly overturns the hope and arrogance of her foe! This cock, lying upon the fox's back, in all his fright spoke to the fox and said, "Sir, if I were as you, so may God help me, I should say,— 'Turn back, all ye proud churls! A very pestilence fall on you! Now that I am come to this wood's edge, the cock shall abide here, in spite of your teeth. I will eat him, in faith, and that at once.'"

"In faith, it shall be done," answered the fox. And as he spoke that word, nimbly the cock broke away from his mouth and flew high upon a tree. And when the fox saw him gone, "Alas! Chanticleer!" quoth he; "alas! I have done you wrong to affright you, when I seized and brought you out of the yard. But, sir, I had no ill intent; come down and I shall make you see it. I shall say the sooth to you, so may God help me!"

"Nay then," quoth the cock, "I curse both of us, and first I curse myself, both blood and flesh, if you beguile me more than once. No more shall your flattery make me sing and shut my two eyes. For he who willfully shuts his eyes when he should see, God let him never thrive!"

"Nay," quoth the fox, "but God give him evil fortune who is so indiscreet as to prate when be should hold his peace!"

Lo, such a thing it is to be negligent and heedless and trust upon flattery! But you who hold this tale foolishness, of naught but a fox and a cock and a hen, take the moral, good sirs. For St. Paul says that all that is written is written for our doctrine, in sooth. Take the fruit and leave the chaff. And now may the good God, if His will be so, as says my lord archbishop, make us all good Christians and bring us to His heavenly bliss.—Amen.

Here is ended the Nun's Priest's Tale.

"Sir Nun's Priest," said our Host, "blessings on your breech for this merry tale of Chanticleer! By my troth, if you were a secular man, a right hearty fellow you would be with dames. See what brawn and what a neck this gentle priest has, and what a chest! He looks with his eyes like a sparrow-hawk. He needs not dye his color with brasil nor Portugal-red. Now may fair befall you for your tale, sir!"

And after that, with a merry look, he said to another as you shall hear.

THE FRANKLIN'S TALE

from *The Canterbury Tales* by Geoffrey Chaucer
translated by John S. P. Tatlock and Percy MacKaye (1912)

Here follow the Words of the Franklin to the Squire, and the Words of the Host to the Franklin.

"In faith, Squire, you have quit yourself well, and like a gentleman. I praise your wit highly, considering your youth," said the Franklin. "I commend you, sir, so feelingly you speak! To my mind there is none in this company shall be your peer in eloquence if you live. God give you good fortune, and send you continuance in virtue, for I have great delight in your speaking. I have a son, and by Saint Trinity I had rather he were a man of such discretion as you, than have twenty pounds' worth of land, though it were fallen to me even now. Fie on possessions unless withal a man's self be worth somewhat! I have chidden my son, and yet shall chide him, because he will not incline to virtue; but his wont is to play at dice and to spend and to lose all that he has. And he had rather talk with a page than commune with any person of gentle birth where he might properly learn gentle manners."

"A straw for your gentle manners! What, Franklin!" quoth our Host; "well you know, verily, that each of you must tell at least a tale or two, or break his word."

"That I well know, sir," quoth the Franklin. "I pray you hold me not in scorn though I speak a word or two to this man."

"Tell on your tale, without more words."

"Gladly, sir Host," quoth he. "I will obey your will. Now hearken to what I tell you. I will not oppose your wish in any way, so far as my wits shall suffice. I pray God my tale may please you; then I shall well know that it is good enough."

The Prologue of the Franklin's Tale.

"These old gentle Britons in their time made lays about divers happenings, rhymed in, their early British tongue; which lays they sang to their instruments of music, or else read them, for their pleasure. And one of them I have in mind, which I will relate with good will as best I can. But, sirs, I am a rude man, and at the beginning I pray you to hold me excused for my homely speech. In sooth, I learned never rhetoric; a thing that I speak must be plain and bare. I slept never on the mount of Parnassus, nor learned Marcus Tullius Cicero. Colors of speech I know none, of a surety; only such colors as grow in the mead, or else such as men dye or paint. Colors of rhetoric be too curious for me, my spirit has no feeling in such matters. But if you list you shall hear my tale."

Here beginneth the Franklin's Tale.

In Armorica, which is called Brittany, there was a knight who loved and served a lady in the best manner he could. And he wrought many a labor, many a great emprise, ere he gained her. For she was one of the fairest women under the sun, and also come of so high kindred that this knight scarce durst for fear tell her his woe and his pain and distress. But at last she took such pity upon his pains; because of his worthiness and chiefest for his humble attentiveness, that privily she agreed to take him for husband and lord, in such lordship as men have over their wives. And that they might live in the more blessedness, he swore to her as a knight, of his own free will, that never at any time in all his life should he take upon him any sovereignty against her will, nor show jealousy toward her, but obey her and follow her will in all things, as any lover shall do toward his lady; save only the name of sovereignty, — that he would have for the honor of his station.

She thanked him, and said with full great humility, "Sir, since of your noble mind you offer me so free a rein, God forbid that of my guilt there were ever war or contention betwixt us two. Sir, I will be your true humble wife till my heart break; take here my pledge."

Thus they were both in quiet and peace. For one thing, sirs. I dare safely say, — friends must comply with one another, if they would hold company long. Love will not be constrained by mastership; when mastery comes, forthwith the god of love beats his wings, and farewell, he is gone! Love is as free as any spirit. Women by their nature desire liberty, and not to be under constraint as a thrall; and so do men, if I shall say sooth. Look who is most patient in love, he has the advantage over all. Patience is a high virtue, of a certainty; for, as these clerks say, it conquers things that rigor could never attain to. Men should not chide or complain at every word. Learn to endure, or else, on my life, ye shall learn it, whether ye will or no. For certainly there is none in this world but sometimes he does or speaks amiss. Wrath, sickness, the stars, wine, woe, changing humors, full often cause a man to act or speak amiss. A man may not be avenged of every wrong; according to the occasion, in every person who knows how to rule his life, there must be moderation. And therefore, that he might live at ease, this wise worthy knight promised forbearance toward her, and she full seriously swore to him that there never should be lack in her. Here men may see a humble and wise agreement; thus she took her servant and her lord, — servant in love, and lord in marriage. Then he was in both lordship and bondage. Bondage? — nay, but on high in lordship, since he has both his lady and love; certainly, his lady, and also his wife, who accepted that law of love. And in this happy state he went home with his wife to his country, not far from Penmark, where was his dwelling, and where he lived in happiness and comfort. Who, unless he had been wedded, could tell the joy, the comfort, and well-being betwixt husband and wife?

This blessed condition lasted a year and more, till the knight of whom I speak, who was called Arveragus of Caer-rhud, laid his plans to go and dwell a year or two in England, which also was called Britain, to seek worship and honor in arms. For he set all his pleasure on such toils. And he dwelt there two years; the book says thus.

Now I will leave Arveragus, and will speak of Dorigen his wife, who loved her husband as her heart's blood. For in his absence she wept and sighed, as these noble wives do (when they will). She mourned, watched, wailed, fasted, lamented; desire for his presence so distracted her that she cared nothing for all this wide world. Her friends, who knew her heavy thoughts, comforted her in all they could. They preached to her; day and night they told her that she was slaying herself without cause, alas! And with all diligence they comforted her all they could, to make her leave her heaviness.

By process of time, ye all know, men may grave in a stone so long that some figure will be imprinted on it. So long they comforted her, that with the aid of hope and reason she received the imprint of their consolation. Wherefore her great sorrow began to assuage; she could not abide ever in such frenzy. And also whilst she was in all this sorrow, Arveragus had sent home to her letters of his welfare, and that he would soon return; else this sorrow had slain her heart. Her friends saw her sorrow began to slacken, and on their knees prayed her for God's love to come and roam about with them, to drive away her dark fantasies. And finally she agreed, for well she saw that it was best.

Now her castle stood hard by the sea, and for diversion she often walked with her friends high upon the shore, whence she saw many a ship and barge sailing upon their course, wherever they would go. But then became that a part of her grief. For full often she said to herself, "Alas! Is there no ship of so many that I see, will bring home my lord? Then were my heart all cured of its bitter, bitter pains."

Another time she would sit there and ponder, and from the shore cast her eyes down. But when she saw the grisly black rocks, her heart would so quake for very fear that she could not hold herself on her feet. Then she would sit down on the green and piteously look into the sea, and with sorrowful, cold sighs say right thus: "Eternal God, who through Thy providence guidest the world by sure government, Thou makest nothing in vain, men say. But, Lord, these grisly, fiendly, black rocks, which seem rather a foul disorder of work than any fair creation by such a perfect, wise, and unchanging God, — why hast Thou wrought this irrational work? For by this work is fostered neither man nor bird nor brute, south or north, east or west. It does no good, to my seeming, but harm. Seest Thou not, Lord, how it destroys mankind? Rocks have slain an hundred thousand bodies of men, although they be not in my memory; which mankind is so fair a part of Thy work that Thou madest it like to Thine own image. Then it should seem Thou hadst a great fondness toward men; but how then may it be that Thou createst to destroy them such means which do no good, but ever harm? I know well that clerks will say as they please by arguments that all is for the best, though I cannot understand the manner. But may that God that made the wind blow guard my lord! This is my conclusion; I leave all disputation to clerks. But would to God that all these black rocks were sunk into hell, for his sake! These rocks slay mine heart for fear."

Thus she would speak to herself, with many a piteous tear. Her friends saw that it was no diversion for her, but only a disquiet, to walk by the sea, and devised for her sports in other places. They led her by rivers and springs and likewise in other delectable places; they danced and they played at chess and backgammon. So on a day in the morning-time, they went to divert them all the long day in a garden hard by, in which they had made their provision of food and other things. And this was on the sixth morning of May, and May with his soft rains had painted this garden full of leaves and flowers. And truly the craft of man's hand had so curiously arrayed this garden that never was a garden of such beauty, unless it were paradise itself. The odor of flowers and the fresh sight would have gladdened any heart that ever was born, unless too great sickness or too great sorrow distressed it; so full was it of delight and beauty. After dinner they began to dance and sing, save only Dorigen, who ever made complaint and moan, because she saw not him go on the dance who was her husband and also her love. But nevertheless she must abide for a time and with good hope let her sorrow pass.

Upon this dance, amongst other men, there danced before Dorigen a squire who was fresher and gayer of apparel than is the month of May, I trust. He sang and danced to surpass any man who is or was since the world was made. He was, to boot, if a man should describe him, one of the best endowed men alive; young, strong, rich, prudent, full of high qualities, well beloved and holden in great honor. And in short, if I am to tell the truth, this servant to Venus, this lusty squire, who was called Aurelius, had loved Dorigen, all without her knowledge, more than any creature two years and more, as was his chance; but never durst he tell her his woe. He drank all his penance without cup. He was in despair, he durst say nothing save that in his songs he would reveal his woe somewhat, as in a general complaining; he said he loved, and was nowise beloved. Of such matter he made many lays, virelays, songs, complaints, and roundels, how he durst not utter his sorrow, but languished like a fury in hell; and die he must, he said, as did Echo for Narcissus, who durst not tell her woe. In other manner than this which I speak of he durst not reveal his passion to her; save that, peradventure, sometimes at dances, where young folk perform their respects, it may well be that he looked upon her face in such wise as a man who asks for favor; but she knew nothing of his meaning.

Nevertheless it befell, ere they went thence, that because he was her neighbor and a man of worship, and she had known him of old, they fell into speech; and Aurelius drew more and more toward his matter, and when he saw his time, he said thus: "Madame, by God That made this world, so I knew it would gladden your heart, I would that the day when your Arveragus went over the sea, I Aurelius had gone whence I never should have returned; for I well know that my service is in vain, my guerdon is but breaking my heart. Have pity upon my bitter pains, madame, for with a word you may slay me or save me — would God that I were buried here at your feet! I have now no time to say more; have mercy, sweet, or you will cause me to die!"

She looked at Aurelius: "Is this your desire?" quoth she. "Say you thus? Never before knew I what was in your mind; but now, Aurelius, I know it. By that God that gave me breath and soul, never in word or deed shall I be an untrue wife, so far as I have my senses. I will be his to whom I am bound. Take this for my final answer." But in sport after that she said thus: "Aurelius, by the high God in heaven, yet would I consent to be your love, since I see you so piteously lamenting; look what day you remove all the rocks, stone by stone, all along Brittany, that they hinder not ship or boat to go, — I say, when you have made the coast so clear of rocks that there is no stone to be seen, then I will love you best of all men. Take here my pledge, so far as my power reaches."

"Is there no other mercy in you?" he said.

"No," quoth she, "by that Lord that made me! For I well know that shall never happen. Let such follies pass out of your heart. What delight should a man ever have to go loving another man's wife, who has her ever at his will?"

Aurelius gave many a sore sigh. Woe was him when he heard this; and with a sorrowful heart he answered, "Madame, this were impossible! Then I must die of a quick, dreadful death." And with that word he turned back.

Then many a one of her other friends came roaming up and down in the paths, and knew naught of this affair, but speedily began new revel; till the bright sun lost his hue, and the horizon had bereft him of his light (this is as much as to say, it was evening). And they went home in joy and contentment, save, alas, wretched Aurelius alone! He went to his house with sorrowful heart; he saw that he could never escape death, and felt his heart grow cold. Up to the heaven he held his hands and set him down on his bare knees, and raving said his orison; for very woe he was out of his wits and knew not what he spake. With piteous heart he began his plaint unto the gods, and first to the sun:

"Apollo," he said, "lord and ruler of every plant, herb, tree, and flower, who givest to each of them his times and seasons, according to thy declination, as thy lodging changes toward north or south; lord Phoebus, cast thy merciful eye upon wretched Aurelius, who am but lost. Behold, lord, my lady has sworn my guiltless death, unless thy benignity have some pity upon my dying heart. For well I know, lord Phoebus, that thou mayst help me best of all save my lady, if thou wilt. Now vouchsafe to hear me tell thee in what wise I may be helped. Thy blessed sister, Lucina the bright, chief goddess and queen of the sea, though Neptunus have his godhead in the sea, yet is she empress over him; thou well knowest, lord, that even as it is her desire to be quickened and lightened by thine orb, wherefore she follows thee eagerly, right so the sea desires of its nature to follow her, being goddess both in the sea and in rivers great and small. Wherefore, lord Phoebus, this is my prayer, — do this miracle or break my heart; that now at this next opposition, which shall

146

be in the sign of the Lion, pray her to bring a flood so great that it shall overtop by at least five fathom the highest rock in Armorican Britain, and let this flood last two years. Then, verily, I may say to my lady, "Keep your promise, the rocks be gone." Lord Phoebus, do this miracle; pray her that she go no faster course than thou; I say, pray thy sister that these two years she go no faster course than thou. Then shall she be ever even at full, and the spring flood-tide last day and night. And, unless she vouchsafe to grant me my dear sovereign lady in such manner, pray her to sink every rock into her own dark region under the ground where Pluto dwelleth, or nevermore shall I gain my lady. Barefoot I will go a pilgrimage to thy temple at Delphi. Lord Phoebus, see the tears on my cheeks, and have some pity on my pains."

And with that he fell down in a swoon and long time lay in a trance. His brother, who knew his trouble, caught him up and brought him to his bed. In this care and torment I let this woeful creature lie despairing. He may choose, for all of me, whether he will live or die.

Arveragus was come home, with other valiant knights, in health and great honor as the flower of chivalry. Oh! now art thou happy, Dorigen, who hast in thine arms thy lusty husband, the vigorous knight, the valiant warrior, who loves thee as his own heart's life. Never thought he to be suspicious whether any person had spoken to her of love whilst he was gone; he had no fear of that. He gave no heed to any such matter, but danced, jousted, and made great cheer toward her. Thus I leave them in happiness and bliss, and will tell of the sick Aurelius.

Two years and more lay wretched Aurelius in languor and mad torment, ere he could walk a step on earth; and no comfort had he in this time, save from his brother, a clerk, who knew of all this woeful matter. For in truth he durst say no word thereof to any other creature. He carried it under his breast more privily than Pamphilus his love for Galatea. His breast was whole, to outward view, but ever in his heart was the keen arrow. And ye well know that in surgery the cure of a wound healed without is perilous, unless men could touch the arrow or get at it.

His brother wept and wailed privily, till at last it came to his mind that whilst he was at Orleans, in France, — as young clerks who are desirous of studying curious arts seek in every nook and corner to learn this special lore, — it came to his mind that, upon a day whilst he studied at Orleans, he saw a book of natural magic, which his fellow, who was then a bachelor of law, had privily left upon his desk, though he were there for a different study; which book spake much of the celestial influences touching the eight-and-twenty mansions which belong to the moon, and such folly as is not worth a fly in our day. For Holy Church's faith which is in our Credo will not suffer any illusion to harm us. And as soon as he remembered this book his heart began to dance for joy, and he said privily to himself, "My brother shall be cured speedily; for I am sure there be arts by which men create divers apparitions, such as these cunning jugglers feign. For often at feasts, I have heard tell, within a large hall these jugglers have made water and a barge come in and row up and down in the hall. Sometimes a grim lion has seemed to come, and sometimes flowers spring as in a meadow, sometimes a vine, with grapes white and red, sometimes a castle of lime and stone. And when they list, straightway they caused it all to pass out; thus it seemed to every man's sight.

Now then, I conclude thus, that if I could find some old comrade at Orleans who is acquainted with these mansions of the moon, or other natural magic besides, he should well cause my brother to possess his love. For by means of an illusion a clerk may make it appear to a man's sight that all the black rocks of Brittany be every one removed, and that ships come and go along the shore, and that this continue a day or two in such form. Then were my brother all cured. Then she must needs keep her promise, or else at least he shall shame her."

Why should I make a longer story? He came to his brother's bed and gave him such encouragement to go to Orleans, that he started up at once, and went on his way forth in hopes to be relieved of his care. When they were almost come to that city, about two or three furlongs away, they met a young clerk roaming by himself who greeted them discreetly in Latin, and then said a marvelous thing. "I know the cause of your coming," quoth he. And ere they went a foot further, he told them all that was in their minds. This clerk of Brittany asked him of the companions whom he had known in old days, and he answered him that they were dead; for which he wept many a tear. Aurelius alighted anon from his horse and went forth home to his house with this magician, who made them well at ease; no victual wanted that might give pleasure. A house so well appointed Aurelius had never seen in his life.

Ere he went to supper, the magician showed him forests, and parks full of wild beasts; there he saw harts with their lofty horns, the largest that eye ever saw. He beheld an hundred of them slain by dogs, and some bleeding from bitter arrow-wounds. When these wild deer vanished, he saw falconers upon a fair river, slaying the heron with their hawks. Then he saw knights jousting on a plain. And after this, the magician did him the pleasure to show him his lady on a dance, in which he himself was dancing, as seemed to him. And when this master who wrought the magic saw that it was time, he clapped his hands, and farewell! all our revel was gone. And yet whilst they saw all this marvelous sight, they stirred never out of the house, but sat still in his study, where his books were, and no one but they three.

This master called his squire to him, and said thus: "Is our supper ready? It is almost an hour, I will be bound, since I bade you make our supper, when these honorable men went with me into my study, where my books be."

"Sir," quoth this squire, "when it please you it is all ready, though you would have it even now."

"Go we to supper, then," quoth he, "that is best. These folk in love must take repose sometime."

After supper they fell into talk over the sum which should be this master's guerdon for removing all the rocks of Brittany and also from the Gironde to the mouth of Seine. He raised difficulties and swore, so God save him! He would not have less than a thousand pound, and he were not right fain to go for that sum.

Aurelius answered straightway, with joyous heart, "Fie on a thousand pound! This wide world, which men say is a ball, would I give, if I were lord of it. This bargain is done, for we be agreed. You shall be paid faithfully, by my word. But look now that you delay us here no longer than tomorrow, for any negligence or sloth."

"Nay," this clerk said, "take here my faith in pledge to you."

To bed went Aurelius when he would, and had repose well-nigh all that night. What for his labor and his hope, his woeful heart had relief from suffering. On the morrow, when it was day, they took the straight road to Brittany, Aurelius and this magician, and dismounted at the place where they would be. And, as books remind me, this was the cold, frosty season of December. Phoebus waxed old and of hue like latten, who in his hot declination shone with his bright beams like burnished gold; but now he was descended into Capricorn, where he shone full pale, I dare well say. The bitter frosts, with sleet and rain, have destroyed the green in every yard. Janus with his double beard sits by the fire and drinks the wine out of his ox-horn; before him stands brawn of the tusked boar, and every lusty man cries, "Noël!"

Aurelius did his master all the cheer and reverence he could, and prayed him to do his diligence to bring him out of his bitter pains, or with a sword he would slit his own heart. This cunning clerk so pitied this man that he sped him all he could, day and night, to watch after a fitting time to work his problem; that is to say, to create an appearance, by such an illusion or crafty sleight — I have no terms of astrology — that she and every person should think and say that the rocks of Brittany were gone, or else sunk under the earth. So at last he found his time to work his jests and his sorry feats, performance of such a cursed superstition. He brought forth his Toledo tables, full well corrected; there lacked naught, neither his tables of *anni collecti* nor of *anni expansi*, nor his roots, nor his other gear, such as his centers, and his arguments, and his tables of proportional parts for his equations. And for his calculations he knew full well how far Alnath in the eighth sphere was pushed from the head of that fixed Aries above, which is reckoned to be in the ninth sphere; full cunningly he calculated by means of all this. When he had found his first mansion, by proportion he knew the remnant, and he well knew the rising of his moon, in which planet's face and term, and all the rest. And he knew full well the moon to be in a mansion favorable to his enterprise, and knew also the other matters to be observed for working such illusions and such cursed practices as heathen folk used in those days. For this reason he no longer tarried, but through his magic it seemed for a week or two that all the rocks were away.

Aurelius, who was still despairing whether he should have his love or fare amiss, waited night and day after this miracle. And when he knew that there was no hindrance, but that every rock was gone, he fell down at his master's feet forthwith and said, "I, Aurelius, woeful wretch, thank you, lord, and Venus my lady, that have helped me from my cold cares." And he took his way forth to the temple where he knew he should see his lady. And when he saw his time, anon he saluted his dear sovereign lady with timid heart and full humble face. Quoth this woeful man, "Mine own lady, whom I most fear and love as best I know how, and whom of all this world I were loathest to displease, — were it not that I have such distress for you that anon I must die here at your feet, I should never tell you how I am encompassed with woe.

But certainly I must either die or make complaint. Guiltless you slay me, for very pain. But though you have no pity for my death, consider ere you break your pledge. For the sake of God in heaven, repent you ere you slay me because I love you. For well you know what you promised, madame; not that I challenge anything of you as of right, my sovereign lady, but only of your grace. Nevertheless, in a garden yonder, at such a spot, you know right well what you promised me, and you plighted your troth in my hand, to love me best; God knows, you said so, though I be unworthy thereof. Madame, I speak it for your honor, more than to save my heart's life; I have done as you bade, and if you will, you may go and see. Do as you list; remember your promise, for, quick or dead, you shall find me right in that garden. It all lies with you, to make me live or die. — But well I know the rocks are gone."

He took his leave, and she stood astonished with not a drop of blood in all her face. She thought never to have come into such a trap. Quoth she, "Alas that ever this should befall! For I never deemed that such a prodigy or marvel could betide, by any possibility. It is against the course of nature."

And home she went a sorrowful person; scarce could she walk for very fear, and for a whole day or two she wept and wailed and swooned, that it was pitiful to behold. But why it was she told no one, for Arveragus was gone out of town. But with pale face and full sorrowful cheer she spake to herself, and said thus in her plaint as I shall tell you. Quoth she, "Alas! I complain on thee, Fortune, who hast bound me unawares in thy chain, from which to escape I know no help save only death or dishonor; one of these twain it behooves me to choose. But nevertheless I had rather forfeit my life than have shame of my body, or lose my fair repute, or know myself false. And by my death, of a surety, I may escape.

"Alas, has not many a noble wife and many a maiden slain herself before this, rather than trespass with her body? Yea, verily; lo! these histories testify it. When the thirty tyrants, full of cursedness, had slain Phidon at a feast in Athens, of their malice they commanded men to arrest his daughters and bring them before them all naked, to fulfill their foul pleasure, and they made them dance in their father's blood upon the pavement. — God give them ill fortune! Wherefore these woeful maidens, in fear of this, privily leaped into a well and drowned themselves, rather than lose their maidenhood; so the books relate. They of Messenia had fifty maidens of Lacedaemonia sought out, with whom they would work their lechery; but of all that band there was none who was not slain, and with good will chose not rather to die than consent to be robbed of her maidenhood. Why should I, then, fear to die?

"Lo also, the tyrant Aristoclides. He loved a maiden named Stymphalis, who, when her father was slain on a night, went straightway to Diana's temple, and laid hold of the image with her two hands, and would never let go. No one could tear her hands from it, till she was slain in that very place. Now since maidens have had such scorn to be defiled with man's base pleasure, methinks a wife ought indeed rather slay herself than be defiled.

"What shall I say of Hasdrubal's wife, who slew herself at Carthage? For when she saw that the Romans had won the city, she took all her children and skipped down into the fire, and chose rather to die than that any Roman dishonored her. Did not Lucrece slay herself at Rome, alas, when she was violated by Tarquin, because she deemed it shame to live when she had lost her honor? The seven maidens of Miletus also for very fear and woe slew themselves rather than the folk of Gaul should violate them. I could tell now more than a thousand stories, I believe, touching this matter. When Abradates was slain, his dear wife slew herself and let her blood flow into Abradates' deep, wide wounds, saying, 'My body, at least, no one shall defile, if I can hinder it.'

"Why should I cite more ensamples hereof, since so many have slain themselves rather than be defiled? I will end thus, that it is better for me to slay myself than so to be defiled. I will be true to Arveragus, or slay myself in some wise, as did the dear daughter of Demotion, because she would not be defiled. O Scedasus, it is full great pity to read how thy daughters died, who slew themselves for the same cause, alas! It was as great pity, or indeed greater, for the Theban maiden that slew herself even for the same grief, to escape Nicanor. Another Theban maiden did likewise; because one of Macedonia had violated her, she redressed her maidenhood by her death. What shall I say of the wife of Niceratus, who for a like cause took her life? How true likewise was his love to Alcibiades, and chose rather to die than to suffer his body to be unburied! Lo, what a wife was Alcestis! What says Homer of Penelope the good? All Greece knows of her chastity. It is written thus of Laodamia, in sooth, that when Protesilaus was slain at Troy, she would live no longer after his days. I may tell the same of noble Portia; she could not live without Brutus, to whom she had given all her whole heart. The perfect wifehood of Artemisia is honored through all heathenesse. O queen Teuta! thy wifely chastity may be a mirror to all wives. The same thing I say of Bilia, of Rhodogune and also of Valeria."

Thus Dorigen made her plaint a day or two, ever purposing to die. But nevertheless Arveragus, this worthy knight, came home the third evening, and asked her why she wept so sore. And she began to weep ever more bitterly.

"Alas that ever I was born! Thus I said," quoth she, "this was my oath," — and she told him what you have already heard; it needs not rehearse it more.

This husband, with cheerful countenance and in friendly wise, answered and said as I shall tell you; "Is there aught else but this, Dorigen?"

"Nay, nay," quoth she, "so may God help me; God forbid there were more; this is too much."

"Yea, wife," he replied; "leave sleeping that which is quiet. It may yet be well today, peradventure. You shall keep your pledge, by my faith! For may God so surely have mercy on me, for the very love I have to you I had far rather be stabbed to the heart, than you should not hold your pledge. Truth is the highest thing that a man may hold." But with that word he burst out weeping forthwith, and said, "I forbid you, on pain of death, ever whilst your life lasts, to tell this matter to any one. I will endure all my woe as best I can, and make no such heavy countenance that folk might deem or guess harm of you."

And he called forth a squire and maid, and said, "Go forth straightway with Dorigen and bring her to such a place." They took their leave and went their way, but they knew not why she went thither. He would tell his mind to no one.

Peradventure in sooth many of you will hold him a foolish man herein, that he would put his wife in jeopardy; hearken to the tale, ere you exclaim upon her. She may have better fortune than you look for; and when you have heard the tale, judge.

This squire Aurelius, who was so amorous of Dorigen, happed by chance to meet her amidst the town, even in the busiest street, as she was bound by the straight way for the garden where she had promised to go. And he also was bound gardenward; for well he ever espied it when she would go out of her house to any place. But thus they met, by chance or good fortune; and he saluted her with joyous mood, and asked whither she went.

And she answered, as if she were half crazed, "To the garden, as my husband bade, to keep my promise, alas! alas!"

Aurelius wondered at this thing, and in his heart had great compassion of her and her lament, and of Arveragus, the worthy knight who had bidden her hold all she had promised, so loath was he that his wife should break her pledge. And he had great sorrow in his heart over it, and he considered on all sides what were best, that he would refrain from his desire rather than to do so high a churlish wretchedness against nobility and all gentle manners. Wherefore he said thus in few words: "Madame, say to Arveragus, your lord, that since I see his great nobility to you (and likewise I well see your distress), that it seemed better to him to suffer shame — and that were pity — than you should break your troth to me, I had rather suffer perpetual woe, than part the love betwixt you. Into your hand, madame, I release, cancelled, every assurance and every bond that you have made to me heretofore from the time when you were born. I plight my troth that I shall never reproach you on the score of any promise. And here I take my leave, of the best and truest wife that in all my days I ever yet knew. But let every woman beware what she promises; let her at least think of Dorigen." Thus of a surety a squire can do a gentle deed, as well as can a knight.

She thanked him upon her bare knees, and went home to her husband and told him all, even as you have heard me say it. And be ye sure, he was so well pleased that I could not tell how much; why should I indite further of this matter? Arveragus and his wife Dorigen led forth their days in sovereign bliss. Never again was there vexation betwixt them. Evermore he cherished her as though she were a queen, and she was true to him. Concerning these two folk ye get no more from me.

Aurelius, who had forfeited all the expense, cursed the time when he was born. "Alas! alas!" quoth he, "that I promised a thousand pounds' weight of refined gold unto this philosopher! How shall I do? I see nothing more but that I am undone. I must needs sell mine heritage and be a beggar. I cannot abide here and shame all my kindred hereabout, unless I may obtain better grace of him. But nevertheless I will seek of him to let me pay at certain times year by year, and will thank him for his great courtesy. I will keep my word, I will not be false."

With sore heart he went to his coffer and brought to this clerk gold of the value of five hundred pounds, I believe, and besought him of his noble courtesy to grant him certain days to pay the remnant, and said, "Master, I dare well boast that I never failed of my word as yet. For verily my debt shall be paid you, whatever befall me, though I go a-begging in my bare kirtle. But would you vouchsafe, upon security, to respite me for two or three years, then it were well with me. For otherwise I must sell mine heritage. There is no more to say."

This philosopher answered gravely and said thus, when he heard these words, "Have I not kept my covenant with you?"

"Yea, certainly, well and truly," quoth he.

"Have you not had your lady even as you desired?"

"No, no," quoth he and sighed sorrowfully.

"What was the cause? Tell me, if you can."

Aurelius began his tale anon, and told him all, as you have heard, it needs not rehearse it again. He said, "Arveragus of his nobility would rather have died in sorrow and woe, than that his wife were false to her troth." He told him also the sorrow of Dorigen, how loath she was to be a wicked wife, and that she had rather have died that day, and that it was through innocence she had sworn her oath. "She never heard tell before of magic illusion; that made me have pity upon her. And even as freely as he sent her to me, so freely I sent her back to him. This is every bit; there is no more to say."

This philosopher answered: "Dear friend, each of you did a gentle deed toward the other. You are a squire, he is a knight. But God in his blessed power forbid but a clerk may verily do a gentle deed as well as any of you. Sir, I release you your thousand pound, as freely as if you were but now crept out of the earth and had never known me ere now. For, sir, I will not take a penny of you for all my art and all my labor. You have paid well for my subsistence. It is enough. And farewell, have good day." And he took his horse and forth he went upon his journey.

Lordings, I would ask you this question now: Which, think ye, was the most generous? Now tell me, ere ye go farther. I can no more; my tale is finished.

Here ended the Franklin's Tale.

HOW ALEXANDER CAME TO THE TREES OF THE SUN AND THE MOON

retold by Robert Steele (1894)

How Alexander Passed through the Land of Darkness and Slew the Basilisk

Alexander and his army entered into a plain full of fair flowers and trees. Now the trees of this land were fruitful and bore all manner of food for man, and amongst them were apples and almonds, vines and pomegranates, and plums and damsons; and it was in this land that the Greeks first ate of damsons, for they did eat of them three days while they were in the forest. But as they went through the wood, they came upon giants twice as high as other men, clad in coats of skin, and covered with long hair. So the Greeks and the Indians were sore afraid lest these giants should fall upon them and slay them, while the giants called one to another, and came together through the trees to gaze on them, for they had never seen men before. When the Greeks saw that these giants were calling to one another and coming together, they drew up in line of battle, and the knights clad in armor mounted their battle horses, and the archers and spearmen prepared their weapons for the onset: for the Greeks had never heard of giants who did no harm to men. But these giants were great stupid oafs who stood gazing with open mouths at Alexander and his men preparing to slay them, and their food was grapes and pomegranates. And when the army was drawn up in line, and all men were ready, Alexander gave the word and they raised a loud shout so that the woods rang again, and the giants turned and fled, for they had never heard sound of man or of trumpet. Then the knights followed them and slew some six hundred of them in the field and in the chase, so that none of them were left in the land round about.

The tale tells that Alexander passed on with his army, still seeking the wonders of the land and finding no man in this part of it, till he came to another river where he halted for many days. And there came men of the land to him, and Alexander asked them of the wonders of the land, so they told him of certain trees near by which grew with the sun, and when it was high they were great, and as the sun fell below the earth so the trees grew smaller and sank down into the soil. But when the king would set out to see this marvel, they told him that no man could go near it for there was a wild man who guarded the wood and suffered no one to pass. Then Alexander sought counsel of his wise men, and they bade him take a fair white maiden such as the wild man had never seen and hold her before him, and so they did, and the wild man became quiet and still at the sight of her, so the Greeks crept up to him and bound him in great chains, and brought him before the King's tent: now this wild man was covered with hair stout and strong, and his arms were great, and his strength was as that of ten men. And when the King had gazed on him they bound him to a tree, and slew him, and burnt him to ashes, for he had slain much folk of that country.

Next day the King and his company came to the place of the trees, and they wondered at the sight, how they grew as the day grew, and the height of them was a spear's length, and on them were fruits like to apples, and men called them the trees of the sun. Now the tent of the King was over against the place where the trees grew, and in the hot sunlight he felt thirst, so he bade one of his churls fetch him an apple, and the man sprang forth to do his bidding, but when he laid his hand on the fruit he fell to the ground as if he was slain. There were birds on those trees among the branches and some men wished to put their hands on them, for they did not fly away from them, but as they did so, flames of fire came out from the trees; and the men of the country told them that no man could touch these trees and live. Then Alexander asked them of the Land of Darkness, for the stone Elmas shone brightly, and he knew that he was drawing near that land: but they said that no man went to that land, for the way was through a desert that none could cross.

Then Alexander chose him out of all his army three hundred young men, able to endure hardship, and they made them ready to go with him to the Land of Darkness, while the army was left in the hand of King Porus; and he gave orders that the young men should carry with them stores of food and water to pass through the desert to the land they sought. Now there was a certain old man in the army named Bushi, who had two sons chosen to go with the King, and he bade them to take him with them to the Land of Darkness, but they said to him that the King had straightly commanded that no old man should go with them. Then said the old man, "O Sons, make strong a box, and put me inside it, and set the box on a mule and carry it with the baggage, and it shall be for your good, for a party without old men to advise can come to no good." So his sons did as he bade them, and closed him in a box, and set him on a mule's back, and carried him with them to the land. And as Alexander went on his way they met men of the land, journeying in the desert, and these told them of the Well of Life, and how a man had drunk of that well, but he could not find his way out of the Land of Darkness, and ever he wandered to and fro, up and down, till at last he gave up the search, and dwelt in a tower alone, and as the years rolled on he grew smaller and smaller, and more and more cruel, and when men came into that land, he slew them and fed on their flesh.

Now when Alexander drew near the Land he came to a desert land, where was neither well nor living thing, and they hastened through it for five days, but on the morrow of the sixth day the sun rose not, and there was no light of day: and so the king knew that he had come on the Land of Darkness, but the tales that he had heard came to his mind, and he feared, for he had no mind to wander through that land without a guide. Then he went back with his men for half a day's journey, and lo! the light of the evening, so he camped in that place and waited for morning light. On the morrow he took counsel with his men, as to the way of return, and he offered great reward to any man who should show the way of a safe journey back, but his young men said, "O King, it is ours to go where thou dost order us, and what thou biddest, that will we do:" and he found no counsel in them. Then the two sons told their father how the King had stopped and asked for counsel, and Bushi bade them bring him before Alexander, and when they feared he bade them be bold, for he had good counsel to give.

The tale tells that the King was sitting sorrowful in his tent that day, for he dared not enter the Land without some means of safe return, and he was unwilling to go back to the army without having reached his object; and when the guards entered and told that an old man sought speech of him, he thought that one of the gods must have come to his help. So he made him to sit in his own seat, for the man was very old and feeble, and asked him what he would. Then Bushi answered and said, "O King, hear the words of an old man; there is no love like the love of a mother for her young. Now thou hast here with thee many asses with their foals. This is my word to thee. Leave here on the borders of the Land, half thy men with their baggage trains, and leave with them the young foals, and go thou with their mothers and the rest of thy men into the Land, and do thy heart's desire: then when thou wilt return from this Land, loosen the mothers and leave them free, and take them for thy guides, and they will lead thee back to the place where their young ones be."

Then Alexander the King praised him greatly, and gave rich reward to the young men, his sons, and he offered to take the old man to the Well of Life, but he would not, for he said, "How should I desire to live for ever, being such a man as I am, for the bitterness of death is past to me." Then he gave counsel to the King that no man should bathe in any well in the land, till he had seen it, for if he did the well would disappear for a year. So Alexander did as the old man Bushi advised him, for he divided his men into two bands, and one he left on the borders of the Land of Darkness, with their baggage and with the young foals, and one he took with him, and the men he took with him he straightly charged to come to him when they found the well, and on no account to bathe in it. So he entered the Land, and the stone Elmas shone with a light like a star, and guided them on the road for three days. But on the fourth day it grew duller, and Alexander knew that he had passed the place of the Well of Life; and he ordered his men to search for the well in all directions, but not to go out of sound of the trumpets which rang out every hour, and to come into the camp when it sounded. Seven times did the trumpet sound, and the scouts came in, but on the seventh time, one of them, Philotus by name, came in with his hair wet, and Alexander knew that he had disobeyed the word of the king, and had bathed in the well. Then said he to him, "O Philotus, canst thou lead me to the well thou hast bathed in," and the man answered, "Yea, Lord;" and they set out together, but no well could be found. Then the wrath of the King burst out, for he knew that he should see the Well no more for a year if he remained in that place, and that all the gray of his expedition was spent for nought but to make this Indian immortal, and he bade men bring great stones, and build them in a pillar round the Indian and close it at the top, and they did so, and he was left alive inside the pillar, for indeed the Greeks could not slay him. This done, Alexander put the reins on the necks of his asses, and they turned and led the way to their young, and in three days he was out of the Land of Darkness and on his way to the army.

In few days the King set out again with his host and went on his way towards the mountain lands, and ever the way led upward till after eleven days' journey they came to a great plain among the mountains, covered with trees and plants, and well watered by noble rivers. The fruits were of the finest savor, and the water was sweeter than milk or mead, and clearer than crystal. So they went on through the land for many days, but they found no man in it, and no houses or temples of the gods; until they came to a high mountain which seemed to reach even to the clouds, and no way was there of crossing it, it was so steep and rugged. But when they came up to this range they found two passes which led through the range, and where they met was a great temple, and the one path led to the East, the way of the sun-rising, and the other to the North. Now there was no man to tell them where these paths led, or what was to be met in them. Then Alexander thought within himself that he would go to the East, for the Gods had predicted that in the East he should learn when and where was the end of his days, and the army of the King went through the pass for seven days.

But on the eighth day, a sudden death fell on many of the men in the host, for when they came to a certain spot or place among the mountains, ever one or another noble knight would fall down suddenly and lie dead on the road, nor did all men who passed the place die, but some only. Then fear came upon all men, and those who had passed the place dared not move either forward or backward, and those who had not passed it would not go forward, nor indeed did the King command them, for all men said, "The wrath of the gods is upon us for coming into this land." So Alexander sought to find the reason for this death, and he went with one of his knights up the mountains at the side of the pass, till he came to a place whence he could see the whole of the pass and the mountains behind it, and looking down into the valley he saw in one of the clefts of the hills a loathly serpent, old and wrinkled, his thin long neck and great head lying on the ground before it. And while the King looked down, the ungainly worm slowly raised its heavy head and looked down on the valley, and let it fall again, and a cry of grief from his men told him that two more of his knights had fallen dead on the pass, and Alexander knew that his eyes saw the Basilisk.

The tale tells that this beast is the most deadly of all serpents, for its venom is such that whatsoever living thing it looks on it slays, yea, the very grass is withered by its deadly breath. And no man may slay it unawares easily, for once a man slew one with a lance, and the venom of it was such that he died from it, though he came no nearer the body than a spear's length. This the king knew and he sought not to slay it with a weapon, but he worked so that the worm should kill itself; for he caused his men to make a shield larger than a man, and on this shield he bade put a bright polished mirror, and he wrapped his feet in linen, and put off his armor, and going softly he bore the shield with its mirror before him, and set it down before the den of the basilisk, and went his way. But the basilisk raised its head as its manner was, and looked before it, and saw its face in the mirror, and the poison of its own look killed it, so it fell dead with its eyes wide open, and lay along the path. Then the knight who was on the mountain watching blew his horn, and all men heard it and rejoiced and praised the brave king who had delivered them from the basilisk.

All this while the march of the host had lain between mountains, and when men climbed to the top they saw nothing but other mountains stretching away as far as they could see, no towns, no villages, no living things, and on the day after the basilisk was slain, the road suddenly stopped among the mountains, and the host could go no further. Then Alexander the King bade them turn back to the parting of the ways, and as they passed the place where the basilisk had been he bade them burn it in asbestos cloth, and take its ashes, for the ashes of the basilisk are a precious thing, able to turn lead into pure gold, but the men found it not, though the great mirror was still there. And at the last they came to the temple at the parting of the ways, and the army lay round the temple for a day to rest, for they were sore wearied with the passage through the Eastward way. The next day at sunrise two aged men came out of the temple, and Alexander spoke with them and they told him of the ways, how that Bacchus, one of the gods, had made this road when he came into India and conquered it, and how he had caused the mountains to come together and block it up, so that no man should pass through by it after. Then Alexander asked them of the Northward way, and they told him how it led to the Trees of the Sun and Moon: and they told of the wonders of the trees, and how they spoke with men's tongues, and told what should be in time to come, and Alexander the King rejoiced.

How Alexander Came to the Trees of the Sun and the Moon, and What They Told Him.

Howbeit Alexander made no sign to them of his joy, for he seemed not to believe the old men, and he said: "Have I spread the might of my name from the East even unto the West to no end but to become a sport to old men and dotards." Then the old men made oath by the gods that this thing was true, and they told the King how that these trees spoke both in the Greek and the Indian language; and Alexander asked them of the way to this marvel, and the men answered: "O King, whosoever thou art, no greater marvel shalt thou see than this we tell thee of. The way to it is a journey of ten days, nor can your army pass because of the narrow paths, and the want of water, but at the most four thousand men with their beasts of burden and their food." Then all the friends of the King and his companions besought him to go and see this great thing, and he made as if he hearkened to their prayers, and consented to go with them. So he left the army with its baggage and the elephants in the hands of King Porus his friend, and set out on the Northward Way to seek the trees, which spoke to men.

Now the Northward Way was like the Eastward one, a narrow road among high mountains, and little ease was there in going through it, and for three days they came to no water, but at noon on the fourth day they came to a spring which flowed out of a cave on the hillside. Then the Indians told Alexander that this cave was sacred to Bacchus, so he entered it and offered up a sacrifice to the god, and prayed him that he might return safe to Macedon, lord of the world, but he got no sign from the god that his prayer was heard. Then on the morrow he set out, and on the tenth day at even they came to the foot of a great cliff, shining in the setting sun from thousands of brilliant points like diamonds, and from chains of red gold leading from step to step up the face of the rock, high up beyond the ken of men. And as the sun shone on it the steps seemed carved from sapphires and rubies, so deep were the blue and red of their color. Then Alexander the king set up altars to the gods of heaven, and offered sacrifices to each one of them, and he and his men lay that night at the foot of the cliff.

Early in the morning he arose, and when he had called to him his twelve tried princes, he began to ascend the steps on the side of the mountain, and as he went up it seemed to him that he was going into the clouds, and when he looked down, the path by which he had come seemed as a silver ribbon among the hills, and the men of his host seemed smaller than bees, and nothing that might happen seemed strange to him, for his joy and lightness of heart. So on and on they went and at length they came to the last of the steps, two thousand five hundred of them, and they found that on the top of the cliff was a wide plain, and in the distance they saw a fair palace set in a garden, and a noble minster shining in the sun like gold. All the plain was full of rich and noble trees bearing precious balm and spices, and many fruits grew on their branches, and the inhabitants of the plain fed on them, for there were many men on the plain, and all men and women were clothed in the skins of panthers or of tigers sewn together, and they spoke in the Indian tongue. As the Greeks drew near the palace they saw it, what a fair home it was, and how it had two broad doors to its hall, and seventy windows of diverse shape, and when they came to the doors they found them covered with beaten gold, and set with fair stones.

But the doors of the palace opened and shut, and there stood before them a negro, ten feet high, with great teeth showing over his lips, his ears pierced and a great pearl in each, and clothed in skins. And when he had saluted them he asked them why they had come to that land, and they said that they wished to see the trees that spoke, and to hear something from them. Then the negro bade them to take three of them, and to put off their shoes, and their weapons and ornaments, and to clothe

159

themselves in fair white linen, and Alexander and two of his companions did so, and the negro brought them within the palace, leaving the rest of their companions outside. And as they went in they marked the fair garden, and in it were golden vines bearing on them grapes of rubies and carbuncles, and they saw how precious a place it was, so that Paradise alone excelled it.

Now when they were come to the inner door of the hall, the negro bowed himself down before them, and opened the door before them, but went not in himself, for that room was the chief of the palace, and when they lifted up their heads they saw before them a couch and on it was a man. Now the hangings of the couch were of golden brocade, and its coverlet was blue, embroidered with shining ones in bright gold, and the bed-head was embroidered with cherubim with glancing wings, and the canopy with the bright seraphim. The curtains were of silk and on them was a fair garden of needlework, and in it were beasts and birds, and the pillars were of the same, and all the points and ornaments were of pearl. The romance tells that he who rested in that room was one of the noblest-looking men that ever had life, with a face bright and bold as fire, his hair was long and gray, and his beard was as white as the driven snow. When the King and his peers saw him they knew that he must be of the blood of the gods and not of mankind, and they knelt down on the ground before him, and saluted him with all reverence. Then he reached out his arms to them, and raised him on the bed, and answered them: "Hail, Alexander," said he, "All hail, thou who wieldest the earth, thou and thy princes are welcome. Sir, thou shalt see with thy sight such marvels as never before man saw; and thou shalt heat of what shall come, things that no man hath heard but thee." Then was the King astonished that his name was known, and he said, "Oh, holy happy man, how dost thou name my name, since thou hast never seen me before?" And the god answered: "Yea, I knew thee ere a word of thy fame had spread over the earth." Then he went on: "Wish ye to look upon the trees that bloom for ever, the trees of the sun and of the moon, that can speak and tell thee of what is to be?" And Alexander the king said, "Yes by my crown, this would I do more than anything else in the world." Then the god said, "Art thou clean of body and mind, thou and thy friends; for no man may enter the place where they are who is not pure of all stain?" and Alexander answered that they were. So the Elder arose from his bed, and cast on him a mantle of gold, and the ground glittered for the glory of his weeds, and he led them to the door, and there stood there two elders like to those Alexander had seen at the Parting of the Ways, and he gave them into their hands, and bade them lead them to the place where they would be. Then he turned and departed, and Alexander and his friends Ptolemy and Antiochus went with the elders.

As they went the elders asked them if they had any metal or rich thing with them, and bade them cast it off, and one of the elders stayed at the door of the minster while the other led them through it, and after that the three Greek lords passed through a wondrous thick wood, full of most precious trees, olives and sycamores, cypresses and cedars, with balm and myrrh trickling down the trunk and all manner of incense and aromatic spices. In this wood they came upon a little round clear space, and when they looked they saw a great tree whereon was neither fruit nor leaves, bark nor bast, and it was one hundred feet high. And on it they saw a bird resting on one of its branches, and the bird was of the size of a peacock, with a crest such as the peacock has, and its cheeks and jaws were red like a fowl, and its breast was of golden feathers, and its back and tail of blue speckled with crimson, and its body of gold and red speckled with gray. Then Alexander the king stayed and considered this bird and wondered at it, and the guide answered his thought: "Why dost thou wait and wonder, yon is the Phoenix, the bird that lives a hundred years, and has no mate:" and he turned them a little way and they saw a spot where two trees grew side by side, the trees of the Sun and the Moon. "Behold now," quoth the guide, "these holy trees; form in thy mind the question thou wouldst ask of them, but say it not in words that can be heard; and thou shalt have an answer in plain words, such as no other oracle gives. And this shall be a sign to thee that the gods are good to thee, since they read thy thoughts and heed not words to tell them thy question."

The tale tells us that these trees were not like others, but their boles and leaves shone like metal, and the tree of the sun was like gold, and the tree of the moon was like silver, and the tree of the sun was the male, and that of the moon the female. Then Alexander asked his guide: "In what way will the trees answer me?" and the Elder answered him: "Truly, O King, the Sun-tree begins to speak in the Indian tongue, and ends in Greek; but the Moon-tree, since it is female, speaks in a contrary manner, for it begins in Greek and finishes in Indian, and thus in two tongues each tells us its mission. of fate." Then he wished to offer sacrifices before the trees to honor them as gods, but the Elder forbade him, for he said that no living thing was to be injured in this place, and no fire must be brought there, but that the only sacrifices offered to the trees were kisses on the tree-boles. And when he heard this Alexander the King knelt down on the ground and kissed the boles of the trees one after the other, and asked within himself whether he should return to Macedon, where his mother dwelt, having conquered all the earth.

Now, when he had, asked this question in his mind, and he and his fellows were kneeling on the ground before the tree, suddenly it began to move, and the leaves began to quiver, though all was still and calm in the forest, and there was a sound of going in the tree-tops, and a sighing as if the wind was rustling through the leaves, and the sighing and moaning of the leaves grew louder, and with a swaying sough this answer came to the King: "O Alexander, unbeaten in war thou art, and shalt be lord of all the world, yet never shalt thou see the soil of thy sires, or return to thy dear land of Macedon; thou shalt see thy mother and thy land no more." When they heard these things the companions of Alexander fell down to the ground as if dead, so great was their grief, and they heard no more of what was said; but Alexander knelt down before the Moon-tree to ask of it a question. Then the Elder came to him and said: "O King, the tree of the Moon answers not till the night has come, and the moon is full in the sky." So the King turned to his companions, and comforted them with his kind words and gifts, and bade them be of good cheer.

When the night was come Alexander rose up again to go before the Moon-tree, and to hear its oracles, and his companions told him of the danger of being unarmed and alone by night, but Alexander feared not, for it was not lawful to slay any one in that forest, neither was there any man in it save the guide and themselves. And having adored the tree and kissed it, he knelt down before it, and thought to ask when and where should be his end. Then at the moment when the rays of the moon made the leaves shine with splendor, he heard a voice from the tree: "Alexander, the end of thy life draws near; this year shall be thine, but in the ninth month of the next thou shalt die at Babylon, deceived by him in whom you fully trust." Then he was filled with grief and he looked at his friends, and he knew that they were ready to die for him if need be, and he thought of the other companions in whom he trusted, and that if he slew them he might save himself, and then he thought of the endless suspicion and sorrow he would live in for the rest of his days, and he remembered the words of the god when he told him that it was not good for men to know the end of their days, and he strengthened his heart and comforted his friends, and he bade them, swear never to reveal the things they had heard, and again they returned to the minster, and found tents thereby where they might rest, and beds of skins, and on an ivory table there was food and drink set for them, fruit and bread, and water from the stream. So they slept and rested.

Then in the morning the Elder woke him from sleep, and led him before the bare tree, and bade him ask of it what he would, and he knelt before it and kissed it, and asked in his mind, "Who is it that shall harm my mother or sisters or myself?" Then he had this answer from the tree: "O mighty lord, if I should tell thee the man who should betray thee it were easy for thee to slay him and to over come thy fate, and the oracles would be made of none effect. Therefore thou shalt die at Babylon, not by iron, as thou deemest, nor by gold, silver, nor by any vile metal, but by poison. Thy mother shall die by the vilest death, and shall lie unburied in the common way, to be eaten by birds and dogs. Thy sisters shall live long and happy lives. Short as thy life shall be, thou shalt be lord of all lands. Now ask no more, but return to thy army and to Porus thy friend." And the Elder came up to him and said: "Let us depart with speed, for the weeping and moaning of thy companions have offended the holy ones of the trees," and Alexander and his companions departed from the forest. Then he asked the Elder who was the god of the palace, and he told the King it was Bacchus, who had sent him to the temple at the Parting of the Ways, and who had welcomed him in the palace. So Alexander came to his peers, and with them went down the golden stairway and joined the host, and hurried on day after day until he came to the Parting of the Ways, and there he found his army under the command of Porus his friend.

And after the army was gathered together, Alexander the King spoke of his journey to the oracles, and how he had climbed the stairway, and how he had been guided by the god, and had asked the trees of his fate, and he told them that the trees had promised him that he should conquer the world, and return to Macedon, and live a long life, and all the army shouted with joy. But the comrades of Alexander and his twelve peers were sad, for they knew what was foretold, yet they said not a word of it, but shouted with the rest. Then Porus the Indian doubted of the truth, and he questioned the king's companions closely, but they told him not of the oracle: howbeit he was assured in his heart that Alexander was to die, and he thought to seize on the empire, and he began to contrive the king's death; and Alexander knew of his questionings, and kept watch over his doings.

3. OLD NORSE

Old Norse shares with Old English a common background. Both of the languages and their respective literatures developed out of the same Germanic history, and some heroes and their exploits are referred to in the writings of both languages. As with surviving Old English literature, what we have of it in Old Norse was written late—much of it dating from the twelfth through the fourteenth centuries.

Two of the most important works of Old Norse literature share the curious name *Edda*, a word of uncertain origin and meaning. The first is a collection of mythological and heroic poems generally known as *The Elder Edda* or *The Poetic Edda*. The second, based in part upon the earlier *Edda*, is known as *The Younger Edda* or *The Prose Edda*. It was compiled in the early thirteenth century by Snorri Sturluson.

Sturluson (1179-1241) was a major figure in medieval Iceland, a politician, poet and historian. Besides his *Edda*, he wrote *Heimskringla*, a history of the kings of Norway, and he is believed also to have written *Egil's Saga*, one of the greatest of the Icelandic family sagas. Sturluson's *Edda* is made up of four parts, a *Prologue*, *Gylfaginning*, *Skaldskaparmal*, and *Hattatal*. Most translations into English include only the *Prologue* and *Gylfaginning*, or "The Deluding of Gylfi," which tells of a Swedish king named Gylfi who hears stories of the Old Norse gods. *Gylfaginning* is the most extensive account of Norse myths and legends that has survived, and the basis for much of our present knowledge of Old Norse mythology. *Skaldskaparmal* is a long essay on the language of poetry, while *Hattatal* discusses the categories of verse-forms.

In Old Norse there was an extensive oral tradition of skaldic poetry, and much of the earliest of it that survives does so only in the form of quotations found in the sagas. The sagas are prose narratives written in medieval Iceland. They are today divided up into several different classifications, some of which are *konungasögur* or "kings' sagas," the most important of which is

Sturluson's *Heimskringla*; *Íslendingasögur* or "sagas of the Icelanders," which are essentially historical novels about certain men and their families—these include *Njal's Saga*, *Egil's Saga*, and *Laxdaela Saga*; and *fornaldarsögur*, or "sagas of ancient times," which are mostly heroic legends and fantastical adventure tales. The *fornaldarsögur* include *The Saga of the Volsungs*, the epic of Sigurd and the slaying of the dragon Fafnir; *The Saga of King Heidrek the Wise*, which contains one of the great riddle-matches in Old Norse literature (the other being in *The Poetic Edda*), here between Heidrek and Gestumblindi, the latter of whom is the god Odin in disguise; and *The Saga of Hrolf Kraki*, which includes the story of a man named Bjorn who has been cursed to be changed into a bear during the daytime and to revert to being a man during the night.

Tolkien studied and taught Old Norse, both the language and its literature, for many years, but he published virtually nothing in this field. From 1926 through the early 1930s Tolkien shared the *Eddas* and several of the Icelandic sagas with his friends, including C. S. Lewis, in a group called the *Kolbítar* ("Coal-biters"), where each person read aloud sections from these works, translating impromptu. There are many elements in Old Norse literature that will be familiar to readers of Tolkien, heroes fighting dragons, riddle-matches, dwarfs, Light-Elves and Dark-Elves, and the divine Æsir who resemble Tolkien's Valar.

For space considerations, I have not included any of the poems from *The Poetic Edda*, but I have included the *Prologue* and *Gylfaginning* from *The Prose Edda*, and *Gylfaginning* itself quotes some of the poems from *The Poetic Edda*, including *Voluspa* with its famous list of dwarf-names from which Tolkien lifted most of the dwarf-names in *The Hobbit*.

To represent the sagas, I have selected one of the *fornaldarsögur*, *The Saga of King Heidrek the Wise*, translated by Nora Kershaw, who is better known under her married name of Nora K. Chadwick. In 1960 Tolkien's third son Christopher published an edition of this saga, in Old Norse with a facing page translation, based on a different manuscript than the one Kershaw translated. Settling on *The Saga of King Heidrek the Wise* was not an easy choice. The other very strong candidate for inclusion was *The Saga of the Volsungs*, but since it is currently easy to procure in translation whereas

The Saga of King Heidrek the Wise is not, I felt compelled to select the more obscure *Heidrek*.

The *Eddas* have been translated many times. For full versions of the *The Poetic Edda*, I would recommend the 1923 translation by Henry Adams Bellows or the 1962 translation by Lee M. Hollander. The abridgement by Paul B. Taylor and W. H. Auden, *The Elder Edda: A Selection* (1969) is interestingly dedicated to J. R. R. Tolkien.

Useful translations of Snorri Sturluson's version include *The Prose Edda of Snorri Sturluson* (1954), translated by Jean I. Young, which includes the *Prologue*, *Gylfaginning*, and some selections from *Skaldskaparmal*. But the only complete translation of all four parts is the one by Anthony Faulkes published as *Edda* (1987).

Of the major sagas, Penguin publishes translations of most of them, including *Egil's Saga* (1976) translated by Hermann Pálsson and Paul Edwards; *Njal's Saga* (2002) translated by Robert Cook; *Laxdaela Saga* (1969) translated by Magnus Magnusson and Hermann Pálsson; and *Eyrbyggja Saga* (1989) translated by Hermann Pálsson and Paul Edwards. Penguin also publishes translations of other sagas, including *The Vinland Sagas* (1965) translated by Magnus Magnusson and Hermann Pálsson; *The Saga of King Hrolf Kraki* (1998) translated by Jesse L. Byock; *King Harald's Saga* (1976) excerpted from Snorri Sturluson's *Heimskringla* and translated by Magnus Magnusson and Hermann Pálsson; *The Saga of the Volsungs* (1990) translated by Jesse L. Byock; and the collections *Seven Viking Romances* (1985) translated by Hermann Pálsson and Paul Edwards; *Hrafnkel's Saga and Other Icelandic Stories* (1971) translated by Hermann Pálsson; and a large omnibus of many of the family sagas, *The Sagas of Icelanders* (2000), with a preface by Jane Smiley. The University of Toronto Press has a fine edition of the other major saga, *Grettir's Saga* (1969) translated by Denton Fox and Hermann Pálsson.

PROLOGUE AND GYLFAGINNING

from *The Prose Edda*, by Snorri Sturluson
translated by Arthur Gilchrist Brodeur (1916)

Prologue

In the beginning God created heaven and earth and all those things which are in them; and last of all, two of human kind, Adam and Eve, from whom the races are descended. And their offspring multiplied among themselves and were scattered throughout the earth. But as time passed, the races of men became unlike in nature: some were good and believed on the right; but many more turned after the lusts of the world and slighted God's command. Wherefore, God drowned the world in a swelling of the sea, and all living things, save them alone that were in the ark with Noah. After Noah's flood eight of mankind remained alive, who peopled the earth; and the races descended from them. And it was even as before: when the earth was full of folk and inhabited of many, then all the multitude of mankind began to love greed, wealth, and worldly honor, but neglected the worship of God. Now accordingly it came to so evil a pass that they would not name God; and who then could tell their sons of God's mighty wonders? Thus it happened that they lost the name of God; and throughout the wideness of the world the man was not found who could distinguish in aught the trace of his Creator. But not the less did God bestow upon them the gifts of the earth: wealth and happiness, for their enjoyment in the world; He increased also their wisdom, so that they knew all earthly matters, and every phase of whatsoever they might see in the air and on the earth.

One thing they wondered and pondered over: what it might mean, that the earth and the beasts and the birds had one nature in some ways, and yet were unlike in manner of life. In this was their nature one: that the earth was cleft into lofty mountain-peaks, wherein water spurted up, and it was not needful to dig longer for water there than in the deep valleys; so it is also with beasts and birds: it is equally far to the blood in the head and the feet. Another quality of the earth is, that in each year grass and flowers grow upon the earth, and in the same year all that growth falls away and withers; it is even so with beasts and birds: hair and feathers grow and fall away each year. This is the third nature of the earth, that when it is opened and dug up, the grass grows straightway on the soil which is uppermost on the earth. Boulders and stones they likened to the teeth and bones of living beings. Thus they recognized that the earth was quick, and had life with some manner of nature of its own; and they understood that she was wondrous old in years and mighty in kind: she nourished all that lived, and she took to herself all that died. Therefore they gave her a name, and traced the number of their generations from her. The same thing, moreover, they learned from their aged kinsmen: that many hundreds of years have been numbered since the same earth yet was, and the same sun and stars of the heavens; but the courses of these were unequal, some having a longer course, and some a shorter.

From things like these the thought stirred within them that there might be some governor of the stars of heaven: one who might order their courses after his will; and that he must be very strong and full of might. This also they held to be true: that if he swayed the chief things of creation, he must have been before the stars of heaven; and they saw that if he ruled the courses of the heavenly bodies, he must also govern the shining of the sun, and the dews of the air, and the fruits of the earth, whatsoever grows upon it; and in like manner the winds of the air and the storms of the sea. They knew not yet where his kingdom was; but this they believed: that he ruled all things on earth and in the sky, the great stars also of the heaven, and the winds of the sea. Wherefore, not only to tell of this fittingly, but also that they might fasten it in memory, they gave names out of their own minds to all things. This belief of theirs has changed in many ways, according as the peoples drifted asunder and their tongues became severed one from another. But all things they discerned with the wisdom of the earth, for the understanding of the spirit was not given to them; this they perceived, that all things were fashioned of some essence.

II

The world was divided into three parts: from the south, extending into the west and bordering on the Mediterranean Sea, — all this part was called Africa, the southern quarter of which is hot, so that it is parched with the sun. The second part, from west to north and bordering on the ocean, is called Europe or Enea; its northern part is so cold that no grass grows upon it, and no man dwells there. From the north and all down over the eastern part, even to the south, is called Asia. In that region of the world is all fairness and pride, and the fruits of the earth's increase, gold and jewels. There also is the center of the earth; and even as the land there is lovelier and better in every way than in other places, so also were the sons of men there most favored with all goodly gifts: wisdom, and strength of the body, beauty, and all manner of knowledge.

III

Near the earth's center was made that goodliest of homes and haunts that ever have been, which is called Troy, even that which we call Turkey. This abode was much more gloriously made than others, and fashioned with more skill of craftsmanship in manifold wise, both in luxury and in the wealth which was there in abundance. There were twelve kingdoms and one High King, and many sovereignties belonged to each kingdom; in the stronghold were twelve chieftains. These chieftains were in every manly part greatly above other men that have ever been in the world. One king among them was called Munon or Mennon; and he was wedded to the daughter of the High King Priam, her who was called Troan; they had a child named Tror, whom we call Thor. He was fostered in Thrace by a certain war-duke called Loricus; but when he was ten winters old he took unto him the weapons of his father. He was as goodly to look upon, when he came among other men, as the ivory that is inlaid in oak; his hair was fairer than gold. When he was twelve winters old he had his full measure of strength; then he lifted clear of the earth ten bear-skins all at one time; and then he slew Duke Loricus, his foster-father, and with him his wife Lora, or Glora, and took into his own hands the realm of Thrace, which we call Thrudheim. Then he went forth far and wide over the lands, and sought out every quarter of the earth, overcoming alone all berserks and giants, and one dragon, greatest of all dragons, and many beasts. In the northern half of his kingdom he found the prophetess that is called Sibyl, whom we call Sif, and wedded her. The lineage of Sif I cannot tell; she was fairest of all women, and her hair was like gold. Their son was Loridi, who resembled his father; his son was Einridi, his son Vingethor, his son Vingenir, his son Moda, his son Magi, his son Sescef, his son Bedvig, his son Athra (whom we call Annar), his son Itrmann, his son Heremod, his son Skjaldun (whom we call Skjold), his son Bjaf (whom we call Bjar), his son Iat, his son Gudolf, his son Finn, his son Friallaf (whom we call Fridleif); his son was he who is named Woden, whom we call Odin: he was a man far-famed for wisdom and every accomplishment. His wife was Frigida, whom we call Frigg.

IV

Odin had second sight, and his wife also; and from their foreknowledge he found that his name should be exalted in the northern part of the world and glorified above the fame of all other kings. Therefore, he made ready to journey out of Turkey, and was accompanied by a great multitude of people, young folk and old, men and women; and they had with them much goods of great price. And wherever they went over the lands of the earth, many glorious things were spoken of them, so that they were held more like gods than men. They made no end to their journeying till they were come north into the land that is now called Saxony; there Odin tarried for a long space, and took the land into his own hand, far and wide.

In that land Odin set up three of his sons for land-wardens. One was named Veggdegg: he was a mighty king and ruled over East Saxony; his son was Vitrgils; his sons were Vitta, Hengest's father, and Sigar, father of Svebdegg, whom we call Svipdag. The second son of Odin was Beldegg, whom we call Baldr: he had the land which is now called Westphalia. His son was Brand, his son Frjodigar, (whom we call Frodi), his son Freovin, his son Wigg, his son Gewis (whom we call Gavir). Odin's third son is named Siggi, his son Rerir. These the forefathers ruled over what is now called France; and thence is descended the house known as Volsungs. From all these are sprung many and great houses.

Then Odin began his way northward, and came into the land which they called Reidgotaland; and in that land he took possession of all that pleased him. He set up over the land that son of his called Skjold, whose son was Fridleif; — and thence descends the house of the Skjoldungs: these are the kings of Denmark. And what was then called Reidgotaland is now called Jutland.

V

After that he went northward, where the land is called Sweden; the king there was named Gylfi. When the king learned of the coming of those men of Asia, who were called Æsir, he went to meet them, and made offer to them that Odin should have such power in his realm as he himself wielded. And such well-being followed ever upon their footsteps, that in whatsoever lands they dwelt were good seasons and peace; and all believed that they caused these things, for the lords of the land perceived that they were unlike other men whom they had seen, both in fairness and also in wisdom.

The fields and the choice lands in that place seemed fair to Odin, and he chose for himself the site of a city which is now called Sigtunir. There he established chieftains in the fashion which had prevailed in Troy; he set up also twelve head-men to be doomsmen over the people and to judge the laws of the land; and he ordained also all laws as, there had been before, in Troy, and according to the customs of the Turks. After that he went into the north, until he was stopped by the sea, which men thought lay around all the lands of the earth; and there he set his son over this kingdom, which is now called Norway. This king was Sæming; the kings of Norway trace their lineage from him, and so do also the jarls and the other mighty men, as is said in the *Haleygjatal*. Odin had with him one of his sons called Yngvi, who was king in Sweden after him; and those houses come from him that are named Ynglings. The Æsir took wives of the land for themselves, and some also for their sons; and these kindreds became many in number, so that throughout Saxony, and thence all over the region of the north, they spread out until their tongue, even the speech of the men of Asia, was the native tongue over all these lands. Therefore men think that they can perceive, from their forefathers' names which are written down, that those names belonged to this tongue, and that the Æsir brought the tongue hither into the northern region, into Norway and into Sweden, into Denmark and into Saxony.

170

But in England there are ancient lists of land-names and place-names which may show that these names came from another tongue than this.

Gylfaginning [The Deluding of Gylfi]

I. King Gylfi ruled the land that men now call Sweden. It is told of him that he gave to a wandering woman, in return for her merry-making, a plow-land in his realm, as much as four oxen might turn up in a day and a night. But this woman was of the kin of the Æsir; she was named Gefiun. She took from the north, out of Jotunheim [Giantland], four oxen which were the soils of a certain giant and, herself, and set them before the plow. And the plow cut so wide and so deep that it loosened up the land; and the oxen drew the land out into the sea and to the westward, and stopped in a certain sound. There Gefiun set the land, and gave it a name, calling it Zealand. And from that time on, the spot whence the land had been torn up is water: it is now called "The Lake" in Sweden; and bays lie in that lake even as the headlands in Zealand. Thus says Bragi, the ancient skald:

> Gefiun drew from Gylfi gladly the wave-trove's free-hold,
> Till from the running beasts sweat reeked, to Denmark's increase;
> The oxen bore, moreover, eight eyes, gleaming brow-lights,
> O'er the field's wide booty, and four heads in their plowing.

II. King Gylfi was a wise man and skilled in magic; he was much troubled that the Æsir-people were so cunning that all things went according to their will. He pondered whether this might proceed from their own nature, or whether the divine powers which they worshipped might ordain such things. He set out on his way to Asgard, going secretly, and clad himself in the likeness of an old man, with which he dissembled. But the Æsir were wiser in this matter, having second sight; and they saw his journeying before ever he came, and prepared against him deceptions of the eye. When he came into the town, he saw there a hall so high that he could not easily make out the top of it: its thatching was laid with golden shields after the fashion of a shingled roof. So also says Thjodolf of Hvinir, that Valhall was thatched with shields:

> On their backs they let beam, sore battered with stones,
> Odin's hall-shingles, the shrewd sea-farers.

In the hall-doorway Gylfi saw a man juggling with anlaces [knives], having seven in the air at one time. This man asked of him his name. He called himself Gangleri, and said he had come by the paths of the serpent, and prayed for lodging for the night, asking: "Who owns the hall?" The other replied that it was their king; "and I will attend thee to see him; then shalt thou thyself ask him concerning his name;" and the man wheeled about before him into the hall, and he went after, and straightway the door closed itself on his heels. There he saw a great room and much people, some with games, some drinking; and some had weapons and were fighting. Then he looked about him, and thought unbelievable many things which he saw; and he said:

> All the gateways ere one goes out
>   Should one scan:
> For 'tis uncertain where sit the unfriendly
>   On the bench before thee.

He saw three high-seats, each above the other, and three men sat thereon, one on each. And he asked what might be the name of those lords. He who had conducted him in answered that the one who, sat on the nethermost high-seat was a king, "and his name is Har [High]; but the next is named Jafnhar [Equally High]; and he who is uppermost is called Thridi [Third]." Then Har asked the newcomer whether his errand were more than for the meat and drink which were always at his command, as for every one there in the Hall of the High One. He answered that he first desired to learn whether there were any wise man there within. Har said, that he should not escape whole from thence unless he were wiser.

> And stand thou forth who speirest [asks];
> Who answers, he shall sit.

III. Gangleri began his questioning thus: "Who is foremost, or oldest, of all the gods?" Har answered: "He is called in our speech All-father, but in the Old Asgard he had twelve names: one is All-father; the second is Herran [Lord] or Herjan [Raider]; the third is Nikar, or Spear-Lord; the fourth is Nikuz, or Striker; the fifth is Knower of Many Things; the sixth, Fulfiller of Wishes; the seventh, Far-Speaking One; the eighth, The Shaker, or He that Putteth the Armies to Flight; the ninth, The Burner; the tenth, The Destroyer; the eleventh, The Protector; the twelfth, Gelding."

Then asked Gangleri: "Where is this god, or what power hath he, or what hath he wrought that is a glorious deed?" Har made answer: "He lives throughout all ages and governs all his realm, and directs all things, great and small." Then said Jafnhar: "He fashioned heaven and earth and air, and all things which are in them." Then spake Thridi: "The greatest of all is this: that he made man, and gave him the spirit, which shall live and never perish, though the flesh-frame rot to mould, or burn to ashes; and all men shall live, such as are just in action, and be with himself in the place called Gimle. But evil men go to Hel and thence down to Niflhel; and that is down in the ninth world." Then said Gangleri: "What did he before heaven and earth were made?" And Har answered: "He was then with the Frost-Giants."

IV. Gangleri said: "What was the beginning, or how began it, or what was before it?" Har answered: "As is told in *Voluspa* [The Wise-woman's Prophecy]:

Erst was the age when nothing was:
Nor sand nor sea, nor chilling stream-waves;
Earth was not found, nor Ether-Heaven, —
A Yawning Gap, but grass was none."

Then said Jafnhar: "It was many ages before the earth was shaped that the Mist-World was made; and midmost within it lies the well that is called Hvergelmir, from which spring the rivers called Svol, Gunnthra, Fjorm, Fimbulthul, Slid and Hrid, Sylg and Ylg, Vid, Leipt; Gjoll is hard by Hel-gates." And Thridi said: "Yet first was the world in the southern region, which was named Muspell; it is light and hot; that region is glowing and burning, and impassable to such as are outlanders and have not their holdings there. He who sits there at the land's-end, to defend the land, is called Surt; he brandishes a flaming sword, and at the end of the world he shall go forth and harry, and overcome all the gods, and burn all the world with fire; thus is said in *Voluspa*:

Surt fares from the south with switch-eating flame, —
On his sword shimmers the sun of the War-Gods;
The rock-crags crash; the fiends are reeling;
Heroes tread Hel-way; Heaven is cloven."

V. Gangleri asked: "How were things wrought, ere the races were and the tribes of men increased?" Then said Har: "The streams called Ice-waves, those which were so long come from the fountain-heads that the yeasty venom upon them had hardened like the slag that runs out of the fire, —these then became ice; and when the ice halted and ceased to run, then it froze over above. But the drizzling rain that rose from the venom congealed to rime, and the rime increased, frost over frost, each over the other, even into Ginnungagap, the Yawning Void." Then spake Jafnhar: "Ginnungagap, which faced toward the northern quarter, became filled with heaviness, and masses of ice and rime, and from within, drizzling rain and gusts; but the southern part of the Yawning Void was lighted by those sparks and glowing masses which flew out of Muspellheim." And Thridi said: "Just as cold arose out of Niflheim, and all terrible things, so also all that looked toward Muspellheim became hot and glowing; but Ginnungagap was as mild as windless air, and when the breath of heat met the rime, so that it melted and dripped, life was quickened from the yeast-drops, by the power of that which sent the heat, and became a man's form. And that man is named Ymir, but the Frost-Giants call him Aurgelimir; and thence are come the races of the Frost-Giants, as it says in *The Shorter Voluspa*:

All the witches spring from Vitolf,
All the warlocks are of Vilmeid,
And the spell-singers spring from Svarthofdi;
All the giants of Ymir come.

But concerning this says Vafthrudnir the giant:

Out of the Ice-waves issued venom-drops,
Waxing until a giant was;
Thence are our kindred come all together, —
So it is they are savage forever."

Then said Gangleri: "How did the races grow thence, or after what fashion was it brought to pass that more men came into being? Or do ye hold him God, of whom ye but now spake?" And Jafnhar answered: "By no means do we acknowledge him God; he was evil and all his kindred: we call them Frost-Giants. Now it is said that when he slept, a sweat came upon him, and there grew under his left hand a man and a woman, and one of his feet begat a son with the other; and thus the races are come; these are the Frost-Giants. The old Frost-Giant, him we call Ymir."

VI. Then said Gangleri: "Where dwelt Ymir, or wherein did he find sustenance?" Har answered: "Straightway after the rime dripped, there sprang from it the cow called Audhumla; four streams of milk ran from her udders, and she nourished Ymir." Then asked Gangleri: "Wherewithal was the cow nourished?" And Har made answer: "She licked the ice-blocks, which were salty; and the first day that she licked the blocks, there came forth from the blocks in the evening a man's hair; the second day, a man's head; the third day the whole man was there. He is named Buri: he was fair of feature, great and mighty. He begat a son called Bor, who wedded the woman named Bestla, daughter of Bolthorn the giant; and they had three sons: one was Odin, the second Vili, the third Ve. And this is my belief, that he, Odin, with his brothers, must be ruler of heaven and earth; we hold that he must be so called; so is that man called whom we know to be mightiest and most worthy of honor, and ye do well to let him be so called."

VII. Then said Gangleri: "What covenant was between them, or which was the stronger?" And Har answered: "The sons of Bor slew Ymir the giant; lo, where he fell there gushed forth so much blood out of his wounds that with it they drowned all the race of the Frost-Giants, save that one, whom giants call Bergelmir, escaped with his household; he went upon his ship [ark], and his wife with him, and they were safe there. And from them are come the races of the Frost-Giants, as is said here:

Untold ages ere earth was shapen,
Then was Bergelmir born;

That first I recall, how the famous wise giant
On the deck of the ship was laid down."

VIII. Then said Gangleri: "What was done then by Bor's sons, if thou believe that they be gods?" Har replied: "In this matter there is no little to be said. They took Ymir and bore him into the middle of the Yawning Void, and made of him the earth: of his blood the sea and the waters; the land was made of his flesh, and the crags of his bones; gravel and stones they fashioned from his teeth and his grinders and from those bones that were broken." And Jafnhar said: "Of the blood, which ran and welled forth freely out of his wounds, they made the sea, when they had formed and made firm the earth together, and laid the sea in a ring round. about her; and it may well seem a hard thing to most men to cross over it." Then said Thridi: "They took his skull also, and made of it the heaven, and set it up over the earth with four corners; and under each corner they set a dwarf: the names of these are East, West, North, and South. Then they took the glowing embers and sparks that burst forth and had been cast out of Muspellheim, and set them in the midst of the Yawning Void, in the heaven, both above and below, to illumine heaven and earth. They assigned places to all fires: to some in heaven, some wandered free under the heavens; nevertheless, to these also they gave a place, and shaped them courses. It is said in old songs, that from these the days were reckoned, and the tale of years told, as is said in *Voluspa*:

The sun knew not where she had housing;
The moon knew not what might he had;
The stars knew not where stood their places.
Thus was it ere the earth was fashioned."

Then said Gangleri: These are great tidings which I now hear; that is a wondrous great piece of craftsmanship, and cunningly made. How was the earth contrived?" And Har answered: "She is ring-shaped without, and round about her without lieth the deep sea; and along the strand of that sea they gave lands to the races of giants for habitation. But on the inner earth they made a citadel round about the world against the hostility of the giants, and for their citadel they raised up the brows of Ymir the giant, and called that place Midgard. They took also his brain and cast it in the air, and made from it the clouds, as is here said:

Of Ymir's flesh the earth was fashioned,
    And of his sweat the sea;
Crags of his bones, trees of his hair,
    And of his skull the sky.
Then of his brows the blithe gods made
    Midgard for sons of men;
And of his brain the bitter-mooded
    Clouds were all created."

IX. Then said Gangleri: "Much indeed they had accomplished then, methinks, when earth and heaven were made, and the sun and the constellations of heaven were fixed, and division was made of days; now whence come the men that people the world?" And Har answered: "When the sons of Bor were walking along the sea-strand, they found two trees, and took up the trees and shaped men of them: the first gave them spirit and life; the second, wit and feeling; the third, form, speech, hearing, and sight. They gave them clothing and names: the male was called Ask, and the female Embla, and of them was mankind begotten, which received a dwelling-place under Midgard. Next they made for themselves in the middle of the world a city which is called Asgard; men call it Troy. There dwelt the gods and their kindred; and many tidings and tales of it have come to pass both on earth and aloft. There is one abode called Hlidskjalf, and when All-father sat in the high-seat there, he looked out over the whole world and saw every man's acts, and knew all things which he saw. His wife was called Frigg daughter of Fjorgvin; and of their blood is come that kindred which we call the races of the Æsir, that have peopled the Elder Asgard, and those kingdoms which pertain to it; and that is a divine race. For this reason must he be called All-father: because he is father of all the gods and of men, and of all that was fulfilled of him and of his might. The Earth was his daughter and his wife; on her he begot the first son, which is Asa-Thor: strength and prowess attend him, wherewith he overcometh all living things.

X. "Norfi or Narfi is the name of a giant that dwelt in Jotunheim: he had a daughter called Night; she was swarthy and dark, as befitted her race. She was given to the man named Naglfari; their son was Aud. Afterward she was wedded to him that was called Annar;

Iord [Earth] was their daughter. Last of all Delling had her, and he was of the race of the Æsir; their son was Day: he was radiant and fair after his father. Then All-father took Night, and Day her son, and gave to them two horses and two chariots, and sent them up into the heavens, to ride round about the earth every two half-days. Night rides before with the horse named Hrimfaxi [frosty-mane], and on each morning he bedews the earth with the foam from his bit. The horse that Day has is called Skinfaxi [shining-mane], and he illumines all the air and the earth from his mane."

XI. Then said Gangleri: "How does he govern the course of the sun or of the moon?" Har answered: "A certain man was named Mundilfari, who had two children; they were so fair and comely that he called his son Moon, and his daughter Sun, and wedded her to the man called Glen. But the gods were incensed at that insolence, and took the brother and sister, and set them up in the heavens; they caused Sun to drive those horses that drew the chariot of the sun, which the gods had fashioned, for the world's illumination, from that glowing stuff which flew out of Muspellheim. Those horses are called thus: Arvak and Alsvinn; and under the shoulders of the horses the gods set two wind-bags to cool them, but in some records that is called 'iron-coolness.' Moon steers the course of the moon, and determines its waxing and waning. He took from the earth two children, called Bil and Hjuki, they that went from the well called Byrgir, bearing on their shoulders the cask called Sæg, and the pole Simul. Their father is named Vidfinn. These children follow Moon, as may be seen from the earth."

XII. Then said Gangleri: "The sun fares swiftly, and almost as if she were afraid: she could not hasten her course any the more if she feared her destruction." Then Har made answer: "It is no marvel that she hastens furiously: close cometh he that seeks her, and she has no escape save to run away." Then said Gangleri: "Who is he that causes her this disquiet?" Har replied: "It is two wolves; and he that runs after her is called Skoll; she fears him, and he shall take her. But he that leaps before her is called Hati Hrodvitnisson. He is eager to seize the moon; and so it must be." Then said Gangleri: "What is the race of the wolves?" Har answered: "A witch dwells to the east of Midgard, in the forest called Ironwood: in that wood dwell the troll-women, who are known as Ironwood-Women. The old witch bears many giants for sons, and all in the shape of wolves; and from this source are these wolves sprung. The saying runs thus: from this race shall come one that shall be mightiest of all, he that is named Moongarm [Moonhound]; he shall be filled with the flesh of all those men that die, and he shall swallow the moon, and sprinkle with blood the heavens and all the lair; thereof shall the sun lose her shining, and the winds in that day shall be unquiet and roar on every side. So it says in *Voluspa*:

Eastward dwells the Old One in Ironwood,
And there gives birth to Fenrir's brethren;
There shall spring of them all a certain one,
The moon's taker in troll's likeness.

He is filled with flesh of fey men.
Reddens the gods' seats with ruddy blood-gouts;
Swart becomes sunshine in summers after,
The weather all shifty. Wit ye yet, or what?"

XIII. Then said Gangleri: "What is the way to heaven from earth?" Then Har answered, and laughed aloud: "Now, that is not wisely asked; has it not been told thee, that the gods made a bridge from earth, to heaven, called Bifrost? Thou must have seen it; it may be that ye call it rainbow.' It is of three colors, and very strong, and made with cunning and with more magic art than other works of craftsmanship. But strong as it is, yet must it be broken, when the sons of Muspell shall go forth harrying and ride it, and swim their horses over great rivers; thus they shall proceed." Then said Gangleri: "To my thinking the gods did not build the bridge honestly, seeing that it could be broken, and they able to make it as they would." Then Har replied: "The gods are not deserving of reproof because of this work of skill: a good

177

bridge is Bifrost, but nothing in this world is of such nature that it may be relied on when the sons of Muspell go a-harrying."

XIV. Then said Gangleri: "What did All-father then do when Asgard was made?" Har answered: "In the beginning he established rulers, and bade them ordain fates with him, and give counsel concerning the planning of the town; that was in the place which is called Ida-field, in the midst of the town. It was their first work to make that court in which their twelve seats stand, and another, the high-seat which All-father himself has. That house is the best-made of any on earth, and the greatest; without and within, it is all like one piece of gold; men call it Gladsheim. They made also a second hall: that was a shrine which the goddesses had, and it was a very fair house; men call it Vingolf. Next they fashioned a house, wherein they placed a forge, and made besides a hammer, tongs, and anvil, and by means of these, all other tools. After this they smithied metal and stone and wood, and wrought so abundantly that metal which is called gold, that they had all their household ware and all dishes of gold; and that time is called the Age of Gold, before it was spoiled by the coming of the Women, even those who came out of Jotunheim. Next after this, the gods enthroned themselves in their seats and held judgment, and called to mind whence the dwarves had quickened in the mould and underneath in the earth, even as do maggots in flesh. The dwarves had first received shape and life in the flesh of Ymir, and were then maggots; but by decree of the gods had become conscious with the intelligence of men, and had human shape. And nevertheless they dwell in the earth and in stones. Modsognir was the first, and Durin the second; so it says in *Voluspa*.

Then strode all the mighty to the seats of judgment,
The gods most holy, and together held counsel,
Who should of dwarves shape the peoples
From the bloody surge and the Blue One's bones. They made many in man's likeness, Dwarves in the earth, as Durin said.

And these, says the Sibyl, are their names:

Nyi and Nidi, Nordri and Sudri,
Austri, Vestri, Althjof, Dvalin;
Nar, Nain, Niping, Dain,
Bifur, Bafur, Bombur, Nori,
Ori, Onar, Oin, Mjodvitnir,
Vigg and Gandalf, Vindalf, Thorin,
Fili, Kili, Fundin, Vali;
Thror, Throin, Thekk, Lit and Vit,
Nyr, Nyrad, Rekk, Radsvid.

And these also are dwarves and dwell in stones, but the first in mould:

Draupnir, Dolgthvari,
Hor, Hugstari, Hledjolf, Gloin;
Dori, Ori, Duf, Andvari,
Heptifili, Har, Sviar.

And these proceed from Svarinshaug to Aurvangar on Joruplain, and thence is Lovar come; these are their names:

Skirfir, Virfir Skafidr, Ai,
Alf, Yngvi, Eikinskjaldi,
Fal, Frosti, Fid, Ginnar."

XV. Then said Gangleri: "Where is the chief abode or holy place of the gods?" Har answered: "That is at the Ash of Yggdrasil; there the gods must give judgment everyday." Then Gangleri asked: "What is to be said concerning that place?" Then said Jafnhar: "The Ash is greatest of all trees and best: its limbs spread out over all the world and stand above heaven. Three roots of the tree uphold it and stand exceeding broad: one is among the Æsir; another among the Frost-Giants, in that place where aforetime was the Yawning Void; the third stands over Niflheim, and under that root is Hvergelmir, and Nidhogg gnaws the root from below. But under that root which turns toward the Frost-Giants is Mimir's Well, wherein wisdom and understanding are stored; and he is called Mimir, who keeps the well. He is full of ancient lore, since he drinks of the well from the Gjallar-Horn. Thither came All-father and craved one drink of the well; but he got it not until he had laid his eye in pledge. So says *Voluspa*:

All know I, Odin, where the eye thou hiddest,
In the wide-renowned well of Mimir;
Mimir drinks mead every morning
From Valfather's wage. Wit ye yet, or what?

The third root of the Ash stands in heaven; and under that root is the well which is very holy, that is called the Well of Urd; there the gods hold their tribunal. Each day the Æsir ride thither up over Bifrost, which is also called the Æsir's Bridge. These are the names of the Æsir's steeds: Sleipnir [The Slipper] is best, which Odin has; he has eight feet. The second is Glad [Bright or Glad], the third Gyllir [Golden], the fourth Glær [Starer], the fifth Skeidbrimir [Fleet Courser], the sixth Silfrintopp [Silver-top], the seventh Sinir [Sinewy], the eighth Gisl [Beam, Ray], the ninth Falhofnir [Hairy-hoof], the tenth. Gulltopp [Gold-top], the eleventh Lettfeti [Light-stepper]. Baldr's horse was burnt with him; and Thor walks to the judgment, and wades those rivers which are called thus:

179

Kormt and Ormt and the Kerlaugs twain,
   Them shall Thor wade
Every day when he goes to doom
   At Ash Yggdrasil;
For the Æsir's Bridge burns all with flame,
   And the holy waters howl."

Then said Gangleri: "Does fire burn over Bifrost?" Har replied: "That which thou seest to be red in the bow is burning fire; the Hill-Giants might go up to heaven, if passage on Bifrost were open to all those who would cross. There are many fair places in heaven, and over everything there a godlike watch is kept. A hall stands there, fair, under the ash by the well, and out of that hall come three maids, who are called thus: Urd [Past], Verdandi [Present], Skuld [Future]; these maids determine the period of men's lives: we call them Norns; but there are many norns: those who come to each child that is born, to appoint his life; these are of the race of the gods, but the second are of the Elf-people, and the third are of the kindred of the dwarves, as it is said here:

   Most sundered in birth I say the Norns are;
      They claim no common kin:
   Some are of Æsir-kin, some are of Elf-kind,
      Some are Dvalin's daughters."

Then said Gangleri: "If the Norns determine the weirds of men, then they apportion exceeding unevenly, seeing that some have a pleasant and luxurious life, but others have little worldly goods or fame; some have long life, others short." Har said: "Good norns and of honorable race appoint good life; but those men that suffer evil fortunes are governed by evil norns."

XVI. Then said Gangleri: "What more mighty wonders are to be told of the Ash?" Har replied: "Much is to be told of it. An eagle sits in the limbs of the Ash, and he has understanding of many a thing; and between his eyes sits the hawk that is called Vedrfolnir. The squirrel called Ratatosk runs up and down the length of the Ash, bearing envious words between the eagle and Nidhogg; and four harts run in the limbs of the Ash and bite the leaves. They are called thus: Dain, Dvalin, Duneyr, Durathror. Moreover, so many serpents are in Hvergelmir with Nidhogg, that no tongue can tell them, as is here said:

   Ash Yggdrasil suffers anguish,
      More than men know of:
   The stag bites above; on the side it rotteth,
      And Nidhogg gnaws from below.

And it is further said:

More serpents lie under Yggdrasil's stock
    Than every unwise ape can think:
Goin and Moin (they're Grafvitnir's sons),
    Grabak and Grafvollud;
Ofnir and Svafnir I think shall aye
    Tear the trunk's twigs.

It is further said that these Norns who dwell by the Well of Urd take water of the well every day, and with it that clay which lies about the well, and sprinkle it over the Ash, to the end that its limbs shall not wither nor rot; for that water is so holy that all things which come there into the well become as white as the film which lies within the egg-shell, —as is here said:

I know an Ash standing called Yggdrasil,
    A high tree sprinkled with snow-white clay;
Thence come the dews in the dale that fall —
    It stands ever green above Urd's Well.

That dew which falls from it onto the earth is called by men honey-dew, and thereon are bees nourished. Two fowls are fed in Urd's Well: they are called Swans, and from those fowls has come the race of birds which is so called."

XVII. Then said Gangleri: "Thou knowest many tidings to tell of the heaven. What chief abodes are there more than at Urd's Well?" Har said: "Many places are there, and glorious. That which is called Alfheim [Elf-home] is one, where dwell the peoples called Light-Elves; but the Dark-Elves dwell down in the earth, and they are unlike in appearance, but by far more unlike in nature. The Light-Elves are fairer to look upon than the sun, but the Dark-Elves are blacker than pitch. Then there is also in that place the abode called Breidablik [Broad-gleaming], and there is not in heaven a fairer dwelling. There, too, is the one called Glitnir [Glittering], whose walls, and all its posts and pillars, are of red gold, but its roof of silver. There is also the abode called Himinbjörg [Heaven-crag]; it stands at heaven's end by the bridge-head, in the place where Bifrost joins heaven. Another great abode is there, which is named Valaskjalf [Seat or shelf of the Fallen]; Odin possesses that dwelling; the gods made it and thatched it with sheer silver, and in this hall is the Hlidskjalf [Gate-seat], the high-seat so called. Whenever All-father sits in that seat, he surveys all lands. At the southern end of heaven is that hall which is fairest of all, and brighter than the sun; it is called Gimle. It shall stand when both heaven and earth have departed; and good men and of righteous conversation shall dwell therein: so it is said in *Voluspa*:

A hall I know standing than the sun fairer,
Thatched with gold in Gimle bright;
There shall dwell the doers of righteousness
And ever and ever enjoy delight."

Then said Gangleri: "What shall guard this place, when the flame of Surt shall consume heaven and earth?" Har answered: "It is sad that another heaven is to the southward and upward of this one, and it is called Andlang [Wide-reaching, extensive]; but the third heaven is yet above that, and it is called Vidblain [Wide-blue], and in that heaven we think this abode is. But we believe that none but Light-Elves inhabit these mansions now."

XVIII. Then said Gangleri: "Whence comes the wind? It is strong, so that it stirs great seas, and it swells fire; but, strong as it is, none may see it, for it is wonderfully shapen." Then said Har: "That I am well able to tell thee. At the northward end of heaven sits the giant called Hræsvelg: he has the plumes of an eagle, and when he stretches his wings for flight, then the wind rises from under his wings, as is here said:

Hræsvelgr is he called who sits at heaven's ending,
Giant in eagle's coat;
From his wings, they say, the wind cometh
All men-folk over."

XIX. Then said Gangleri: "Why is there so much difference, that summer should be hot, but winter cold?" Har answered: "A wise man would not ask thus, seeing that all are able to tell this; but if thou alone art become-so slight of understanding as not to have heard it, then I will yet permit that thou shouldst rather ask foolishly once, than that thou shouldst be kept longer in ignorance of a thing which it is proper to know. He is called Svasud [Delightful] who is father of Summer; and he is of pleasant nature, so that from his name whatsoever is pleasant is called 'sweet.'

But the father of Winter is variously called Vindljoni [Wind-bringer] or Vindsval [Wind-chill]; he is the son of Vasad [Wet and sleety]; and these were kinsmen grim and chilly-breasted, and Winter has their temper."

XX. Then said Gangleri: "Who are the Æsir, they in whom it behoves men to believe?" Har answered: "The divine Æsir are twelve." Then said Jafnhar: "Not less holy are the Asynjur, the goddesses, and they are of no less authority." Then said Thridi: "Odin is highest and eldest of the Æsir: he rules all things, and mighty as are the other gods, they all serve him as children obey a father. Frigg is his wife, and she knows all the fates of men, though she speaks no prophecy, — as is said here, when Odin himself spake with him of the Æsir whom men call Loki:

Thou art mad now, Loki, and reft of mind,—
   Why, Loki, leav'st thou not off?
Frigg, methinks, is wise in all fates,
   Though herself say them not!

Odin is called All-father because he is father of all the gods. He is also called Father of the Slain, because all those that fall in battle are the sons of his adopt on; for them he appoints Valhall [Hall of the Slain] and Vingolf [Friendly Floor], and they are then called Champions. He is also called God of the Hanged, God of Gods, God of Cargoes; and he has also been named in many more ways, after he had come to King Geirrod:

We were called Grim and Gangleri,
   Herjan, Hjalmberi;
Thekk, Thridi, Thud, Ud,
   Helblindi, Har.

Sad, Svipal, Sann-getal,
   Herteit, Hnikar;
Bileyg, Baleyg, Bolverk, Fjolnir,
   Grimnir, Glapsvid, Fjolsvid.

Sidhott, Sidskegg, Sigfod, Hnikud,
   Alfod, Atrid, Farmatyr;
Oski, Omi, Jafnhar, Biflindi,
   Gondlir, Harbard.

Svidur, Svidrir, Jalk, Kjalar, Vidur,
   Thror, Ygg, Thund;
Vak, Skilfing, Vafud, Hroptatyr,
   Gaut, Veratyr."

Then said Gangleri: "Exceeding many names have ye given him; and, by my faith, it must indeed be a goodly wit that knows all the lore and the examples of what chances have brought about each of these names." Then Har made answer: "It is truly a vast sum of knowledge to gather together and set forth fittingly. But it is briefest to tell thee that most of his names have been given him by reason of this chance: there being so many branches of tongues in the world, all peoples believed that it was needful for them to turn his name into their own tongue, by which they might the better invoke him and entreat him on their own behalf. But some occasions for these names arose in his wanderings; and that matter is recorded in tales. Nor canst thou ever be called a wise man if thou shalt not be able to tell of those great events."

XXI. Then said Gangleri: "What are the names of the other Æsir, or what is their office, or what deeds of renown have they done?" Har answered: "Thor is the foremost of them, he that is called Thor of the Æsir, or Oku-Thor; he is strongest of all the gods and men. He has his realm in the place called Thrudvangar [Plains of Strength] and his hall is called Bilskirnir; in that hall are five hundred rooms and forty. That is the greatest house that men know of; it is thus said in *Grimnismal* [The Ballad of Grimnir]:

> Five hundred floors and more than forty,
>   So reckon I Bilskirnir with bending ways;
> Of those houses that I know of hall-roofed,
>   My son's I know the most.

Thor has two he-goats, that are called Tooth-Gnasher and Tooth-Gritter, and a chariot wherein he drives, and the he-goats draw the chariot; therefore is he called Oku-Thor. He has also three things of great price: one is the hammer Mjollnir, which the Frost-Giants and the Hill-Giants know, when it is raised on high; and that is no wonder, it has bruised many a skull among their fathers or their kinsmen. He has a second costly thing, best of all: the girdle of might; and when he clasps it about him, then the godlike strength within him is increased by half. Yet a third thing he has, in which there is much virtue: his iron gloves; he cannot do without them when he uses his hammer-shaft. But no one is so wise that he can tell all his mighty works; yet I can tell thee so much tidings of him that the hours would be spent before all that I know were told."

XXII. Then said Gangleri: "I would ask tidings of more Æsir." Har replied: "The second son of Odin is Baldr, and good things are to be said of him. He is best, and all praise him; he is so fair of feature, and so bright, that light shines from him. A certain herb is so white that it is likened to Baldr's brow; of all grasses it is whitest, and by it thou mayest judge his fairness, both in hair and in body. He is the wisest of the Æsir, and the fairest-spoken and most gracious; and that quality attends him, that none may gainsay his judgments. He dwells in the place called Breidablik, which is in heaven; in that place may nothing unclean be, even as is said here:

> Breidablik 'tis called, where Baldr has
>   A hall made for himself:
> In that land where I know lie
>   Fewest baneful runes.

XXIII. "The third among the Æsir is he that is called Njord: he dwells in heaven, in the abode called Noatun. He rules the course of the wind, and stills sea and fire; on him shall men call for voyages and for hunting. He is so prosperous and abounding in wealth, that he may give them great plenty of lands or of gear; and him shall men invoke for such things. Njord is not of the race of the Æsir: he was reared in the land of the Vanir, but the Vanir delivered him as hostage to the gods, and took for hostage in exchange him that men call Hœnir; he became an atonement between the gods and the Vanir. Njord has to wife the woman called Skadi, daughter of Thjazi the giant. Skadi would fain dwell in the abode which her father had had, which is on certain mountains, in the place called Thrymheim; but Njord would be near the sea. They made a compact on these terms: they should be nine nights in Thrymheim, but the second nine at Noatun. But when Njord came down from the mountain back to Noatun, he sang this lay:

> Loath were the hills to me, I was not long in them,
>   Nights only nine;
> To me the wailing of wolves seemed ill,
>   After the song of swans.

Then Skadi sang this:

> Sleep could I never on the sea-beds,
>   For the wailing of waterfowl;
> He wakens me, who comes from the deep —
>   The sea-mew every morn.

Then Skadi went up onto the mountain, and dwelt in Thrymheim. And she goes for the more part on snowshoes and with a bow and arrow, and shoots beasts; she is called Snowshoe-Goddess or Lady of the Snowshoes. So it is said:

> Thrymheim 'tis called, where Thjazi dwelt,
>   He the hideous giant;
> But now Skadi abides, pure bride of the gods,
>   In her father's ancient freehold.

XXIV. "Njord in Noatun begot afterward two children: the son was called Freyr, and the daughter Freyja; they were fair of face and mighty. Freyr is the most renowned of the Æsir; he rules over the rain and the shining of the sun, and therewithal the fruit of the earth; and it is good to call on him for fruitful seasons and peace. He governs also the prosperity of men. But Freyja is the most renowned of the goddesses; she has in heaven the dwelling called Folkvanga [Folk-plain], and wheresoever she rides to the strife, she has one-half of the kill, and Odin half, as is here said:

> Folkvanga 'tis called, where Freyja rules
>   Degrees of seats in the hall;

Half the kill she keepeth each day,
And half Odin hath.

Her hall Sessrumnir [Seat-roomy] is great and fair. When she goes forth, she drives her cats and sits in a chariot; she is most conformable to man's prayers, and from her name comes the name of honor, Fru, by which noblewomen are called. Songs of love are well-pleasing to her; it is good to call on her for furtherance in love."

XXV. Then said Gangleri: "Great in power do these Æsir seem to me; nor is it a marvel, that much authority attends you who are said to possess understanding of the gods, and know which one men should call on for what boon soever. Or are the gods yet more?" Har said: "Yet remains that one of the Æsir who is called Tyr: he is most daring, and best in stoutness of heart, and he has much authority over victory in battle; it is good for men of valor to invoke him. It is a proverb, that he is Tyr-valiant, who surpasses other men and does not waver. He is wise, so that it is also said, that he that is wisest is Tyr-prudent. This is one token of his daring: when the Æsir enticed Fenris-Wolf to take upon him the fetter Gleipnir, the wolf did not believe them, that they would loose him, until they laid Tyr's hand into his mouth as a pledge. But when the Æsir would not loose him, then he bit off the hand at the place now called 'the wolf's joint;' and Tyr is one-handed, and is not called a reconciler of men.

XXVI. "One is called Bragi: he is renowned for wisdom, and most of all for fluency of speech and skill with words. He knows most of skaldship, and after him skaldship is called *brag*, and from his name that one is called *brag*-man or -woman, who possesses eloquence surpassing others, of women or of men. His wife is Idun: she guards in her chest of ash those apples which the gods must taste whensoever they grow old; and then they all become young, and so it shall be even unto Ragnarok." Then said Gangleri: "A very great thing, methinks, the gods entrust to the watchfulness and good faith of Idun." Then said Har, laughing loudly: "'Twas near being desperate once; I may be able to tell thee of it, but now thou shalt first hear more of the names of the Æsir.

XXVII. "Heimdall is the name of one: he is called the White God. He is great and holy; nine maids, all sisters, bore him for a son. He is also called Hallinskidi [Ram] and Gullintanni [Golden-teeth]; his teeth were of gold, and his horse is called Gold-top. He dwells in the place called Himinbjorg [Heaven-fells], hard by Bifrost: he is the warder of the gods, and sits there by heaven's end to guard the bridge from the Hill-Giants. He needs less sleep than a bird; he sees equally well night and day a hundred leagues from him, and hears how grass grows on the earth or wool on sheep, and everything that has a louder sound. He has that trumpet which is called Gjallar-Horn, and its blast is heard throughout all worlds. Heimdall's sword is called Head. It is said further:

Himinbjorg 'tis called, where Heimdall, they say,
    Aye has his housing;
There the gods' sentinel drinks in his snug hall
    Gladly good mead.

And furthermore, he himself says in *Heimdalar-galdr* [Heimdall's Spell]:

I am of nine mothers the offspring,
Of sisters nine am I the son.

XXVIII. "One of the Æsir is named Hod: he is blind. He is of sufficient strength, but the gods would desire that no occasion should rise of naming this god, for the work of his hands shall long be held in memory among gods and men.

XXIX. "Vidar is the name of one, the silent god. He has a thick shoe. He is nearly as strong as Thor; in him the gods have great trust in all struggles.

XXX. "One is called Ali or Vali, son of Odin and Rind: he is daring in fights, and a most fortunate marksman.

XXXI. "One is called Ull, son of Sif, step-son of Thor; he is so excellent a bowman, and so swift on snowshoes, that none may contend with him. He is also fair of aspect and has the accomplishments of a warrior; it is well to call on him in single-combats.

XXXII. "Forseti is the name of the son of Baldr and Nanna daughter of Nep: he has that hall in heaven which is called Glitnir. All that come to him with such quarrels as arise out of law-suits, all these return thence reconciled. That is the best seat of judgment among gods and men; thus it is said here:

A hall is called Glitnir, with gold 'tis pillared,
    And with silver thatched the same;
There Forseti bides the full day through,
    And puts to sleep all suits.

XXXIII. "Also numbered among the Æsir is he whom some call the mischief-monger of the Æsir, and the first father of falsehoods, and blemish of all gods and men: he is named Loki or Lopt, son of Farbauti the giant; his mother was Laufey or Nal; his brothers are Byleist and Helblindi. Loki is beautiful and comely to look upon, evil in spirit, very fickle in habit. He surpassed other men in that wisdom which is called 'sleight,' and had artifices for all occasions; he would ever bring the Æsir into great hardships, and then get them out with crafty counsel. His wife was called Sigyn, their son Nari or Narfi.

187

XXXIV. Yet more children had Loki. Angrboda was the name of a certain giantess in Jotunheim, with whom Loki gat three children: one was Fenris-Wolf, the second Jormungand — that is the Midgard Serpent, — the third is Hel. But when the gods learned that this kindred was nourished in Jotunheim, and when the gods perceived by prophecy that from this kindred great misfortune should befall them; and since it seemed to all that there was great prospect of ill — (first from the mother's blood, and yet worse from the father's) — then All-father sent gods thither to take the children and bring them to him. When they came to him, straightway he cast the serpent into the deep sea, where he lies about all the land; and this serpent grew so greatly that he lies in the midst of the ocean encompassing all the land, and bites upon his own tail. Hel he cast into Niflheim, and gave to her power over nine worlds, to apportion all abodes among those that were sent to her: that is, men dead of sickness or of old age. She has great possessions there; her walls are exceeding high and her gates great. Her hall is called Sleet-Cold; her dish, Hunger; Famine is her knife; Idler, her thrall; Sloven, her maidservant; Pit of Stumbling, her threshold, by which one enters; Disease, her bed; Gleaming Bale, her bed-hangings. She is half blue-black and half flesh-color (by which she is easily recognized), and very lowering and fierce.

The Wolf the Æsir brought up at home, and Tyr alone dared go to him to give him meat. But when the gods saw. how much he grew every day, and when all prophecies declared that he was fated to be their destruction, then the Æsir seized upon this way of escape: they made a very strong fetter, which they called Leyding, and brought it before the Wolf, bidding him try his strength against the fetter. The Wolf thought that no overwhelming odds, and let them do with him as they would. The first time the Wolf lashed out against it, the fetter broke; so he was loosed out of Leyding. After this, the Æsir made a second fetter, stronger by half, which they called Dromi, and bade the Wolf try that fetter, saying he would become very famous for strength, if such huge workmanship should not suffice to hold him. But the Wolf thought that this fetter was very strong; he considered also that strength had increased in him since the time he broke Leyding: it came into his mind, that he must expose himself to danger, if he would become famous. So he let the fetter be laid upon him. Now when the Æsir declared themselves ready, the Wolf shook himself, dashed the fetter against the earth and struggled fiercely with it, spurned against it, and broke the fetter, so that the fragments flew far. So he dashed himself out of Dromi. Since then it passes as a proverb, 'to loose out of Leyding,' or 'to dash out of Dromi,' when anything is exceeding hard.

"After that the Æsir feared that they should never be able to get the Wolf bound. Then All-father sent him who is called Skirnir, Freyr's messenger, down into the region of the Black Elves, to certain dwarves, and caused to be made the fetter named Gleipnir. It was made of six things: the noise a cat makes in foot-fall, the beard of a woman, the roots of a rock, the sinews of a bear, the breath of a fish, and the spittle of a bird. And though thou understand not these matters already, yet now thou mayest speedily find certain proof herein, that no lie is told thee: thou must have seen that a woman has no beard, and no sound comes from the leap of a cat, and there are no roots under a rock; and by my troth, all that I have told thee is equally true, though there be some things which thou canst not put to the test."

Then said Gangleri: "This certainly I can perceive to be true: these things which thou hast taken for proof, I can see; but how was the fetter fashioned?" Har answered: "That I am well able to tell thee. The fetter was soft and smooth as a silken ribbon, but as sure and strong as thou shalt now hear. Then, when the fetter was brought to the Æsir, they thanked the messenger well for his errand. Then the Æsir went out upon the lake called Amsvartnir, to the island called Lyngvi, and summoning the Wolf with them, they showed him the silken ribbon and bade him burst it, saying that it was somewhat stouter than appeared from its thickness. And each passed it to the others, and tested it with the strength of their hands and it did not snap; yet they said the Wolf could break it. Then the Wolf answered: 'Touching this matter of the ribbon, it seems to me that I shall get no glory of it, though I snap asunder so slender a band; but if it be made with cunning and wiles, then, though it seem little, that band shall never come upon my feet.' Then the Æsir answered that he could easily snap apart a slight silken band, he who had before broken great fetters of iron, — 'but if thou shalt not be able to burst this band, then thou wilt not be able to frighten the gods; and then we shall unloose thee.' The Wolf said: 'If ye bind me so that I shall not get free again, then ye will act in such a way that it will be late ere I receive help from you; I am unwilling that this band should be laid upon me. Yet rather than that ye should impugn my courage, let some one of you lay his hand in my mouth, for a pledge that this is done in good faith.' Each of the Æsir looked at his neighbor, and none was willing to part with his hand, until Tyr stretched out his right hand and laid it in the Wolf's mouth. But when the Wolf lashed out, the fetter became hardened; and the more he struggled against it, the tighter the band was. Then all laughed except Tyr: he lost his hand.

"When the Æsir saw that the Wolf was fully bound, they took the chain that was fast to the fetter, and which is called Gelgja, and passed it through a great rock — it is called Gjoll — and fixed the rock deep down into the earth. Then they took a great stone and drove it yet deeper into the earth — it was called Thviti — and used the stone for a fastening-pin. The Wolf gaped terribly, and thrashed about and strove to bite them; they thrust into his mouth a certain sword: the guards caught in his lower jaw, and the point in the upper; that is his gag. He howls hideously, and slaver runs out of his mouth: that is the river called Van; there he lies till Ragnarok." Then said Gangleri: "Marvellous ill children did Loki beget, but all these brethren are of great might. Yet why did not the Æsir kill the Wolf, seeing they had expectation of evil from him?" Har answered: "So greatly did the gods esteem their holy place and sanctuary, that they would not stain it with the Wolf's blood; though (so say the prophecies) he shall be the slayer of Odin."

XXXV. Then said Gangleri: "Which are the Asynjur? Har said: "Frigg is the foremost: she has that estate which is called Fensalir, and it is most glorious. The second is Saga: she dwells at Sokkvabekk, and that is a great abode. The third is Fir: she is the best physician. The fourth is Gefjun: she is a virgin, and they that die maidens attend her. The fifth is Fulla: she also is a maid, and goes with loose tresses and a golden band about her head; she bears the ashen coffer of Frigg, and has charge over her footgear, and knows her secret counsel. Freyja is most gently born (together with Frigg): she is wedded to the man named Od. Their daughter is Hnoss: she is so fair, that those things which are fair and precious are called *hnossir* [treasures]. Od went away on long journeys, and Freyja weeps for him, and her tears are red gold. Freyja has many names, and this is the cause thereof: that she gave herself sundry names, when she went out among unknown peoples seeking Od: she is called Mardoll and Horn, Gefn, Syr. Freyja had the necklace Brisinga-men. She is also called Lady of the Vanir. The seventh is Sjofn: she is most diligent in turning the thoughts of men to love, both of women and of men; and from her name love-longing is called *sjafni*. The eighth is Lofn: she is so gracious and kindly to those that call upon her, that she wins All-father's or Frigg's permission for the coming together of mankind in marriage, of women and of men, though it were forbidden before, or seem flatly denied; from her name such permission is called 'leave,' and thus also she is much 'loved' of men. The ninth is Var: she harkens to the oaths and compacts made between men and women; wherefore such covenants are called 'vows.' She also takes vengeance on those who perjure themselves. The tenth is Vor: she is wise and of searching spirit, so that none can conceal anything from her; it is a saying, that a woman becomes 'ware' of that of which she is informed. The eleventh is Syn: she keeps the door in the hall, and locks it before those who should not go in; she is also set at trials as a defence against such suits as she wishes to refute: thence is the expression, that *syn* is set forward, when a man denies. The twelfth is Hlin: she is established as keeper over those men whom Frigg desires to preserve from any danger; thence comes the saying, that he who escapes 'leans.' Snotra is thirteenth: she is prudent and of gentle bearing; from her name a woman or a man who is moderate is called *snotr*. The fourteenth is Gna: her Frigg sends into divers lands on her errands; she has that horse which runs over sky and sea and is called Hofvarpnir [Hoof-Tosser]. Once when she was riding, certain of the Vanir saw her course in the air; then one spake:

> What flieth there? What fareth there,
> Or glideth in the air?

She made answer:

> I fly not, though I fare
> And in the air glide
> On Hofvarpnir, him that Hamskerpir
> Gat with Gardrofa.

From Gna's name that which soars high is said to *gnæfa* [to tower]. Sol and Bil are reckoned among the Asynjur, but their nature has been told before.

XXXVI. "There are also those others whose office it is to serve in Valhall, to bear drink and mind the table-service and ale-flagons; thus are they named in *Grimnismal*:

> Hrist and Mist I would have bear the horn to me,
> Skeggjold and Skogul;
> Hild and Thrud, Hlokk and Herfjotur,
> Goll and Geirahod,
> Randgrid and Radgrid and Reginleif —
> These bear the Einherjar ale.

These are called Valkyries: them Odin sends to every battle; they determine men's feyness and award victory. Gud and Rota and the youngest Norn, she who is called Skuld, ride ever to take the slain and decide fights. Jord, the mother of Thor, and Rind, Vali's mother, are reckoned among the Asynjur.

XXXVII. "A certain man was called Gymir, and his wife Aurboda: she was of the stock of the Hill-Giants; their daughter was Gerd, who was fairest of all women. It chanced one day that Freyr had gone to Hlidskjalf, and gazed over all the world; but when he looked over into the northern region, he saw on an estate a house great and fair. And toward this house went a woman; when she raised her hands and opened the door before her, brightness gleamed from her hands, both over sky and sea, and all the worlds were illumined of her. Thus his overweening pride, in having presumed to sit in that holy seat, was avenged upon him, that he went away full of sorrow. When he had come home, he spake not, he slept not, he drank not; no man dared speak to him. Then Njord summoned to him Skirnir, Freyr's foot-page, and bade him go to Freyr and beg speech of him and ask for whose sake he was so bitter that he would not speak with men. But Skirnir said he would go, albeit unwillingly; and said that evil answers were to be expected of Freyr.

"But when he came to Freyr, straightway he asked why Freyr was so downcast, and spake not with men. Then Freyr answered and said that he had seen a fair woman; and for her sake he was so full of grief that he would not live long if he were not to obtain her. 'And now thou shalt go and woo her on my behalf and have her hither, whether her father will or no. I will reward thee well for it.' Then Skirnir answered thus: he would go on his errand, but Freyr should give him his own sword — which is so good that it fights of itself; — and Freyr did not refuse, but gave him the sword. Then Skirnir went forth and wooed the woman for him, and received her promise; and nine nights later she was to come to the place called Barey, and then go to the bridal with Freyr. But when Skirnir told Freyr his answer, then he sang this lay:

Long is one night, long is the second;
How can I wait through three?
Often a month to me seemed less
Than this one night of waiting.

This was to blame for Freyr's being so weaponless, when he fought with Beli, and slew him with the horn of a hart." Then said Gangleri: "'Tis much to be wondered at, that such a great chief as Freyr is would give away his sword, not having another equally good. It was a great privation to him, when he fought with him called Beli; by my faith, he must have rued that gift." Then answered Har: "There was small matter in that, when he and Beli met; Freyr could have killed him with his hand. It shall come to pass that Freyr will think a worse thing has come upon him, when he misses his sword on that day that the Sons of Muspell go a-harrying."

XXXVIII. Then said Gangleri: "Thou sayest that all those men who have fallen in battle from the beginning of the world are now come to Odin in Valhall. What has he to give them for food? I should think that a very great host must be there." Then Har answered: "That which thou sayest is true: a very mighty multitude is there, but many more shall be, notwithstanding which it will seem all too small, in the time when the Wolf shall come. But never is so vast a multitude in Valhall that the flesh of that boar shall fail, which is called Sæhrimnir; he is boiled every day and is whole at evening. But this question which thou askest now: I think it likelier that few may be so wise as to be able to report truthfully concerning it. His name who roasts is Andhrimnir, and the kettle is Eldhrimnir; so it is said here:

Andhrimnir has in Eldhrimnir
  Sæhrimnir sodden,
Best of hams; yet how few know
  With what food the champions are fed."

Then said Gangleri: "Has Odin the same fare as the champions?" Har answered: "That food which stands on his board he gives to two wolves which he has, called Geri [Ravener] and Freki [Glutton]; but no food does he need; wine is both food and drink to him; so it says here:

Geri and Freki the war-mighty glutteth,
  The glorious God of Hosts;
But on wine alone the weapon-glorious
  Odin aye liveth.

The ravens sit on his shoulders and say into his ear all the tidings which they see or hear; they are called thus: Hugin [Thought] and Munin [Memory]. He sends them at day-break to fly about all the world, and they come back at undern-meal;

thus he is acquainted with many tidings. Therefore men call him Raven-God, as is said:

> Hugin and Munin hover each day
>   The wide earth over;
> I fear for Hugin lest he fare not back, —
>   Yet watch I more for Munin."

XXXIX. Then said Gangleri: "What have the champions to drink, that may suffice them as abundantly as the food? Or is water drunk there?'" Then said Har: "Now thou askest strangely; as if All-father would invite to him kings or earls or other men of might and would give them water to drink! I know, by my faith! that many a man comes to Valhall who would think he had bought his drink of water dearly, if there were not better cheer to be had there, he who before had suffered wounds and burning pain unto death. I can tell thee a different tale of this. The she-goat, she who is called Heidrun, stands up in Valhall and bites the needles from the limb of that tree which is very famous, and is called Lerad; and from her udders mead runs so copiously, that she fills a tun every day. That tun is so great that all the champions become quite drunk from it." Then said Gangleri: "That is a wondrous proper goat for them; it must be an exceeding good tree from which she eats." Then spake Har: "Even more worthy of note is the hart Eikthyrni, which stands in Valhall and bites from the limbs of the tree; and from his horns distils such abundant exudation that it comes down into Hvergelmir, and from thence fall those rivers called thus: Sid, Vid, Sokin, Eikin, Svol, Gunnthra, Fjorm, Fimbulthul, Gipul, Gopul, Gomul, Geirvimul. Those fall about the abodes of the Æsir; these also are recorded: Thyn, Vin, Tholl, Holl, Grad, Gunnthrain, Nyt, Not, Nonn, Hronn, Vina, Vegsvinn, Thjodnuma."

XL. Then said Gangleri: "These are marvellous tidings which thou now tellest. A wondrous great house Valhall must be; it must often be exceeding crowded before the doors." Then Har answered: "Why dost thou not ask how many doors there are in the hall, or how great? If thou hearest that told, then thou wilt say that it is strange indeed if whosoever will may not go out and in; but it may be said truly that it is no more crowded to find place therein than to enter into it; here thou mayest read in *Grimnismal*:

> Five hundred doors and forty more
>   So I deem stand in Valhall;
> Eight hundred champions go out at each door
>   When they fare to fight with the Wolf."

XLI. Then said Gangleri: "A very mighty multitude of men is in Valhall, so that, by my faith, Odin is a very great chieftain, since he commands so large an army. Now what is the sport of the champions, when they are not fighting?" Har replied: "Every day, as soon as they are clothed, they straightway put on their armor and go out into the court and fight, and fell each other. That is their sport; and when the time draws near to undern-meal, they ride home to Valhall and sit down to drink, even as is said here:

> All the Einherjar in Odin's court
>   Deal out blows every day;
> The slain they choose and ride from the strife,
>   Sit later in love together.

But what thou hast said is true: Odin is of great might. Many examples are found in proof of this, as is here said in the words of the Æsir themselves:

> Ash Yggdrasil's trunk of trees is foremost,
> And Skidbladnir of ships;
> Odin of Æsir, of all steeds Sleipnir,
> Bifrost of bridges, and Bragi of skalds;
> Habrok of hawks, and of hounds Garm."

XLII. Then said Gangleri: "Who owns that horse Sleipnir, or what is to be said of him?" Har answered: "Thou hast no knowledge of Sleipnir's points, and thou knowest not the circumstances of his begetting; but it will seem to thee worth the telling. It was early in the first days of the gods' dwelling here, when the gods had established the Midgard and made Valhall; there came at that time a certain wright and offered to build them a citadel in three seasons, so good that it should be staunch and proof against the Hill-Giants and the Frost-Giants, though they should come in over Midgard. But he demanded as wages that he should have possession of Freyja, and would fain have had the sun and the moon. Then the Æsir held parley and took counsel together; and a bargain was made with the wright, that he should have that which he demanded, if he should succeed in completing the citadel in one winter. On the first day of summer, if any part of the citadel were left unfinished, he should lose his reward; and he was to receive help from no man in the work. When they told him these conditions, he asked that they would give him leave to have the help of his stallion, which was called Svadilfari; and Loki advised it, so that the wright's petition was granted. He set to work the first day of winter to make the citadel, and by night he hauled stones with the stallion's aid; and it seemed very marvellous to the Æsir what great rocks that horse drew, for the horse did more rough work by half than did the wright. But there were strong witnesses to their bargain, and many oaths, since it seemed unsafe to the giant to be among the Æsir without truce, if Thor should come home. But Thor had then gone away into the eastern region to fight trolls.

"Now when the winter drew nigh unto its end, the building of the citadel was far advanced; and it was so high and strong that it could not be taken. When it lacked three days of summer, the work had almost reached the gate of the stronghold. Then the gods sat down in their judgment seats, and sought means of evasion, and asked one another who had advised giving Freyja into Jotunheim, or so destroying the air and the heaven as to take thence the sun and the moon and give them to the giants. The gods agreed that he must have counselled this who is wont to give evil advice, Loki Laufeyarson, and they declared him deserving of an ill death, if he could not hit upon a way of losing the wright his wages; and they threatened Loki with violence. But when he became frightened, then he swore oaths, that he would so contrive that the wright should lose his wages, cost him what it might.

"That same evening, when the wright drove out after stone with the stallion Svadilfari, a mare bounded forth from a certain wood and whinnied to him. The stallion, perceiving what manner of horse this was, straightway became frantic, and snapped the traces asunder, and leaped over to the mare, and she away to the wood, and the wright after, striving to seize the stallion. These horses ran all night, and the wright stopped there that night; and afterward, at day, the work was not done as it had been before. When the wright saw that the work could not be brought to an end, he fell into giant's fury. Now that the Æsir saw surely that the hill-giant was come thither, they did not regard their oaths reverently, but called on Thor, who came as quickly. And straightway the hammer Mjollnir was raised aloft; he paid the wright's wage, and not with the sun and the moon. Nay, he even denied him dwelling in Jotunheim, and struck but the one first blow, so that his skull was burst into small crumbs, and sent him down bellow under Niflhel. But Loki had such dealings with Svadilfari, that somewhat later he gave birth to a foal, which was gray and had eight feet; and this horse is the best among gods and men. So is said in *Voluspa*:

Then all the Powers strode to the seats of judgment,
The most holy gods council held together:
Who had the air all with evil envenomed,
Or to the Ettin-race Od's maid given.

Broken were oaths then, bond and swearing,
Pledges all sacred which passed between them;
Thor alone smote there, swollen with anger:
He seldom sits still when such he hears of."

XLIII. Then said Gangleri: "What is to be said of Skidbladnir, that which is best of ships? Is there no ship equally great?" Har replied: "Skidbladnir is best of ships and made with most skill of craftsmanship; but Naglfar is the largest ship; Muspell has it. Certain dwarves, sons of Ivaldi, made Skidbladnir and gave the ship to Freyr. It is so great that all the Æsir may man it, with their weapons and armaments, and it has a favoring wind as soon as the sail is hoisted, whithersoever it is bound; but when there is no occasion for going to sea in it, it is made of so many things and with so much cunning that then it may be folded together like a napkin and kept in one's pouch."

XLIV. Then spake Gangleri: "'A good ship is Skidbladnir, but very great magic must have been used upon it before it got to be so fashioned. Has Thor never experienced such a thing, that he has found in his path somewhat so mighty or so powerful that it has overmatched him through strength of magic?" Then said Har: "Few men, I ween, are able to tell of this; yet many a thing has seemed to him hard to overcome. Though there may have been something so powerful or strong that Thor might not have succeeded in winning the victory, yet it is not necessary to speak of it; because there are many examples to prove, and because all are bound to believe, that Thor is mightiest." Then said Gangleri: "It seems to me that I must have asked you touching this matter what no one is able to tell of. Then spake Jafnhar: "We have heard say concerning some matters which seem to us incredible, but here sits one near at hand who will know how to tell true tidings of this. Therefore thou must believe that he will not lie for the first time now, who never lied before." Gangleri said: "Here will I stand and listen, if any answer is forthcoming to this word; but otherwise I pronounce you overcome, if ye cannot tell that which I ask you."

Then spake Thridi: "Now it is evident that he is resolved to know this matter, though it seem not to us a pleasant thing to tell. This is the beginning of this tale: Oku-Thor drove forth with his he-goats and chariot, and with him that As called Loki; they came at evening to a husbandman's, and there received a night's lodging. About evening, Thor took his he-goats and slaughtered them both; after that they were flayed and borne to the caldron. When the cooking was done, then Thor and his companion sat down to supper. Thor invited to meat with him the husbandman and his wife, and their children: the husbandman's son was called Thjalfi, and the daughter Roskva. Then Thor laid the goat-hides farther away from the fire, and said that the husbandman and his servants should cast the bones on the goat-hides. Thjalfi, the husbandman's son, was holding a thigh-bone of the goat, and split it with his knife and broke it for the marrow.

"Thor tarried there overnight; and in the interval before day he rose up and clothed himself, took the hammer Mjollnir, swung it up, and hallowed the goat-hides; straightway the he-goats rose up, and then one of them was lame in a hind leg. Thor discovered this, and declared that the husbandman or his household could not have dealt wisely with the bones of the goat: be knew that the thighbone was broken. There is no need to make a long story of it; all may know how frightened the husbandman must have been when he saw how Thor let his brows sink down before his eyes; but when he looked at the eyes, then it seemed to him that he must fall down before their glances alone. Thor clenched his hands on the hammer-shaft so that the knuckles whitened; and the husbandman and all his household did what was to be expected: they cried out lustily, prayed for peace, offered in recompense all that they had. But when he saw their terror, then the fury departed from him, and he became appeased, and took of them in atonement their children, Thjalfi and Roskva, who then became his bond-servants; and they follow him ever since.

XLV. "Thereupon he left his goats behind, and began his journey eastward toward Jotunheim and clear to the sea; and then he went out over the sea, that deep one; but when he came to land, he went up, and Loki and Thjalfi and Roskva with him. Then, when they had walked a little while, there stood before them a great forest; they walked all that day till dark. Thjalfi was swiftest-footed of all men; he bore Thor's bag, but there was nothing good for food. As soon as it had become dark, they sought themselves shelter for the night, and found before them a certain hall, very great: there was a door in the end, of equal width with the hall, wherein they took up quarters for the night. But about midnight there came a great earthquake: the earth rocked under them exceedingly, and the house trembled. Then Thor rose up and called to his companions, and they explored farther, and found in the middle of the hall a side-chamber on the right hand, and they went in thither. Thor sat down in the doorway, but the others were farther in from him, and they were afraid; but Thor gripped his hammer-shaft and thought to defend himself. Then they heard a great humming sound, and a crashing.

"But when it drew near dawn, then Thor went out and saw a man lying a little way from him in the wood; and that man was not small; he slept and snored mightily. Then Thor thought he could perceive what kind of noise it was which they had heard during the night. He girded himself with his belt of strength, and his divine power waxed; and on the instant the man awoke and rose up swiftly; and then, it is said, the first time Thor's heart failed him, to strike him with the hammer. He asked him his name, and the man called himself Skrymir, — 'but I have no need,' he said, 'to ask thee for thy name; I know that thou art Asa-Thor. But what? Hast thou dragged away my glove?' Then Skrymir stretched out his hand and took up the glove; and at once Thor saw that it was that which he had taken for a hall during the night; and as for the side-chamber, it was the thumb of the glove. Skrymir asked whether Thor would have his company, and Thor assented to this. Then Skrymir took and unloosened his provision wallet and made ready to eat his morning meal, and Thor and his fellows in another place. Skrymir then proposed to them to lay their supply of food together, and Thor assented. Then Skrymir bound all the food in one bag and laid it on his own back; he went before during the day, and stepped with very great strides; but late in the evening Skrymir found them night-quarters under a certain great oak. Then Skrymir said to Thor that he would lay him down to sleep, — 'and do ye take the provision-bag and make ready for your supper.'

"Thereupon Skrymir slept and snored hard, and Thor took the provision-bag and set about to unloose it; but such things must be told as will seem incredible: he got no knot loosened and no thong-end stirred, so as to be looser than before. When he saw that this work might not avail, then he became angered, gripped the hammer Mjollnir in both hands, and strode with great strides to that place where Skrymir lay, and smote him in the head. Skrymir awoke, and asked whether a leaf had fallen upon his head; or whether they had eaten and were ready for bed? Thor replied that they were just then about to go to sleep; then they went under another oak. It must be told thee, that there was then no fearless sleeping. At midnight Thor heard how Skrymir snored and slept fast, so that it thundered in the woods; then he stood up and went to him, shook his hammer eagerly and hard, and smote down upon the middle of his crown: he saw that the face of the hammer sank deep into his head. And at that moment Skrymir awoke arid said: 'What is it now? Did some acorn fall on my head? Or what is the news with thee, Thor?' But Thor went back speedily, and replied that he was then but new-wakened; said that it was then midnight, and there was yet time to sleep.

"Thor meditated that if he could get to strike him a third blow, never should the giant see himself again; he lay now and watched whether Skrymir were sleeping soundly yet. A little before day, when he perceived that Skrymir must have fallen asleep, he stood up at once and rushed over to him, brandished his hammer with all his strength, and smote upon that one of his temples which was turned up. But Skrymir sat up and stroked his cheek, and said: 'Some birds must be sitting in the tree above me; I imagined, when I awoke, that some dirt from the twigs fell upon my head. Art thou awake, Thor? It will be time to arise and clothe us; but now ye have no long journey forward to the castle called Utgard. I have heard how ye have whispered among yourselves that I am no little man in stature; but ye shall see taller men, if ye come into Utgard. Now I will give you wholesome advice: do not conduct yourselves boastfully, for the henchmen of Utgarda-Loki will not well endure big words from such swaddling-babes. But if not so, then turn back, and I think it were better for you to do that; but if ye will go forward, then turn to the east. As for me, I hold my way north to these hills, which ye may how see.' Skrymir took the provision-bag and cast it on his back, and turned from them across the forest; and it is not recorded that the Æsir bade him god-speed.

XLVI. "Thor turned forward on his way, and his fellows, and went onward till mid-day. Then they saw a castle standing in a certain plain, and set their necks down on their backs before they could see up over it. They went to the castle; and there was a grating in front of the castle-gate, and it was closed. Thor went up to the grating, and did not succeed in opening it; but when they struggled to make their way in, they crept between the bars and came in that way. They saw a great hall and went thither; the door was open; then they went in, and saw there many men on two benches, and most of them were big enough. Thereupon they came before the king Utgarda-Loki and saluted him; but he looked at them in his own good time, and smiled scornfully over his teeth, and said: 'It is late to ask tidings of a long journey; or is it otherwise than I think: that this toddler is Oku-Thor? Yet thou mayest be greater than thou appearest to me. What manner of accomplishments are those, which thou and thy fellows think to be ready for? No one shall be here with us who knows not some kind of craft or cunning surpassing most men.'

"Then spoke the one who came last, 'Who was called Loki: 'I know such a trick, which I am ready to try: that there is no one within here who shall eat his food more quickly than I.' Then Utgarda-Loki answered: 'That is a feat, if thou accomplish it; and this feat shall accordingly be put to the proof.' He called to the farther end of the bench, that he who was called Logi should come forth on the floor and try his prowess against Loki. Then a trough was taken and borne in upon the hall-floor and filled with flesh; Loki sat down at the one end and Logi at the other, and each ate as fast as he could, and they met in the middle of the trough. By that time Loki had eaten all the meat from the bones, but Logi likewise had eaten all the meat, and the bones with it, and the trough too; and now it seemed to all as if Loki had lost the game.

"Then Utgarda-Loki asked what yonder young man could play at; and Thjalfi answered that he would undertake to run a race with whomsoever Utgarda-Loki would bring up. Then Utgarda-Loki said that that was a good accomplishment, and that there was great likelihood that he must be well endowed with fleetness if he were to perform that feat; yet he would speedily see to it that the matter should be tested. Then Utgarda-Loki arose and went out; and there was a good course to run on over the level plain. Then Utgarda-Loki called to him a certain lad, who was named Hugi, and bade him run a match against Thjalfi. Then they held the first heat; and Hugi was so much ahead that he turned back to meet Thjalfi at the end of the course. Then said Utgarda-Loki: 'Thou wilt need to lay thyself forward more, Thjalfi, if thou art to win the game; but it is none the less true that never have any men come hither who seemed to me fleeter of foot than this.' Then they began another heat; and when Hugi had reached the course's end, and was turning back, there was still a long bolt-shot to Thjalfi. Then spake Utgarda-Loki: 'Thjalfi appears to me to run this course well, but I do not believe of him now that he will win the game. But it will be made manifest presently, when they run the third heat.' Then they began the heat; but when Hugi had come to the end of the course and turned back, Thjalfi had not yet reached mid-course. Then all said that that game had been proven.

"Next, Utgarda-Loki asked Thor what feats there were which he might desire to show before them: such great tales as men have made of his mighty works. Then Thor answered that he would most willingly undertake to contend with any in drinking. Utgarda-Loki said that might well be; he went into the hall and called his serving-boy, and bade him bring the sconce-horn which the henchmen were wont to drink off. Straightway the serving-lad came forward with the horn and put it into Thor's hand. Then said Utgarda-Loki: 'It is held that this horn is well drained if it is drunk off in one drink, but some drink it off in two; but no one is so poor a man at drinking that it fails to drain off in three.' Thor looked upon the horn, and it did not seem big to him; and yet it was somewhat long. Still he was very thirsty; he took and drank, and swallowed enormously, and thought that he should not need to bend oftener to the horn. But when his breath failed, and he raised his head from the horn and looked to see how it had gone with the drinking, it seemed to him that there was very little space by which the drink was lower now in the horn than before. Then said Utgarda-Loki: 'It is well drunk, and not too much; I should not have believed, if it had been told me, that Asa-Thor could not drink a greater draught. But I know that thou wilt wish to drink it off in another draught.' Thor answered nothing; he set the horn to his mouth, thinking now that he should drink a greater drink, and struggled with the draught until his breath gave out; and yet he saw that the tip of the horn would not come up so much as he liked. When he took the horn from his mouth and looked into it, it seemed to him then as if it had decreased less than the former time; but now there was a clearly apparent lowering in the horn. Then said Utgarda-Loki: 'How now, Thor? Thou wilt not shrink from one more drink than may he well for thee? If thou now drink the third draught from the horn, it seems to me as if this must he esteemed the greatest; but thou canst not be called so great a man here among us as the Æsir call thee, if thou give not a better account of thyself in the other games than it seems to me may come of this.' Then Thor became angry, set-the horn to his mouth, and drank with all his might, and struggled with the drink as much as he could; and when he looked into the horn, at least some space had been made. Then he gave up the horn and would drink no more.

"Then said Utgarda-Loki: Now it is evident that thy prowess is not so great as we thought it to be; but wilt thou try thy hand at more games? It may readily be seen that thou gettest no advantage hereof.' Thor answered: "will make trial of yet other games; but it would have seemed wonderful to me, when I was at home with the Æsir, if such drinks had been called so little. But what game will ye now offer me?' Then said Utgarda-Loki: 'Young lads here are wont to do this (which is thought of small consequence): lift my cat up from the earth; but I should not have been able to speak of such a thing to Asa-Thor if I had not seen that thou hast far less in thee than I had thought.' Thereupon there leaped forth on the hall-floor a gray cat, and a very big one; and Thor went to it and took it with his hand down under the middle of the belly and lifted up. But the cat bent into an arch just as Thor stretched up his hands; and when Thor reached up as high as he could at the very utmost, then the cat lifted up one foot, and Thor got this game no further advanced. Then said Utgarda-Loki: 'This game went even as I had foreseen; the cat is very great, whereas Thor is low and little beside the huge men who are here with us.'

"Then said Thor: 'Little as ye call me, let any one come up now and wrestle with me; now I am angry.' Then Utgarda-Loki answered, looking about him on the benches, and spake: 'I see no such man here within, who would not hold it a disgrace to wrestle with thee;' and yet he said: 'Let us see first; let the old woman my nurse be called hither, Elli, and let Thor wrestle with her if he will. She has thrown such men as have seemed to me no less strong than Thor.' Straightway there came into the hall an old woman, stricken in years. Then Utgarda-Loki said that she should grapple with Asa-Thor. There is no need to make a long matter of it: that struggle went in such wise that the harder Thor strove in gripping, the faster she stood; then the old woman essayed a hold, and then Thor became totty on his feet, and their tuggings were very hard. Yet it was not long before Thor fell to his knee, on one foot. Then Utgarda-Loki went up and bade them cease the wrestling, saying that Thor should not need to challenge more men of his body-guard to wrestling. By then it had passed toward night; Utgarda-Loki showed Thor and his companions to a seat, and they tarried there the night long in good cheer.

XLVII. "But at morning, as soon as it dawned, Thor and his companions arose, clothed themselves, and were ready to go away. Then came there Utgarda-Loki and caused a table to be set for them; there was no lack of good cheer, meat and drink. So soon as they had eaten, he went out from the castle with them; and at parting Utgarda-Loki spoke to Thor and asked how he thought his journey had ended, or whether he had met any man mightier than himself. Thor answered that he could not say that he had not got much shame in their dealings together. 'But yet I know that ye will call me a man of little might, and I am ill-content with that.' Then said Utgardi-Loki: 'Now I will tell thee the truth, now that thou art come out of the castle; and if I live and am able to prevail, then thou shalt never again come into it. And this I know, by my troth! that thou shouldst never have come into it, If I had known before that thou haddest so much strength in thee, and that thou shouldst so nearly have had us in great peril. But I made ready against thee eye-illusions; and I came upon you the first time in the wood, and when thou wouldst have unloosed the provision-bag, I had bound it with iron, and thou didst not find where to undo it. But next thou didst smite me three blows with the hammer; and the first was least, and was yet so great that it would have sufficed to slay me, if it had come upon me. Where thou sawest near my hall a saddle-backed mountain, cut at the top into threesquare dales, and one the deepest, those were the marks of thy hammer. I brought the saddle-back before the blow, but thou didst not see that. So it was also with the games, in which ye did contend against my henchmen: that was the first, which Loki did; he was very hungry and ate zealously, but he who was called Logi was "wild-fire," and he burned the trough no less swiftly than the meat. But when Thjalfi ran the race with him called Hugi, that was my "thought," and it was not to be expected of Thjalfi that he should match swiftness with it.

" 'Moreover, when thou didst drink from the horn, and it seemed to thee to go slowly, then, by my faith, that was a wonder which I should not have believed possible: the other end of the horn was out in the sea, but thou didst not perceive it. But now, when thou comest to the sea, thou shalt be able to mark what a diminishing thou hast drunk in the sea: this is henceforth called "ebb-tides."'

"And again he said: 'It seemed to me not less noteworthy when thou didst lift up the cat; and to tell thee truly, then all were afraid who saw how thou didst lift one foot clear of the earth. That cat was not as it appeared to thee: it was the Midgard Serpent, which lies about all the land, and scarcely does its length suffice to encompass the earth with head and tail. So high didst thou stretch up thine arms that it was then but a little way more to heaven. It was also a great marvel concerning the wrestling-match, when thou didst withstand so long, and didst not fall more than on one knee, wrestling with Elli; since none such has ever been and none shall be, if he become so old as to abide "Old Age," that she shall not cause him to fall. And

201

now it is truth to tell that we must part; and it will be better on both sides that ye never come again to seek me. Another time I will defend my castle with similar wiles or with others, so that ye shall get no power over me.'

"When Thor had heard these sayings, he clutched his hammer and brandished it aloft; but when he was about to launch it forward, then he saw Utgarda-Loki nowhere. Then he turned back to the castle, purposing to crush it to pieces; and he saw there a wide and fair plain, but no castle. So he turned back and went his way, till he was come back again to Thrudvangar. But it is a true tale that then he resolved to seek if he might bring about a meeting between himself and the Midgard Serpent, which afterward came to pass. Now I think no one knows how to tell thee more truly concerning this journey of Thor's."

XLVIII. Then said Gangleri: "Very mighty is Utgarda-Loki, and he deals much in wiles and in magic; and his might may be seen in that he had such henchmen as have great prowess. Now did Thor ever take vengeance for this?" Har answered: "It is not unknown, though one be not a scholar, that Thor took redress for this journey of which the tale has but now been told; and he did not tarry at home long before he made ready for his journey so hastily that he had with him no chariot and no he-goats and no retinue. He went out over Midgard in the guise of a young lad, and came one evening at twilight to a certain giant's, who was called Hymir. Thor abode as guest there overnight; but at dawn Hymir arose and clothed himself and made ready to row to sea a-fishing. Then Thor sprang up and was speedily ready, and asked Hymir to let him row to sea with him. But Hymir said that Thor would be of little help to him, being so small and a youth, 'And thou wilt freeze, if I stay so long and so far out as I am wont.' But Thor said that he would be able to row far out from land, for the reason that it was not certain whether he would be the first to ask to row back. Thor became so enraged at the giant that he was forthwith ready to let his hammer crash against him; but he forced himself to forbear, since he purposed to try his strength in another quarter. He asked Hymir what they should have for bait, but Hymir bade him get bait for himself. Then Thor turned away thither where he, saw a certain herd of oxen, which Hymir owned; he took the largest ox, called Himinbrjot [Heaven-bellower], and cut off its head and went therewith to the sea. By that time Hymir had shoved out the boat.

"Thor went aboard the skiff and sat down in the stern-seat, took two oars and rowed; and it seemed to Hymir that swift progress came of his rowing. Hymir rowed forward in the bow, and the rowing proceeded rapidly; then Hymir said that they had arrived at those fishing-banks where he was wont to anchor and angle for flat-fish. But Thor said that he desired to row much further, and they took a sharp pull; then Hymir said that they had come so far that it was perilous to abide out farther because of the Midgard Serpent. Thor replied that they would row a while yet, and so he did; but Hymir was then sore afraid. Now as soon as Thor had laid by the oars, he made ready a very strong fishing-line, and the hook was no less large and strong. Then Thor put the ox-head on the hook and cast it overboard, and the hook went to the bottom; and it is telling thee the truth to say that then Thor beguiled the Midgard Serpent no less than Utgarda-Loki had mocked Thor, at the time when he lifted up the Serpent in his hand.

"The Midgard Serpent snapped at the ox-head, and the hook caught in its jaw; but when the Serpent was aware of this, it dashed away so fiercely that both Thor's fists crashed against the gunwale. Then Thor was angered, and took upon him his divine strength, braced his feet so strongly that he plunged through the ship with both feet, and dashed his feet against the bottom; then he drew the Serpent up to the gunwale. And it may be said that no one has seen very fearful sights who might not see that: bow Thor flashed fiery glances at the Serpent, and the Serpent in turn stared up toward him from below and blew venom. Then, it is said, the giant Hymir grew pale, became yellow, and was sore afraid, when he saw the Serpent, and how the sea rushed out and in through the boat. In the very moment when Thor clutched his hammer and raised it on high, then the giant fumbled for his fish-knife and hacked off Thor's line at the gunwale, and the Serpent sank down into the sea. Thor hurled his hammer after it; and men say that he struck off its head against the bottom; but I think it were true to tell thee that the Midgard Serpent yet lives and lies in the encompassing sea. But Thor swung his fist and brought it against Hymir's ear, so that he plunged overboard, and Thor saw the soles of his feet. And Thor waded to land."

XLIX. Then spake Gangleri: "Have any more matters of note befallen among the Æsir? A very great deed of valor did Thor achieve on that journey." Har made answer: "Now shall be told of those tidings which seemed of more consequence to the Æsir. The beginning of the story is this, that Baldr the Good dreamed great and perilous dreams touching his life. When he told these dreams to the Æsir, then they took counsel together: and this was their decision: to ask safety for Baldr from all kinds of dangers. And Frigg took oaths to this purport, that fire and water should spare Baldr, likewise iron and metal of all kinds, stones, earth, trees, sicknesses, beasts, birds, venom, serpents. And when that was done and made known, then it was a diversion of Baldr's and the Æsir, that he should stand up in the Thing [the legislative assembly of Iceland], and all the others should some shoot at him, some hew at him, some beat him with stones; but whatsoever was done hurt him not at all, and that seemed to them all a very worshipful thing.

"But when Loki Laufeyarson saw this, it pleased him ill that Baldr took no hurt. He went to Fensalir to Frigg, and made himself into the likeness of a woman. Then Frigg asked if that woman knew what the Æsir did at the Thing. She said that all were shooting at Baldr, and moreover, that he took no hurt. Then said Frigg: 'Neither weapons nor trees may hurt Baldr: I have taken oaths of them all.' Then the woman asked: 'Have all things taken oaths to spare Baldr?' and Frigg answered: 'There grows a tree-sprout alone westward of Valhall: it is called Mistletoe; I thought it too young to ask the oath of.' Then straightway the woman turned away; but Loki took Mistletoe and pulled it up and went to the Thing.

"Hod stood outside the ring of men, because he was blind. Then spake Loki to him: 'Why dost thou not shoot at Baldr?' He answered: 'Because I see not where Baldr is; and for this also, that I am weaponless.' Then said Loki: 'Do thou also after the manner of other men, and show Baldr honor as the other men do. I will direct thee where he stands; shoot at him with this wand.' Hod took Mistletoe and shot at Baldr, being guided by Loki: the shaft flew through Baldr, and he fell dead to the earth; and that was the greatest mischance that has ever befallen among gods and men.

"Then, when Baldr was fallen, words failed all the, Æsir, and their hands likewise to lay hold of him; each looked at the other, and all were of one mind as to him who had. wrought the work, but none might take vengeance, so great a sanctuary was in that place. But when the Æsir tried to speak, then it befell first that weeping broke out, so that none might speak to the others with words concerning his grief. But Odin bore that misfortune by so much the worst, as he had most perception of how great harm and loss for the Æsir were in the death of Baldr.

"Now when the gods had come to themselves, Frigg spake, and asked who there might be among the Æsir who would fain have for his own all her love and favor: let him ride the road to Hel, and seek if he may find Baldr, and offer Hel a ransom if she will let Baldr come home to Asgard. And he is named Hermod the Bold, Odin's son, who undertook that embassy. Then Sleipnir was taken, Odin's steed, and led forward; and Hermod mounted on that horse and galloped off.

"The Æsir took the body of Baldr and brought it to the sea. Hringhorni is the name of Baldr's ship: it was greatest of all ships; the gods would have launched it and made Baldr's pyre thereon, but the ship stirred not forward. Then word was sent to Jotunheim after that giantess who is called Hyrrokkin. When she had come, riding a wolf and having a viper for bridle, then she leaped off the steed; and Odin called to four berserks to tend the steed; but they were not able to hold it until they had felled it. Then Hyrrokkin went to the prow of the boat and thrust it out at the first push, so that fire burst from the rollers, and all lands trembled. Thor became angry and clutched his hammer, and would straightway have broken her head, had not the gods prayed for peace for her.

"Then was the body of Baldr borne out on shipboard; and when his wife, Nanna the daughter of Nep, saw that, straightway her heart burst with grief, and she died; she was borne to the pyre, and fire was kindled. Then Thor stood by and hallowed the pyre with Mjollnir; and before his feet ran a certain dwarf which was named Lit; Thor kicked at him with his foot and thrust him into the fire, and he burned. People of many races visited this burning: First is to be told of Odin, how Frigg and the Valkyries went with him, and his ravens; but Freyr drove in his chariot with the boar called Gullinbursti [Gold-mane], or Slidrugtanni [Fearful-tusk], and Heimdall rode the horse called Gulltopp [Gold-top], and Freyja drove her cats. Thither came also much people of the Frost-Giants and the Hill-Giants. Odin laid on the pyre that gold ring which is called Draupnir; this quality attended it, that every ninth night there dropped from it eight gold rings of equal weight. Baldr's horse was led to the bale-fire with all his trappings.

"Now this is to be told concerning Hermod, that he rode nine nights through dark dales and deep, so that he saw not before he was come to the river Gjoll and rode onto the Gjoll-Bridge; which bridge is thatched with glittering gold. Modgud is the maiden called who guards the bridge; she asked him his name and race, saying that the day before there had ridden over the bridge five companies of dead men; but the bridge thunders no less under thee alone, and thou hast not the color of dead men. Why ridest thou hither on Hel-way?' He answered: 'I am appointed to ride to Hel to seek out Baldr. Hast thou perchance seen Baldr on Hel-way?' She said that Baldr had ridden there over Gjoll's Bridge, — 'but down and north lieth Hel-way.'

'Then Hermod rode on till he came to Hel-gate; he dismounted from his steed and made his girths fast, mounted and pricked him with his spurs; and the steed leaped so hard over the gate that he came nowise near to it. Then Hermod rode home to the hall and dismounted from his steed, went into the hall, and saw sitting there in the high-seat Baldr, his brother; and Hermod tarried there overnight. At morn Hermod prayed Hel that Baldr might ride home with him, and told her how great weeping was among the Æsir. But Hel said that in this wise it should be put to the test, whether Baldr were so all-beloved as had been said: 'If all things in the world, quick and dead, weep for him, then he shall go back to the Æsir; but he shall remain with Hel if any gainsay it or will not weep.' Then Hermod arose; but Baldr led him out of the hall, and took the ring Draupnir and sent it to Odin for a remembrance. And Nanna sent Frigg a linen smock, and yet more gifts, and to Fulla a golden finger-ring.

"Then Hermod rode his way back, and came into Asgard, and told all those tidings which he had seen and heard. Thereupon the Æsir sent over all the world messengers to pray that Baldr be wept out of Hel; and all men did this, and quick things, and the earth, and stones, and trees, and all metals, — even as thou must have seen that these things weep when they come out of frost and into the heat. Then, when the messengers went home, having well wrought their errand, they found, in a certain cave, where a giantess sat: she called herself Thokk. They prayed her to weep Baldr out of Hel; she answered:

> Thokk will weep waterless tears
>   For Baldr's bale-fare;
> Living or dead, I loved not the churl's son;
>   Let Hel hold to that she hath!

And men deem that she who was there was Loki Laufeyarson, who hath wrought most ill among the Æsir."

L. Then said Gangleri: "Exceeding much Loki had brought to pass, when he had first been cause that Baldr was slain, and then that he was not redeemed out of Hel. Was any vengeance taken on him for this?" Har answered: "This thing was repaid him in such wise that he shall remember it long. When the gods had become as wroth with him as was to be looked for, he ran off and hid himself in a certain mountain; there he made a house with four doors, so that he could see out of the house in all directions. Often throughout the day he turned himself into the likeness of a salmon and hid himself in the place called Franangr-Falls; then he would ponder what manner of wile the gods would devise to take him in the water-fall. But when he sat in the house, he took twine of linen and knitted meshes as a net is made since; but a fire burned before him. Then he saw that the Æsir were close upon him; and Odin had seen from Hlidskjalf where he was. He leaped up at once and out into the river, but cast the net into the fire.

"When the Æsir had come to the house, he went in first who was wisest of all, who is called Kvasir; and when he saw in the fire the white ash where the net had burned, then he perceived that that thing must be a device for catching fish, and told it to the Æsir. Straightway they took hold, and made themselves a net after the pattern of the one which they perceived, by the burnt-out ashes, that Loki had made. When the net was ready, then the Æsir went to the river and cast the net into the fall; Thor held one end of the net, and all of the Æsir held the other, and they drew the net. But Loki darted ahead and lay down between two stones; they drew the net over him, and perceived that something living was in front of it. A second time they went up to the fall and cast out the net, having bound it to something so heavy that nothing should be able to pass under it. Then Loki swam ahead of the net; but when he saw that it was but a short distance to the sea, then he jumped up over the net-rope and ran into the fall. Now the Æsir saw where he went, and went up again to the fall and divided the company into two parts, but Thor waded along in mid-stream; and so they went out toward the sea. Now Loki saw a choice of two courses: it was a mortal peril to dash out into the sea; but this was the second — to leap over the net again. And so he did: he leaped as swiftly as he could over the net-cord. Thor clutched at him and got hold of him, and he slipped in Thor's hand, so that the hand stopped at the tail; and for this reason the salmon has a tapering back.

"Now Loki was taken truceless, and was brought with them into a certain cave. Thereupon they took three flat stones, and set them on edge and drilled a hole in each stone. Then were taken Loki's sons, Vili and Nari or Narfi; the Æsir changed Vali into the form of a wolf, and he tore asunder Narfi his brother. And the Æsir took his entrails and bound Loki with them over the three stones: one stands under his shoulders, the second under his loins, the third under his boughs; and those bonds were turned to iron. Then Skadi took a venomous serpent and fastened it up over him, so that the venom should drip from the serpent into his face. But Sigyn, his wife, stands near him and holds a basin under the venom-drops; and when the basin is full, she goes and pours out the venom, but in the meantime the venom drips into his face. Then he writhes against it with such force that all the earth trembles: ye call that 'earthquakes.' There he lies in bonds till Ragnarok."

LI. Then said Gangleri: "What tidings are to be told concerning Ragnarok? Never before have I heard aught said of this." Har answered: "Great tidings are to be told of it, and much. The first is this, that there shall come that winter which is called the *fimbul*-winter [Terrible-winter]: in that time snow shall drive from all quarters; frosts shall be great then, and winds sharp; there shall be no virtue in the sun. Those winters shall proceed three in succession, and no summer between; but first shall come three other winters, such that over all the world there shall be mighty battles. In that time brothers shall slay each other for greed's sake, and none shall spare father or son in manslaughter and in incest; so it says in *Voluspa*:

Brothers shall strive and slaughter each other;
Own sisters' children shall sin together;
Ill days among men, many a whoredom:
An axe-age, a sword-age, shields shall be cloven;
A wind-age, a wolf-age, ere the world totters.

Then shall happen what seems great tidings: the Wolf shall swallow the sun; and this shall seem to men a great harm. Then the other wolf shall seize the moon, and he also shall work great ruin; the stars shall vanish from the heavens. Then shall come to pass these tidings also: all the earth shall tremble so, and the crags, that trees shall be torn up from the earth, and the crags fall to ruin; and all fetters and bonds shall be broken and rent. Then shall Fenris-Wolf get loose; then the sea shall gush forth upon the land, because the Midgard Serpent stirs in giant wrath and advances up onto the land. Then that too shall happen, that Naglfar shall be loosened, the ship which is so named. (It is made of dead men's nails; wherefore a warning is desirable, that if a man die with unshorn nails, that man adds much material to the ship Naglfar, which gods and men were fain to have finished late.) Yet in this sea-flood Naglfar shall float. Hrym is the name of the giant who steers Naglfar. Fenris-Wolf shall advance with gaping mouth, and his lower jaw shall be against the earth, but the upper against heaven, — he would gape yet more if there were room for it; fires blaze from his eyes and nostrils. The Midgard Serpent shall blow venom so that he shall sprinkle all the air and water; and he is very terrible, and shall be on one side of the Wolf. In this din shall the heaven be cloven, and the Sons of Muspell ride thence: Surt shall ride first, and both before him and after him burning fire; his sword is exceeding good: from it radiance shines brighter than from the sun; when they ride over Bifrost, then the bridge shall break, as has been told before. The Sons of Muspell shall go forth to that field which is called Vigrid, thither shall come Fenris-Wolf also and the Midgard Serpent; then Loki and Hrym shall come there also, and with him all the Frost-Giants. All the champions of Hel follow Loki; and the Sons of Muspell shall have a company by themselves, and it shall be very bright. The field Vigrid is a hundred leagues wide each way.

"When these tidings come to pass, then shall Heimdall rise up and blow mightily in the Gjallar-Horn, and awaken all the gods; and they shall hold council together. Then Odin shall ride to Mimir's Well and take counsel of Mimir for himself and his host. Then the Ash of Yggdrasil shall tremble, and nothing then shall be without fear in heaven or in earth. Then shall the Æsir put on their war-weeds, and all the Champions, and advance to the field: Odin rides first with the gold helmet and a fair byrnie, and his spear, which is called Gungnir. He shall go forth against Fenris-Wolf, and Thor stands forward on his other side, and can be of no avail to him, because he shall have his hands full to fight against the Midgard Serpent. Freyr shall contend with Surt, and a hard encounter shall there be between them before Freyr falls: it is to be his death that he lacks that good sword of his, which he gave to Skirnir. Then shall the dog Garm be loosed, which is bound before Gnipa's Cave: he is the greatest monster; he shall do battle with Tyr, and each become the other's slayer. Thor shall put to death the Midgard Serpent, and shall stride away nine paces from that spot; then shall he fall dead to the earth, because of the venom which the Snake has blown at him. The Wolf shall swallow Odin; that shall be his ending But straight thereafter shall Vidar stride forth and set one foot upon the lower jaw of the Wolf: on that foot he has the shoe, materials for which have been gathering throughout all time. (They are the scraps of leather which men cut out: of their shoes at toe or heel; therefore he who desires in his heart to come to the Æsir's help should cast those scraps away.) With one hand he shall seize the Wolf's upper jaw and tear his gullet asunder; and that is the death of the Wolf. Loki shall have battle with Heimdall, and each be the slayer of the other. Then straightway shall Surt cast fire over the earth and burn all the world; so is said in *Voluspa*:

> High blows Heimdall, the horn is aloft;
> Odin communes with Mimir's head;
> Trembles Yggdrasil's towering Ash;
> The old tree wails when the Ettin is loosed.

> What of the Æsir? What of the Elf-folk?
> All Jotunheim echoes, the Æsir are at council;
> The dwarves are groaning before their stone doors,
> Wise in rock-walls; wit ye yet, or what?

> Hrym sails from the east, the sea floods onward;
> The monstrous Beast twists in mighty wrath;
> The Snake beats the waves, the Eagle is screaming;
> The gold-beak tears corpses, Naglfar is loosed.

> From the east sails the keel; come now Muspell's folk
> Over the sea-waves, and Loki steereth;
> There are the warlocks all with the Wolf, —
> With them is the brother of Byleist faring.

Surt fares from southward with switch-eating flame;
On his sword shimmers the sun of the war-gods;
The rocks are falling, and fiends are reeling,
Heroes tread Hel-way, heaven is cloven.

Then to the Goddess a second grief cometh,
When Odin fares to fight with the Wolf,
And Beli's slayer, the bright god, with Surt;
There must fall Frigg's beloved.

Odin's son goeth to strife with the Wolf, —
Vidar, speeding to meet the slaughter-beast;
The sword in his hand to the heart he thrusteth
Of the fiend's offspring; avenged is his Father.

Now goeth Hlodyn's glorious son
Not in flight from the Serpent, of fear unheeding;
All the earth's offspring must empty the homesteads,
When furiously smiteth Midgard's defender.

The sun shall be darkened, earth sinks in the sea, —
Glide from the heaven the glittering stars;
Smoke-reek rages and reddening fire:
The high heat licks against heaven itself.

And here it says yet so:

Vigrid hight the field where in fight shall meet
 Surt and the cherished gods;
An hundred leagues it has on each side:
 Unto them that field is fated."

LII. Then said Gangleri: 'What shall come to pass afterward, when all the world is burned, and dead are all the gods and all the champions and all mankind? Have ye not said before, that every man shall live in some world throughout all ages?" Then Thridi answered: "In that time the good abodes shall be many, and many the ill; then it shall be best to be in Gimle in Heaven. Moreover, there is plenteous abundance of good drink, for them that esteem that a pleasure, in the hall which is called Brimir: it stands in Okolnir. That too is a good hall which stands in Nida Fells, made of red gold; its name is Sindri. In these halls shall dwell good men and pure in heart.

"On Nastrand [Corpse-strands] is a great hall and evil, and its doors face to the north: it is all woven of serpent-backs like a wattle-house; and all the snake-heads turn into the house and blow venom, so that along the hall run rivers of venom; and they who have broken oaths, and murderers, wade those rivers, even as it says here:

> I know a hall standing far from the sun,
> In Nastrand: the doors to northward are turned;
> Venom-drops fall down from the roof-holes;
> That hall is bordered with backs of serpents.

> There are doomed to wade the weltering streams
> Men that are mansworn, and they that murderers are.

> But it is worst in Hvergelmir:

> There the cursed snake tears dead men's corpses."

LIII. Then spake Gangleri: "Shall any of the gods live then, or shall there be then any earth or heaven?" Har answered: "In that time the earth shall emerge out of the sea, and shall then be green and fair; then shall the fruits of it be brought forth unsown. Vidar and Vali shall be living, inasmuch as neither sea nor the fire of Surt shall have harmed them; and they shall dwell at Ida-Plain, where Asgard was before. And then the sons of Thor, Modi and Magni, shall come there, and they shall have Mjollnir there. After that Baldr shall come thither, and Hod, from Hel; then all shall sit down together and hold speech. with one another, and call to mind their secret wisdom, and speak of those happenings which have been before: of the Midgard Serpent and of Fenris-Wolf. Then they shall find in the grass those golden chess-pieces which the Æsir had had; thus is it said:

> In the deities' shrines shall dwell Vidar and Vali,
>   When the Fire of Surt is slackened;
> Modi and Magni shall have Mjollnir
>   At the ceasing of Thor's strife.

In the place called Hoddmimir's Holt there shall lie hidden during the Fire of Surt two of mankind, who are called thus: Lif and Lifthrasir, and for food they shall have the morning-dews. From these folk shall come so numerous an offspring that all the world shall be peopled, even as is said here:

> Lif and Lifthrasir, these shall lurk hidden
>   In the Holt of Hoddmimir;
> The morning dews their meat shall be;
>   Thence are gendered the generations.

And it may seem wonderful to thee, that the sun shall have borne a daughter not less fair than herself; and the daughter shall then tread in the steps of her mother, as is said here:

> The Elfin-beam shall bear a daughter,
>   Ere Fenris drags her forth;
> That maid shall go, when the great gods die,
>   To ride her mother's road.

But now, if thou art able to ask yet further, then indeed I know not whence answer shall come to thee, for I never heard any man tell forth at greater length the course of the world; and now avail thyself of that which thou hast heard."

LIV. Thereupon Gangleri heard great noises on every side of him; and then, when he had looked about him more, lo, he stood out of doors on a level plain, and saw no hall there and no castle. Then he went his way forth and came home into his kingdom, and told those tidings which he had seen and heard; and after him each man told these tales to the other.

But the Æsir sat them down to speak together, and took counsel and recalled all these tales which had been told to him. And they gave these same names that were named before to those men and places that were there, to the end that when long ages should have passed away, men should not doubt thereof, that those Æsir that were but now spoken of, and these to whom the same names were then given, were all one. There Thor was so named, and he is the old Asa-Thor.

He is Oku-Thor, and to him are ascribed those mighty works which Hector wrought in Troy. But this is the belief of men: that the Turks told of Ulysses, and called him Loki, for the Turks were his greatest foes.

THE SAGA OF KING HEIDREK THE WISE (OR THE SAGA OF HERVÖR AND HEIDREK)

translated by N. Kershaw (1921)

Here begins the Saga of King Heidrek the Wise.

I. It is said that in the days of old the northern part of Finnmark was called Jötunheimar, and that there was a country called Ymisland to the south between it and the Halogaland. These lands were then the home of many giants and half-giants; for there was a great intermixture of races at the time, because the giants took wives from among the people of Ymisland.

There was a king in Jötunheimar called Guthmund. He was a mighty man among the heathen. He dwelt at a place called Grund in the region of Glasisvellir. He was wise and mighty. He and his men lived for many generations, and so heathen men believed that the fields of immortality lay in his realm; and whoever went there cast off sickness or old age and became immortal.

After Guthmund's death, people worshipped him and called him their god. His son's name was Höfund. He had second sight and was wise of understanding, and was judge of all suits throughout the neighboring kingdoms. He never gave an unjust judgment, and no-one dared violate his decision.

There was a man called Hergrim who was a giant dwelling in the rocks. He carried off from Ymisland Ama the daughter of Ymir, and afterwards married her. Their son Thorngrim Halftroll took from Jötunheimar Ögn Alfasprengi, and afterwards married her. Their son was called Grim. She had been betrothed to Starkath Aludreng, who had eight hands; but she was carried off while he was away to the north of Elivagar. When he came home he slew Hergrim in single combat; but Ögn ran herself through with a sword rather than marry Starkath. After that

212

Starkath carried off Alfhild the daughter of King Alf from Alfheimar, but he was afterwards slain by Thor.

Then Alfhild went to her kinsfolk, and Grim was with her till he went raiding and he became a great warrior. He married Bauggerth the daughter of Starkath Aludrenga and set up his dwelling on an island off Halogaland called Bolm. He was called Ey-grim Bolm. His son by Bauggerth was called Arngrim the Berserk, who afterwards lived in Bolm and was a very famous man.

II. There was a King called Sigrlami who was said to be a son of Odin. His son Svafrlami succeeded the kingdom after his father and was a very great warrior. One day as the king rode a-hunting he got separated from his men, and at sunset he came upon a big stone and two dwarfs beside it. The king banned them with his graven sword from entering the stone. The dwarfs begged him to spare their lives.

The King said, "What are your names?"

One of them said his name was Dvalin and the other, Dulin.

The King said: "As you are the most cunning of all dwarfs, you must make me a sword, the best you can. The hilt and the grip must be of gold, and it must cut iron as easily as if it were cloth, and never rust; and it must bring victory to whoever uses it in battle and single combat."

They agreed to this, and the King rode away.

And when the appointed day came, the King rode to the stone. The dwarfs were outside, and they handed to the King a sword which was very beautiful.

But as Dvalin was standing in the doorway of the stone, he said: "Your sword, Svafrlami, will be the death of a man every time it is drawn; and moreover, it will be the instrument of three pieces of villainy; and to you yourself also it shall bring death."

Then the king struck at the dwarfs with the sword. But they sprang into the stone, and the sword came down on it — sinking so deep that both the ridges of the blade were hidden; for the door into the stone closed as they disappeared: The King called the sword "Tyrfing," and ever afterwards, he carried it in battle and single combat, and was always victorious.

The King had a daughter who was called Eyfura, an exceedingly beautiful and clever girl.

At that time, Arngrim was raiding among the Perms in the Baltic. He raided the kingdom of King Svafrlami and fought against him. They met face to face, and King Svafrlami struck at Arngrim who parried the blow with his shield; but the lower part of the shield was cut away and the sword plunged into the earth. Then Arngrim struck off he king's hand, so that he had to let Tyrfing fall. Arngrim caught up Tyrfing and cut down first the king, and then many others. He took great booty there, and carried off Eyfura, the king's daughter, and took her to his home in Bolm.

By her he had twelve sons. The eldest was Angantyr, then Hervarth, then Hjörvarth, Sæming and Hrani, Brami, Barri, Reifnir, Tind, and Bui, and the two Haddings who only did one man's work between them because they were twins and the youngest of the family; whereas Angantyr, who was a head taller than other men, did the work of two. They were all berserks, and were unequalled in strength and courage. Even when they went marauding there were never more than just the twelve brothers on one ship. They raided far and wide in many lands, and had much success and won great renown. Angantyr had Tyrfing, and Sæming Mistletoe, Hervarth had Hrotti, and each of the others possessed a sword famous in combat. And it was their custom, when they had only their own men with them, to land when they felt the berserks' fury coming upon them, and wrestle with trees or great rocks; for they had been known to slay their own men and disable their ship. Great tales were told about them and they became very famous.

III. One Yule Eve at Bolm, Angantyr made a vow over the pledge cup, as the custom then was, that he would wed Ingibjörg the daughter of King Yngvi of Uppsala — the cleverest and most beautiful maiden in all Northlands — or perish in the attempt and marry no-one else. No more of their vows are recorded.

Tyrfing had this characteristic, that whenever it was unsheathed it shone like a sunbeam, even in the dark, and could only be sheathed with human blood still warm upon it. Never did he whose blood was shed by Tyrfing live to see another day. It is very famous in all stories of the olden days.

Next summer, the brothers went to Uppsala in Sweden, and when they had entered the hall, Angantyr told the King of his vow and that he intended to wed his daughter.

Everybody in the hall listened. Angantyr asked the King to declare what was to be the result of their errand, whereupon Hjalmar the stout-hearted rose from the table, and addressed the king: "Call to mind, Sire, how much honor I have won for you since I came into your kingdom, and how many times I have risked my life for you. In return for these my service I beg that you will give me your daughter in marriage. And moreover I consider myself more deserving a favorable answer than these berserks, who do harm to everyone."

The King pondered over the matter, and found it difficult to decide the question in such a way as to give rise to as little trouble as possible, and he answered at last: "My wish is that Ingibjörg should choose for herself the husband she prefers."

She replied: "If you want to marry me to anyone, then I would rather have a man whose good qualities I know already than one whom I have known by hearsay, and nothing but evil at that."

Angantyr said: "I will not bandy words with you; for I can see that you love Hjalmar. But as for you, Hjalmar, come south to Samso and meet me in single combat. If you do not appear next mid-summer you will be a coward in the eyes of all men."

Hjalmar said that he would not fail to come and fight, and the sons of Arngrim went home to their father and told him what happened. He replied that this was the first time he had ever felt any anxiety on their behalf.

They spent the winter at home, and in the spring made ready to start, going first to Earl Bjartmar, where a feast was made for them. And during the evening Angantyr asked the Earl for the hand of his daughter, and in this as in the rest they got their wish. The wedding took place, and afterwards the sons of Arngrim prepared to set out. But the night before they left, Angantyr had a dream which he related to the Earl: "I dreamed that I and my brothers were in Samso. We found many birds there and killed all that we saw. Then I dreamed that as we were setting out again upon the island, two eagles flew towards us. I went against one and we had a stiff encounter; and at last we sank down and had no strength left in us. But the eagle fought with my eleven brothers and overcame them all."

The Earl said: "The death of mighty men has been revealed to you in this dream."

Then Angantyr and his brother went away and came to Samso, and went ashore to look fore Hjalmar; and the story of their adventures there is related in the *Saga of Örvar-Odd*. First they came to Munarvagar, where they slew all the men from the two ships of Hjalmar and Odd; and afterwards they went ashore and encountered Hjalmar and Odd themselves on the island. Odd slew Angantyr's eleven brothers, and Hjalmar slew Angantyr, and afterwards died there himself on his wounds.

Then Odd had all the rest of them placed in great barrows with all the weapons; but Hjalmar's body he took home to Sweden. And when Ingibjörg the King's daughter saw Hjalmar's body, she fell down dead, and they were both laid together in one barrow at Uppsala.

IV. The story goes on to say that a girl was born to the daughter of Earl Bjartmar. Everyone advised exposing the child, saying that if she resembled her father's kinsmen she would not have a womanly disposition. The Earl, however, had her sprinkled with water and he brought her up, and called her Hervör, saying that the line of Arngrim's sons would not be extinguished if she were left alive.

She grew up to be a beautiful girl. She was tall and strong, and trained herself in the use of bow, shield, and sword. But as soon as she could do anything it was oftener harm than good; and when she had been checked she ran away to the woods and killed people to provide herself with money. And when the Earl heard of it, he had her caught and brought home, where she remained for at time.

One day she went to the Earl and said; "I want to go away because I am not happy here."

A little while after she departed alone, dressed and armed like a man, and joined some vikings and stayed with them for a time, calling herself Hervarth. Shortly afterwards the chief of the vikings died, and Hervarth took command of the band.

One day when they sailed to Samso, Hervarth landed; but her men would not follow her, saying that it was not safe for anyone to be out of doors there by night. Hervarth declared that there was likely to be much treasure in the barrows. She landed on the island towards sunset, but they lay off in Munarvagar. She met a shepherd boy and asked him for information.

He said: "You are a stranger to the island; but come home with me, for it is unsafe for anyone to be out of doors here after sunset; and I am in a hurry to get home."

Hervarth replied: "Tell me where are 'Hjörarth's Barrows,' as they are called."

"You must surely be mad," replied the boy, "if you want to explore by night what no-one dare visit at mid-day. Burning flame plays over them as soon as the sun has set."

But Hervarth insisted that she would visit the barrows — whereupon the shepherd said: "I see that you are a brave man though not a wise one, so I will give you my necklace if you will come home with me."

But Hervarth replied: "Even if you give me all you have you will not hold me back."

And when the sun had set, loud rumblings were heard all over the island, and flames leapt out of the barrows. Then the shepherd grew frightened and took to his heels and ran to the wood as fast as he could, without once looking back. Here is a poem giving an account of his talk with Hervör:

Driving his flocks at the fall of day,
In Munarvagar along the bay,
  A shepherd met a maid.—
"Who comes to our island here alone?
Haste to seek shelter, the day is done,
  The light will quickly fade."
"I will not seek for a resting place:
A stranger am I to the island race.—
  But tell me quick I pray,
Ere thou goest hence, if I may descry
Where the tombs of the children of Arngrim lie:
  O tell me, where are they?"

"Forebear from such questions utterly!
Foolish and rash must thou surely be,
  And in a desperate plight!
Let us haste from these horrors as fast as we can,
For abroad it is ghastly for children of men
  To wander about in the night."

"My necklace of gold is the price I intend
To pay for thy guidance; for I am the friend
  Of vikings, and will not be stayed."
"No treasures so costly, nor rings of red gold
Shall take me their thrall, or my footsteps withhold,
  That thereby my flight be gainsaid.

"Foolish is he who comes here alone
In the fearsome dark when the sun has gone
   And the flames are mounting high;—
When earth and fen are alike ablaze,
And tombs burst open before thy gaze:
   O faster let us hie!"

"Let us never heed for the snorting blaze,
Nor fear, though over the island ways
   Dart tongues of living light.
Let us not lightly give way to fear
Of the noble warriors buried here,
   But talk with them tonight."

But the shepherd lad fled fast away,
Nor stayed to hear what the youth would say,
   But into the forest sped;
While in Hervör's breast rose proud and high
Her hard-knit heart, as she saw near by
   The dwellings of the dead.

She could now see the fires of the barrows and the ghosts standing outside; and she approached the barrows fearlessly and passed through the fires as if they had been merely smoke, until she reached the barrow of the berserks. Then she cried:

V. "Awaken, Anganatyr, hearken to me!
The only daughter of Tofa and thee
   Is here and bids thee awake!
Give me from out the barrow's shade
The keen-edged sword which the dwarfs once made
   For Svafrlami's sake.

Hervarth, Hjörvarth, Angantyr,
And Hrani, under the tree-roots here,
   I bid you now appear;—
Clad in harness and coat of mail,
With shield and broadsword of biting steel,
   Helmet and reddened spear!

The sons of Arngrim are changed indeed
To heaps of dust, and Eyfura's seed
   Has crumbled into mould.—
In Munarvagar will no one speak

To her who has come thus far to seek
   Discourse with the men of old?

Hervarth, Hjörvarth, Angantyr
And Hrani, great be your torment here
   If ye will not hear my words.
Give me the blade that Dvalin made;
It is ill becoming the ghostly dead
   To keep such costly swords!

In your tortured ribs shall my curses bring
A maddening itch and a frenzied sting,
   Till ye writhe in agonies,
As if ye were laid to your final rest
Where the ants are swarming within their nest,
   And reveling in your thighs!"

Then answered Angantyr:
"O Hervör, daughter, why dost thou call
Words full of cursing upon us all?
   Thou goest to meet thy doom!
Mad art thou grown, and thy wits are fled;
Thy mind is astray, that thou wak'st the dead
   —The dwellers in the tomb.

No father buried me where I lie,
Nor other kinsman . . .
The only two who remained unslain
Laid hold on Tyrfing, but now again
   One only possesses the sword."

She answered:
"Nought save the truth shalt thou tell to me!
May the ancient gods deal ill with thee
   If thou harbor Tyrfing there!
Thine only daughter am I, and yet
Unwilling thou art that I should get
   That which belongs to thine heir!"

It now seemed as if the barrows, which had opened, were surrounded with
an unbroken ring of flame. Then Angantyr cried:

"The barrows are opening! Before thy gaze

The round of the island is all ablaze,
   And the gate of Hell stands wide.
There are specters abroad that are ghastly to see.
Return, little maiden, right hastily
   To thy ship that waits on the tide."

She replied:
"No funeral fire that burns by night
Can make me tremble with affright,
   Or fear of awful doom.
Thy daughter's heart can know no fear,
Though a ghost before her should appear
   In the doorway of the tomb."

Angantyr:
"O Hervör, Hervör, hearken to me!
Nought save the truth will I tell to thee
   That will surely come about!
Believe me, maiden, Tyrfing will be
A curse upon all thy progeny
   Till thy race be blotted out.

A son shalt thou bear, as I prophesy,
Who shall fight with Tyrfing mightily,
   And trust to Tyrfing's might.
I tell thee Heidrek shall be his name,
The noblest man and of greatest fame
   Of all under Heaven's light."

Hervör:
"On all you dead this curse I cry:—
Moldering and rotting shall ye lie
   With the spirits in the tomb!
Out of the barrow, Angantyr,
Give me the keen-edged Tyrfing here,
   The sword called 'Hjalmar's Doom' !"

Angantyr:
"Surely unlike to a mortal thou
To wander about from howe to howe,
   And stand in the doorway here!
In the horror of night-time, my little maid,
Thou comest with helmet and byrnie and blade,

And shakest thy graven spear!"
Hervör:
"A mortal maiden is she who comes,
Arousing the corpses within their tombs,
  And will not be denied:—
Give me from out the barrow's shade
The keen-edged sword that the dwarf-folk made,
  Which it ill becomes thee to hide!"

Angantyr:
"The sword that the death-stroke to Hjalmar gave
Lies under my shoulders within the grave,
  And wrapped about with flame.
But that maiden lives not in any land
Who dare grasp the weapon within her hand
  For any hope of fame."

Hervör:
"There lives, O Angantyr, a maid
Who yearns to handle the keen-edged blade,
  And such a maid am I!
And what care I though the tombs firs blaze!
They sink and tremble before my gaze,
  They quiver out and die!"

Angantyr:
"O Hervör, 'tis folly and madness dire
To rush wide-eyed through the flaming fire
  With courage undismayed.
Rather by far will I give to thee
The accursed sword, though unwillingly,
  My little, tender maid."

Hervör:
"O son of the vikings, well hast thou done
In giving me Tyrfing from out the tomb;
  And happier am I today
That I now grasp Tyrfing within my hands
Than if I were queen of the broad Northlands,
  And conqueror of Noroway."

Angantyr:
"Vain is thy rapture, my luckless maid!

Thy hopes are false. All too soon will fade
  The flush of joy from thy face.
Try, child, to listen; I am warning thee! —
This sword is the sword of destiny,
  The destroyer of all thy race!"

Hervör:
"Away, away to my 'ocean-steed'!
The daughter of princes is glad indeed,
  O glad at heart today!
And what care I for the destiny
Of children as yet undreamed by me?—
  Let them quarrel as they may!"

Angantyr:
"Thou shalt have and enjoy without sorrow or pain
The blade which proved to Hjalmar's bane,
  If thou draw it not from its sheath.
Worse than a plague is this cursed thing.
Touch not its edges, for poisons cling
  Above it and beneath.

Farewell, yet fain would I give to thee
The life that has passed from my brothers and me,
  O daughter, 'tis truth I say!
—The strength and vigor and hardihood,
—All that we had that was great and good,
  That has vanished and passed away!"

Hervör:
"Farewell, farewell to all you dead!
Farewell! I would that I were sped!
  Farewell all you in the mound! . . .
Surely in terror I drew my breath
Between the Worlds of Life and Death
  When the grave fires girt me round!"

Then she returned towards her ships; but when dawn came, she saw that they had departed. The vikings had been scared by the rumblings and the flames on the island. She got a ship to carry her away; but nothing is told of her voyage till she came to Guthmund in Glasisvellir, where she remained all through the winter, still calling herself Hervarth.

221

VI. One day Guthmund was playing chess, and when the game was almost up, he asked if anyone could advise him as to his moves. So Hervarth went up to him and began to direct his moves; and it was not long before Guthmund began to win. Then somebody took up Tyrfing and drew it. When Hervarth saw this, he snatched the sword out of his hands, and slew him, and then left the room. They wanted to rush out in pursuit, but Guthmund said: "Don't stir—you will not be avenged on the man so easily as you think, for you don't know who he is. This woman-man will cost you dear before you take his life."

After that Hervör spent a long time in piracy and had great success. And when she grew tired of that she went home to the Earl, her mother's father. There she behaved like other girls, working at her embroidery and fine needlework.

Höfund, the son of Guthmund, heard of this and went and asked for the hand of Hervör, and was accepted; and he took her home.

Höfund was a very wise man and so just in his judgments that he never swerved from giving a correct decision, whether the persons involved were natives or foreigners. And it is from him that the 'höfund' or judge of law-suits takes his name in every realm.

He and Hervör had two sons. One was called Angantyr, the other Heidrek. They were both big strong men—sensible and handsome. Angantyr resembled his father in character and was kindly disposed towards everyone. Höfund loved him very much, as indeed did everybody. But however much good he did, Heidrek did still more evil. He was Hervör's favorite. His foster-father was called Gizur.

One day Höfund held a feast and invited all the chief men in his kingdom except Heidrek. This greatly displeased him, but he put in an appearance all the same, declaring that he would do them some mischief. And when he entered the hall, Angantyr rose and went to meet him and invited him to sit beside him. Heidrek was not cheerful, but he sat till late in the evening after Angantyr had gone; and then he turned to the men who sat on either side of him and worked upon them by his conversation in such a way that they became infuriated with each other. But when Angantyr came back he told them to be quiet. But when Angantyr went out a second time, Heidrek reminded them of his words, and worked upon them to such an extent that one of them struck the other. Then Angantyr returned and persuaded them to keep the peace till morning. And the third time Angantyr went away, Heidrek asked the man who had been struck why he had not the courage to avenge himself. And so effective did his persuasion prove that he who had been struck sprang up and slew his companion. When Angantyr returned, he was displeased at what had taken place. And when Höfund heard of it, he told Heidrek that he must either leave his kingdom or forfeit his life.

So Heidrek went out, and his brother with him. Then his mother came up and gave him Tyrfing. And Heidrek said to her: "I don't know when I shall be able to show as much difference in my treatment of my father and mother as they do in their treatment of me. My father proclaims me and outlaw while my mother has given me Tyrfing, which is more account to me than a great territory. But I shall do that very thing that will most distress my father."

He then drew the sword, which gleamed and flashed brilliantly, and then he got into a great rage and showed the berserk's fury coming upon him. The two brothers were alone. Now since Tyrfing had to be the death of a man every time it was drawn, Heidrek dealt this brother his death-blow. Höfund was told of it, and Heidrek escaped at once to the woods. Höfund had a funeral feast made for his son Angantyr, and he was lamented by everybody.

Heidrek got little joy of his deed and lived in the woods for a long time, shooting deer and bears for food. And when he came to think over his position, he reflected that there would be but a poor tale to tell if no-one was to know what had become of him; and it occurred to him that he could even yet become a man famous for deeds of prowess like his ancestors before him. So he went home and sought out his mother and begged her to ask his father to give him some sound advice before they parted. She went to Höfund and asked him to give their son sound advice. Höfund replied that he would give him a little, but added that it would turn out to his disadvantage nevertheless; he said however that he would not ignore his request: "In the first place he must not aid a man who has slain his liege lord. Secondly, he must not protect a man who has slain one of his comrades. Thirdly, his wife ought not to be always leaving home to visit her relatives. Fourthly, he ought not to stay out late with his sweetheart. Fifthly, he should not ride his best horse when he is in a hurry. Sixthly, he ought not to bring up the child of a man in a better position than himself. Seventhly, let him always be cheerful towards one who comes for hospitality. Eighthly, he should never lay Tyrfing on the ground.—Yet he will not get any benefit from this advice."

His mother repeated these maxims to him.

Heidrek replied: "This advice must have been given me in a spiteful spirit. It will not be of any use to me."

His mother gave him a mark of gold at parting, and bade him always bear in mind how sharp his sword was, and how great renown had been won by everyone who had borne it—what great protection its sharp edges afforded to him who wielded it in battle or single combat, and what great success it always had.—Then they parted.

He went on his way; and when he had gone a short distance he came upon some men who were leading a man in bonds. Heidrek asked what the man had done, and they replied that he had betrayed his liege lord. He asked if they would accept money as his ransom, and they said they were willing to do so. He ransomed the man for half his gold mark.

The man then offered to serve him, but Heidrek replied: "You would not be faithful to a stranger like me, seeing that you betrayed your liege lord to whom you owed many benefits."

Shortly after he again came upon some men, of whom one was in bonds. He asked what this man had done, and they replied that he had murdered one of his comrades. He freed him with the other half of his gold mark. This man also offered to serve him, but Heidrek declined.

After that he went on his way till he came to Reithgotaland, where he went to the King who ruled there. His name was Harold, and he was an old man at the time. Heidrek remained for a time with the King, who gave him a cordial welcome.

VII. There were two Earls who had plundered the kingdom of King Harold and made it subject to them, and because he was old he paid them tribute every year. Heidrek grew intimate with the King, and eventually it came about that he became the commander of his army and betook himself to raiding, and soon made himself famous for his victories. He proceeded to make war on the Earls who had subdued King Harold's kingdom, and a stiff fight took place between them. Heidrek fought with Tyrfing and, as in the past, no-one could withstand it, for it cut through steel as easily as cloth; and the result was that he slew both the Earls and put all their army to flight. He then went throughout the kingdom and brought it under King Harold and took hostages, and then returned home. And as a mark of great honor, King Harold went himself to meet him, and he acquired great fame from this. The King gave him his daughter Helga in marriage and with her half his kingdom. Heidrek had the defense of the whole realm in his hands; and this arrangement lasted for a time.

King Harold had a son in his old age. Heidrek also had a son, who was called Angantyr. Presently a great famine began in Reithgotaland (which is now called Jutland) and it threatened to destroy all the inhabitants. So they tried divination, and the answer was that there would be no plenty in Reithgotaland until the noblest boy in the land hand been sacrificed. Heidrek said that that was King Harold's son, but the King declared that Heidrek's son was the noblest; and there was no escape from this dilemma save by referring it to Höfund, whose decisions were always just.

Thereupon Heidrek went to visit his father, who made him welcome. He asked his father's decision about this question. Höfund pronounced Heidrek's son to be the noblest in that land.

"What compensation do you adjudge to me for my loss?" asked Heidrek.

"You shall claim for yourself in compensation every second man in the retinue of King Harold. Beyond that there is no need to give you advice, considering your character and the army that you have under you."

Then Heidrek went back and summoned a meeting, and told them his father's opinion: "He decided that it was my son who must be sacrificed; and as compensation to me he adjudged to me every second man of those who are with King Harold, and I want you to swear an oath that this shall be done."

And they did so. Then the people demanded that he should give up his son and get them a better harvest. Heidrek then talked with his men after the force had been divided, and demanded fresh oaths of allegiance from them. These they gave, swearing to follow him whether at home or abroad, for whatever purpose he wished.

224

Then said he: "It appears to me that Odin will have been well compensated for one boy if he gets in place of him King Harold and his son and all his host!"

He then bade his men raise his standard and make an attack on King Harold and slay him and all his host, declaring that he was giving this host to Odin instead of his own son. He caused the altars to be reddened with the blood of King Harold and his son Halfdan, while the Queen took her own life in the temple of the Dis.

Heidrek was now accepted as King throughout the realm. He made love to Sifka the daughter of Humli, a prince from the land of the Huns. Their son was called Hlöth. He was brought up with his mother's father.

VIII. King Heidrek went out raiding and marched against the land of the Saxons with a great host. The King of the Saxons sent men to meet him and they made peace with one another, and the King invited Heidrek to a banquet. Heidrek accepted the invitation. The result of this banquet was that Heidrek sought the hand of the King's daughter and married her, receiving much property and land as her dowry; and with that King Heidrek went home to his kingdom. She often used to ask to go to visit her father, and Heidrek was indulgent to her in this matter. Her stepson Angantyr used to go with her.

On one occasion when Heidrek was returning from a raid, he lay in hiding off the land of the Saxons. He landed during the night and entered the building in which his wife was sleeping. He had only one companion with him. All the sentries were asleep. He found a handsome man asleep bedside his wife. He took his son Angantyr and carried him away with him, and returned to his ship, having first cut off a lock of the man's hair.

Next morning he lay to in the King's berth, and all the people went to greet him; and a feast was prepared in his honor. A little later he had a meeting called and asked if anything was known of his son. The Queen alleged that he had died suddenly. He asked her to guide him to his tomb, and when she said that that would only increase his grief, he replied that he did not mind that. A search was made accordingly, and a dog was found wrapped in a shroud. Heidrek remarked that his son had not changed for the better. Then the King caused the man whom he had found asleep to be brought forward, and he proved to be a bondman. Thereupon Heidrek put away his wife, and then went home to his kingdom.

One summer as Heidrek was away raiding, he went into the land of Huns and harried there, and Humli his father-in-law fled before him. Heidrek there captured great booty and also Sifka, the daughter of King Humli, and then returned home to his kingdom. Their son was called Hlöth, as we said before. He sent her home shortly after. He also captured another woman called Sifka from Finland. She was the loveliest woman ever seen.

One summer he sent men east to Holmgarth to offer to bring up the child of King Hrollaug, the most powerful king of the time. This he did because he was anxious to act exactly contrary to the whole of his father's advice. Messengers came to Holmgarth and told their errand to the King, who had a young son called Horlaug.

The King replied: "Is it likely that I shall send him my son to bring up, when he has betrayed King Harold his father-in-law and his other relatives and friends?"

But the Queen urged: "Do not be so hasty in refusing this, for if you do not accept his offer the result will certainly be war. I expect it will fare with you as with many another, and war with him will be no trifle. Moreover he has a sword which nothing can withstand, and the man who wields it will always be victorious."

So the King resolved to send his son to Heidrek; and Heidrek was pleased with him and brought him up and loved him much.

Heidrek's father had also counseled him not to tell secrets to his sweetheart.

IX. Every summer King Heidrek went raiding; he always went into the Baltic where he had King Hrollaug's friendly country at hand. On one occasion King Hrollaug invited him to a feast, and Heidrek consulted his friends as to whether he should accept the invitation. They all tried to dissuade him, bidding him bear in mind his father's maxims.

"All his maxims will I disregard," he replied, and sent word to the King that he would be present at the feast.

He divided his host into three parts. One he ordered to guard the ships, the second accompanied him, while the third he ordered to go on shore and conceal themselves in a wood near the house in which the feast was to be held, and to be on the look out in case he should need help. Heidrek went to the feast, and the next day, when the Kings were seated, Heidrek asked where the King's son, his foster-child, was. A search was made for him, but he could not be found. Heidrek was greatly distressed and retired to bed early; and when Sifka joined him she asked why he was distressed.

"That is a difficult matter to talk about," replied he, "because my life is at stake if it becomes known."

She promised to keep the secret, adding: "Tell me for the sake of the love that is between us."

So Heidrek began: "As I was riding to the forest yesterday looking for sport, I caught sight of a wild boar and made a thrust at him with my spear; but I missed my aim and the shaft snapped. Then I leapt down from my horse and drew Tyrfing, which was effective as usual, and I slew the boar. But when I looked round there was no-one by except the King's son. But it is a peculiarity of Tyrfing that it must be sheathed with human blood still warm upon it, so I slew the lad. Now this will be the end of me if King Hrollaug hears of it, because we have only a small force here."

Next morning when Sifka came to the Queen, the Queen asked her why Heidrek had been depressed. She said that she did not dare to tell. But the Queen persuaded her to change her mind, so she told the Queen all that Heidrek had told her.

"These are terrible tidings," cried the Queen, and went off in deep grief and told the King; but she added:

"Yet Heidrek has done this against his will."

"Your advice has turned out as I expected," said the King as he left the hall to give orders to his men to arm.

Heidrek had a shrewd notion as to what Sifka had said, and ordered his men to arm themselves secretly, and then to go out in small detachments and try to find out what was happening.

A little later King Hrollaug came in and asked Heidrek to come and have a private talk with him. And when they entered a garden, some men sprang at Heidrek and seized him and cast him into fetters and bound him securely; and he recognized the two men who bound him most tightly as the men whose lives he had saved. The King ordered him to be taken to the forest and hanged. There were two hundred and forty of them all told, and when they entered the forest, King Heidrek's men sprang out at them with his weapons and standard and a trumpet which they blew as they attacked their foes. Their companions concealed in the woods heard the noise and came out to meet King Heidrek's men. And when the natives saw that, they all took to their heels; but most of them were slain. The Goths took their King and released him. Heidrek went to his ships after that, taking with him the King's son whom he had left with the men concealed in the wood.

King Hrollaug now summoned a very large force, and King Heidrek raided in his kingdom wherever he went.

Then said King Hrollaug to the Queen: "Your advice has turned out badly for me. I find that our son is with Heidrek, and in his present state of anger he will think nothing of making and end of him in his criminal way, just as he slew his own innocent brother."

"We have been far too easily convinced," replied the Queen. "You saw how popular he was, when no-one would fetter him except two bad men; and our son is taken good care of. This has been a trick of his to make trial of you, and you offered him a poor return for bringing up your child. Send men to him now, and offer to make it up with him, and to give him so much of your territories as you may agree upon with him; and offer him your daughter too, if we can recover our son. That will be better than that you should part from him in enmity. And even if he already has wide territory, he has not a wife as beautiful as she."

"I had not intended to offer her to anyone," replied the King; "but as you are so wise, you shall decide."

Messengers were sent accordingly to King Heidrek to bring about a reconciliation. A council was held and a reconciliation effected by Heidrek's marrying Hergerth, the daughter of King Hrollaug; and she brought him as her dowry Wendland, the province which lies nearest to Reithgotaland.

On one occasion the King was riding his best horse as he was conducting Sifka home. It was late in the evening, and when the King came to a river his horse fell dead. Shortly afterwards, when Sifka attempted to embrace him, he threw her down and broke her leg. Afterwards King Heidrek settled down in his own kingdom and became a great sage.

X. They had a daughter called Hervör who was brought up by a man called Ormar. She was a most beautiful girl, but as tall and strong as a man, and trained herself in the use of bows and arrows.

There was a great man in Reithgotaland called Gestumblindi, who was not on good terms with King Heidrek.

In the King's retinue there were seven men whose duty it was to decide all the disputes that arose in that country.

King Heidrek worshipped Frey, and he used to give Frey the biggest boar he could find. They regarded it as so sacred that in all important cased they used to take the oath on its bristles. It was the custom to sacrifice this boar at the 'sacrifice of the herd.' On Yule Eve the 'boar of the herd' was led into the hall before the King. Then men laid their hands on his bristles and made solemn vows. King Heidrek himself made a vow that however deeply a man should have wronged him, if he came into his power he should not be deprived of the chance of receiving a trial by the King's judges; but he should get off scot free if he could propound riddles which the King could not answer. But when people tried to ask the King riddles, not one was put to him which he could not solve.

The King sent a message to Gestumblindi bidding him come to him on an appointed day; otherwise the King said that he would send to fetch him. Neither alternative pleased Gestumblindi, because he knew himself to be no match for the King in a contest of words; neither did he think he had much to hope from a trial before the judges, for his offences were many. On the other hand, he knew that if the King had to send men to bring him it would cost him his life. Then he proceeded to sacrifice to Odin and to ask his help, promising him great offerings.

One evening a stranger visited Gestumblindi, and said that he also was called Gestumblindi. They were so much alike that neither could be distinguished from the other. They exchanged clothes, and the landowner went into hiding, and everyone thought the stranger was the landowner himself.

This man went to visit the King and greeted him. The King looked at him and was silent.

Gestumblindi said: "I am come, Sire, to make my peace with you."

"Will you stand trial by the judges?" asked the King.

"Are there no other means of escape?" asked Gestumblindi.

"If," replied the King, "you can ask me riddles which I cannot answer, you shall go free."

"I am not likely to be able to do that," replied Gestumblindi; "yet the alternative is severe."

"Do you prefer the trial?" asked the King.

"Nay," said he, "I would rather ask riddles."

"That is quite in order," said the King, "and much depends on the issue. If you can get the better of me you shall marry my daughter and none shall gainsay you. Yet I don't imagine you are very clever, and it has never yet happened that I have been unable to solve the riddles that have been put to me."

Then a chair was placed for Gestumblindi, and the people began to listen eagerly to the words of wisdom. Gestumblindi began as follows:

XI. "I would that I had that which I had yesterday. Guess O King, what that was:—Exhauster of men, retarder of words, yet originator of speech. King Heidrek, read me this riddle!"

Heidrek replied: "Your riddle is a good one, Gestumblindi. I have guessed it. —Give him some ale. That is what confounds many people's reason. Some are made garrulous by it, but some become confused in their speech."

Gestumblindi said: "I went from home, I made my way from home, I looked upon a road of roads. A road was beneath me, a road above and a road on every side. King Heidrek, read me this riddle!"

Heidrek replied: "Your riddle is a good one, Gestumblindi. I have guessed it. You went over a bridge, and the course of the river was beneath it , and birds were flying over your head and on either side of you; that was their road; you saw a salmon in the river, and that was his road."

Gestumblindi said: "What was the drink that I had yesterday? It was neither wine nor water, mead nor ale, nor any kind of food; and yet I went away with my thirst quenched. King Heidrek, read me this riddle!"

Heidrek replied: "Your riddle is a good one, Gestumblindi. I have guessed it. You lay in the shade and cooled your lips in dew. But if you are the Gestumblindi I took you for, you are a more intelligent man than I expected; for I had heard that your conversation showed no brains, yet now you are setting to work cleverly."

Gestumblindi said: "I expect that I shall soon come to grief; yet I should like you to listen a while longer." Then he continued: "Who is that clanging one who traverses hard paths which he has trod before? He kisses very rapidly, has two mouths and walks on gold alone. King Heidrek, read me this riddle!"

Heidrek replied: "Your riddle is a good one, Gestumblindi. I have guessed it. That is the goldsmith's hammer, with which gold is forged."

Gestumblindi said: "What is that huge one that passes over the earth, swallowing lakes and pools? He fears the wind, but he fears not man, and carries on hostilities against the sun. King Heidrek, read me this riddle!"

Heidrek replied: "Your riddle is a good one, Gestumblindi. I have guessed it. That is fog. One cannot see the sea because of it. Yet as soon as the wind blows, the fog lifts; but men can do nothing to it. Fog kills the sunshine. You have a cunning way of asking riddles and conundrums, whoever you are."

Gestumblindi said: "What is the huge one that controls many things and of which half faces towards Hell? It saves people's lives and grapples with the earth, if it has a trusty friend. King Heidrek, read me this riddle!"

Heidrek replied: "Your riddle is a good one, Gestumblindi. I have guessed it. That is an anchor with its thick strong cable. It controls many a ship, and grips the earth with one of its flukes which is pointing towards Hell. It is a means of safety to many people. Greatly do I marvel at your readiness of speech and wisdom."

Gestumblindi said: "Ah, but I am now almost at the end of my riddles; yet everyone is eager to save his life. — What lives in high mountains? What falls in deep valleys? What lives without breathing? What is never silent? King Heidrek, read me this riddle!"

Heidrek replied: "Your riddle is a good one, Gestumblindi. I have guessed it. A raven always lives in high mountains, and dew falls in deep valleys, a fish lives without breathing, and the booming waterfall is never silent."

"Things are now becoming serious," said Gestumblindi, "and I do not know what is going to happen. —What is the marvel which I have seen outside Delling's doorway? It points its head towards Hell and turns its feet to the sun. King Heidrek, read me this riddle!"

Heidrek replied: "Your riddle is a good one, Gestumblindi. I have guessed it. That is a leek. It head grows down into the ground, and its blades upward into the air."

Gestumblindi said: "What is the marvel which I have seen outside Delling's doorway?—Two restless, lifeless things boiling a wound-leek. King Heidrek, read me this riddle!"

Heidrek replied: "Your riddle is a good one, Gestumblindi. I have guessed it. That is the smith's bellows which have breath, yet not life."

Gestumblindi said: "What is the marvel which I have seen outside Delling's doorway?—White fliers smiting the rock, and black fliers burying themselves in sand! King Heidrek, read me this riddle!"

Heidrek replied: "Your riddle is a good one, Gestumblindi. I have guessed it. But now your riddles are growing trivial. That is hail and rain; for hail beats upon the street; whereas rain-drops fall into the sand and sink into the earth."

Gestumblindi said: "What is the marvel which I have seen outside Delling's doorway? I saw a black hog wallowing in mud, yet no bristles were standing up on his back. King Heidrek, read me this riddle!"

Heidrek replied: "Your riddle is a good one, Gestumblindi. I have guessed it. That is a dung-beetle. But we have talked too long when dung-beetles come to exercise the wits of great men."

Gestumblindi said: " 'It is best to put off misfortune'; and though there are some who overlook this truth, many will want to go on trying. I myself too see now that I shall have to look out for every possible way of escape. What is the marvel which I have seen outside Delling's doorway? This creature has ten tongues, twenty eyes, forty feet, and walks with difficulty. King Heidrek, read me this riddle!"

Heidrek replied: "Your riddle is a good one, Gestumblindi. I have guessed it. That was a sow with nine little pigs."

Then the King had the sow killed and they found they had killed with her nine little pigs, as Gestumblindi had said.

Then the King said: "I am beginning to suspect that I have to deal with a cleverer man than myself in this business; but I don't know who you can be."

Gestumblindi said: "I am such as you can see; and I am very anxious to save my life and be quit of this task."

"You must go on asking riddles," replied the King, "till you have exhausted your stock, or else till I fail to solve them."

Gestumblindi said: "What is the marvel which I have seen outside Delling's doorway? It flies high, with a whistling sound like the whirring of an eagle. Hard it is to clutch, O King. King Heidrek, read me this riddle!"

Heidrek replied: "Your riddle is a good one, Gestumblindi. I have guessed it. That is an arrow," said the King.

Gestumblindi said: "What is the marvel which I have seen outside Delling's doorway? It has eight feet and four eyes, and carries its knees higher than its body. King Heidrek, read me this riddle!"

Heidrek replied: "I notice firstly that you have a long hood; and secondly that you look downwards more than most people, since you observe every creature of the earth.—That is a spider."

Gestumblindi said: "What is the marvel which I have seen outside Delling's doorway? It shines upon men in every land; and yet wolves are always struggling for it. King Heidrek, read me this riddle!"

Heidrek replied: "Your riddle is a good one, Gestumblindi. I have guessed it. It is the sun. It gives light to every land and shines down on all men. But the wolves are called Skalli and Hatti. Those are the wolves who accompany the sun, one in front and one behind."

Gestumblindi said: "What is the marvel which I have seen outside Delling's doorway? It was harder than horn, blacker than the raven, whiter than the membrane of an egg, straighter than a shaft. King Heidrek, read me this riddle!"

Heidrek replied: "Your riddle is a good one, Gestumblindi. I have guessed it. You saw an agate, and a sunbeam penetrated the house and shone upon it. But since you seem to be a learned man, can you not propound your riddles without beginning them in the same way?"

Gestumblindi said: "Two bond-women, fair-haired brides, were carrying ale to the store-room. The cask was not turned by hands, nor clinched by hammers; and he who made it strutted about outside the islands. King Heidrek, read me this riddle!"

Heidrek replied: "Your riddle is a good one, Gestumblindi. I have guessed it. These are eider ducks laying their eggs. The eggs are not made with hammer or hands, and the hand-maidens put the ale into the egg-shell."

Gestumblindi said: "He who has got but a little sword and is very short of learning has to look out for help. I would like to talk still further. —Who are those ladies of the lofty mountain? A woman begets by a woman; a maid has a son by a maid; and these good-wives have no husbands. King Heidrek, read me this riddle!"

Heidrek replied: "Your riddle is a good one, Gestumblindi. I have guessed it. They are two Angelicas joined together, and a young angelica shoot is growing between them."

Gestumblindi said: "Who are the girls who fight without weapons around their lord? The dark red ones always protect him, and the fair ones seek to destroy him. King Heidrek, read me this riddle!"

Heidrek replied: "Your riddle is a good one, Gestumblindi. I have guessed it. That is a game of chess. The pieces smite one another without weapons around the king, and the red assist him."

Gestumblindi said: "Who are the merry-maids who glide over the land for their father's pleasure? They bear a white shield in winter and a black one in summer. King Heidrek, read me this riddle!"

Heidrek replied: "Your riddle is a good one, Gestumblindi. I have guessed it. Those are ptarmigan."

Gestumblindi said: "Who are the damsels who go sorrowing for their father's pleasure? These white-hooded ladies have shining hair, and are very wide awake in a gale. King Heidrek, read me this riddle!"

Heidrek replied: "Your riddle is a good one, Gestumblindi. I have guessed it. Those are the billows, which are called Ægir's maidens."

Gestumblindi said: "Who are the maidens who go about many together for their father's pleasure? They have brought trouble to many; and these good-wives have no husbands. King Heidrek, read me this riddle!"

Heidrek replied: "Your riddle is a good one, Gestumblindi. I have guessed it. Those are billows like the last."

Gestumblindi said: "Who are the brides who go about the reefs and trail along the firths? These white-hooded ladies have a hard bed and do not play much when the weather is calm. King Heidrek, read me this riddle!"

Heidrek replied: "Your riddle is a good one, Gestumblindi. I have guessed it. Those again are Ægir's maidens; but your pleading has now become so weak that you will have to stand trial by the judges."

Gestumblindi said: "I am loath to do so; and yet I fear that it will very soon come to that. I saw a barrow-dweller pass by, a corpse sitting on a corpse, the blind riding on the blind towards the ocean-path. Lifeless was the steed. King Heidrek, read me this riddle!"

Heidrek replied: "Your riddle is a good one, Gestumblindi. I have guessed it. It is that you came to a river; and an ice-floe was floating along the stream, and on it a dead horse was lying, and on the horse was a dead snake; and thus the blind was carrying the blind when they were all three together."

Gestumblindi said: "What is the beast which slays people's flocks and is girt around with iron? It has eight horns, yet no head, and it runs when it can. King Heidrek, read me this riddle!"

Heidrek replied: "Your riddle is a good one, Gestumblindi. I have guessed it. That is the *Hunn* in chess. It has the same name as the bear. It runs as soon as it is thrown."

Gestumblindi said: "What is the beast which protects the Danes? Its back is bloody, but it shields men, encounters spears and saves men's lives. Man fits his hand to its body. King Heidrek, read me this riddle!"

Heidrek replied: "Your riddle is a good one, Gestumblindi. I have guessed it. That is a shield. It protects many people and often has a bloody back."

Gestumblindi said: "A 'nose-goose' (i.e. duck) in former days had grown very big when eager for young. She gathered together her building timber: 'biters of straw' sheltered her, and 'drink's echoing cavern' was above her. King Heidrek, read me this riddle!"

Heidrek replied: "Your riddle is a good one, Gestumblindi. I have guessed it. There a duck was sitting on her eggs between the jaws of an ox, which you call 'biters of straw.' The 'echoing cavern' is the skull, and the 'building timber,' the nest."

Gestumblindi said: "Four walking, four hanging, two pointing the way, two warding off the dogs, one, generally dirty, dangling behind! King Heidrek, read me this riddle!"

Heidrek replied: "Your riddle is a good one, Gestumblindi. I have guessed it. That is a cow. She has four feet and four udders, two horns and two eyes, and the tail dangles behind."

Gestumblindi said: "Who is that solitary one who sleeps in the gray ash, and is made from stone only? This greedy one has neither father nor mother. There will he spend his life. King Heidrek, read me this riddle!"

Heidrek replied: "Your riddle is a good one, Gestumblindi. I have guessed it. That is a spark struck by a flint and hidden in the hearth."

Gestumblindi said: "I saw a horse standing . . . "

Then the King said: "My retinue shall read this riddle."

They made many guesses, but not particularly good ones. And when the King saw that they could do nothing he said: "What you call a 'horse' is a piece of linen, and his 'mare' is the weaver's rod; and the linen is shaken up and down."

Gestumblindi said: "Who are the thanes who ride to the meeting, sixteen of them together? They send their men far and wide to make homes of their own. King Heidrek, read me this riddle!"

Heidrek replied: "Your riddle is a good one, Gestumblindi. I have guessed it. That is 'King Itrek's game.'"

Gestumblindi said: "In summer time at sunset I saw the King's body-guard awake and very joyful. The nobles were drinking their ale in silence, but the ale-butts stood screaming. King Heidrek, read me this riddle!"

Heidrek replied: "Your riddle is a good one, Gestumblindi. I have guessed it. That is a sow with her litter. When the little pigs are feeding, she squeals and they are silent. —But I can't imagine who you are who can compose such things so deftly out of such unpromising materials!"

The King then silently made a sign that the door of the hall was to be closed.

Gestumblindi said: "I saw maidens like dust. Rocks were their beds. They were black and swarthy in the sunshine, but the darker it grew, the fairer they appeared. King Heidrek, read me this riddle!"

Heidrek replied: "Your riddle is a good one, Gestumblindi. I have guessed it. They are pale embers on the hearth."

Gestumblindi said: "I sat on a sail, and saw dead men carrying a channel of blood in the bark of a tree. King Heidrek, read me this riddle!"

Heidrek replied: "Your riddle is a good one, Gestumblindi. I have guessed it. You sat on a wall, and watched a hawk flying and carrying an eider duck in its claws."

Gestumblindi said: "Who are those two who have ten feet, three eyes and one tail? King Heidrek, read me this riddle!"

Heidrek replied: "You are hard up when you have to turn back to things of long ago to bring forward against me. That is Odin riding his horse Sleipnir. It had eight feet and Odin two, and they had three eyes—Sleipnir two and Odin one."

Gestumblindi said: "Tell me lastly, Heidrek, if you are wiser than any other prince, what did Odin whisper in Balder's ear, before he was placed upon the pyre?"

The King replied: "I am sure it was something scandalous and cowardly and thoroughly contemptible. You are the only person who knows the words which you spoke, you evil and wretched creature."

Then the King drew Tyrfing, and struck at Gestumblindi; but he changed himself into a falcon and flew out through the window of the hall. And the sword struck the tail of the falcon; and that is why it has had a short tail ever since, according to heathen superstition. But Odin had now become wroth with the King for striking at him; and that night he was slain.

XII. It is said that King Heidrek had some slaves, nine in all, whom he had taken in a freebooting expedition in the West. They came of noble families, and chafed against their captivity. One night, when King Heidrek lay in bed, attended by only a handful of men, the slaves armed themselves and went to the building in which he lay. They first slew the sentries, and then went and broke into the King's chamber, and slew the King and all who were within. They took the sword Tyrfing, and all the treasure that they found there, and carried everything off with them.

For a while, no one knew who had done the deed or how vengeance was to be taken. Then Angantyr the son of King Heidrek had a meeting called, and by that assembly he was proclaimed King over all the territories that King Heidrek had held. And at the same meeting he swore a solemn oath that he would never sit on his father's throne until he had avenged him.

Shortly after the meeting, Angantyr went away by himself and traveled far and wide searching for these men. One evening he was walking down to the sea along a river called Graf. There he saw three men in a fishing-boat, and presently he saw one of the men catch fish, and heard him call to one of his companions to hand him a bait-knife to cut off the fish's head. The man replied that he could not spare it. Then the first man said:

"Take down the sword from over there by the rudder, and hand it to me."
And he took it and unsheathed it, and cut off the fish's head, and then spoke
a verse:

"This pike at the mouth of the river
Has paid the penalty
For the slaughter inflicted on Heidrek,
'Neath the Mountains of Harvathi."

Angantyr immediately perceived that it was Tyrfing, and went off at once to the
wood and waited there till it was dark. And the fishermen rowed to the land, and
went to a tent which they had, and lay down and went to sleep. And when it was close
on midnight, Angantyr went up to them and pulled down the tent on top of the
slaves and slew all nine of them, and carried off the sword Tyrfing as a sign that he
had avenged his father. He then went home and had a great funeral feast held to his
father's memory on the banks of the Dnieper, at a place called Arheimar. The kings
who ruled at the time were as follows: Humli ruled the Huns, Gizur the Gautar,
Angantyr the Goths, Valdar the Danes, Kjar the Gauls; Alrek the Bold ruled the
English people.

Hlöth the son of King Heidrek was brought up at the court of King Humli, his
grandfather. He was a very handsome and valiant man. There was an old saying at
that time that a man was "born with weapons or horses." And the explanation is that
it referred to the weapons which were being forged at the time when the man was
born; also to any sheep, beasts, oxen and horses that were born about the same time.
These were all given to high-born men as an honor to them, as is here related about
Hlöth the son of Heidrek:

"In the land of the Huns was Hlöth born
In a holy forest glade,
With ring-bedizened helmet,
With dagger and keen-edged blade,
With byrnie and with broadsword,
And noble prancing steed."

Then Hlöth learnt of the death of his father, and also that this brother Angantyr
had been made King over all the territory which their father had held. Then King
Humli and Hlöth resolved that Hlöth should go and request his brother Angantyr
to allow him a share of his father's property, and that he should try first by fair
words—as is said here:

"Hlöth, the heir of Heidrek,
Came riding from the East,
To where Angantyr was holding

235

King Heidrek's funeral feast.
He came to his court in Arheimar
Where the Gothic people dwell,
Demanding his share of the heritage left
By the King when he journeyed to Hell."

Hlöth now arrived in Arheimar with a great host as it says here:

"He found a warrior hastening
Towards the lofty hall;
And unto this late traveler
Did Hlöth his greeting call:
O man, make haste to enter
This hall that towers so high!
Bid Angantyr speed,
For great is the need
We hold a colloquy."

The men entered and went up to Angantyr's table and saluted the King, saying:

"Hlöth, thy warlike brother,
King Heidrek's valiant heir,
Has sent me hither to thee,
And bidden me declare
That he wishes to hold converse;
And though he be young indeed,
Yet he looks a mighty champion,
Seated high upon his steed."

And when the King heard that, he flung down his knife upon the table and arose from the feast; and he put on his corslet and took a white shield in one hand and the sword Tyrfing in the other. Then a great din arose in the hall, as is said in the poem:

"Then a murmur arose from the warriors,
And all in the hall drew near,
As the warder reported the message of Hlöth:
—Everyone lent an ear;
And the men all awaited with quivering breath
The message of Angantyr."

Then Angantyr said: "Hail, brother! You are welcome! Come in and drink with us, and let us first drink mead in memory of our father, to the honor and glory of us all with full ceremony."

236

Hlöth said: "We are come hither for a different purpose than to fill our stomachs."

The Hlöth cried:

"Of all the possessions of Heidrek
The half do I now demand;
—His spear and blade and treasures,
His cattle and his land,
His handmaids and his bondmen,
And the children to them born,
And the murmuring mill that the bondwomen turn
As they wearily grind the corn.

And half of the far-famed Mirkwood,
And half of the holy grave
Far off mid the Gothic peoples,—
These also will I have.—
Half of the noble pillar
That stands on Dnieper's shore;
And of Heidrek's castles, land and folk,
And half of his golden store!"

Cried Angantyr:

"The white-shining shield shall be cloven, brother,
And spear on spear shall ring;
And many a helmet be lowered, brother,
In battle for this thing,
Ere I give thee half my heritage,
Or half of the sword Tyrfing."

But Angantyr added:

"I will offer thee wealth in plenty,
And all thy heart's desire
In store of costly treasure,
And rings of golden fire;
Twelve hundred squires will I give thee,
Twelve hundred prancing steeds;
Twelve hundred men
To attend on them
And arm them for mighty deeds.
And every man whom I give thee

Shall receive a richer store
Of rings and costly treasures
Than ever he had before.—
To every man a maiden!
To every maid a ring!
I will clasp a necklace round her throat,
A necklace fit for a king!

I will case thee all in silver
As thou sittest on thy throne;
And a third of the Gothic peoples
Shall be thine to rule alone;
With gold shalt thou be covered
As thou farest through the land.—
Thou shalt dazzle the sight
As thou walk'st in the light
Like the flame of a fiery brand."

XIII. Gizur, a liegeman from the Grytingar, King Heidrek's foster-father, was with King Angantyr. He was a very old man at that time. And when he heard King Angantyr's suggestion, he thought that he was offering too much and said:

"King Angantyr is generous
And royal his offering!
For thy mother was merely a bondmaid
Though thou hadst for thy father a King.
And though thou art only an outcast,
Yet a seat of honor was thine,
When the Prince was dividing his treasure and land,
And his portion to each did assign."

Hlöth grew very angry at being called an outcast and the child of a bondwoman, if he accepted his brother's offer; so he departed at once with all his men and returned home to King Humli, his mother's father, in the land of the Huns. And he told Humli that Angantyr his brother had not granted him an equal share. King Humli enquired as to all that had passed between them, and was very angry that Hlöth, the son of his daughter, should be called the son of a bondmaid, and he cried:

"We will stay in our homes for the winter,
And as princes are wont when they dine,
We will hold high converse together,
Quaffing the costly wine.
We will call on the Hunnish people

238

To arm them with spear and with shield.—
They shall march to the fight
Right royally dight,
And conquer their foes in the field."

Then he added:

"We will summon a mighty host, Hlöth,
And shield on shield will clang,
As the warriors arm them from twelve years old,
And the wild colts gallop along.
And the Huns shall mass
Ere the winter pass,
And assemble a countless throng."

That winter, King Humli and Hlöth remained quiet, but the following spring they collected such a large army that the land of the Huns was swept bare of fighting men. All those of twelve years old and upwards, who were fit for military service and could carry arms, joined the army, and all the horses of two years old and upwards. The host was now so big that thousands and nothing less than thousands could be counted in the legions. And a commander was set over every "thousand," and a standard was set up over every legion. And there were five "thousand" in each legion, each "thousand" containing thirteen "hundreds," and each "hundred" four times forty men; and these legions were thirty three in number.

When these troops had assembled, they rode thorough the forest which was called Mirkwood, and which separated the land of the Huns from that of the Goths. And when they emerged from the forest, they came upon a thickly inhabited country with level fields; and on these plains there was a fine fortress. It was under the command of Hervör, the sister of Angantyr and Hlöth, and Ormar, her foster-father was with her. They had been appointed to defend the land against the Hunnish host, and they had a large army there.

XIV. It happened one morning at sunrise that as Hervör was standing on the summit of a tower over the gate of the fortress, she looked southwards towards the forest, and saw clouds of dust arising from a great body of horses, by which the sun was hidden for a long time. Next she saw a gleam beneath the dust, as though she were gazing on a mass of gold—fair shields overlaid with gold, gilded helmets and white corslets. Then she perceived that it was the Hunnish host coming on in vast numbers. She descended hastily and called her trumpeter, and bade him sound the assembly.

Then said Hervör: "Take your weapons and arm for battle; and do thou, Ormar, ride against the Huns and offer them battle before the Southern Gate."

Ormar replied: "I will certainly take my shield and ride with the companies of the Goths. I will challenge the Huns and offer them battle before the Southern Gate."

Then Ormar rode out of the fortress against the Huns. He called loudly bidding them ride up to the fort, saying: "Outside the gate of the fortress, in the plains to the south—there will I offer you battle. Let those who arrive first await their foes!"

Then Ormar rode back to the fortress, and found Hervör and all her host armed and ready. They rode forthwith out of the fort with all their host against the Huns, and a great battle began between them. But the Hunnish host was far superior in numbers, so that Hervör's troops began to suffer heavy losses; and in the end Hervör fell, and a great part of her army round about her. And when Ormar saw her fall, he fled with all those who still survived. Ormar rode day and night as fast as he could to King Angantyr in Arheimar. The Huns then proceeded to ravage and burn throughout the land.

And when Ormar came into the presence of King Angantyr, he cried:

"From the south have I journeyed hither
To bear these tidings to thee:—
The whole of the forest of Mirkwood
Is burnt up utterly;
And the land of the Goths is drenched with blood
As our warriors fall and die."

Then he continued:

"All of thy noblest warriors
On the field are lying dead.
King Heidrek's daughter fell by the sword;
She drooped and bowed her head.
Thy sister Hervör is now no more.—
By the Huns was her life-blood shed.
O prouder and lighter the maiden's step
As she wielded spear and sword
Than if she were sped to her trysting place,
Or her seat at the bridal-board!"

When King Angantyr heard that, he drew back his lips, and it was some time before he spoke. Then he said: "In no brotherly wise hast thou been treated, my noble sister!"

Then he surveyed his retinue, and his band of men was but small; then he cried:

"The Gothic warriors were many,
As they sat and drank the mead;

240

But now when many are called for,
The array is poor indeed!
Not a man in the host will adventure—
Though I offer a rich reward—
To take his shield,
And ride to the field,
To seek out the Hunnish horde."

Then Gizur the Old cried:

"I will crave no single farthing,
Nor ringing coin of gold;
I will take my shield
And ride to the field
To the Huns with their myriads untold.
And the message of war that you send to the host
Will I carry, and there unfold."

It was a rule with King Heidrek that if his army was invading a land, and the King of that land had set up hazel stakes to mark the spot on which the battle was to take place, then the vikings should not go raiding till the battle had been fought.

Gizur armed himself with good weapons and leapt on his horse as if he had been a young man. Then he cried to the King: "Where shall I challenge the host of the Huns to battle?"

King Angantyr replied: "Challenge them to battle at Dylgia and on Dunheith, and upon all the heights of Jösur, where the Goths have often won renown by glorious victories!"

Then Gizur rode away until he came to the host of the Huns. He rode just within earshot, and then called loudly, crying:

"Your host is panic stricken,
And your prince is doomed to fall;
Though your banners are waving high in the air,
Yet Odin is wroth with you all.
Come forth to the Jösur Mountains,
On Dylgia and Dunheith come fight;
For I make a sure boast,
In the heart of your host
The javelin of Odin will light!"

When Hlöth heard Gizur's words, he cried: "Lay hold upon Gizur of the Grytingar, Angantyr's man, who has come from Arheimar!"

King Humli said: "We must not injure heralds who travel about unattended."

Gizur cried: "You Hunnish dogs are not going to overcome us with guile."

Then Gizur struck spurs into his horse and rode back to King Angantyr, and went up to him and saluted him. The King asked him if he had parleyed with the Huns.

Gizur replied: "I spoke with them and I challenged them to meet us on the battle-field of Dunheith and in the valleys of Dylgia."

Angantyr asked how big the army of the Huns was.

"Their host is very numerous," replied Gizur. "There are six legions in all, and five 'thousands' in every legion, and each 'thousand' contains thirteen 'hundreds,' and in every 'hundred' there are a hundred and sixty men."

Angantyr asked further questions about the host of the Huns.

He then sent men in all directions to summon every man who was willing to support him and could bear weapons. He then marched to Dunheith with his army, and it was a very great host. There the host of the Huns came against him with an army half as big again as his own.

XV. Next day they began their battle, and they fought together the whole day, and at evening they went to their quarters. They continued fighting for eight days, but the princes were then still all unwounded, though none could count the number of the slain. But both day and night troops came thronging round Angantyr's banner from all quarters; and so it came about that his army never grew less.

The battle now became fiercer than ever. The Huns were desperate, for they now saw that their only chance of escaping annihilation lay in victory, and that sorry would be their lot if they had to ask for quarter from the Goths. The Goths on the other hand were defending their freedom and their native land against the Huns; so they stood fast and encouraged one another to fight on. Then towards the close of the day the Goths made so fierce and attack that the line of the Huns recoiled before it. And when Angantyr saw that, he pressed forward from behind the rampart of shields into the forefront of the battle, and grasping Tyrfing in his hand, mowed down both men and horses. Then the ranks fell apart in front of the Kings of the Huns, and Hlöth exchanged blows with his brother. There fell Hlöth and King Humli, and then the Huns took flight. The Goths cut them down and made such a great slaughter that the rivers were dammed with the bodies and diverted from their courses, and the valleys were full of dead men and horses. Angantyr then went to search among the slain, and found his brother Hlöth. Then he cried:

"I offered thee wealth unstinted, brother,
And treasures manifold,—
Riches of cattle and land, brother,
Riches of glittering gold;
But now thou hast wagered and lost in the battle
Thy desires and glories untold.

A curse has fallen upon us, brother,
I have dealt destruction to thee;
And ne'er shall the deed be forgotten, brother;
Full ill is the norns' decree!"

XVI. Angantyr ruled Reithgotaland as King for a long time. He was powerful and generous and a great warrior, and lines of kings are sprung from him.
He had a son called Heidrek Wolfskin who ruled after him for a long time in Reithgotaland. Heidrek had a daughter called Hild, who was the mother of Halfdan the Valiant, the father of Ivar Vithfathmi. Ivar Vithfathmi went with his army into the Swedish kingdom, as is told in the Sagas of the Kings. And King Ingjald the Wicked was panic-stricken at the approach of his army, and burned the roof over himself and all his retinue at a place called Ræning. Ivar Vithfathmi then conquered all Sweden. He also subdued Denmark and Courland and the land of the Saxons and Estonia, and all the eastern realms as far as Russia. He also ruled the land of the Saxons in the West and conquered the part of England which was called Northumbria.
Then he conquered all Denmark and set over it King Valdar, to whom he married his daughter Alfhild. Their sons were Harold Hilditönn and Randver who afterwards fell in England. And when Valdar died in Denmark, Randver got possession of the Danish kingdom and made himself King over it. And King Harold Hilditönnn got himself proclaimed King of Gautland, and he afterwards conquered all the kingdoms already mentioned, which King Ivar Vithfathmi had held.
King Randver married Asa, the daughter of King Harold of the Red Moustache from Norway. Their son was Sigurth Hring. King Randver died suddenly, and Sigurth Hring succeeded to the Kingdom of Denmark. He fought against King Harold Hilditönn at the Battle of Bravöll in East Gautland, and there King Harold fell, and a great multitude of his army with him. This battle and the one which Angantyr and his brother Hlöth fought at Dunheith are the battles which have been most famous in stories of old. Never were any greater slaughters made.
King Sigurth Hring ruled the Kingdom of the Danes till the day of his death; and his son Ragnar Lothbrok succeeded him.
Harold Hilditönn had a son called Eystein the Wicked, who succeeded the Swedish realm after his father, and ruled it until he was slain by the sons of Ragnar Lothbrok, as is related in the Saga of Ragnar Lothbrok. The sons of Ragnar Lothbrok conquered all the Swedish Kingdom; and after the death of King Ragnar, his son, Björn Ironside, inherited Sweden, and Sigurth Denmark, Hvitserk the Eastern Realm, and Ivar the Boneless England.
The sons of Björn Ironside were Eric and Refil. The latter was a warrior-prince and sea-king. King Eric ruled the Swedish Realm after his father, and lived but a short time. Then Eric the son of Refil succeeded to the Kingdom. He was a great warrior and a very powerful King. The sons of Eric Björnsson were Önund of Uppsala and King Björn. Then the Swedish Realm again came to be divided between brothers. They succeeded to the Kingdom on the death of Eric Refilssson.

King Björn built a house called "Barrow," and he himself was called Björn of the Barrow. Bragi the poet was with him. King Önund had a son called Eric, and he succeeded to the throne at Uppsala after his father . He was a mighty King. In his days Harold the Fair-haired made himself King of Norway. He was the first to unite the whole of that country under his sway.

Eric at Uppsala had a son called Björn, who came to the throne after his father and ruled for a long time. The sons of Björn, Eric the Victorious, and Olaf succeeded to the kingdom after their father. Olaf was the father of Styrbjörn the Strong. In their days King Harold the Fair-haired died. Styrbjörn fought against King Eric his father's brother at Fyrisvellir, and there Styrbjörn fell. Then Eric ruled Sweden till the day of his death. He married Sigrith the Ambitious. They had as son called Olaf who was accepted as King in Sweden after King Eric. He was only a child at the time and the Swedes carried him about with them, and for this reason they called him "Skirt-King," and then, later, Olaf the Swede. He ruled for a long time and was a powerful King. He was the first king of Sweden to be converted, and in his days, Sweden was nominally Christian.

King Olaf the Swede had a son called Önund who succeeded him. He died in his bed. In his day fell King Olaf the Saint at Stiklestad. Olaf the Swede had another son called Eymund, who came to the throne after his brother. In his day the Swedes neglected the Christian religion, but he was King for only a short time.

There was a great man of noble family in Sweden called Steinkel. His mother's name was Astrith, the daughter of Njal the son of Fin the Squinter, from Halogaland; and his father was Rögnvald the Old. Steinkel was an Earl in Sweden at first, and then after the death of Eymund, the Swedes elected him their King. Then the throne passed out of the line of the ancient kings of Sweden. Steinkel was a mighty prince. He married the daughter of King Eymund. He died in his bed in Sweden about the time that King Harold fell in England.

Steinkel had a son called Ingi, who became King of Sweden after Haakon. Ingi was King of Sweden for a long time, and was popular and a good Christian. He tried to put an end to heathen sacrifices in Sweden and commanded all the people to accept Christianity; yet the Swedes held to their ancient faith. King Ingi married a woman called Mær who had a brother called Svein. King Ingi liked Svein better than any other man, and Svein became thereby the greatest man in Sweden. The Swedes considered that King Ingi was violating the ancient law of the land when he took exception to many things which Steinkel his father had permitted, and at an assembly held between the Swedes and King Ingi, they offered him two alternatives, either to follow the old order, or else to abdicate. Then King Ingi spoke up and said that he would not abandon the true faith; whereupon the Swedes raised a shout and pelted him with stones, and drove him from the assembly.

Svein, the King's brother-in-law, remained behind in the assembly, and offered the Swedes to do sacrifices on their behalf if they would give him the Kingdom. They all agreed to accept Svein's offer, and he was then recognized as King over all Sweden. A horse was then brought to the assembly and hewn in pieces and cut up for eating, and the sacred tree was smeared with blood. Then all the Swedes abandoned Christianity, and sacrifices started again. They drove King Ingi away; and he went into Vestergötland. Svein the Sacrificer was King of Sweden for three years.

King Ingi set off with his retinue and some of his followers, though it was but a small force. He then rode eastwards by Småland and into Östergötland and then into Sweden. He rode both day and night, and came upon Svein suddenly in the early morning. They caught him in his house and set it on fire and burned the band of men who were within.

There was a baron called Thjof who was burnt inside. He had been previously in the retinue of Svein the Sacrificer. Svein himself left the house, but was slain immediately.

Thus Ingi once more received the Kingdom of Sweden; and he re-established Christianity and ruled the Kingdom till the end of his life, when he died in his bed.

King Steinkel had, besides Ingi, another son Hallstein who reigned along with his brother. Hallstein's sons were Philip and Ingi, and they succeeded to the Kingdom of Sweden after King Ingi the elder. Philip married Ingigerth, the daughter of King Harold the son of Sigurth. He reigned for only a short time.

4. CELTIC

A few months after the publication of *The Hobbit* in 1937, Tolkien's publisher invited him to submit further works for consideration. Tolkien submitted several things, including some related to his invented mythology. The publisher's reader commented on one of the latter items, "The Geste of Beren and Luthien," as containing "eye-splitting Celtic names," and said "it has something of that mad, bright-eyed beauty that perplexes all Anglo-Saxons in face of Celtic art."

After these comments were sent to Tolkien, he responded in a letter of December 16, 1937: "Needless to say they are not Celtic! Neither are the tales. I do know Celtic things (many in their original languages Irish and Welsh), and feel for them a certain distaste: largely for their fundamental unreason. They have bright colour, but are like a broken stained glass window reassembled without design. They are in fact 'mad' as your reader says—but I don't believe I am." (Carpenter, *The Letters of J. R. R. Tolkien*, p. 26.)

Nearly twenty years later, in his lecture "English and Welsh" given at Oxford on October 21, 1955 (the day after the publication of the third volume of *The Lord of the Rings*), Tolkien commented on the recent appearance of his large work by stating that it "contains, in the way of presentation that I find most natural, much of what I personally have received from the study of things Celtic." (Tolkien, *The Monsters and the Critics*, p. 162.)

It is difficult to pin down Celtic influences on Tolkien to specific works. The Celtic motifs which influenced Tolkien are more general—the Celtic Otherworld with its god-like beings, and the idea of the blessed islands in the west (where Frodo at the end of *The Lord of the Rings*, like King Arthur in the various Arthurian legends, is taken to be healed).

Many of the ancient Celtic stories and poems are preserved in manuscripts from the thirteenth and fourteenth centuries, the Welsh compilations having names like the White Book of Rhydderch, the Black Book of Carmarthen, and the Red Book of Hergest, while one of the similar Irish collections is known as the Yellow Book of Lecan. It is easy to see where Tolkien came up with the idea for his Red Book of Westmarch.

The Red Book of Hergest contains, among other poems and prose, around a dozen tales that have since become known as the *Mabinogion*. This is a misnomer, for only four of the tales themselves are actually labeled as parts of the "mabinogi." The mistaken attribution was begun by Lady Charlotte Guest, who first translated the tales into English over the years 1838 through 1849, and since then the title has become widely known even though it isn't correct.

In the Welsh section I have included all four branches of the *Mabinogion* proper, along with one other tale usually published in the full collection, "Kilhwich and Olwen." This tale has similarities with Tolkien's story of Beren and Luthien, in the series of impossible tasks that the man must perform in order to secure the hand of the woman he loves.

In terms of Irish Celtic materials, I have selected the story of "The Second Battle of Mag Tured (Moytura)," one of the mythological stories of the Tuatha De Danann (the Peoples of the Goddess Danu, or Anu), who were said to have come to Ireland from the north of Europe, where they had excelled in learning arts and magic. The Tuatha De Danann were considered to be large and beautiful beings who mingled with mortals and yet remained superior to them. "The Second Battle of Mag Tured (Moytura)" almost reads like an outtake from *The Silmarillion* in both style and content.

Readers interested in more of the tales of the *Mabinogion* are encouraged to seek out the full of Lady Guest's translation, or that by Gwyn Jones and Thomas Jones, both of which have been published with illustrations by Alan Lee (the Jones' version in 1982, and the Guest version in 2000). Besides having illustrated both *The Hobbit* and *The Lord of the Rings*, Alan Lee was one of the conceptual designers on the Peter Jackson *Lord of the Rings* films. Most Tolkien fans will no doubt find Alan Lee illustrations to the *Mabinogion*

to be enchanting. Another fine translation is that by Patrick K. Ford, published as *The Mabinogi and Other Medieval Welsh Tales* (1977).

For more Irish Celtic tales, a fine omnibus, *Ancient Irish Tales* edited by Tom Peete Cross and Clark Harris Slover, was published in 1936. This selection of about forty tales also includes 'The Voyage of Bran Son of Febal," one of the class of Irish stories called *imrama* or "voyages." Tolkien himself wrote a poem called "Imram" about the voyage and death of St. Brendan. It is published in the *Sauron Defeated* (pp. 296-299).

THE FOUR BRANCHES
OF THE MABINOGION

translated by Lady Charlotte Guest (1849)

I. Pwyll Prince of Dyved

Pwyll Prince of Dyved was lord of the seven Cantrevs of Dyved; and once upon a time he was at Narberth his chief palace, and he was minded to go and hunt, and the part of his dominions in which it pleased him to hunt was Glyn Cuch. So he set forth from Narbeth that night, and went as far as Llwyn Diarwyd. And that night he tarried there, and early on the morrow he rose and came to Glyn Cuch; when he let loose the dogs in the wood, and sounded the horn, and began the chase. And as he followed the dogs, he lost his companions; and whilst he listened to the hounds, he heard the cry of other hounds, a cry different from his own, and coming in the opposite direction.

And he beheld a glade in the wood forming a level plain, and as his dogs came to the edge of the glade, he saw a stag before the other dogs. And lo, as it reached the middle of the glade, the dogs that followed the stag overtook it and brought it down. Then looked he at the color of the dogs, staying not to look at the stag, and of all the hounds that he had seen in the world, he had never seen any that were like unto these. For their hair was of a brilliant shining white, and their ears were red; and as the whiteness of their bodies shone, so did the redness of their ears glisten. And he came towards the dogs, and drove away those that had brought down the stag, and set his own dogs upon it.

And as he was setting on his dogs he saw a horseman coming towards him upon a large light-gray steed, with a hunting horn round his neck, and clad in garments of gray woolen in the fashion of a hunting garb. And the horseman drew near and spoke unto him thus. "Chieftain," said he, "I know who thou art, and I greet thee not." "Peradventure," said Pwyll, "thou art of such dignity that thou shouldest not do so." "Verily," answered he, "it is not my dignity that prevents me." "What is it then, O Chieftain?" asked he. "By Heaven, it is by reason of thine own ignorance and want of courtesy." "What discourtesy, Chieftain, hast thou seen in me?" "Greater discourtesy saw I never in man," said he, "than to drive away the dogs that were killing the stag and to set upon it thine own. This was discourteous, and though I may not be revenged upon thee, yet I declare to Heaven that I will do thee more dishonor than the value of an hundred stags." "O Chieftain," he replied, "if I have done ill I will redeem thy friendship." "How wilt thou redeem it?" "According as thy dignity may be, but I know not who thou art?" "A crowned king am I in the land whence I come." "Lord," said he, "may the day prosper with thee, and from what land comest thou?" "From Annwvyn," answered he; "Arawn, a King of Annwvyn, am I." "Lord," said he, "how may I gain thy friendship?" "After this manner mayest thou," he said. "There is a man whose dominions are opposite to mine, who is ever warring against me, and he is Havgan, a King of Annwvyn, and by ridding me of this oppression, which thou canst easily do, shalt thou gain my friendship." "Gladly will I do this," said he. "Show me how I may." "I will show thee. Behold thus it is thou mayest. I will make firm friendship with thee; and this will I do. I will send thee to Annwvyn in my stead, and I will give thee the fairest lady thou didst ever behold to be thy companion, and I will put my form and semblance upon thee, so that not a page of the chamber, nor an officer, nor any other man that has always followed me shall know that it is not I. And this shall be for the space of a year from tomorrow, and then we will meet in this place." "Yes," said he; "but when I shall have been there for the space of a year, by what means shall I discover him of whom thou speakest?" "One year from this night," he answered, "is the time fixed between him and me that we should meet at the Ford; be thou there in my likeness, and with one stroke that thou givest him, he shall no longer live. And if he ask thee to give him another, give it not, how much soever he may entreat thee, for when I did so, he fought with me next day as well as ever before." "Verily," said Pwyll, "what shall I do concerning my kingdom?" Said Arawn, "I will cause that no one in all thy dominions, neither man nor woman, shall know that I am not thou, and I will go there in thy stead." "Gladly then," said Pwyll, "will I set forward." "Clear shall be thy path, and nothing shall detain thee, until thou come into my dominions, and I myself will be thy guide!"

So he conducted him until he came in sight of the palace and its dwellings. "Behold," said he, "the Court and the kingdom in thy power. Enter the Court, there is no one there who will know thee, and when thou seest what service is done there, thou wilt know the customs of the Court."

So he went forward to the Court, and when he came there, he beheld sleeping-rooms, and halls, and chambers, and the most beautiful buildings ever seen. And he went into the hall to disarray, and there came youths and pages and disarrayed him, and all as they entered saluted him. And two knights came and drew his hunting-dress from about him, and clothed him in a vesture of silk and gold. And the hall was prepared, and behold he saw the household and the host enter in, and the host was the most comely and the best equipped that he had ever seen. And with them came in likewise the Queen, who was the fairest woman that he had ever yet beheld. And she had on a yellow robe of shining satin; and they washed and went to the table, and sat, the Queen upon one side of him, and one who seemed to be an Earl on the other side.

And he began to speak with the Queen, and he thought, from her speech, that she was the seemliest and most noble lady of converse and of cheer that ever was. And they partook of meat, and drink, with songs and with feasting; and of all the Courts upon the earth, behold this was the best supplied with food and drink, and vessels of gold and royal jewels.

And the year he spent in hunting, and minstrelsy, and feasting, and diversions, and discourse with his companions until the night that was fixed for the conflict. And when that night came, it was remembered even by those who lived in the furthest part of his dominions, and he went to the meeting, and the nobles of the kingdom with him. And when he came to the Ford, a knight arose and spake thus. "Lords," said he, "listen well. It is between two kings that this meeting is, and between them only. Each claimeth of the other his land and territory, and do all of you stand aside and leave the fight to be between them."

Thereupon the two kings approached each other in the middle of the Ford, and encountered, and at the first thrust, the man who was in the stead of Arawn struck Havgan on the center of the boss of his shield, so that it was cloven in twain, and his armor was broken, and Havgan himself was borne to the ground an arm's and a spear's length over the crupper of his horse, and he received a deadly blow. "O Chieftain," said Havgan, "what right hast thou to cause my death? I was not injuring thee in anything, and I know not wherefore thou wouldest slay me. But, for the love of Heaven, since thou hast begun to slay me, complete thy work." "Ah, Chieftain," he replied, "I may yet repent doing that unto thee, slay thee who may, I will not do so." "My trusty Lords," said Havgan, "bear me hence. My death has come. I shall be no more able to uphold you." "My Nobles," also said he who was in the semblance of Arawn, "take counsel and know who ought to be my subjects." "Lord," said the Nobles, "all should be, for there is no king over the whole of Annwvyn but thee." "Yes," he replied, "it is right that he who comes humbly should be received graciously, but he that doth not come with obedience, shall be compelled by the force of swords." And thereupon he received the homage of the men, and he began to conquer the country; and the next day by noon the two kingdoms were in his power. And thereupon he went to keep his tryst, and came to Glyn Cuch.

And when he came there, the King of Annwvyn was there to meet him, and each of them was rejoiced to see the other. "Verily," said Arawn, "may Heaven reward thee for thy friendship towards me. I have heard of it. When thou comest thyself to thy dominions," said he, "thou wilt see that which I have done for thee." "Whatever thou hast done for me, may Heaven repay it thee."

Then Arawn gave to Pwyll Prince of Dyved his proper form and semblance, and he himself took his own; and Arawn set forth towards the Court of Annwvyn; and he was rejoiced when he beheld his hosts, and his household, whom he had not seen so long; but they had not known of his absence, and wondered no more at his coming than usual. And that day was spent in joy and merriment; and he sat and conversed with his wife and his nobles. And when it was time for them rather to sleep than to carouse, they went to rest.

Pwyll Prince of Dyved came likewise to his country and dominions, and began to inquire of the nobles of the land, how his rule had been during the past year, compared with what it had been before. "Lord," said they, "thy wisdom was never so great, and thou wast never so kind or so free in bestowing thy gifts, and thy justice was never more worthily seen than in this year." "By Heaven," said he, "for all the good you have enjoyed, you should thank him who hath been with you; for behold, thus hath this matter been." And thereupon Pwyll related the whole unto them. "Verily, Lord," said they, "render thanks unto Heaven that thou hast such a fellowship, and withhold not from us the rule which we have enjoyed for this year past." "I take Heaven to witness that I will not withhold it," answered Pwyll.

And thenceforth they made strong the friendship that was between them, and each sent unto the other horses, and greyhounds, and hawks, and all such jewels as they thought would be pleasing to each other. And by reason of his having dwelt that year in Annwvyn, and having ruled there so prosperously, and united the two kingdoms in one day by his valor and prowess, he lost the name of Pwyll Prince of Dyved, and was called Pwyll Chief of Annwvyn from that time forward.

Once upon a time, Pwyll was at Narberth his chief palace, where a feast had been prepared for him, and with him was a great host of men. And after the first meal, Pwyll arose to walk, and he went to the top of a mound that was above the palace, and was called Gorsedd Arberth. "Lord," said one of the Court, "it is peculiar to the mound that whosoever sits upon it cannot go thence, without either receiving wounds or blows, or else seeing a wonder." "I fear not to receive wounds and blows in the midst of such a host as this, but as to the wonder, gladly would I see it. I will go therefore and sit upon the mound."

And upon the mound he sat. And while he sat there, they saw a lady, on a pure white horse of large size, with a garment of shining gold around her, coming along the highway that led from the mound; and the horse seemed to move at a slow and even pace, and to be coming up towards the mound. "My men," said Pwyll, "is there any among you who knows yonder lady?" "There is not, Lord," said they. "Go one of you and meet her, that we may know who she is." And one of them arose, and as he came upon the road to meet her, she passed by, and he followed as fast as he could, being on foot; and the greater was his speed, the further was she from him. And when he saw that it profited him nothing to follow her, he returned to Pwyll, and said unto him, "Lord, it is idle for any one in the world to follow her on foot." "Verily," said Pwyll, "go unto the palace, and take the fleetest horse that thou seest, and go after her."

And he took a horse and went forward. And he came to an open level plain, and put spurs to his horse; and the more he urged his horse, the further was she from him. Yet she held the same pace as at first. And his horse began to fail; and when his horse's feet failed him, he returned to the place where Pwyll was. "Lord," said he, "it will avail nothing for any one to follow yonder lady. I know of no horse in these realms swifter than this, and it availed me not to pursue her." "Of a truth," said Pwyll, "there must be some illusion here. Let us go towards the palace." So to the palace they went, and they spent that day. And the next day they arose, and that also they spent until it was time to go to meat. And after the first meal, "Verily," said Pwyll, "we will go the same party as yesterday to the top of the mound. And do thou," said he to one of his young men, "take the swiftest horse that thou knowest in the field." And thus did the young man. And they went towards the mound, taking the horse with them. And as they were sitting down they beheld the lady on the same horse, and in the same apparel, coming along the same road. "Behold," said Pwyll, "here is the lady of yesterday. Make ready, youth, to learn who she is." "My lord," said he, "that will I gladly do." And thereupon the lady came opposite to them. So the youth mounted his horse; and before he had settled himself in his saddle, she passed by, and there was a clear space between them. But her speed was no greater than it had been the day before. Then he put his horse into an amble, and thought that notwithstanding the gentle pace at which his horse went, he should soon overtake her.

But this availed him not; so he gave his horse the reins. And still he came no nearer to her than when he went at a foot's pace. And the more he urged his horse, the further was she from him. Yet she rode not faster than before. When he saw that it availed not to follow her, he returned to the place where Pwyll was. "Lord," said he, "the horse can no more than thou hast seen." "I see indeed that it avails not that any one should follow her. And by Heaven," said he, "she must needs have an errand to some one in this plain, if her haste would allow her to declare it. Let us go back to the palace." And to the palace they went, and they spent that night in songs and feasting, as it pleased them.

And the next day they amused themselves until it was time to go to meat. And when meat was ended, Pwyll said, "Where are the hosts that went yesterday and the day before to the top of the mound?" "Behold, Lord, we are here," said they. "Let us go," said he, "to the mound, to sit there. And do thou," said he to the page who tended his horse, "saddle my horse well, and hasten with him to the road, and bring also my spurs with thee." And the youth did thus. And they went and sat upon the mound; and ere they had been there but a short time, they beheld the lady coming by the same road, and in the same manner, and at the same pace. "Young man," said Pwyll, "I see the lady coming; give me my horse." And no sooner had he mounted his horse than she passed him. And he turned after her and followed her. And he let his horse go bounding playfully, and thought that at the second step or the third he should come up with her. But he came no nearer to her than at first. Then he urged his horse to his utmost speed, yet he found that it availed nothing to follow her. Then said Pwyll, "O maiden, for the sake of him whom thou best lovest, stay for me." "I will stay gladly," said she, "and it were better for thy horse hadst thou asked it long since." So the maiden stopped, and she threw back that part of her head dress which covered her face. And she fixed her eyes upon him, and began to talk with him.

"Lady," asked he, "whence comest thou, and whereunto dost thou journey?" "I journey on mine own errand," said she, "and right glad am I to see thee." "My greeting be unto thee," said he. Then he thought that the beauty of all the maidens, and all the ladies that he had ever seen, was as nothing compared to her beauty. "Lady," he said, "wilt thou tell me aught concerning thy purpose?" "I will tell thee," said she. "My chief quest was to seek thee." "Behold," said Pwyll, "this is to me the most pleasing quest on which thou couldst have come; and wilt thou tell me who thou art?" "I will tell thee, Lord," said she. "I am Rhiannon, the daughter of Heveydd Hên, and they sought to give me to a husband against my will. But no husband would I have, and that because of my love for thee, neither will I yet have one unless thou reject me. And hither have I come to hear thy answer." "By Heaven," said Pwyll, "behold this is my answer. If I might choose among all the ladies and damsels in the world, thee would I choose." "Verily," said she, "if thou art thus minded, make a pledge to meet me ere I am given to another." "The sooner I may do so, the more pleasing will it be unto me," said Pwyll, "and wheresoever thou wilt, there will I meet with thee." "I will that thou meet me this day twelvemonth at the palace of Heveydd. And I will cause a feast to be prepared, so that it be ready against thou come." "Gladly," said he, "will I keep this tryst." "Lord," said she, "remain in health, and be mindful that thou keep thy promise; and now I will go hence." So they parted, and he went back to his hosts and to them of his household. And whatsoever questions they asked him respecting the damsel, he always turned the discourse upon other matters. And when a year from that time was gone, he caused a hundred knights to equip themselves and to go with him to the palace of Heveydd Hên. And he came to the palace, and there was great joy concerning him, with much concourse of people and great rejoicing, and vast preparations for his coming. And the whole Court was placed under his orders.

And the hall was garnished and they went to meat, and thus did they sit; Heveydd Hên was on one side of Pwyll, and Rhiannon on the other. And all the rest according to their rank. And they ate and feasted and talked one with another, and at the beginning of the carousal after the meat, there entered a tall auburn-haired youth, of royal bearing, clothed in a garment of satin. And when he came into the hall, he saluted Pwyll and his companions. "The greeting of Heaven be unto thee, my soul," said Pwyll, "come thou and sit down." "Nay," said he, "a suitor am I, and I will do mine errand." "Do so willingly," said Pwyll. "Lord," said he, "my errand is unto thee, and it is to crave a boon of thee that I come." "What boon soever thou mayest ask of me, as far as I am able, thou shalt have." "Ah," said Rhiannon, "wherefore didst thou give that answer?" "Has he not given it before the presence of these nobles?" asked the youth. "My soul," said Pwyll, "what is the boon thou askest?" "The lady whom best I love is to be thy bride this night; I come to ask her of thee, with the feast and the banquet that are in this place." And Pwyll was silent because of the answer which he had given. "Be silent as long as thou wilt," said Rhiannon. "Never did man make worse use of his wits than thou hast done." "Lady," said he, "I knew not who he was." "Behold this is the man to whom they would have given me against my will," said she. "And he is Gwawl the son of Clud, a man of great power and wealth, and because of the word thou hast spoken, bestow me upon him lest shame befall thee." "Lady," said he, "I understand not thine answer. Never can I do as thou sayest." "Bestow me upon him," said she, "and I will cause that I shall never be his." "By what means will that be?" asked Pwyll. "In thy hand will I give thee a small bag," said she. "See that thou keep it well, and he will ask of thee the banquet, and the feast, and the preparations which are not in thy power. Unto the hosts and the household will I give the feast. And such will be thy answer respecting this. And as concerns myself, I will engage to become his bride this night twelvemonth. And at the end of the year be thou here," said she, "and bring this bag with thee, and let thy hundred knights be in the orchard up yonder. And when he is in the midst of joy and feasting, come thou in by thyself, clad in ragged garments, and holding thy bag in thy hand, and ask nothing but a bagful of food, and I will cause that if all the meat and liquor that are in these seven Cantrevs were put into it, it would be no fuller than before. And after a great deal has been put therein, he will ask thee whether thy bag will ever be full. Say thou then that it never will, until a man of noble birth and of great wealth arise and press the food in the bag with both his feet, saying, 'Enough has been put therein;' and I will cause him to go and tread down the food in the bag, and when he does so, turn thou the bag, so that he shall be up over his head in it, and then slip a knot upon the thongs of the bag. Let there be also a good bugle horn about thy neck, and as soon as thou hast bound him in the bag, wind thy horn, and let it be a signal between thee and thy knights. And when they hear the sound of the horn, let them come down upon the palace." "Lord," said Gwawl, "it is meet that I have an answer to my request." "As much of that thou hast asked as it is in my power to give, thou shalt have," replied Pwyll. "My soul," said Rhiannon unto him, "as for the feast and the banquet that are here, I have bestowed them upon the men of Dyved, and the household, and the warriors that are with us. These can I not suffer to be given to any. In a year from tonight a banquet shall be prepared for thee in this palace, that I may become thy bride."

So Gwawl went forth to his possessions, and Pwyll went also back to Dyved. And they both spent that year until it was the time for the feast at the palace of Heveydd Hên. Then Gwawl the son of Clud set out to the feast that was prepared for him, and he came to the palace, and was received there with rejoicing. Pwyll, also, the Chief of Annwvyn, came to the orchard with his hundred knights, as Rhiannon had commanded him, having the bag with him. And Pwyll was clad in coarse and ragged garments, and wore large clumsy old shoes upon his feet. And when he knew that the carousal after the meat had begun, he went towards the hall, and when he came into the hall, he saluted Gwawl the son of Clud, and his company, both men and women. "Heaven prosper thee," said Gwawl, "and the greeting of Heaven be unto thee." "Lord," said he, "may Heaven reward thee, I have an errand unto thee." "Welcome be thine errand, and if thou ask of me that which is just, thou shalt have it gladly." "It is fitting," answered he. "I crave but from want, and the boon that I ask is to have this small bag that thou seest filled with meat." "A request within reason is this," said he, "and gladly shalt thou have it. Bring him food." A great number of attendants arose and began to fill the bag, but for all that they put into it, it was no fuller than at first. "My soul," said Gwawl, "will thy bag be ever full?" "It will not, I declare to Heaven," said he, "for all that may be put into it, unless one possessed of lands, and domains, and treasure, shall arise and tread down with both his feet the food that is within the bag, and shall say, 'Enough has been put therein.'" Then said Rhiannon unto Gwawl the son of Clud, "Rise up quickly." "I will willingly arise," said he. So he rose up, and put his two feet into the bag. And Pwyll turned up the sides of the bag, so that Gwawl was over his head in it. And he shut it up quickly and slipped a knot upon the thongs, and blew his horn. And thereupon behold his household came down upon the palace. And they seized all the host that had come with Gwawl, and cast them into his own prison. And Pwyll threw off his rags, and his old shoes, and his tattered array; and as they came in, every one of Pwyll's knights struck a blow upon the bag, and asked, "What is here?" "A Badger," said they. And in this manner they played, each of them striking the bag, either with his foot or with a staff. And thus played they with the bag. Every one as he came in asked, "What game are you playing at thus?" "The game of Badger in the Bag," said they. And then was the game of Badger in the Bag first played.

"Lord," said the man in the bag, "if thou wouldest but hear me, I merit not to be slain in a bag." Said Heveydd Hên, "Lord, he speaks truth. It were fitting that thou listen to him, for he deserves not this." "Verily," said Pwyll, "I will do thy counsel concerning him." "Behold this is my counsel then," said Rhiannon; "thou art now in a position in which it behoves thee to satisfy suitors and minstrels; let him give unto them in thy stead, and take a pledge from him that he will never seek to revenge that which has been done to him. And this will be punishment enough." "I will do this gladly," said the man in the bag. "And gladly will I accept it," said Pwyll, "since it is the counsel of Heveydd and Rhiannon." "Such then is our counsel," answered they. "I accept it," said Pwyll. "Seek thyself sureties." "We will be for him," said Heveydd, "until his men be free to answer for him." And upon this he was let out of the bag, and his liegemen were liberated. "Demand now of Gwawl his sureties," said Heveydd, "we know which should be taken for him." And Heveydd numbered the sureties. Said Gwawl, "Do thou thyself draw up the covenant." "It will suffice me that it be as Rhiannon said," answered Pwyll. So unto that covenant were the sureties pledged. "Verily, Lord," said Gwawl, "I am greatly hurt, and I have many bruises. I have need to be anointed; with thy leave I will go forth. I will leave nobles in my stead, to answer for me in all that thou shalt require." "Willingly," said Pwyll, "mayest thou do thus." So Gwawl went towards his own possessions.

And the hall was set in order for Pwyll and the men of his host, and for them also of the palace, and they went to the tables and sat down. And as they had sat that time twelvemonth, so sat they that night. And they ate, and feasted, and spent the night in mirth and tranquility. And the time came that they should sleep, and Pwyll and Rhiannon went to their chamber.

And next morning at the break of day, "My Lord," said Rhiannon, "arise and begin to give thy gifts unto the minstrels. Refuse no one today that may claim thy bounty." "Thus shall it be gladly," said Pwyll, "both today and every day while the feast shall last." So Pwyll arose, and he caused silence to be proclaimed, and desired all the suitors and the minstrels to show and to point out what gifts were to their wish and desire. And this being done, the feast went on, and he denied no one while it lasted. And when the feast was ended, Pwyll said unto Heveydd, "My Lord, with thy permission I will set out for Dyved tomorrow." "Certainly," said Heveydd, "may Heaven prosper thee. Fix also a time when Rhiannon may follow thee." "By Heaven," said Pwyll, "we will go hence together." "Willest thou this, Lord?" said Heveydd. "Yes, by Heaven," answered Pwyll.

And the next day, they set forward towards Dyved, and journeyed to the palace of Narberth, where a feast was made ready for them. And there came to them great numbers of the chief men and the most noble ladies of the land, and of these there was none to whom Rhiannon did not give some rich gift, either a bracelet, or a ring, or a precious stone. And they ruled the land prosperously both that year and the next.

And in the third year the nobles of the land began to be sorrowful at seeing a man whom they loved so much, and who was moreover their lord and their foster-brother, without an heir. And they came to him. And the place where they met was Preseleu, in Dyved. "Lord," said they, "we know that thou art not so young as some of the men of this country, and we fear that thou mayest not have an heir of the wife whom thou hast taken. Take therefore another wife of whom thou mayest have heirs. Thou canst not always continue with us, and though thou desire to remain as thou art, we will not suffer thee." "Truly," said Pwyll, "we have not long been joined together, and many things may yet befall. Grant me a year from this time, and for the space of a year we will abide together, and after that I will do according to your wishes." So they granted it. And before the end of a year a son was born unto him. And in Narberth was he born; and on the night that he was born, women were brought to watch the mother and the boy. And the women slept, as did also Rhiannon, the mother of the boy. And the number of the women that were brought into the chamber was six. And they watched for a good portion of the night, and before midnight every one of them fell asleep, and towards break of day they awoke; and when they awoke, they looked where they had put the boy, and behold he was not there. "Oh," said one of the women, "the boy is lost?" "Yes," said another, "and it will be small vengeance if we are burnt or put to death because of the child."

Said one of the women, "Is there any counsel for us in the world in this matter?" "There is," answered another, "I offer you good counsel." "What is that?" asked they. "There is here a stag-hound bitch, and she has a litter of whelps. Let us kill some of the cubs, and rub the blood on the face and hands of Rhiannon, and lay the bones before her, and assert that she herself hath devoured her son, and she alone will not be able to gainsay us six." And according to this counsel it was settled. And towards morning Rhiannon awoke, and she said, "Women, where is my son?" "Lady," said they, "ask us not concerning thy son, we have nought but the blows and the bruises we got by struggling with thee, and of a truth we never saw any woman so violent as thou, for it was of no avail to contend with thee. Hast thou not thyself devoured thy son? Claim him not therefore of us." "For pity's sake," said Rhiannon; "the Lord God knows all things. Charge me not falsely. If you tell me this from fear, I assert before Heaven that I will defend you." "Truly," said they, "we would not bring evil on ourselves for any one in the world." "For pity's sake," said Rhiannon, "you will receive no evil by telling the truth." But for all her words, whether fair or harsh, she received but the same answer from the women.

And Pwyll the chief of Annwvyn arose, and his household, and his hosts. And this occurrence could not be concealed, but the story went forth throughout the land, and all the nobles heard it. Then the nobles came to Pwyll, and besought him to put away his wife, because of the great crime which she had done. But Pwyll answered them, that they had no cause wherefore they might ask him to put away his wife, save for her having no children. "But children has she now had, therefore will I not put her away; if she has done wrong, let her do penance for it."

So Rhiannon sent for the teachers and the wise men, and as she preferred doing penance to contending with the women, she took upon her a penance. And the penance that was imposed upon her was, that she should remain in that palace of Narberth until the end of seven years, and that she should sit every day near unto a horse-block that was without the gate. And that she should relate the story to all who should come there, whom she might suppose not to know it already; and that she should offer the guests and strangers, if they would permit her, to carry them upon her back into the palace. But it rarely happened that any would permit. And thus did she spend part of the year.

Now at that time Teirnyon Twryv Vliant was Lord of Gwent Is Coed, and he was the best man in the world. And unto his house there belonged a mare, than which neither mare nor horse in the kingdom was more beautiful. And on the night of every first of May she foaled, and no one ever knew what became of the colt. And one night Teirnyon talked with his wife: "Wife," said he, "it is very simple of us that our mare should foal every year, and that we should have none of her colts." "What can be done in the matter?" said she. "This is the night of the first of May," said he. "The vengeance of Heaven be upon me, if I learn not what it is that takes away the colts." So he caused the mare to be brought into a house, and he armed himself, and began to watch that night. And in the beginning of the night, the mare foaled a large and beautiful colt. And it was standing up in the place. And Teirnyon rose up and looked at the size of the colt, and as he did so he heard a great tumult, and after the tumult behold a claw came through the window into the house, and it seized the colt by the mane. Then Teirnyon drew his sword, and struck off the arm at the elbow, so that portion of the arm together with the colt was in the house with him. And then did he hear a tumult and wailing, both at once. And he opened the door, and rushed out in the direction of the noise, and he could not see the cause of the tumult because of the darkness of the night, but he rushed after it and followed it. Then he remembered that he had left the door open, and he returned. And at the door behold

CELTIC

there was an infant boy in swaddling-clothes, wrapped around in a mantle of satin. And he took up the boy, and behold he was very strong for the age that he was of.

Then he shut the door, and went into the chamber where his wife was. "Lady," said he, "art thou sleeping?" "No, lord," said she, "I was asleep, but as thou camest in I did awake." "Behold, here is a boy for thee if thou wilt," said he, "since thou hast never had one." "My lord," said she, "what adventure is this?" "It was thus," said Teirnyon; and he told her how it all befell. "Verily, lord," said she, "what sort of garments are there upon the boy?" "A mantle of satin," said he. "He is then a boy of gentle lineage," she replied. "My lord," she said, "if thou wilt, I shall have great diversion and mirth. I will call my women unto me, and tell them that I have been pregnant." "I will readily grant thee to do this," he answered. And thus did they, and they caused the boy to be baptized, and the ceremony was performed there; and the name which they gave unto him was Gwri Wallt Euryn, because what hair was upon his head was as yellow as gold. And they had the boy nursed in the Court until he was a year old. And before the year was over he could walk stoutly. And he was larger than a boy of three years old, even one of great growth and size. And the boy was nursed the second year, and then he was as large as a child six years old. And before the end of the fourth year, he would bribe the grooms to allow him to take the horses to water. "My lord," said his wife unto Teirnyon, "where is the colt which thou didst save on the night that thou didst find the boy?" "I have commanded the grooms of the horses," said he, "that they take care of him." "Would it not be well, lord," said she, "if thou wert to cause him to be broken in, and given to the boy, seeing that on the same night that thou didst find the boy, the colt was foaled and thou didst save him?" "I will not oppose thee in this matter," said Teirnyon. "I will allow thee to give him the colt." "Lord," said she, "may Heaven reward thee; I will give it him." So the horse was given to the boy. Then she went to the grooms and those who tended the horses, and commanded them to be careful of the horse, so that he might be broken in by the time that the boy could ride him.

And while these things were going forward, they heard tidings of Rhiannon and her punishment. And Teirnyon Twryv Vliant, by reason of the pity that he felt on hearing this story of Rhiannon and her punishment, inquired closely concerning it, until he had heard from many of those who came to his court. Then did Teirnyon, often lamenting the sad history, ponder within himself, and he looked steadfastly on the boy, and as he looked upon him, it seemed to him that he had never beheld so great a likeness between father and son, as between the boy and Pwyll the Chief of Annwvyn. Now the semblance of Pwyll was well known to him, for he had of yore been one of his followers. And thereupon he became grieved for the wrong that he did, in keeping with him a boy whom he knew to be the son of another man. And the first time that he was alone with his wife, he told her that it was not right that they should keep the boy with them, and suffer so excellent a lady as Rhiannon to be punished so greatly on his account, whereas the boy was the son of Pwyll the Chief of Annwvyn. And Teirnyon's wife agreed with him, that they should send the boy to Pwyll. "And three things, lord," said she, "shall we gain thereby. Thanks and gifts

259

for releasing Rhiannon from her punishment; and thanks from Pwyll for nursing his son and restoring him unto him; and thirdly, if the boy is of gentle nature, he will be our foster-son, and he will do for us all the good in his power." So it was settled according to this counsel.

And no later than the next day was Teirnyon equipped, and two other knights with him. And the boy, as a fourth in their company, went with them upon the horse which Teirnyon had given him. And they journeyed towards Narberth, and it was not long before they reached that place. And as they drew near to the palace, they beheld Rhiannon sitting beside the horseblock. And when they were opposite to her, "Chieftain," said she, "go not further thus, I will bear every one of you into the palace, and this is my penance for slaying my own son and devouring him." "Oh, fair lady," said Teirnyon, "think not that I will be one to be carried upon thy back." "Neither will I," said the boy. "Truly, my soul," said Teirnyon, "we will not go." So they went forward to the palace, and there was great joy at their coming. And at the palace a feast was prepared, because Pywll was come back from the confines of Dyved. And they went into the hall and washed, and Pwyll rejoiced to see Teirnyon. And in this order they sat. Teirnyon between Pwyll and Rhiannon, and Teirnyon's two companions on the other side of Pwyll, with the boy between them. And after meat they began to carouse and to discourse. And

Teirnyon's discourse was concerning the adventure of the mare and the boy, and how he and his wife had nursed and reared the child as their own. "And behold here is thy son, lady," said Teirnyon. "And whosoever told that lie concerning thee, has done wrong. And when I heard of thy sorrow, I was troubled and grieved. And I believe that there is none of this host who will not perceive that the boy is the son of Pwyll," said Teirnyon. "There is none," said they all, "who is not certain thereof." "I declare to Heaven," said Rhiannon, "that if this be true, there is indeed an end to my trouble." "Lady," said Pendaran Dyved, "well hast thou named thy son Pryderi, and well becomes him the name of Pryderi son of Pwyll Chief of Annwvyn." "Look you," said Rhiannon, "will not his own name become him better?" "What name has he?" asked Pendaran Dyved. "Gwri Wallt Euryn is the name that we gave him." "Pryderi," said Pendaran, "shall his name be." "It were more proper," said Pwyll, "that the boy should take his name from the word his mother spoke when she received the joyful tidings of him." And thus was it arranged.

"Teirnyon," said Pwyll, "Heaven reward thee that thou hast reared the boy up to this time, and, being of gentle lineage, it were fitting that he repay thee for it." "My lord," said Teirnyon, "it was my wife who nursed him, and there is no one in the world so afflicted as she at parting with him. It were well that he should bear in mind what I and my wife have done for him." "I call Heaven to witness," said Pwyll, "that while I live I will support thee and thy possessions, as long as I am able to preserve my own. And when he shall have power, he will more fitly maintain them than I. And if this counsel be pleasing unto thee, and to my nobles, it shall be that, as thou hast reared him up to the present time, I will give him to be brought up by Pendaran Dyved, from henceforth. And you shall be companions, and shall both be foster-fathers unto him." "This is good counsel," said they all. So the boy was given to Pendaran Dyved, and the nobles of the land were sent with him. And Teirnyon Twryv Vliant, and his companions, set out for his country, and his possessions, with love and gladness. And he went not without being offered the fairest jewels and the fairest horses, and the choicest dogs; but he would take none of them.

Thereupon they all remained in their own dominions. And Pryderi, the son of Pwyll the Chief of Annwvyn, was brought up carefully as was fit, so that he became the fairest youth, and the most comely, and the best skilled in all good games, of any in the kingdom. And thus passed years and years, until the end of Pwyll the Chief of Annwvyn's life came, and he died.

And Pryderi ruled the seven Cantrevs of Dyved prosperously, and he was beloved by his people, and by all around him. And at length he added unto them the three Cantrevs of Ystrad Tywi, and the four Cantrevs of Cardigan; and these were called the Seven Cantrevs of Seissyllwch. And when he made this addition, Pryderi the son of Pwyll the Chief of Annwvyn desired to take a wife. And the wife he chose was Kicva, the daughter of Gwynn Gohoyw, the son of Gloyw Wallt Lydan, the son of Prince Casnar, one of the nobles of this Island.

And thus ends this portion of the Mabinogion.

II. Branwen the Daughter of Llyr

Here is the Second Portion of the Mabinogi

Bendigeid Vran, the son of Llyr, was the crowned king of this island, and he was exalted from the crown of London. And one afternoon he was at Harlech in Ardudwy, at his Court, and he sat upon the rock of Harlech, looking over the sea. And with him were his brother Manawyddan the son of Llyr, and his brothers by the mother's side, Nissyen and Evnissyen, and many nobles likewise, as was fitting to see around a king. His two brothers by the mother's side were the sons of Eurosswydd, by his mother, Penardun, the daughter of Beli son of Manogan. And one of these youths was a good youth and of gentle nature, and would make peace between his kindred, and cause his family to be friends when their wrath was at the highest; and this one was Nissyen; but the other would cause strife between his two brothers when they were most at peace. And as they sat thus, they beheld thirteen ships coming from the south of Ireland, and making towards them, and they came with a swift motion, the wind being behind them, and they neared them rapidly. "I see ships afar," said the king, "coming swiftly towards the land. Command the men of the Court that they equip themselves, and go and learn their intent." So the men equipped themselves and went down towards them. And when they saw the ships near, certain were they that they had never seen ships better furnished. Beautiful flags of satin were upon them. And behold one of the ships outstripped the others, and they saw a shield lifted up above the side of the ship, and the point of the shield was upwards, in token of peace. And the men drew near that they might hold converse. Then they put out boats and came towards the land. And they saluted the king. Now the king could hear them from the place where he was, upon the rock above their heads. "Heaven prosper you," said he, "and be ye welcome. To whom do these ships belong, and who is the chief amongst you?" "Lord," said they, "Matholwch, king of Ireland, is here, and these ships belong to him." "Wherefore comes he?" asked the king, "and will he come to the land?" "He is a suitor unto thee, lord," said they, "and he will not land unless he have his boon." "And what may that be?" inquired the king. "He desires to ally himself with thee, lord," said they, "and he comes to ask Branwen the daughter of Llyr, that, if it seem well to thee, the Island of the Mighty may be leagued with Ireland, and both become more powerful." "Verily," said he, "let him come to land, and we will take counsel thereupon." And this answer was brought to Matholwch. "I will go willingly," said he. So he landed, and they received him joyfully; and great was the throng in the palace that night, between his hosts and those of the Court; and next day they took counsel, and they resolved to bestow Branwen upon Matholwch. Now she was one of the three chief ladies of this island, and she was the fairest damsel in the world.

And they fixed upon Aberffraw as the place where she should become his bride. And they went thence, and towards Aberffraw the hosts proceeded; Matholwch and his host in their ships; Bendigeid Vran and his host by land, until they came to Aberffraw. And at Aberffraw they began the feast and sat down. And thus sat they. The King of the Island of the Mighty and Manawyddan the son of Llyr, on one side, and Matholwch on the other side, and Branwen the daughter of Llyr beside him. And they were not within a house, but under tents. No house could ever contain Bendigeid Vran. And they began the banquet and caroused and discoursed. And when it was more pleasing to them to sleep than to carouse, they went to rest, and that night Branwen became Matholwch's bride.

And next day they arose, and all they of the Court, and the officers began to equip and to range the horses and the attendants, and they ranged them in order as far as the sea.

And behold one day, Evnissyen, the quarrelsome man of whom it is spoken above, came by chance into the place, where the horses of Matholwch were, and asked whose horses they might be. "They are the horses of Matholwch king of Ireland, who is married to Branwen, thy sister; his horses are they." "And is it thus they have done with a maiden such as she, and moreover my sister, bestowing her without my consent? They could have offered no greater insult to me than this," said he. And thereupon he rushed under the horses and cut off their lips at the teeth, and their ears close to their heads, and their tails close to their backs, and wherever he could clutch their eyelids, he cut them to the very bone, and he disfigured the horses and rendered them useless.

And they came with these tidings unto Matholwch, saying that the horses were disfigured, and injured so that not one of them could ever be of any use again. "Verily, lord," said one, "it was an insult unto thee, and as such was it meant." "Of a truth, it is a marvel to me, that if they desire to insult me, they should have given me a maiden of such high rank and so much beloved of her kindred, as they have done." "Lord," said another, "thou seest that thus it is, and there is nothing for thee to do but to go to thy ships." And thereupon towards his ships he set out.

And tidings came to Bendigeid Vran that Matholwch was quitting the Court without asking leave, and messengers were sent to inquire of him wherefore he did so. And the messengers that went were Iddic the son of Anarawd, and Heveydd Hir. And these overtook him and asked of him what he designed to do, and wherefore he went forth. "Of a truth," said he, "if I had known I had not come hither. I have been altogether insulted, no one had ever worse treatment than I have had here. But one thing surprises me above all." "What is that?" asked they. "That Branwen the daughter of Llyr, one of the three chief ladies of this island, and the daughter of the King of the Island of the Mighty, should have been given me as my bride, and that after that I should have been insulted; and I marvel that the insult was not done me before they had bestowed upon me a maiden so exalted as she." "Truly, lord, it was not the will of any that are of the Court," said they, "nor of any that are of the council, that thou shouldest have received this insult; and as thou hast been insulted, the dishonor is greater unto Bendigeid Vran than unto thee." "Verily," said he, "I think so. Nevertheless he cannot recall the insult." These men returned with that answer to the place where Bendigeid Vran was, and they told him what reply Matholwch had given them. "Truly," said he, "there are no means by which we may prevent his going away at enmity with us, that we will not take." "Well, lord," said they, "send after him another embassy." "I will do so," said he. "Arise, Manawyddan son of Llyr, and Heveydd Hir, and Unic Glew Ysgwyd, and go after him, and tell him that he shall have a sound horse for every one that has been injured. And beside that, as an atonement for the insult, he shall have a staff of silver, as large and as tall as himself, and a plate of gold of the breadth of his face. And show unto him who it was that did this, and that it was done against my will; but that he who did it is my brother, by the mother's side, and therefore it would be hard for me to put him to death. And let him come and meet me," said he, "and we will make peace in any way he may desire."

The embassy went after Matholwch, and told him all these sayings in a friendly manner, and he listened thereunto. "Men," said he, "I will take counsel." So to the council he went. And in the council they considered that if they should refuse this, they were likely to have more shame rather than to obtain so great an atonement. They resolved therefore to accept it, and they returned to the Court in peace.

Then the pavilions and the tents were set in order after the fashion of a hall; and they went to meat, and as they had sat at the beginning of the feast, so sat they there. And Matholwch and Bendigeid Vran began to discourse; and behold it seemed to Bendigeid Vran, while they talked, that Matholwch was not so cheerful as he had been before. And he thought that the chieftain might be sad, because of the smallness of the atonement which he had, for the wrong that had been done him. "Oh, man," said Bendigeid Vran, "thou dost not discourse tonight so cheerfully as thou wast wont. And if it be because of the smallness of the atonement, thou shalt add thereunto whatsoever thou mayest choose, and tomorrow I will pay thee the horses." "Lord," said he, "Heaven reward thee." "And I will enhance the atonement," said Bendigeid Vran, "for I will give unto thee a cauldron, the property of which is, that if one of thy men be slain today, and be cast therein, tomorrow he will be as well as ever he was at the best, except that he will not regain his speech." And thereupon he gave him great thanks, and very joyful was he for that cause.

And the next morning they paid Matholwch the horses as long as the trained horses lasted. And then they journeyed into another commot, where they paid him with colts until the whole had been paid, and from thenceforth that commot was called Talebolion.

And a second night sat they together. "My lord," said Matholwch, whence hadst thou the cauldron which thou hast given me?" "I had it of a man who had been in thy land," said he, "and I would not give it except to one from there." "Who was it?" asked he. "Llassar Llaesgyvnewid; he came here from Ireland with Kymideu Kymeinvoll, his wife, who escaped from the Iron House in Ireland, when it was made red hot around them, and fled hither. And it is a marvel to me that thou shouldst know nothing concerning the matter." "Something I do know," said he, "and as much as I know I will tell thee. One day I was hunting in Ireland, and I came to the mound at the head of the lake, which is called the Lake of the Cauldron. And I beheld a huge yellow-haired man coming from the lake with a cauldron upon his back. And he was a man of vast size, and of horrid aspect, and a woman followed after him. And if the man was tall, twice as large as he was the woman, and they came towards me and greeted me. 'Verily,' asked I, 'wherefore are you journeying?' 'Behold, this,' said he to me, 'is the cause that we journey. At the end of a month and a fortnight this woman will have a son; and the child that will be born at the end of the month and the fortnight will be a warrior fully armed.' So I took them with me and maintained them. And they were with me for a year. And that year I had them with me not grudgingly. But thenceforth was there murmuring, because that they were with me. For, from the beginning of the fourth month they had begun to make themselves hated and to be disorderly in the land; committing outrages, and molesting and harassing the nobles and ladies; and thenceforward my people rose up and besought me to part with them, and they bade me to choose between them and my dominions. And I applied to the council of my country to know what should be done concerning them; for of their own free will they would not go, neither could they be compelled against their will, through fighting. And [the people of the country] being in this strait, they caused a chamber to be made all of iron. Now when the chamber was ready, there came there every smith that was in Ireland, and every one who owned tongs and hammer. And they caused coals to be piled up as high as the top of the chamber. And they had the man, and the woman, and the children, served with plenty of meat and drink; but when it was known that they were drunk, they began to put fire to the coals about the chamber, and they blew it with bellows until the house was red hot all around them. Then was there a council held in the center of the floor of the chamber. And the man tarried until the plates of iron were all of a white heat; and then, by reason of the great heat, the man dashed against the plates with his shoulder and struck them out, and his wife followed him; but except him and his wife none escaped thence. And then I suppose, lord," said Matholwch unto Bendigeid Vran, "that he came over unto thee." "Doubtless he came here," said he, "and gave unto me the cauldron." "In what manner didst thou receive them?" "I dispersed them through every part of my dominions, and they have become numerous and are prospering everywhere, and they fortify the places where they are with men and arms, of the best that were ever seen."

That night they continued to discourse as much as they would, and had minstrelsy and carousing, and when it was more pleasant to them to sleep than to sit longer, they went to rest. And thus was the banquet carried on with joyousness; and when it was finished, Matholwch journeyed towards Ireland, and Branwen with him, and they went from Aber Menei with thirteen ships, and came to Ireland. And in Ireland was there great joy because of their coming. And not one great man or noble lady visited Branwen unto whom she gave not either a clasp, or a ring, or a royal jewel to keep, such as it was honorable to be seen departing with. And in these things she spent that year in much renown, and she passed her time pleasantly, enjoying honor and friendship. And in the meanwhile it chanced that she became pregnant, and in due time a son was born unto her, and the name that they gave him was Gwern the son of Matholwch, and they put the boy out to be foster-nursed, in a place where were the best men of Ireland.

And behold in the second year a tumult arose in Ireland, on account of the insult which Matholwch had received in Cambria, and the payment made him for his horses. And his foster-brothers, and such as were nearest unto him, blamed him openly for that matter. And he might have no peace by reason of the tumult until they should revenge upon him this disgrace. And the vengeance which they took was to drive away Branwen from the same chamber with him, and to make her cook for the Court; and they caused the butcher after he had cut up the meat to come to her and give her every day a blow on the ear, and such they made her punishment.

"Verily, lord," said his men to Matholwch, "forbid now the ships and the ferry boats and the coracles, that they go not into Cambria, and such as come over from Cambria hither, imprison them that they go not back for this thing to be known there." And he did so; and it was thus for no less than three years.

And Branwen reared a starling in the cover of the kneading trough, and she taught it to speak, and she taught the bird what manner of man her brother was. And she wrote a letter of her woes, and the despite with which she was treated, and she bound the letter to the root of the bird's wing, and sent it towards Britain. And the bird came to this island, and one day it found Bendigeid Vran at Caer Seiont in Arvon, conferring there, and it alighted upon his shoulder and ruffled its feathers, so that the letter was seen, and they knew that the bird had been reared in a domestic manner.

Then Bendigeid Vran took the letter and looked upon it. And when he had read the letter he grieved exceedingly at the tidings of Branwen's woes. And immediately he began sending messengers to summon the island together. And he caused sevenscore and four countries to come unto him, and he complained to them himself of the grief that his sister endured. So they took counsel. And in the council they resolved to go to Ireland, and to leave seven men as princes here, and Caradawc, the son of Bran, as the chief of them, and their seven knights. In Edeyrnion were these men left. And for this reason were the seven knights placed in the town. Now the names of these seven men were, Caradawc the son of Bran, and Heveydd Hir, and Unic Glew Ysgwyd, and Iddic the son of Anarawc Gwalltgrwn, and Fodor the son of Ervyll, and Gwlch Minascwrn, and Llassar the son of Llaesar Llaesgygwyd, and Pendaran Dyved as a young page with them. And these abode as seven ministers to take charge of this island; and Caradawc the son of Bran was the chief amongst them.

Bendigeid Vran, with the host of which we spoke, sailed towards Ireland, and it was not far across the sea, and he came to shoal water. It was caused by two rivers; the Lli and the Archan were they called; and the nations covered the sea. Then he proceeded with what provisions he had on his own back, and approached the shore of Ireland.

Now the swineherds of Matholwch were upon the seashore, and they came to Matholwch. "Lord," said they, "greeting be unto thee." "Heaven protect you," said he, "have you any news?" "Lord," said they, "we have marvelous news, a wood have we seen upon the sea, in a place where we never yet saw a single tree." "This is indeed a marvel," said he; "saw you aught else?" "We saw, lord," said they, "a vast mountain beside the wood, which moved, and there was a lofty ridge on the top of the mountain, and a lake on each side of the ridge. And the wood, and the mountain, and all these things moved." "Verily," said he, "there is none who can know aught concerning this, unless it be Branwen."

Messengers then went unto Branwen. "Lady," said they, "what thinkest thou that this is?" "The men of the Island of the Mighty, who have come hither on hearing of my ill-treatment and my woes." "What is the forest that is seen upon the sea?" asked they. "The yards and the masts of ships," she answered. "Alas," said they, "what is the mountain that is seen by the side of the ships?" "Bendigeid Vran, my brother," she replied, "coming to shoal water; there is no ship that can contain him in it." "What is the lofty ridge with the lake on each side thereof?" "On looking towards this island he is wroth, and his two eyes, one on each side of his nose, are the two lakes beside the ridge."

The warriors and the chief men of Ireland were brought together in haste, and they took counsel. "Lord," said the nobles unto Matholwch, "there is no other counsel than to retreat over the Linon (a river which is in Ireland), and to keep the river between thee and him, and to break down the bridge that is across the river, for there is a loadstone at the bottom of the river that neither ship nor vessel can pass over." So they retreated across the river, and broke down the bridge.

Bendigeid Vran came to land, and the fleet with him by the bank of the river. "Lord," said his chieftains, "knowest thou the nature of this river, that nothing can go across it, and there is no bridge over it?" "What," said they, "is thy counsel concerning a bridge?" "There is none," said he, "except that he who will be chief, let him be a bridge. I will be so," said he. And then was that saying first uttered, and it is still used as a proverb. And when he had lain down across the river, hurdles were placed upon him, and the host passed over thereby.

And as he rose up, behold the messengers of Matholwch came to him, and saluted him, and gave him greeting in the name of Matholwch, his kinsman, and showed how that of his goodwill he had merited of him nothing but good. "For Matholwch has given the kingdom of Ireland to Gwern the son of Matholwch, thy nephew and thy sister's son. And this he places before thee, as a compensation for the wrong and despite that has been done unto Branwen. And Matholwch shall be maintained wheresoever thou wilt, either here or in the Island of the Mighty." Said Bendigeid Vran, "Shall not I myself have the kingdom? Then peradventure I may take counsel concerning your message. From this time until then no other answer will you get from me." "Verily," said they, "the best message that we receive for thee, we will convey it unto thee, and do thou await our message unto him." "I will wait," answered he, "and do you return quickly."

The messengers set forth and came to Matholwch. "Lord," said they, "prepare a better message for Bendigeid Vran. He would not listen at all to the message that we bore him." "My friends," said Matholwch, "what may be your counsel?" "Lord," said they, "there is no other counsel than this alone. He was never known to be within a house, make therefore a house that will contain him and the men of the Island of the Mighty on the one side, and thyself and thy host on the other; and give over thy kingdom to his will, and do him homage. So by reason of the honor thou doest him in making him a house, whereas he never before had a house to contain him, he will make peace with thee." So the messengers went back to Bendigeid Vran, bearing him this message.

And he took counsel, and in the council it was resolved that he should accept this, and this was all done by the advice of Branwen, and lest the country should be destroyed. And this peace was made, and the house was built both vast and strong. But the Irish planned a crafty device, and the craft was that they should put brackets on each side of the hundred pillars that were in the house, and should place a leathern bag on each bracket, and an armed man in every one of them. Then Evnissyen came in before the host of the Island of the Mighty, and scanned the house with fierce and savage looks, and descried the leathern bags which were around the pillars. "What is in this bag?" asked he of one of the Irish. "Meal, good soul," said he. And Evnissyen felt about it until he came to the man's head, and he squeezed the head until he felt his fingers meet together in the brain through the bone. And he left that one and put his hand upon another, and asked what was therein. "Meal," said the Irishman. So he did the like unto every one of them, until he had not left alive, of all the two hundred men, save one only; and when he came to him, he asked what was there. "Meal, good soul," said the Irishman. And he felt about until he felt the head, and he squeezed that head as he had done the others. And, albeit he found that the head of this one was armed, he left him not until he had killed him. And then he sang an Englyn:

"There is in this bag a different sort of meal,
The ready combatant, when the assault is made
By his fellow-warriors, prepared for battle."

Thereupon came the hosts unto the house. The men of the Island of Ireland entered the house on the one side, and the men of the Island of the Mighty on the other. And as soon as they had sat down there was concord between them; and the sovereignty was conferred upon the boy. When the peace was concluded, Bendigeid Vran called the boy unto him, and from Bendigeid Vran the boy went unto Manawyddan, and he was beloved by all that beheld him. And from Manawyddan the boy was called by Nissyen the son of Eurosswydd, and the boy went unto him lovingly. "Wherefore," said Evnissyen, "comes not my nephew the son of my sister unto me? Though he were not king of Ireland, yet willingly would I fondle the boy." "Cheerfully let him go to thee," said Bendigeid Vran, and the boy went unto him cheerfully. "By my confession to Heaven," said Evnissyen in his heart, "unthought of by the household is the slaughter that I will this instant commit."

Then he arose and took up the boy by the feet, and before any one in the house could seize hold of him, he thrust the boy headlong into the blazing fire. And when Branwen saw her son burning in the fire, she strove to leap into the fire also, from the place where she sat between her two brothers. But Bendigeid Vran grasped her with one hand, and his shield with the other. Then they all hurried about the house, and never was there made so great a tumult by any host in one house as was made by them, as each man armed himself. Then said Morddwydtyllyon, "The gadflies of Morddwydtyllyon's Cow!" And while they all sought their arms, Bendigeid Vran supported Branwen between his shield and his shoulder.

Then the Irish kindled a fire under the cauldron of renovation, and they cast the dead bodies into the cauldron until it was full, and the next day they came forth fighting-men as good as before, except that they were not able to speak. Then when Evnissyen saw the dead bodies of the men of the Island of the Mighty nowhere resuscitated, he said in his heart, "Alas! woe is me, that I should have been the cause of bringing the men of the Island of the Mighty into so great a strait. Evil betide me if I find not a deliverance therefrom." And he cast himself among the dead bodies of the Irish, and two unshod Irishmen came to him, and, taking him to be one of the Irish, flung him into the cauldron. And he stretched himself out in the cauldron, so that he rent the cauldron into four pieces, and burst his own heart also.

In consequence of that the men of the Island of the Mighty obtained such success as they had; but they were not victorious, for only seven men of them all escaped, and Bendigeid Vran himself was wounded in the foot with a poisoned dart. Now the seven men that escaped were Pryderi, Manawyddan, Gluneu Eil Taran, Taliesin, Ynawc, Grudyen the son of Muryel, and Heilyn the son of Gwynn Hen.

And Bendigeid Vran commanded them that they should cut off his head. "And take you my head," said he, "and bear it even unto the White Mount, in London, and bury it there, with the face towards France. And a long time will you be upon the road. In Harlech you will be feasting seven years, the birds of Rhiannon singing unto you the while. And all that time the head will be to you as pleasant company as it ever was when on my body. And at Gwales in Penvro you will be fourscore years, and you may remain there, and the head with you uncorrupted, until you open the door that looks towards Aber Henvelen, and towards Cornwall. And after you have opened that door, there you may no longer tarry, set forth then to London to bury the head, and go straight forward."

So they cut off his head, and these seven went forward therewith. And Branwen was the eighth with them, and they came to land at Aber Alaw, in Talebolyon, and they sat down to rest. And Branwen looked towards Ireland and towards the Island of the Mighty, to see if she could descry them. "Alas," said she, "woe is me that I was ever born; two islands have been destroyed because of me!" Then she uttered a loud groan, and there broke her heart. And they made her a four-sided grave, and buried her upon the banks of the Alaw.

Then the seven men journeyed forward towards Harlech, bearing the head with them; and as they went, behold there met them a multitude of men and of women. "Have you any tidings?" asked Manawyddan. "We have none," said they, "save that Caswallawn the son of Beli has conquered the Island of the Mighty, and is crowned king in London." "What has become," said they, "of Caradawc the son of Bran, and the seven men who were left with him in this island?" "Caswallawn came upon them, and slew six of the men, and Caradawc's heart broke for grief thereof; for he could see the sword that slew the men, but knew not who it was that wielded it. Caswallawn had flung upon him the Veil of Illusion, so that no one could see him slay the men, but the sword only could they see. And it liked him not to slay Caradawc, because he was his nephew, the son of his cousin. And now he was the third whose heart had broke through grief. Pendaran Dyved, who had remained as a young page with these men, escaped into the wood," said they.

Then they went on to Harlech, and there stopped to rest, and they provided meat and liquor, and sat down to eat and to drink. And there came three birds, and began singing unto them a certain song, and all the songs they had ever heard were unpleasant compared thereto; and the birds seemed to them to be at a great distance from them over the sea, yet they appeared as distinct as if they were close by, and at this repast they continued seven years.

And at the close of the seventh year they went forth to Gwales in Penvro. And there they found a fair and regal spot overlooking the ocean; and a spacious hall was therein. And they went into the hall, and two of its doors were open, but the third door was closed, that which looked towards Cornwall. "See, yonder," said Manawyddan, "is the door that we may not open." And that night they regaled themselves and were joyful. And of all they had seen of food laid before them, and of all they had heard of, they remembered nothing; neither of that, nor of any sorrow whatsoever. And there they remained fourscore years, unconscious of having ever spent a time more joyous and mirthful. And they were not more weary than when first they came, neither did they, any of them, know the time they had been there. And it was not more irksome to them having the head with them, than if Bendigeid Vran had been with them himself. And because of these fourscore years, it was called the entertaining of the noble head. The entertaining of Branwen and Matholwch was in the time that they went to Ireland.

One day said Heilyn the son of Gwynn, "Evil betide me, if I do not open the door to know if that is true which is said concerning it." So he opened the door and looked towards Cornwall and Aber Henvelen. And when they had looked, they were as conscious of all the evils they had ever sustained, and of all the friends and companions they had lost, and of all the misery that had befallen them, as if all had happened in that very spot; and especially of the fate of their lord. And because of their perturbation they could not rest, but journeyed forth with the head towards London. And they buried the head in the White Mount, and when it was buried, this was the third goodly concealment; and it was the third ill-fated disclosure when it was disinterred, inasmuch as no invasion from across the sea came to this island while the head was in that concealment.

And thus is the story related of those who journeyed over from Ireland.

In Ireland none were left alive, except five pregnant women in a cave in the Irish wilderness; and to these five women in the same night were born five sons, whom they nursed until they became grown-up youths. And they thought about wives, and they at the same time desired to possess them, and each took a wife of the mothers of their companions, and they governed the country and peopled it.

And these five divided it amongst them, and because of this partition are the five divisions of Ireland still so termed. And they examined the land where the battles had taken place, and they found gold and silver until they became wealthy.

And thus ends this portion of the Mabinogi, concerning the blow given to Branwen, which was the third unhappy blow of this island; and concerning the entertainment of Bran, when the hosts of sevenscore countries and ten went over to Ireland to revenge the blow given to Branwen; and concerning the seven years' banquet in Harlech, and the singing of the birds of Rhiannon, and the sojourning of the head for the space of fourscore years.

III. Manawyddan the Son of Llyr

Here is the Third Portion of the Mabinogi

When the seven men of whom we spoke above had buried the head of Bendigeid Vran, in the White Mount an London, with its face towards France; Manawyddan gazed upon the town of London, and upon his companions, and heaved a great sigh; and much grief and heaviness came upon him. "Alas, Almighty Heaven, woe is me," he exclaimed, "there is none save myself without a resting-place this night." "Lord," said Pryderi, "be not so sorrowful. Thy cousin is king of the Island of the Mighty, and though he should do thee wrong, thou hast never been a claimant of land or possessions. Thou art the third disinherited prince." "Yea," answered he, "but although this man is my cousin, it grieveth me to see any one in the place of my brother Bendigeid Vran, neither can I be happy in the same dwelling with him." "Wilt thou follow the counsel of another?" said Pryderi. "I stand in need of counsel," he answered, "and what may that counsel be?" "Seven Cantrevs remain unto me," said Pryderi, "wherein Rhiannon my mother dwells. I will bestow her upon thee and the seven Cantrevs with her, and though thou hadst no possessions but those Cantrevs only, thou couldst not have seven Cantrevs fairer than they. Kicva, the daughter of Gwynn Gloyw, is my wife, and since the inheritance of the Cantrevs belongs to me, do thou and Rhiannon enjoy them, and if thou ever desire any possessions thou wilt take these." "I do not, Chieftain," said he; "Heaven reward thee for thy friendship." "I would show thee the best friendship in the world if thou wouldst let me." "I will, my friend," said he, "and Heaven reward thee. I will go with thee to seek Rhiannon and to look at thy possessions." "Thou wilt do well," he answered. "And I believe that thou didst never hear a lady discourse better than she, and when she was in her prime none was ever fairer. Even now her aspect is not uncomely."

They set forth, and, however long the journey, they came at length to Dyved, and a feast was prepared for them against their coming to Narberth, which Rhiannon and Kicva had provided. Then began Manawyddan and Rhiannon to sit and to talk together, and from their discourse his mind and his thoughts became warmed towards her, and he thought in his heart he had never beheld any lady more fulfilled of grace and beauty than she. "Pryderi," said he, "I will that it be as thou didst say." "What saying was that?" asked Rhiannon. "Lady," said Pryderi, "I did offer thee as a wife to Manawyddan the son of Llyr." "By that will I gladly abide," said Rhiannon. "Right glad am I also," said Manawyddan; "may Heaven reward him who hath shown unto me friendship so perfect as this."

And before the feast was over she became his bride. Said Pryderi, "Tarry ye here the rest of the feast, and I will go into Lloegyr to tender my homage unto Caswallawn the son of Beli." "Lord," said Rhiannon, "Caswallawn is in Kent, thou mayest therefore tarry at the feast, and wait until he shall be nearer." "We will wait," he answered. So they finished the feast. And they began to make the circuit of Dyved, and to hunt, and to take their pleasure. And as they went through the country, they had never seen lands more pleasant to live in, nor better hunting grounds, nor greater plenty of honey and fish. And such was the friendship between those four, that they would not be parted from each other by night nor by day.

And in the midst of all this he went to Caswallawn at Oxford, and tendered his homage; and honorable was his reception there, and highly was he praised for offering his homage.

And after his return, Pryderi and Manawyddan feasted and took their ease and pleasure. And they began a feast at Narberth, for it was the chief palace; and there originated all honor. And when they had ended the first meal that night, while those who served them ate, they arose and went forth, and proceeded all four to the Gorsedd of

Narberth, and their retinue with them. And as they sat thus, behold, a peal of thunder, and with the violence of the thunderstorm, lo there came a fall of mist, so thick that not one of them could see the other. And after the mist it became light all around. And when they looked towards the place where they were wont to see cattle, and herds, and dwellings, they saw nothing now, neither house, nor beast, nor smoke, nor fire, nor man, nor dwelling; but the houses of the Court empty, and desert, and uninhabited, without either man or beast within them. And truly all their companions were lost to them, without their knowing aught of what had befallen them, save those four only.

"In the name of Heaven," cried Manawyddan, "where are they of the Court, and all my host beside these? Let us go and see." So they came into the hall, and there was no man; and they went on to the castle and to the sleeping-place, and they saw none; and in the mead-cellar and in the kitchen there was nought but desolation. So they four feasted, and hunted, and took their pleasure. Then they began to go through the land and all the possessions that they had, and they visited the houses and dwellings, and found nothing but wild beasts. And when they had consumed their feast and all their provisions, they fed upon the prey they killed in hunting, and the honey of the wild swarms. And thus they passed the first year pleasantly, and the second; but at the last they began to be weary.

"Verily," said Manawyddan, "we must not bide thus. Let us go into Lloegyr, and seek some craft whereby we may gain our support." So they went into Lloegyr, and came as far as Hereford. And they betook themselves to making saddles. And Manawyddan began to make housings, and he gilded and colored them with blue enamel, in the manner that he had seen it done by Llasar Llaesgywydd. And he made the blue enamel as it was made by the other man. And therefore is it still called Calch Lasar [blue enamel], because Llasar Llaesgywydd had wrought it.

And as long as that workmanship could be had of Manawyddan, neither saddle nor housing was bought of a saddler throughout all Hereford; till at length every one of the saddlers perceived that they were losing much of their gain, and that no man bought of them, but him who could not get what he sought from Manawyddan. Then they assembled together, and agreed to slay him and his companions.

Now they received warning of this, and took counsel whether they should leave the city. "By Heaven," said Pryderi, "it is not my counsel that we should quit the town, but that we should slay these boors." "Not so," said Manawyddan, "for if we fight with them, we shall have evil fame, and shall be put in prison. It were better for us to go to another town to maintain ourselves." So they four went to another city.

"What craft shall we take?" said Pryderi. "We will make shields," said Manawyddan. "Do we know anything about that craft?" said Pryderi. "We will try," answered he. There they began to make shields, and fashioned them after the shape of the good shields they had seen; and they enamelled they, as them had done the saddles. And they prospered in that place, so that not a shield was asked for in the whole town, but such as was had of them. Rapid therefore was their work, and numberless were the shields they made. But at last they were marked by the craftsmen, who came together in haste, and their fellow-townsmen with them, and agreed that they should seek to slay them. But they received warning, and heard how the men had resolved on their destruction. "Pryderi," said Manawyddan, "these men desire to slay us." "Let us not endure this from these boors, but let us rather fall upon them and slay them." "Not so," he answered; "Caswallawn and his men will hear of it, and we shall be undone. Let us go to another town." So to another town they went.

"What craft shall we take?" said Manawyddan. "Whatsoever thou wilt that we know," said Pryderi. "Not so," he replied, "but let us take to making shoes, for there is not courage enough among cordwainers either to fight with us or to molest us." "I know nothing thereof," said Pryderi. "But I know," answered Manawyddan; "and I will teach thee to stitch. We will not attempt to dress the leather, but we will buy it ready dressed and will make the shoes from it."

So he began by buying the best cordwal that could be had in the town, and none other would he buy except the leather for the soles; and he associated himself with the best goldsmith in the town, and caused him to make clasps for the shoes, and to gild the clasps, and he marked how it was done until he learnt the method. And therefore was he called one of the three makers of Gold Shoes; and, when they could be had from him, not a shoe nor hose was bought of any of the cordwainers in the town. But when the cordwainers perceived that their gains were failing (for as Manawyddan shaped the work, so Pryderi stitched it), they came together and took counsel, and agreed that they would slay them.

"Pryderi," said Manawyddan, "these men are minded to slay us." "Wherefore should we bear this from the boorish thieves?" said Pryderi. "Rather let us slay them all." "Not so," said Manawyddan, "we will not slay them, neither will we remain in Lloegyr any longer. Let us set forth to Dyved and go to see it."

So they journeyed along until they came to Dyved, and they went forward to Narberth. And there they kindled fire and supported themselves by hunting. And thus they spent a month. And they gathered their dogs around them, and tarried there one year.

And one morning Pryderi and Manawyddan rose up to hunt, and they ranged their dogs and went forth from the palace. And some of the dogs ran before them and came to a small bush which was near at hand; but as soon as they were come to the bush, they hastily drew back and returned to the men, their hair bristling up greatly. "Let us go near to the bush," said Pryderi, "and see what is in it." And as they came near, behold, a wild boar of a pure white color rose up from the bush. Then the dogs, being set on by the men, rushed towards him; but he left the bush and fell back a little way from the men, and made a stand against the dogs without retreating from them, until the men had come near. And when the men came up, he fell back a second time, and betook him to flight. Then they pursued the boar until they beheld a vast and lofty castle, all newly built, in a place where they had never before seen either stone or building. And the boar ran swiftly into the castle and the dogs after him. Now when the boar and the dogs had gone into the castle, they began to wonder at finding a castle in a place where they had never before seen any building whatsoever. And from the top of the Gorsedd they looked and listened for the dogs. But so long as they were there they heard not one of the dogs nor aught concerning them.

"Lord," said Pryderi, "I will go into the castle to get tidings of the dogs." "Truly," he replied, "thou wouldst be unwise to go into this castle, which thou hast never seen till now. If thou wouldst follow my counsel, thou wouldst not enter therein. Whosoever has cast a spell over this land has caused this castle to be here." "Of a truth," answered Pryderi, "I cannot thus give up my dogs." And for all the counsel that Manawyddan gave him, yet to the castle he went.

When he came within the castle, neither man nor beast, nor boar nor dogs, nor house nor dwelling saw he within it. But in the center of the castle floor he beheld a fountain with marble work around it, and on the margin of the fountain a golden bowl upon a marble slab, and chains hanging from the air, to which he saw no end.

And he was greatly pleased with the beauty of the gold, and with the rich workmanship of the bowl, and he went up to the bowl and laid hold of it. And when he had taken hold of it his hands stuck to the bowl, and his feet to the slab on which the howl was placed, and all his joyousness forsook him, so that he could not utter a word. And thus he stood.

And Manawyddan waited for him till near the close of the day. And late in the evening, being certain that he should have no tidings of Pryderi or of the dogs, he went back to the palace. And as he entered, Rhiannon looked at him. "Where," said she, "are thy companion and thy dogs?" "Behold," he answered, "the adventure that has befallen me." And he related it all unto her. "An evil companion hast thou been," said Rhiannon, "and a good companion hast thou lost." And with that word she went out, and proceeded towards the castle according to the direction which he gave her. The gate of the castle she found open. She was nothing daunted, and she went in. And as she went in, she perceived Pryderi laying hold of the bowl, and she went towards him. "Oh, my lord," said she, "what dost thou do here?" And she took hold of the bowl with him; and as she did so her hands became fast to the bowl, and her feet to the slab, and she was not able to utter a word. And with that, as it became night, lo, there came thunder upon them, and a fall of mist, and thereupon the castle vanished, and they with it.

When Kicva the daughter of Gwynn Gloyw saw that there was no one in the palace but herself and Manawyddan, she sorrowed so that she cared not whether she lived or died. And Manawyddan saw this. "Thou art in the wrong," said he, "if through fear of me thou grievest thus. I call Heaven to witness that thou hast never seen friendship more pure than that which I will bear thee, as long as Heaven will that thou shouldst be thus. I declare to thee that were I in the dawn of youth I would keep my faith unto Pryderi, and unto thee also will I keep it. Be there no fear upon thee, therefore," said he, "for Heaven is my witness that thou shalt meet with all the friendship thou canst wish, and that it is in my power to show thee, as long as it shall please Heaven to continue us in this grief and woe." "Heaven reward thee," she said, "and that is what I deemed of thee." And the damsel thereupon took courage and was glad.

"Truly, lady," said Manawyddan, "it is not fitting for us to stay here, we have lost our dogs, and we cannot get food. Let us go into Lloegyr; it is easiest for us to find support there." "Gladly, lord," said she, "we will do so." And they set forth together to Lloegyr.

"Lord," said she, "what craft wilt thou follow? Take up one that is seemly." "None other will I take," answered he, "save that of making shoes, as I did formerly." "Lord," said she, "such a craft becomes not a man so nobly born as thou." "By that however will I abide," said he.

So he began his craft, and he made all his work of the finest leather he could get in the town, and, as he had done at the other place, he caused gilded clasps to be made for the shoes. And except himself all the cordwainers in the town were idle, and without work. For as long as they could be had from him, neither shoes nor hose were bought elsewhere. And thus they tarried there a year, until the cordwainers became envious, and took counsel concerning him. And he had warning thereof, and it was told him how the cordwainers had agreed together to slay him.

"Lord," said Kicva, "wherefore should this be borne from these boors?" "Nay," said he, "we will go back unto Dyved." So towards Dyved they set forth.

Now Manawyddan, when he set out to return to Dyved, took with him a burden of wheat. And he proceeded towards Narberth, and there he dwelt. And never was he better pleased than when he saw Narberth again, and the lands where he had been wont to hunt with Pryderi and with Rhiannon. And he accustomed himself to fish, and to hunt the deer in their covert. And then he began to prepare some ground, and he sowed a croft, and a second, and a third. And no wheat in the world ever sprung up better. And the three crofts prospered with perfect growth, and no man ever saw fairer wheat than it.

And thus passed the seasons of the year until the harvest came. And he went to look at one of his crofts, and behold it was ripe. "I will reap this tomorrow," said he. And that night he went back to Narberth, and on the morrow in the gray dawn he went to reap the croft, and when he came there he found nothing but the bare straw. Every one of the ears of the wheat was cut from off the stalk, and all the ears carried entirely away, and nothing but the straw left. And at this he marveled greatly.

Then he went to look at another croft, and behold that also was ripe. "Verily," said he, "this will I reap tomorrow. And on the morrow he came with the intent to reap it, and when he came there he found nothing but the bare straw. "Oh, gracious Heaven," he exclaimed, "I know that whosoever has begun my ruin is completing it, and has also destroyed the country with me."

Then he went to look at the third croft, and when he came there, finer wheat had there never been seen, and this also was ripe. "Evil betide me," said he, "if I watch not here tonight. Whoever carried off the other corn will come in like manner to take this. And I will know who it is." So he took his arms, and began to watch the croft. And he told Kicva all that had befallen. "Verily," said she, "what thinkest thou to do?" "I will watch the croft tonight," said he.

And he went to watch the croft. And at midnight, lo, there arose the loudest tumult in the world. And he looked, and behold the mightiest host of mice in the world, which could neither be numbered nor measured. And he knew not what it was until the mice had made their way into the croft, and each of them climbing up the straw and bending it down with its weight, had cut off one of the ears of wheat, and had carried it away, leaving there the stalk, and he saw not a single stalk there that had not a mouse to it. And they all took their way, carrying the ears with them.

In wrath and anger did he rush upon the mice, but he could no more come up with them than if they had been gnats, or birds in the air, except one only, which though it was but sluggish, went so fast that a man on foot could scarce overtake it. And after this one he went, and he caught it and put it in his glove, and tied up the opening of the glove with a string, and kept it with him, and returned to the palace. Then he came to the hall where Kicva was, and he lighted a fire, and hung the glove by the string upon a peg. "What hast thou there, lord?" said Kicva. "A thief," said he, "that I found robbing me." "What kind of thief may it be, lord, that thou couldst put into thy glove?" said she. "Behold I will tell thee," he answered. Then he showed her how his fields had been wasted and destroyed, and how the mice came to the last of the fields in his sight. "And one of them was less nimble than the rest, and is now in my glove; tomorrow I will hang it, and before Heaven, if I had them, I would hang them all." "My lord," said she, "this is marvelous; but yet it would be unseemly for a man of dignity like thee to be hanging such a reptile as this. And if thou doest right, thou wilt not meddle with the creature, but wilt let it go." "Woe betide me," said he, "if I would not hang them all could I catch them, and such as I have I will hang." "Verily, lord," said she, "there is no reason that I should succor this reptile, except to prevent discredit unto thee. Do therefore, lord, as thou wilt." "If I knew of any cause in the world wherefore thou shouldst succor it, I would take thy counsel concerning it," said Manawyddan, "but as I know of none, lady, I am minded to destroy it." "Do so willingly then," said she.

And then he went to the Gorsedd of Narberth, taking the mouse with him. And he set up two forks on the highest part of the Gorsedd. And while he was doing this, behold he saw a scholar coming towards him, in old and poor and tattered garments. And it was now seven years since he had seen in that place either man or beast, except those four persons who had remained together until two of them were lost.

"My lord," said the scholar, "good day to thee." "Heaven prosper thee, and my greeting be unto thee. And whence dost thou come, scholar?" asked he. "I come, lord, from singing in Lloegyr; and wherefore dost thou inquire?" "Because for the last seven years," answered he, "I have seen no man here save four secluded persons, and thyself this moment." "Truly, lord," said he, "I go through this land unto mine own. And what work art thou upon, lord?" "I am hanging a thief that I caught robbing me," said he. "What manner of thief is that?" asked the scholar. "I see a creature in thy hand like unto a mouse, and ill does it become a man of rank equal to thine to touch a reptile such as this. Let it go forth free." "I will not let it go free, by Heaven," said he; "I caught it robbing me, and the doom of a thief will I inflict upon it, and I will hang it." "Lord," said he, "rather than see a man of rank equal to thine at such a work as this, I would give thee a pound which I have received as alms, to let the reptile go forth free." "I will not let it go free," said he, "by Heaven, neither will I sell it." "As thou wilt, lord," he answered; "except that I would not see a man of rank equal to thine touching such a reptile, I care nought." And the scholar went his way.

And as he was placing the crossbeam upon the two forks, behold a priest came towards him upon a horse covered with trappings. "Good day to thee, lord," said he. "Heaven prosper thee," said Manawyddan; "thy blessing." "The blessing of Heaven be upon thee. And what, lord, art thou doing?" "I am hanging a thief that I caught robbing me," said he. "What manner of thief, lord?" asked he. "A creature," he answered, "in form of a mouse. It has been robbing me, and I am inflicting upon it the doom of a thief." "Lord," said he, "rather than see thee touch this reptile, I would purchase its freedom." "By my confession to Heaven, neither will I sell it nor set it free." "It is true, lord, that it is worth nothing to buy; but rather than see thee defile thyself by touching such a reptile as this, I will give thee three pounds to let it go." "I will not, by Heaven," said he, "take any price for at. As it ought, so shall it be hanged." "Willingly, lord, do thy good pleasure." And the priest went his way.

Then he noosed the string around the mouse's neck, and as he was about to draw it up, behold, he saw a bishop's retinue with his sumpter-horses, and his attendants. And the bishop himself came towards him. And he stayed his work. "Lord bishop," said he, "thy blessing." "Heaven's blessing be unto thee," said he; "what work art thou upon?" "Hanging a thief that I caught robbing me," said he. "Is not that a mouse that I see in thy hand?" "Yes," answered he. "And she has robbed me." "Aye," said he, "since I have come at the doom of this reptile, I will ransom it of thee. I will give thee seven pounds for it, and that rather than see a man of rank equal to thine destroying so vile a reptile as this. Let it loose and thou shalt have the money." "I declare to Heaven that I will not set it loose." "If thou wilt not loose it for this, I will give thee four-and-twenty pounds of ready money to set it free." "I will not set it free, by Heaven, for as much again," said he. "If thou wilt not set it free for this, I will give thee all the horses that thou seest in this plain, and the seven loads of baggage, and the seven horses that they are upon." "By Heaven, I will not," he replied. "Since for this thou wilt not, do so at what price soever thou wilt." "I will do so," said he. "I will that Rhiannon and Pryderi be free," said he. "That thou shalt have," he answered. "Not yet will I loose the mouse, by Heaven." "What then wouldst thou?" "That the charm and the illusion be removed from the seven Cantrevs of Dyved." "This shalt thou have also; set therefore the mouse free." "I will not set it free, by Heaven," said he. "I will know who the mouse may be." "She is my wife." "Even though she be, I will not set her free. Wherefore came she to me?" "To despoil thee," he answered. "I am Llwyd the son of Kilcoed, and I cast the charm over the seven Cantrevs of Dyved. And it was to avenge Gwawl the son of Clud, from the friendship I had towards him, that I cast the charm. And upon Pryderi did I revenge Gwawl the son of Clud, for the game of Badger in the Bag, that Pwyll Pen Annwvyn played upon him, which he did unadvisedly in the Court of Heveydd Hên. And when it was known that thou wast come to dwell in the land, my household came and besought me to transform them into mice, that they might destroy thy corn. And it was my own household that went the first night. And the second night also they went, and they destroyed thy two crofts. And the third night came unto me my wife and the ladies of the Court, and besought me to transform them. And I transformed them. Now she is pregnant. And had she not been pregnant thou wouldst not have been able to overtake her; but since this has taken place, and she has been caught, I will restore thee Pryderi and Rhiannon; and I will take the charm and illusion from off Dyved. I have now told thee who she is. Set her therefore free." "I will not set her free, by Heaven," said he. "What wilt thou more?" he asked. "I will that there be no more charm upon the seven Cantrevs of Dyved, and that none shall be put upon it henceforth." "This thou shalt have," said he. "Now set her free." "I will not, by my faith," he answered. "What wilt thou furthermore?" asked he. "Behold," said he, "this will I have; that vengeance be never taken for this, either upon Pryderi or Rhiannon, or upon me." "All this shalt thou have. And truly thou hast done wisely in asking this. Upon thy head would have lighted all this trouble." "Yea," said he, "for fear thereof was it, that I required this." "Set now my wife at liberty." "I will not, by Heaven," said he, "until I see Pryderi and Rhiannon with me free." "Behold, here they come," he answered.

And thereupon behold Pryderi and Rhiannon. And he rose up to meet them, and greeted them, and sat down beside them. "Ah, Chieftain, set now my wife at liberty," said the bishop. "Hast thou not received all thou didst ask?" "I will release her gladly," said he. And thereupon he set her free.

Then Llwyd struck her with a magic wand, and she was changed back into a young woman, the fairest ever seen.

"Look around upon thy land," said he, "and then thou wilt see it all tilled and peopled, as it was in its best state." And he rose up and looked forth. And when he looked he saw all the lands tilled, and full of herds and dwellings. "What bondage," he inquired, "has there been upon Pryderi and Rhiannon?" "Pryderi has had the knockers of the gate of my palace about his neck, and Rhiannon has had the collars of the asses, after they have been carrying hay, about her neck."

And such had been their bondage.

And by reason of this bondage is this story called the Mabinogi of Mynnweir and Mynord.

And thus ends this portion of the Mabinogi.

IV. Math the Son of Mathonwy

This is the Fourth Portion of the Mabinogi

Math the son of Mathonwy was lord over Gwynedd, and Pryderi the son of Pwyll was lord over the one-and-twenty Cantrevs of the South; and these were the seven Cantrevs of Dyved, and the seven Cantrevs of Morganwc, the four Cantrevs of Ceredigiawn, and the three of Ystrad Tywi.

At that time, Math the son of Mathonwy could not exist unless his feet were in the lap of a maiden, except only when he was prevented by the tumult of war. Now the maiden who was with him was Goewin, the daughter of Pebin of Dôl Pebin, in Arvon, and she was the fairest maiden of her time who was known there.

And Math dwelt always at Caer Dathyl, in Arvon, and was not able to go the circuit of the land, but Gilvaethwy the son of Don, and Eneyd the son of Don, his nephews, the sons of his sisters, with his household, went the circuit of the land in his stead.

Now the maiden was with Math continually, and Gilvaethwy the son of Don set his affections upon her, and loved her so that he knew not what he should do because of her, and therefrom behold his hue, and his aspect, and his spirits changed for love of her, so that it was not easy to know him.

One day his brother Gwydion gazed steadfastly upon him. "Youth," said he, "what aileth thee?" "Why," replied he, "what seest thou in me?" "I see," said he, "that thou hast lost thy aspect and thy hue; what, therefore, aileth thee?" "My lord brother," he answered, "that which aileth me, it will not profit me that I should own to any." "What may it be, my soul?" said he. "Thou knowest," he said, "that Math the son of Mathonwy has this property, that if men whisper together, in a tone how low soever, if the wind meet it, it becomes known unto him." "Yes," said Gwydion, "hold now thy peace, I know thy intent, thou lovest Goewin."

When he found that his brother knew his intent, he gave the heaviest sigh in the world. "Be silent, my soul, and sigh not," he said. "It is not thereby that thou wilt succeed. I will cause," said he, "if it cannot be otherwise, the rising of Gwynedd, and Powys, and Deheubarth, to seek the maiden. Be thou of glad cheer therefore, and I will compass it."

So they went unto Math the son of Mathonwy. "Lord," said Gwydion, "I have heard that there have come to the South some beasts, such as were never known in this island before." "What are they called?" he asked. "Pigs, lord." "And what kind of animals are they?" "They are small animals, and their flesh is better than the flesh of oxen." "They are small, then?" "And they change their names. Swine are they now called." "Who owneth them?" "Pryderi the son of Pwyll; they were sent him from Annwvyn, by Arawn the king of Annwvyn, and still they keep that name, half hog, half pig." "Verily," asked he, "and by what means may they be obtained from him?" "I will go, lord, as one of twelve, in the guise of bards, to seek the swine." "But it may be that he will refuse you," said he. "My journey will not be evil, lord," said he; "I will not come back without the swine." "Gladly," said he, "go thou forward."

So he and Gilvaethwy went, and ten other men with them. And they came into Ceredigiawn, to the place that is now called Rhuddlan Teivi, where the palace of Pryderi was. In the guise of bards they came in, and they were received joyfully, and Gwydion was placed beside Pryderi that night.

"Of a truth," said Pryderi, "gladly would I have a tale from some of your men yonder." "Lord," said Gwydion, "we have a custom that the first night that we come to the Court of a great man, the chief of song recites. Gladly will I relate a tale." Now Gwydion was the best teller of tales in the world, and he diverted all the Court that night with pleasant discourse and with tales, so that he charmed every one in the Court, and it pleased Pryderi to talk with him.

And after this, "Lord," said he unto Pryderi, "were it more pleasing to thee, that another should discharge my errand unto thee, than that I should tell thee myself what it is?" "No," he answered, "ample speech hast thou." "Behold then, lord," said he, "my errand. It is to crave from thee the animals that were sent thee from Annwvyn." "Verily," he replied, "that were the easiest thing in the world to grant, were there not a covenant between me and my land concerning them. And the covenant is that they shall not go from me, until they have produced double their number in the land." "Lord," said he, "I can set thee free from those words, and this is the way I can do so; give me not the swine tonight, neither refuse them unto me, and tomorrow I will show thee an exchange for them."

And that night he and his fellows went unto their lodging, and they took counsel. "Ah, my men," said he, "we shall not have the swine for the asking." "Well," said they, "how may they be obtained?" "I will cause them to be obtained," said Gwydion.

Then he betook himself to his arts, and began to work a charm. And he caused twelve chargers to appear, and twelve black greyhounds, each of them white-breasted, and having upon them twelve collars and twelve leashes, such as no one that saw them could know to be other than gold. And upon the horses twelve saddles, and every part which should have been of iron was entirely of gold, and the bridles were of the same workmanship. And with the horses and the dogs he came to Pryderi.

"Good day unto thee, lord," said he. "Heaven prosper thee," said the other, "and greetings be unto thee." "Lord," said he, "behold here is a release for thee from the word which thou spakest last evening concerning the swine; that thou wouldst neither give nor sell them. Thou mayest exchange them for that which is better. And I will give these twelve horses, all caparisoned as they are, with their saddles and their bridles, and these twelve greyhounds, with their collars and their leashes as thou seest, and the twelve gilded shields that thou beholdest yonder." Now these he had formed of fungus. "Well," said he, "we will take counsel." And they consulted together, and determined to give the swine to Gwydion, and to take his horses and his dogs and his shields.

Then Gwydion and his men took their leave, and began to journey forth with the pigs. "Ah, my comrades," said Gwydion, "it is needful that we journey with speed. The illusion will not last but from the one hour to the same tomorrow." And that night they journeyed as far as the upper part of Ceredigiawn, to the place which, from that cause, is called Mochdrev still. And the next day they took their course through Melenydd, and came that night to the town which is likewise for that reason called Mochdrev between Keri and Arwystli. And thence they journeyed forward; and that night they came as far as that Commot in Powys, which also upon account thereof is called Mochnant, and there tarried they that night. And they journeyed thence to the Cantrev of Rhos, and the place where they were that night is still called Mochdrev.

"My men," said Gwydion, "we must push forward to the fastnesses of Gwynedd with these animals, for there is a gathering of hosts in pursuit of us." So they journeyed on to the highest town of Arllechwedd, and there they made a sty for the swine, and therefore was the name of Creuwyryon given to that town. And after they had made the sty for the swine, they proceeded to Math the son of Mathonwy, at Caer Dathyl. And when they came there, the country was rising. "What news is there here?" asked Gwydion. "Pryderi is assembling one-and-twenty Cantrevs to pursue after you," answered they. "It is marvelous that you should have journeyed so slowly." "Where are the animals whereof you went in quest?" said Math. "They have had a sty made for them in the other Cantrev below," said Gwydion.

Thereupon, lo, they heard the trumpets and the host in the land, and they arrayed themselves and set forward and came to Penardd in Arvon.

And at night Gwydion the son of Don, and Gilvaethwy his brother, returned to Caer Dathyl; and Gilvaethwy took Math the son of Mathonwy's couch. And while he turned out the other damsels from the room discourteously, he made Goewin unwillingly remain.

And when they saw the day on the morrow, they went back unto the place where Math the son of Mathonwy was with his host; and when they came there, the warriors were taking counsel in what district they should await the coming of Pryderi, and the men of the South. So they went in to the council. And it was resolved to wait in the strongholds of Gwynedd, in Arvon. So within the two Maenors they took their stand, Maenor Penardd and Maenor Coed Alun. And there Pryderi attacked them, and there the combat took place. And great was the slaughter on both sides; but the men of the South were forced to flee. And they fled unto the place which is still called Nantcall. And thither did they follow them, and they made a vast slaughter of them there, so that they fled again as far as the place called Dol Pen Maen, and there they halted and sought to make peace.

And that he might have peace, Pryderi gave hostages, Gwrgi Gwastra gave he and three-and-twenty others, sons of nobles. And after this they journeyed in peace even unto Traeth Mawr; but as they went on together towards Melenryd, the men on foot could not be restrained from shooting. Pryderi despatched unto Math an embassy to pray him to forbid his people, and to leave it between him and Gwydion the son of Don, for that he had caused all this. And the messengers came to Math. "Of a truth," said Math, "I call Heaven to witness, if it be pleasing unto Gwydion the son of Don, I will so leave it gladly. Never will I compel any to go to fight, but that we ourselves should do our utmost."

"Verily," said the messengers, "Pryderi saith that it were more fair that the man who did him this wrong should oppose his own body to his, and let his people remain unscathed." "I declare to Heaven, I will not ask the men of Gwynedd to fight because of me. If I am allowed to fight Pryderi myself, gladly will I oppose my body to his." And this answer they took back to Pryderi. "Truly," said Pryderi, "I shall require no one to demand my rights but myself."

Then these two came forth and armed themselves, and they fought. And by force of strength, and fierceness, and by the magic and charms of Gwydion, Pryderi was slain. And at Maen Tyriawc, above Melenryd, was he buried, and there is his grave.

And the men of the South set forth in sorrow towards their own land; nor is it a marvel that they should grieve, seeing that they had lost their lord, and many of their best warriors, and for the most part their horses and their arms.

The men of Gwynedd went back joyful and in triumph. "Lord," said Gwydion unto Math, "would it not be right for us to release the hostages of the men of the South, which they pledged unto us for peace? for we ought not to put them in prison." "Let them then be set free," saith Math. So that youth, and the other hostages that were with him, were set free to follow the men of the South.

Math himself went forward to Caer Dathyl. Gilvaethwy the son of Don, and they of the household that were with him, went to make the circuit of Gwynedd as they were wont, without coming to the Court. Math went into his chamber, and caused a place to be prepared for him whereon to recline, so that he might put his feet in the maiden's lap. "Lord," said Goewin, "seek now another to hold thy feet, for I am now a wife." "What meaneth this?" said he. "An attack, lord, was made unawares upon me; but I held not my peace, and there was no one in the Court who knew not of it. Now the attack was made by thy nephews, lord, the sons of thy sister, Gwydion the son of Don, and Gilvaethwy the son of Don; unto me they did wrong, and unto thee dishonor." "Verily," he exclaimed, "I will do to the utmost of my power concerning this matter. But first I will cause thee to have compensation, and then will I have amends made unto myself. As for thee, I will take thee to be my wife, and the possession of my dominions will I give unto thy hands."

And Gwydion and Gilvaethwy came not near the Court, but stayed in the confines of the land until it was forbidden to give them meat and drink. At first they came not near unto Math, but at the last they came. "Lord," said they, "good day to thee." "Well," said he, "is it to make me compensation that ye are come?" "Lord," they said, "we are at thy will." "By my will I would not have lost my warriors, and so many arms as I have done. You cannot compensate me my shame, setting aside the death of Pryderi. But since ye come hither to be at my will, I shall begin your punishment forthwith."

Then he took his magic wand, and struck Gilvaethwy, so that he became a deer, and he seized upon the other hastily lest he should escape from him. And he struck him with the same magic wand, and he became a deer also. "Since now ye are in bonds, I will that ye go forth together and be companions, and possess the nature of the animals whose form ye bear. And this day twelvemonth come hither unto me."

At the end of a year from that day, lo there was a loud noise under the chamber wall, and the barking of the dogs of the palace together with the noise. "Look," said he, "what is without." "Lord," said one, "I have looked; there are there two deer, and a fawn with them." Then he arose and went out. And when he came he beheld the three animals. And he lifted up his wand. "As ye were deer last year, be ye wild hogs each and either of you, for the year that is to come." And thereupon he struck them with the magic wand. "The young one will I take and cause to be baptized." Now the name that he gave him was Hydwn. "Go ye and be wild swine, each and either of you, and be ye of the nature of wild swine. And this day twelvemonth be ye here under the wall."

At the end of the year the barking of dogs was heard under the wall of the chamber. And the Court assembled, and thereupon he arose and went forth, and when he came forth he beheld three beasts. Now these were the beasts that he saw; two wild hogs of the woods, and a well-grown young one with them. And he was very large for his age.

"Truly," said Math, "this one will I take and cause to be baptized." And he struck him with his magic wand, and he become a fine fair auburn-haired youth, and the name that he gave him was Hychdwn. "Now as for you, as ye were wild hogs last year, be ye wolves each and either of you for the year that is to come." Thereupon he struck them with his magic wand, and they became wolves. "And be ye of like nature with the animals whose semblance ye bear, and return here this day twelvemonth beneath this wall."

And at the same day at the end of the year, he heard a clamor and a barking of dogs under the wall of the chamber. And he rose and went forth. And when he came, behold, he saw two wolves, and a strong cub with them. "This one will I take," said Math, "and I will cause him to be baptized; there is a name prepared for him, and that is Bleiddwn. Now these three, such are they:

The three sons of Gilvaethwy the false,
The three faithful combatants,
Bleiddwn, Hydwn, and Hychdwn the Tall."

Then he struck the two with his magic wand, and they resumed their own nature. "Oh men," said he, "for the wrong that ye did unto me sufficient has been your punishment and your dishonor. Prepare now precious ointment for these men, and wash their heads, and equip them." And this was done.

And after they were equipped, they came unto him. "Oh men," said he, "you have obtained peace, and you shall likewise have friendship. Give your counsel unto me, what maiden I shall seek." "Lord," said Gwydion the son of Don, "it is easy to give thee counsel; seek Arianrod, the daughter of Don, thy niece, thy sister's daughter."

And they brought her unto him, and the maiden came in. "Ha, damsel," said he, "art thou the maiden?" "I know not, lord, other than that I am." Then he took up his magic wand, and bent it. "Step over this," said he, "and I shall know if thou art the maiden." Then stepped she over the magic wand, and there appeared forthwith a fine chubby yellow-haired boy. And at the crying out of the boy, she went towards the door. And thereupon some small form was seen; but before any one could get a second glimpse of it, Gwydion had taken it, and had flung a scarf of velvet around it and hidden it. Now the place where he hid it was the bottom of a chest at the foot of his bed.

"Verily," said Math the son of Mathonwy, concerning the fine yellow-haired boy, "I will cause this one to be baptized, and Dylan is the name I will give him."

So they had the boy baptized, and as they baptized him he plunged into the sea. And immediately when he was in the sea, he took its nature, and swam as well as the best fish that was therein. And for that reason was he called Dylan, the son of the Wave. Beneath him no wave ever broke. And the blow whereby he came to his death, was struck by his uncle Govannon. The third fatal blow was it called.

As Gwydion lay one morning on his bed awake, he heard a cry in the chest at his feet; and though it was not loud, it was such that he could hear it. Then he arose in haste, and opened the chest: and when he opened it, he beheld an infant boy stretching out his arms from the folds of the scarf, and casting it aside. And he took up the boy in his arms, and carried him to a place where he knew there was a woman that could nurse him. And he agreed with the woman that she should take charge of the boy. And that year he was nursed.

And at the end of the year he seemed by his size as though he were two years old. And the second year he was a big child, and able to go to the Court by himself. And when he came to the Court, Gwydion noticed him, and the boy became familiar with him, and loved him better than any one else. Then was the boy reared at the Court until he was four years old, when he was as big as though he had been eight.

And one day Gwydion walked forth, and the boy followed him, and he went to the Castle of Arianrod, having the boy with him; and when he came into the Court, Arianrod arose to meet him, and greeted him and bade him welcome. "Heaven prosper thee," said he. "Who is the boy that followeth thee?" she asked. "This youth, he is thy son," he answered. "Alas," said she, "what has come unto thee that thou shouldst shame me thus, wherefore dost thou seek my dishonor, and retain it so long as this?" "Unless thou suffer dishonor greater than that of my bringing up such a boy as this, small will be thy disgrace." "What is the name of the boy?" said she. "Verily," he replied, "he has not yet a name." "Well," she said, "I lay this destiny upon him, that he shall never have a name until he receives one from me." "Heaven bears me witness," answered he, "that thou art a wicked woman. But the boy shall have a name how displeasing soever it may be unto thee. As for thee, that which afflicts thee is that thou art no longer called a damsel." And thereupon he went forth in wrath, and returned to Caer Dathyl and there he tarried that night.

And the next day he arose and took the boy with him, and went to walk on the seashore between that place and Aber Menei. And there he saw some sedges and seaweed, and he turned them into a boat. And out of dry sticks and sedges he made some Cordovan leather, and a great deal thereof, and he colored it in such a manner that no one ever saw leather more beautiful than it. Then he made a sail to the boat, and he and the boy went in it to the port of the castle of Arianrod. And he began forming shoes and stitching them, until he was observed from the castle. And when he knew that they of the castle were observing him, he disguised his aspect, and put another semblance upon himself, and upon the boy, so that they might not be known. "What men are those in yonder boat?" said Arianrod. "They are cordwainers," answered they. "Go and see what kind of leather they have, and what kind of work they can do."

So they came unto them. And when they came he was coloring some Cordovan leather, and gilding it. And the messengers came and told her this. "Well," said she, "take the measure of my foot, and desire the cordwainer to make shoes for me." So he made the shoes for her, yet not according to the measure, but larger. The shoes then were brought unto her, and behold they were too large. "These are too large," said she, "but he shall receive their value. Let him also make some that are smaller than they." Then he made her others that were much smaller than her foot, and sent them unto her. "Tell him that these will not go on my feet," said she. And they told him this. "Verily," said he, "I will not make her any shoes, unless I see her foot." And this was told unto her. "Truly," she answered, "I will go unto him."

So she went down to the boat, and when she came there, he was shaping shoes and the boy stitching them. "Ah, lady," said he, "good day to thee." "Heaven prosper thee," said she. "I marvel that thou canst not manage to make shoes according to a measure." "I could not," he replied, "but now I shall be able."

Thereupon behold a wren stood upon the deck of the boat, and the boy shot at it, and hit it in the leg between the sinew and the bone. Then she smiled. "Verily," said she, "with a steady hand did the lion aim at it." "Heaven reward thee not, but now has he got a name. And a good enough name it is. Llew Llaw Gyffes be he called henceforth."

Then the work disappeared in seaweed and sedges, and he went on with it no further. And for that reason was he called the third Gold-shoemaker. "Of a truth," said she, "thou wilt not thrive the better for doing evil unto me." "I have done thee no evil yet," said he. Then he restored the boy to his own form. "Well," said she, "I will lay a destiny upon this boy, that he shall never have arms and armor until I invest him with them." "By Heaven," said he, "let thy malice be what it may, he shall have arms."

Then they went towards Dinas Dinllev, and there he brought up Llew Llaw Gyffes, until he could manage any horse, and he was perfect in features, and strength, and stature. And then Gwydion saw that he languished through the want of horses and arms. And he called him unto him. "Ah, youth," said he, "we will go tomorrow on an errand together. Be therefore more cheerful than thou art." "That I will," said the youth.

Next morning, at the dawn of day, they arose. And they took way along the sea coast, up towards Bryn Arycn. And at the top of Cevn Clydno they equipped themselves with horses, and went towards the Castle of Arianrod. And they changed their form, and pricked towards the gate in the semblance of two youths, but the aspect of Gwydion was more staid than that of the other. "Porter," said he, "go thou in and say that there are here bards from Glamorgan." And the porter went in. "The welcome of Heaven be unto them, let them in," said Arianrod.

With great joy were they greeted. And the hall was arranged, and they went to meat. When meat was ended, Arianrod discoursed with Gwydion of tales and stories. Now Gwydion was an excellent teller of tales. And when it was time to leave off feasting, a chamber was prepared for them, and they went to rest.

In the early twilight Gwydion arose, and he called unto him his magic and his power. And by the time that the day dawned, there resounded through the land uproar, and trumpets and shouts. When it was now day, they heard a knocking at the door of the chamber, and therewith Arianrod asking that it might be opened. Up rose the youth and opened unto her, and she entered and a maiden with her. "Ah, good men," she said, "in evil plight are we." "Yes, truly," said Gwydion, "we have heard trumpets and shouts; what thinkest thou that they may mean?" "Verily," said she, "we cannot see the color of the ocean by reason of all the ships, side by side. And they are making for the land with all the speed they can. And what can we do?" said she. "Lady," said Gwydion, "there is none other counsel than to close the castle upon us, and to defend it as best we may." "Truly," said she, "may Heaven reward you. And do you defend it. And here may you have plenty of arms."

And thereupon went she forth for the arms, and behold she returned, and two maidens, and suits of armor for two men, with her. "Lady," said he, "do you accouter this stripling, and I will arm myself with the help of thy maidens. Lo, I hear the tumult of the men approaching." "I will do so, gladly." So she armed him fully, and that right cheerfully. "Hast thou finished arming the youth?" said he. "I have finished," she answered. "I likewise have finished," said Gwydion. "Let us now take off our arms, we have no need of them." "Wherefore?" said she. "Here is the army around the house." "Oh, lady, there is here no army." "Oh," cried she, "whence then was this tumult?" "The tumult was but to break thy prophecy and to obtain arms for thy son. And now has he got arms without any thanks unto thee." "By Heaven," said Arianrod, "thou art a wicked man. Many a youth might have lost his life through the uproar thou hast caused in this Cantrev today. Now will I lay a destiny upon this youth," she said, "that he shall never have a wife of the race that now inhabits this earth." "Verily," said he, "thou wast ever a malicious woman, and no one ought to support thee. A wife shall he have notwithstanding."

They went thereupon unto Math the son of Mathonwy, and complained unto him most bitterly of Arianrod. Gwydion showed him also how he had procured arms for the youth. "Well," said Math, "we will seek, I and thou, by charms and illusion, to form a wife for him out of flowers. He has now come to man's stature, and he is the comeliest youth that was ever beheld." So they took the blossoms of the oak, and the blossoms of the broom, and the blossoms of the meadow-sweet, and produced from them a maiden, the fairest and most graceful that man ever saw. And they baptized her, and gave her the name of Blodeuwedd.

After she had become his bride, and they had feasted, said Gwydion, "It is not easy for a man to maintain himself without possessions." "Of a truth," said Math, "I will give the young man the best Cantrev to hold." "Lord," said he, "what Cantrev is that?" "The Cantrev of Dinodig," he answered. Now it is called at this day Eivionydd and Ardudwy. And the place in the Cantrev where he dwelt, was a palace of his in a spot called Mur y Castell, on the confines of Ardudwy. There dwelt he and reigned, and both he and his sway were beloved by all.

One day he went forth to Caer Dathyl, to visit Math the son of Mathonwy. And on the day that he set out for Caer Dathyl, Blodeuwedd walked in the Court. And she heard the sound of a horn. And after the sound of the horn, behold a tired stag went by, with dogs and huntsmen following it. And after the dogs and the huntsmen there came a crowd of men on foot. "Send a youth," said she, "to ask who yonder host may be." So a youth went, and inquired who they were. "Gronw Pebyr is this, the lord of Penllyn," said they. And thus the youth told her.

Gronw Pebyr pursued the stag, and by the river Cynvael he overtook the stag and killed it. And what with flaying the stag and baiting his dogs, he was there until the night began to close in upon him. And as the day departed and the night drew near, he came to the gate of the Court. "Verily," said Blodeuwedd, "the Chieftain will speak ill of us if we let him at this hour depart to another land without inviting him in." "Yes, truly, lady," said they, "it will be most fitting to invite him."

Then went messengers to meet him and bid him in. And he accepted her bidding gladly, and came to the Court, and Blodeuwedd went to meet him, and greeted him, and bade him welcome. "Lady," said he, "Heaven repay thee thy kindness."

When they had disaccoutered themselves, they went to sit down. And Blodeuwedd looked upon him, and from the moment that she looked on him she became filled with his love. And he gazed on her, and the same thought came unto him as unto her, so that he could not conceal from her that he loved her, but he declared unto her that he did so. Thereupon she was very joyful. And all their discourse that night was concerning the affection and love which they felt one for the other, and which in no longer space than one evening had arisen. And that evening passed they in each other's company.

The next day he sought to depart. But she said, "I pray thee go not from me today." And that night he tarried also. And that night they consulted by what means they might always be together. "There is none other counsel," said he, "but that thou strive to learn from Llew Llaw Gyffes in what manner he will meet his death. And this must thou do under the semblance of solicitude concerning him."

The next day Gronw sought to depart. "Verily," said she, "I will counsel thee not to go from me today." "At thy instance will I not go," said he, "albeit, I must say, there is danger that the chief who owns the palace may return home." "Tomorrow," answered she, "will I indeed permit thee to go forth."

The next day he sought to go, and she hindered him not. "Be mindful," said Gronw, "of what I have said unto thee, and converse with him fully, and that under the guise of the dalliance of love, and find out by what means he may come to his death."

That night Llew Llaw Gyffes returned to his home. And the day they spent in discourse, and minstrelsy, and feasting. And at night they went to rest, and he spoke to Blodeuwedd once, and he spoke to her a second time. But, for all this, he could not get from her one word. "What aileth thee?" said he, "art thou well?" "I was thinking," said she, "of that which thou didst never think of concerning me; for I was sorrowful as to thy death, lest thou shouldst go sooner than I." "Heaven reward thy care for me," said he, "but until Heaven take me I shall not easily be slain" "For the sake of Heaven, and for mine, show me how thou mightest be slain. My memory in guarding is better than thine." "I will tell thee gladly," said he. "Not easily can I be slain, except by a wound. And the spear wherewith I am struck must be a year in the forming. And nothing must be done towards it except during the sacrifice on Sundays." "Is this certain?" asked she. "It is in truth," he answered. "And I cannot be slain within a house, nor without. I cannot be slain on horseback nor on foot." "Verily," said she, "in what manner then canst thou be slain?" "I will tell thee," said he. "By making a bath for me by the side of a river, and by putting a roof over the cauldron, and thatching it well and tightly, and bringing a buck, and putting it beside the cauldron. Then if I place one foot on the buck's back, and the other on the edge of the cauldron, whosoever strikes me thus will cause my death." "Well," said she, "I thank Heaven that it will be easy to avoid this."

No sooner had she held this discourse than she sent to Gronw Pebyr. Gronw toiled at making the spear, and that day twelvemonth it was ready. And that very day he caused her to be informed thereof.

"Lord," said Blodeuwedd unto Llew, "I have been thinking how it is possible that what thou didst tell me formerly can be true; wilt thou show me in what manner thou couldst stand at once upon the edge of a cauldron and upon a buck, if I prepare the bath for thee?" "I will show thee," said he.

Then she sent unto Gronw, and bade him be in ambush on the hill which is now called Bryn Kyvergyr, on the bank of the river Cynvael. She caused also to be collected all the goats that were in the Cantrev, and had them brought to the other side of the river, opposite Bryn Kyvergyr.

And the next day she spoke thus. "Lord," said she, "I have caused the roof and the bath to be prepared, and lo! they are ready." "Well," said Llew, "we will go gladly to look at them."

The day after they came and looked at the bath. "Wilt thou go into the bath, lord?" said she. "Willingly will I go in," he answered. So into the bath he went, and he anointed himself. "Lord," said she, "behold the animals which thou didst speak of as being called bucks." "Well," said he, "cause one of them to be caught and brought here."

And the buck was brought. Then Llew rose out of the bath, and put on his trousers, and he placed one foot on the edge of the bath and the other on the buck's back.

Thereupon Gronw rose up from the hill which is called Bryn Kyvergyr, and he rested on one knee, and flung the poisoned dart and struck him on the side, so that the shaft started out, but the head of the dart remained in. Then he flew up in the form of an eagle and gave a fearful scream. And thenceforth was he no more seen.

As soon as he departed Gronw and Blodeuwedd went together unto the palace that night. And the next day Gronw arose and took possession of Ardudwy. And after he had overcome the land, he ruled over it, so that Ardudwy and Penllyn were both under his sway.

Then these tidings reached Math the son of Mathonwy. And heaviness and grief came upon Math, and much more upon Gwydion than upon him. "Lord," said Gwydion, "I shall never rest until I have tidings of my nephew." "Verily," said Math, "may Heaven be thy strength." Then Gwydion set forth and began to go forward. And he went through

Gwynedd and Powys to the confines. And when he had done so, he went into Arvon, and came to the house of a vassal, in Maenawr Penardd. And he alighted at the house, and stayed there that night. The man of the house and his household came in, and last of all came there the swineherd. Said the man of the house to the swineherd, "Well, youth, hath thy sow come in tonight?" "She hath," said he, "and is this instant returned to the pigs." "Where doth this sow go to?" said Gwydion. "Every day, when the sty is opened, she goeth forth and none can catch sight of her, neither is it known whither she goeth more than if she sank into the earth." "Wilt thou grant unto me," said Gwydion, "not to open the sty until I am beside the sty with thee?" "This will I do, right gladly," he answered.

That night they went to rest; and as soon as the swineherd saw the light of day, he awoke Gwydion. And Gwydion arose and dressed himself, and went with the swineherd, and stood beside the sty. Then the swineherd opened the sty. And as soon as he opened it, behold she leaped forth, and set off with great speed. And Gwydion followed her, and she went against the course of a river, and made for a brook, which is now called Nant y Llew. And there she halted and began feeding. And Gwydion came under the tree, and looked what it might be that the sow was feeding on. And he saw that she was eating putrid flesh and vermin. Then looked he up to the top of the tree, and as he looked he beheld on the top of the tree an eagle, and when the eagle shook itself, there fell vermin and putrid flesh from off it, and these the sow devoured. And it seemed to him that the eagle was Llew. And he sang an Englyn:

"Oak that grows between the two banks;
Darkened is the sky and hill!
Shall I not tell him by his wounds,
That this is Llew?"

Upon this the eagle came down until he reached the center of the tree. And Gwydion sang another Englyn:

"Oak that grows in upland ground,
Is it not wetted by the rain? Has it not been drenched
By nine score tempests?
It bears in its branches Llew Llaw Gyffes!"

Then the eagle came down until he was on the lowest branch of the tree, and thereupon this Englyn did Gwydion sing:

"Oak that grows beneath the steep;
Stately and majestic is its aspect!
Shall I not speak it?
That Llew will come to my lap?"

And the eagle came down upon Gwydion's knee. And Gwydion struck him with his magic wand, so that he returned to his own form. No one ever saw a more piteous sight, for he was nothing but skin and bone.

Then he went unto Caer Dathyl, and there were brought unto him good physicians that were in Gwynedd, and before the end of the year he was quite healed.

"Lord," said he unto Math the son of Mathonwy, "it is full time now that I have retribution of him by whom I have suffered all this woe." "Truly," said Math, "he will never be able to maintain himself in the possession of that which is thy right." "Well," said Llew, "the sooner I have my right, the better shall I be pleased."

Then they called together the whole of Gwynedd, and set forth to Ardudwy. And Gwydion went on before and proceeded to Mur y Castell. And when Blodeuwedd heard that he was coming, she took her maidens with her, and fled to the mountain. And they passed through the river Cynvael, and went towards a court that there was upon the mountain, and through fear they could not proceed except with their faces looking backwards, so that unawares they fell into the lake. And they were all drowned except Blodeuwedd herself, and her Gwydion overtook. And he said unto her, "I will not slay thee, but I will do unto thee worse than that. For I will turn thee into a bird; and because of the shame thou hast done unto Llew Llaw Gyffes, thou shalt never show thy face in the light of day henceforth; and that through fear of all the other birds. For it shall be their nature to attack thee, and to chase thee from wheresoever they may find thee. And thou shalt not lose thy name, but shalt be always called Blodeuwedd." Now Blodeuwedd is an owl in the language of this present time, and for this reason is the owl hateful unto all birds. And even now the owl is called Blodeuwedd.

Then Gronw Pebyr withdrew unto Penllyn, and he dispatched thence an embassy. And the messengers he sent asked Llew Llaw Gyffes if he would take land, or domain, or gold, or silver, for the injury he had received. "I will not, by my confession to Heaven," said he. "Behold this is the least that I will accept from him; that he come to the spot where I was when he wounded me with the dart, and that I stand where he did, and that with a dart I take my aim at him. And this is the very least that I will accept."

And this was told unto Gronw Pebyr. "Verily," said he, "is it needful for me to do thus? My faithful warriors, and my household, and my foster-brothers, is there not one among you who will stand the blow in my stead?" "There is not, verily," answered they. And because of their refusal to suffer one stroke for their lord, they are called the third disloyal tribe even unto this day. "Well," said he, "I will meet it."

Then they two went forth to the banks of the river Cynvael, and Gronw stood in the place where Llew Llaw Gyffes was when he struck him, and Llew in the place where Gronw was. Then said Gronw Pebyr unto Llew, "Since it was through the wiles of a woman that I did unto thee as I have done, I adjure thee by Heaven to let me place between me and the blow, the slab thou seest yonder on the river's bank." "Verily," said Llew, "I will not refuse thee this." "Ah," said he, "may Heaven reward thee." So Gronw took the slab and placed it between him and the blow.

Then Llew flung the dart at him, and it pierced the slab and went through Gronw likewise, so that it pierced through his back. And thus was Gronw Pebyr slain. And there is still the slab on the bank of the river Cynvael, in Ardudwy, having the hole through it. And therefore is it even now called Llech Gronw. A second time did Llew Llaw Gyffes take possession of the land, and prosperously did he govern it. And, as the story relates, he was lord after this over Gwynedd. And thus ends this portion of the Mabinogi.

KILHWCH AND OLWEN, OR THE TWRCH TRWYTH

translated by Lady Charlotte Guest (1848)

Kilydd the son of Prince Kelyddon desired a wife as a helpmate, and the wife that he chose was Goleuddydd, the daughter of Prince Anlawdd. And after their union, the people put up prayers that they might have an heir. And they had a son through the prayers of the people. From the time of her pregnancy Goleuddydd became wild, and wandered about, without habitation; but when her delivery was at hand, her reason came back to her. Then she went to a mountain where there was a swineherd, keeping a herd of swine. And through fear of the swine the queen was delivered. And the swineherd took the boy, and brought him to the palace; and he was christened, and they called him Kilhwch, because he had been found in a swine's burrow. Nevertheless the boy was of gentle lineage, and cousin unto Arthur; and they put him out to nurse.

After this the boy's mother, Goleuddydd, the daughter of Prince Anlawdd, fell sick. Then she called her husband unto her, and said to him, "Of this sickness I shall die, and thou wilt take another wife. Now wives are the gift of the Lord, but it would be wrong for thee to harm thy son. Therefore I charge thee that thou take not a wife until thou see a briar with two blossoms upon my grave." And this he promised her. Then she besought him to dress her grave every year, that nothing might grow thereon. So the queen died. Now the king sent an attendant every morning to see if anything were growing upon the grave. And at the end of the seventh year the master neglected that which he had promised to the queen.

One day the king went to hunt, and he rode to the place of burial to see the grave, and to know if it were time that he should take a wife; and the king saw the briar. And when he saw it, the king took counsel where he should find a wife. Said one of his counselors, "I know a wife that will suit thee well, and she is the wife of King Doged." And they resolved to go to seek her; and they slew the king, and brought away his wife and one daughter that she had along with her. And they conquered the king's lands.

On a certain day, as the lady walked abroad, she came to the house of an old crone that dwelt in the town, and that had no tooth in her head. And the queen said

292

to her, "Old woman, tell me that which I shall ask thee, for the love of Heaven. Where are the children of the man who has carried me away by violence?" Said the crone, "He has not children." Said the queen, "Woe is me, that I should have come to one who is childless!" Then said the hag, "Thou needest not lament on account of that, for there is a prediction he shall have an heir by thee, and by none other. Moreover, be not sorrowful, for he has one son."

The lady returned home with joy; and she asked her consort, "Wherefore hast thou concealed thy children from me?" The king said, "I will do so no longer." And he sent messengers for his son, and he was brought to the Court. His stepmother said unto him, "It were well for thee to have a wife, and I have a daughter who is sought of every man of renown in the world." "I am not yet of an age to wed," answered the youth. Then said she unto him, "I declare to thee, that it is thy destiny not to be suited with a wife until thou obtain Olwen, the daughter of Yspaddaden Penkawr." And the youth blushed, and the love of the maiden diffused itself through all his frame, although he had never seen her. And his father inquired of him, "What has come over thee, my son, and what aileth thee?" "My stepmother has declared to me that I shall never have a wife until I obtain Olwen, the daughter of Yspaddaden Penkawr." "That will be easy for thee," answered his father. "Arthur is thy cousin. Go, therefore, unto Arthur, to cut thy hair, and ask this of him as a boon."

And the youth pricked forth upon a steed with head dappled gray, of four winters old, firm of limb, with shell-formed hoofs, having a bridle of linked gold on his head, and upon him a saddle of costly gold. And in the youth's hand were two spears of silver, sharp, well-tempered, headed with steel, three ells in length, of an edge to wound the wind, and cause blood to flow, and swifter than the fall of the dewdrop from the blade of reed-grass upon the earth when the dew of June is at the heaviest. A gold-hilted sword was upon his thigh, the blade of which was of gold, bearing a cross of inlaid gold of the hue of the lightning of heaven: his war-horn was of ivory. Before him were two brindled white-breasted greyhounds, having strong collars of rubies about their necks, reaching from the shoulder to the ear. And the one that was on the left side bounded across to the right side, and the one on the right to the left, and like two sea-swallows sported around him. And his courser cast up four sods with his four hoofs, like four swallows in the air, about his head, now above, now below. About him was a four-cornered cloth of purple, and an apple of gold was at each corner, and every one of the apples was of the value of an hundred kine. And there was precious gold of the value of three hundred kine upon his shoes, and upon his stirrups, from his knee to the tip of his toe. And the blade of grass bent not beneath him, so light was his courser's tread as he journeyed towards the gate of Arthur's Palace.

Spoke the youth, "Is there a porter?" "There is; and if thou holdest not thy peace, small will be thy welcome. I am Arthur's porter every first day of January. And during every other part of the year but this, the office is filled by Huandaw, and Gogigwc, and Llacskenym, and Pennpingyon, who goes upon his head to save his feet, neither towards the sky nor towards the earth, but like a rolling stone upon the floor of the court." "Open the portal." "I will not open it." "Wherefore not?" "The knife is in the meat, and the drink is in the horn, and there is revelry in Arthur's Hall, and none may enter therein but the son of a king of a privileged country, or a craftsman bringing his craft. But there will be refreshment for thy dogs, and for thy horses; and for thee there will be collops cooked and peppered, and luscious wine and mirthful songs, and food for fifty men shall be brought unto thee in the guest chamber, where the stranger and the sons of other countries eat, who come not unto the precincts of the Palace of Arthur. Thou wilt fare no worse there than thou wouldest with Arthur in the Court. A lady shall smooth thy couch, and shall lull thee with songs; and early tomorrow morning, when the gate is open for the multitude that come hither today, for thee shall it be opened first, and thou mayest sit in the place that thou shalt choose in Arthur's Hall, from the upper end to the lower." Said the youth, "That will I not do. If thou openest the gate, it is well. If thou dost not open it, I will bring disgrace upon thy Lord, and evil report upon thee. And I will set up three shouts at this very gate, than which none were ever more deadly, from the top of Pengwaed in Cornwall to the bottom of Dinsol, in the North, and to Esgair Oervel, in Ireland. And all the women in this Palace that are pregnant shall lose their offspring; and such as are not pregnant, their hearts shall be turned by illness, so that they shall never bear children from this day forward." "What clamor soever thou mayest make," said Glewlwyd Gavaelvawr, "against the laws of Arthur's Palace shalt thou not enter therein, until I first go and speak with Arthur."

Then Glewlwyd went into the Hall. And Arthur said to him, "Hast thou news from the gate?"—"Half of my life is past, and half of thine. I was heretofore in Kaer Se and Asse, in Sach and Salach, in Lotor and Fotor; and I have been heretofore in India the Great and India the Lesser; and I was in the battle of Dau Ynyr, when the twelve hostages were brought from Llychlyn. And I have also been in Europe, and in Africa, and in the islands of Corsica, and in Caer Brythwch, and Brythach, and Verthach; and I was present when formerly thou didst slay the family of Clis the son of Merin, and when thou didst slay Mil Du the son of Ducum, and when thou didst conquer Greece in the East. And I have been in Caer Oeth and Annoeth, and in Caer Nevenhyr; nine supreme sovereigns, handsome men, saw we there, but never did I behold a man of equal dignity with him who is now at the door of the portal." Then said Arthur, "If walking thou didst enter in here, return thou running. And every one that beholds the light, and every one that opens and shuts the eye, let them shew him respect, and serve him, some with gold-mounted drinking-horns, others with collops cooked and peppered, until food and drink can be prepared for him. It is unbecoming to keep such a man as thou sayest he is, in the wind and the rain." Said Kai, "By the hand of my friend, if thou wouldest follow my counsel, thou wouldest not break through the laws of the Court because of him." "Not so, blessed Kai. It is an honor to us to be resorted to, and the greater our courtesy the greater will be our renown, and our fame, and our glory."

And Glewlwyd came to the gate, and opened the gate before him; and although all dismounted upon the horseblock at the gate, yet did he not dismount, but rode in upon his charger. Then said Kilhwch, "Greeting be unto thee, Sovereign Ruler of this Island; and be this greeting no less unto the lowest than unto the highest, and be it equally unto thy guests, and thy warriors, and thy chieftains—let all partake of it as completely as thyself. And complete be thy favor, and thy fame, and thy glory, throughout all this Island." "Greeting unto thee also," said Arthur; "sit thou between two of my warriors, and thou shalt have minstrels before thee, and thou shalt enjoy the privileges of a king born to a throne, as long as thou remainest here. And when I dispense my presents to the visitors and strangers in this Court, they shall be in thy hand at my commencing." Said the youth, "I came not here to consume meat and drink; but if I obtain the boon that I seek, I will requite it thee, and extol thee; and if I have it not, I will bear forth thy dispraise to the four quarters of the world, as far as thy renown has extended." Then said Arthur, "Since thou wilt not remain here, chieftain, thou shalt receive the boon whatsoever thy tongue may name, as far as the wind dries, and the rain moistens, and the sun revolves, and the sea encircles, and the earth extends; save only my ship; and my mantle; and Caledvwlch, my sword; and Rhongomyant, my lance; and Wynebgwrthucher, my shield; and Carnwenhau, my dagger; and Gwenhwyvar, my wife. By the truth of Heaven, thou shalt have it cheerfully, name what thou wilt." "I would that thou bless my hair." "That shall be granted thee."

And Arthur took a golden comb, and scissors, whereof the loops were of silver, and he combed his hair. And Arthur inquired of him who he was. "For my heart warms unto thee, and I know that thou art come of my blood. Tell me, therefore, who thou art." "I will tell thee," said the youth. "I am Kilhwch, the son of Kilydd, the son of Prince Kelyddon, by Goleuddydd, my mother, the daughter of Prince Anlawdd." "That is true," said Arthur; "thou art my cousin. Whatsoever boon thou mayest ask, thou shalt receive, be it what it may that thy tongue shall name." "Pledge the truth of Heaven and the faith of thy kingdom thereof." "I pledge it thee, gladly." "I crave of thee then, that thou obtain for me Olwen, the daughter of Yspaddaden Penkawr; and this boon I likewise seek at the hands of thy warriors. I seek it from Kai, and Bedwyr, and Greidawl Galldonyd, and Gwythyr the son of Greidawl, and Greid the son of Eri, and Kynddelig Kyvarwydd, and Tathal Twyll Goleu, and Maelwys the son of Baeddan, and Crychwr the son of Nes, and Cubert the son of Daere, and Percos the son of Poch, and Lluber Beuthach, and Corvil Bervach, and Gwynn the son of Nudd, and Edeyrn the son of Nudd, and Gadwy the son of Geraint, and Prince Fflewddur Fflam, and Ruawn Pebyr the son of Dorath, and Bradwen the son of Moren Mynawc, and Moren Mynawc himself, and Dalldav the son of Kimin Côv, and the son of Alun Dyved, and the son of Saidi, and the son of Gwryon, and Uchtryd Ardywad Kad, and Kynwas Curvagyl, and Gwrhyr Gwarthegvras, and Isperyr Ewingath, and Gallcoyt Govynynat, and Duach, and Grathach, and Nerthach, the sons of Gwawrddur Kyrvach (these men came forth from the confines of hell), and Kilydd Canhastyr, and Canastyr Kanllaw, and Cors Cant-Ewin, and Esgeir Gulhwch Govynkawn, and Drustwrn Hayarn, and Glewlwyd Gavaelvawr, and Lloch Llawwynnyawc, and Aunwas Adeiniawc, and Sinnoch the son of Seithved, and Gwennwynwyn the son of Naw, and Bedyw the son of Seithved, and Gobrwy the son of Echel Vorddwyttwll, and Echel Vorddwyttwll himself, and Mael the son of Roycol, and Dadweir Dallpenn, and Garwyli the son of Gwythawc Gwyr, and Gwythawc Gwyr himself, and Gormant the son of Ricca, and Menw the son of Teirgwaedd, and Digon the son of Alar, and Selyf the son of Smoit, and Gusg the son of Atheu, and Nerth the son of Kedarn, and Drudwas the son of Tryffin, and Twrch the son of Perif, and Twrch the son of Annwas, and Iona king of France, and Sel the son of Selgi, and Teregud the son of Iaen, and Sulyen the son of Iaen, and Bradwen the son of Iaen, and Moren the son of Iaen, and Siawn the son of Iaen, and Cradawc the son of Iaen. (They were men of Caerdathal, of Arthur's kindred on his father's side.) Dirmyg the son of Kaw, and Justic the son of Kaw, and Etmic the son of Kaw, and Anghawd the son of Kaw, and Ovan the son of Kaw, and Kelin the son of Kaw, and Connyn the son of Kaw, and Mabsant the son of Kaw, and Gwyngad the son of Kaw, and Llwybyr the son of Kaw, and Coth the son of Kaw, and Meilic the son of Kaw, and Kynwas the son of Kaw, and Ardwyad the son of Kaw, and Ergyryad the son of Kaw, and Neb the son of Kaw, and Gilda the son of Kaw, and Calcas the son of Kaw, and Hueil the son of Kaw (he never yet made a request at the hand of any Lord). And Samson Vinsych, and Taliesin the chief of the bards, and Manawyddan the son of Llyr, and Llary the son of Prince Kasnar, and Ysperni the son of Fflergant king of Armorica, and Saranhon the son of Glythwyr, and Llawr Eilerw, and Annyanniawc the son of Menw the son of Teirgwaedd, and Gwynn the son of Nwyvre, and Fflam the son of Nwyvre, and Geraint the son of Erbin, and Ermid the son of Erbin, and Dyvel the son of Erbin, and Gwynn the son of Ermid, and Kyndrwyn the son of Ermid, and Hyveidd Unllenn, and Eiddon Vawr Vrydic, and Reidwn Arwy, and Gormant the son of Ricca (Arthur's brother by his mother's side; the Penhynev of Cornwall was his father), and Llawnrodded Varvawc, and Nodawl Varyf Twrch, and Berth the son of Kado, and Rheidwn the son of Beli, and Iscovan Hael, and Iscawin the son of Panon, and Morvran the son of Tegid (no one struck him in the battle of Camlan by reason of his ugliness; all thought he was an auxiliary devil. Hair had he upon him like the hair of a stag). And Sandde Bryd Angel (no one touched him with a spear in the battle of Camlan because of his beauty; all thought he was a ministering angel). And Kynwyl Sant (the third man that escaped from the battle of Camlan, and he was the last who parted from Arthur on Hengroen his horse). And Uchtryd the son of Erim, and Eus the son of Erim, and Henwas Adeinawg the son of Erim, and Henbedestyr the son of Erim, and Sgilti Yscawndroed the son of Erim. (Unto these three men belonged these three qualities,—With Henbedestyr there was not any one who could keep pace, either on horseback or on foot; with Henwas Adeinawg, no four-footed beast could run the distance of an acre, much less could it go beyond it; and as to Sgilti Yscawndroed, when he intended to go upon a message for his Lord, he never sought to find a path, but knowing whither he was to go, if his way lay through a wood he went along the tops of the trees. During his whole life, a blade of reed grass bent not beneath his feet, much less did one ever break, so lightly did he tread.) Teithi Hên the son of Gwynhan (his dominions were swallowed up by the sea, and he himself hardly escaped, and he came to Arthur; and his knife had this peculiarity, that from the time that he came there no haft would ever remain upon it, and owing to this a sickness came over him, and he pined away during the remainder of his life, and of this he died). And Carneddyr the son of Govynyon Hen, and Gwenwynwyn the son of Nav Gyssevin, Arthur's champion, and Llysgadrudd Emys, and Gwrbothu Hên (uncles unto Arthur were they, his mother's brothers). Kulvanawyd the son of Goryon, and Llenlleawg Wyddel from the headland of Ganion, and Dyvynwal Moel, and Dunard king of the North, Teirnon Twryf Bliant, and Tegvan Gloff, and Tegyr Talgellawg, Gwrdinal the son of Ebrei, and Morgant Hael, Gwystyl the son of Rhun the son of Nwython, and Llwyddeu the son of Nwython, and Gwydre the son of Llwyddeu (Gwenabwy the daughter of [Kaw] was his mother, Hueil his uncle stabbed him, and hatred was between Hueil and Arthur because of the wound). Drem the son of Dremidyd (when the gnat arose in the morning with the sun, he could see it from Gelli Wic in Cornwall, as far off as Pen Blathaon in North Britain). And Eidyol the son of Ner, and Glwyddyn Saer (who constructed Ehangwen, Arthur's Hall). Kynyr Keinvarvawc (when he was told he had a son born he said to his wife, 'Damsel, if thy son be mine, his heart will be always cold, and there will be no warmth in his hands; and he will have another peculiarity, if he is my son he will always be stubborn; and he will have another peculiarity, when he carries a burden, whether it be large or small, no one will be able to see it, either before him or at his back; and he will have another peculiarity, no one will be able to resist fire and water so well as he will; and he will have another peculiarity, there will never be a servant or an officer equal to him'). Henwas, and Henwyneb (an old companion to Arthur). Gwallgoyc (another; when he came to a town, though there were three hundred houses in it, if he wanted anything, he would not let sleep come to the eyes of any one whilst he remained there). Berwyn the son of Gerenhir, and Paris king of France, and Osla Gyllellvawr (who bore a short broad dagger. When Arthur and his hosts came before a torrent, they would seek for a narrow place where they might pass the water, and would lay the sheathed dagger across the torrent, and it would form a bridge sufficient for the armies of the three Islands of Britain, and of the three islands adjacent, with their spoil). Gwyddawg the son of Menestyr (who slew Kai, and whom Arthur slew, together with his brothers, to revenge Kai). Garanwyn the son of Kai, and Amren the son of Bedwyr, and Ely Amyr, and Rheu Rhwyd Dyrys, and Rhun Rhudwern, and Eli, and Trachmyr (Arthur's chief huntsmen). And Llwyddeu the son of Kelcoed, and Hunabwy the son of Gwryon, and Gwynn Godyvron, and Gweir Datharwenniddawg, and Gweir the son of Cadell the son of Talaryant, and Gweir Gwrhyd Ennwir, and Gweir Paladyr Hir (the uncles of Arthur, the brothers of his mother). The sons of Llwch Llawwynnyawg (from beyond the raging sea). Llenlleawg Wyddel, and Ardderchawg Prydain. Cas the son of Saidi, Gwrvan Gwallt Avwyn, and Gwyllennhin the king of France, and Gwittart the son of Oedd king of Ireland. Garselit Wyddel, Panawr Pen Bagad, and Ffleudor the son of Nav, Gwynnhyvar mayor of Cornwall and Devon (the ninth man that rallied the battle of Camlan). Keli and Kueli, and Gilla Coes Hydd (he would clear three hundred acres at one bound: the chief leaper of Ireland was he). Sol, and Gwadyn Ossol, and Gwadyn Odyeith. (Sol could stand all day upon one foot. Gwadyn Ossol, if he stood upon the top of the highest mountain in the world, it would become a level plain under his feet. Gwadyn Odyeith, the soles of his feet emitted sparks of fire when they struck upon things hard, like the heated mass when drawn out of the forge. He cleared the way for Arthur when he came to any stoppage.) Hirerwm and

Hiratrwm. (The day they went on a visit three Cantrevs provided for their entertainment, and they feasted until noon and drank until night, when they went to sleep. And then they devoured the heads of the vermin through hunger, as if they had never eaten anything. When they made a visit they left neither the fat nor the lean, neither the hot nor the cold, the sour nor the sweet, the fresh nor the salt, the boiled nor the raw.) Huarwar the son of Aflawn (who asked Arthur such a boon as would satisfy him. It was the third great plague of Cornwall when he received it. None could get a smile from him but when he was satisfied). Gware Gwallt Euryn. The two cubs of Gast Rhymi, Gwyddrud and Gwyddneu Astrus. Sugyn the son of Sugnedydd (who would suck up the sea on which were three hundred ships so as to leave nothing but a dry strand. He was broad-chested). Rhacymwri, the attendant of Arthur (whatever barn he was shown, were there the produce of thirty ploughs within it, he would strike it with an iron flail until the rafters, the beams, and the boards were no better than the small oats in the mow upon the floor of the barn). Dygyflwng and Anoeth Veidawg. And Hir Eiddyl, and Hir Amreu (they were two attendants of Arthur). And Gwevyl the son of Gwestad (on the day that he was sad, he would let one of his lips drop below his waist, while he turned up the other like a cap upon his head). Uchtryd Varyf Draws (who spread his red untrimmed beard over the eight-and-forty rafters which were in Arthur's Hall). Elidyr Gyvarwydd. Yskyrdav and Yscudydd (two attendants of Gwenhwyvar were they. Their feet were swift as their thoughts when bearing a message). Brys the son of Bryssethach (from the Hill of the Black Fernbrake in North Britain). And Grudlwyn Gorr. Bwlch, and Kyfwlch, and Sefwlch, the sons of Cleddyf Kyfwlch, the grandsons of Cleddyf Difwlch. (Their three shields were three gleaming glitterers; their three spears were three pointed piercers; their three swords were three grinding gashers; Glas, Glessic, and Gleisad. Their three dogs, Call, Cuall, and Cavall. Their three horses, Hwyrdyddwd, and Drwgdyddwd, and Llwyrdyddwg. Their three wives, Och, and Garym, and Diaspad. Their three grandchildren, Lluched, and Neved, and Eissiwed. Their three daughters, Drwg, and Gwaeth, and Gwaethav Oll. Their three hand-maids, Eheubryd the daughter of Kyfwlch, Gorascwrn the daughter of Nerth, Ewaedan the daughter of Kynvelyn Keudawd Pwyll the half-man.) Dwnn Diessic Unbenn, Eiladyr the son of Pen Llarcau, Kynedyr Wyllt the son of Hettwn Talaryant, Sawyl Ben Uchel, Gwalchmai the son of Gwyar, Gwalhaved the son of Gwyar, Gwrhyr Gwastawd Ieithoedd (to whom all tongues were known), and Kethcrwm the Priest. Clust the son of Clustveinad (though he were buried seven

298

cubits beneath the earth, he would hear the ant fifty miles off rise from her nest in the morning). Medyr the son of Methredydd (from Gelli Wic he could, in a twinkling, shoot the wren through the two legs upon Esgeir Oervel in Ireland). Gwiawn Llygad Cath (who could cut a haw from the eye of the gnat without hurting him). Ol the son of Olwydd (seven years before he was born his father's swine were carried off, and when he grew up a man he tracked the swine, and brought them back in seven herds). Bedwini the Bishop (who blessed Arthur's meat and drink). For the sake of the golden-chained daughters of this island. For the sake of Gwenhwyvar its chief lady, and Gwennhwyach her sister, and Rathtyeu the only daughter of Clemenhill, and Rhelemon the daughter of Kai, and Tannwen the daughter of Gweir Datharweniddawg. Gwenn Alarch the daughter of Kynwyl Canbwch. Eurneid the daughter of Clydno Eiddin. Eneuawc the daughter of Bedwyr. Enrydreg the daughter of Tudvathar. Gwennwledyr the daughter of Gwaledyr Kyrvach. Erddudnid the daughter of Tryffin. Eurolwen the daughter of Gwdolwyn Gorr. Teleri the daughter of Peul. Indeg the daughter of Garwy Hir. Morvudd the daughter of Urien Rheged. Gwenllian Deg the majestic maiden. Creiddylad the daughter of Lludd Llaw Ereint. (She was the most splendid maiden in the three Islands of the mighty, and in the three Islands adjacent, and for her Gwythyr the son of Greidawl and Gwynn the son of Nudd fight every first of May until the day of doom.) Ellylw the daughter of Neol Kynn-Crog (she lived three ages). Essyllt Vinwen and Essyllt Vingul." And all these did Kilhwch the son of Kilydd adjure to obtain his boon.

Then said Arthur, "Oh! chieftain, I have never heard of the maiden of whom thou speakest, nor of her kindred, but I will gladly send messengers in search of her. Give me time to seek her." And the youth said, "I will willingly grant from this night to that at the end of the year to do so." Then Arthur sent messengers to every land within his dominions to seek for the maiden; and at the end of the year Arthur's messengers returned without having gained any knowledge or intelligence concerning Olwen more than on the first day. Then said Kilhwch, "Every one has received his boon, and I yet lack mine. I will depart and bear away thy honor with me." Then said Kai, "Rash chieftain! dost thou reproach Arthur? Go with us, and we will not part until thou dost either confess that the maiden exists not in the world, or until we obtain her." Thereupon Kai rose up. Kai had this peculiarity, that his breath lasted nine nights and nine days under water, and he could exist nine nights and nine days without sleep. A wound from Kai's sword no physician could heal. Very subtle was Kai. When it pleased him he could render himself as tall as the highest tree in the forest. And he had another peculiarity,— so great was the heat of his nature, that, when it rained hardest, whatever he carried remained dry for a handbreadth above and a handbreadth below his hand; and when his companions were coldest, it was to them as fuel with which to light their fire.

And Arthur called Bedwyr, who never shrank from any enterprise upon which Kai was bound. None was equal to him in swiftness throughout this island except Arthur and Drych Ail Kibddar. And although he was one-handed, three warriors could not shed blood faster than he on the field of battle. Another property he had; his lance would produce a wound equal to those of nine opposing lances.

And Arthur called to Kynddelig the Guide, "Go thou upon this expedition with the chieftain." For as good a guide was he in a land which he had never seen as he was in his own.

He called Gwrhyr Gwalstawt Ieithoedd, because he knew all tongues.

He called Gwalchmai the son of Gwyar, because he never returned home without achieving the adventure of which he went in quest. He was the best of footmen and the best of knights. He was nephew to Arthur, the son of his sister, and his cousin.

And Arthur called Menw the son of Teirgwaedd, in order that if they went into a savage country, he might cast a charm and an illusion over them, so that none might see them whilst they could see every one.

They journeyed until they came to a vast open plain, wherein they saw a great castle, which was the fairest of the castles of the world. And they journeyed that day until the evening, and when they thought they were nigh to the castle, they were no nearer to it than they had been in the morning. And the second and the third day they journeyed, and even then scarcely could they reach so far. And when they came before the castle, they beheld a vast flock of sheep, which was boundless and without an end. And upon the top of a mound there was a herdsman, keeping the sheep. And a rug made of skins was upon him; and by his side was a shaggy mastiff, larger than a steed nine winters old. Never had he lost even a lamb from his flock, much less a large sheep. He let no occasion ever pass without doing some hurt and harm. All the dead trees and bushes in the plain he burnt with his breath down to the very ground.

Then said Kai, "Gwrhyr Gwalstawt Ieithoedd, go thou and salute yonder man." "Kai," said he, "I engaged not to go further than thou thyself." "Let us go then together," answered Kai. Said Menw the son of Teirgwaedd, "Fear not to go thither, for I will cast a spell upon the dog, so that he shall injure no one." And they went up to the mound whereon the herdsman was, and they said to him, "How dost thou fare, O herdsman?" "No less fair be it to you than to me." "Truly, art thou the chief?" "There is no hurt to injure me but my own." "Whose are the sheep that thou dost keep, and to whom does yonder castle belong?" "Stupid are ye, truly! Through the whole world is it known that this is the castle of Yspaddaden Penkawr." "And who art thou?" "I am called Custennin the son of Dyfnedig, and my brother Yspaddaden Penkawr oppressed me because of my possessions. And ye also, who are ye?" "We are an embassy from Arthur, come to seek Olwen the daughter of Yspaddaden Penkawr." "Oh men! the mercy of Heaven be upon you, do not that for all the world. None who ever came hither on this quest has returned alive." And the herdsman rose up. And as he arose, Kilhwch gave unto him a ring of gold. And he sought to put on the ring, but it was too small for him, so he placed it in the finger of his glove. And he went home, and gave the glove to his spouse to keep. And she took the ring from the glove when it was given her, and she said, "Whence came this ring, for thou art not wont to have good fortune?" "I went," said he, "to the sea to seek for fish, and lo, I saw a corpse borne by the waves. And a fairer corpse than it did I never behold. And from its finger did I take this ring." "O man! does the sea permit its dead to wear jewels? Show me then this body." "Oh wife, him to whom this ring belonged thou shalt see here in the evening." "And who is he?" asked the woman, "Kilhwch the son of Kilydd, the son of Prince Kelyddon, by Goleuddydd the daughter of Prince Anlawdd, his mother, who is come to seek Olwen as his wife." And when she heard that, her feelings were divided between the joy that she had that her nephew, the son of her sister, was coming to her, and sorrow because she had never known any one depart alive who had come on that quest.

And they went forward to the gate of Custennin the herdsman's dwelling. And when she heard their footsteps approaching, she ran out with joy to meet them. And Kai snatched a billet out of the pile. And when she met them she sought to throw her arms about their necks. And Kai placed the log between her two hands, and she squeezed it so that it became a twisted coil. "Oh woman," said Kai, "if thou hadst squeezed me thus, none could ever again have set their affections on me. Evil love were this." They entered into the house, and were served; and soon after they all went forth to amuse themselves. Then the woman opened a stone chest that was before the chimney-corner, and out of it arose a youth with yellow curling hair. Said Gwrhyr, "It is a pity to hide this youth. I know that it is not his own crime that is thus visited upon him." "This is but a remnant," said the woman. "Three-and-twenty of my sons has Yspaddaden Penkawr slain, and I have no more hope of this one than of the others." Then said Kai, "Let him come and be a companion with me, and he shall not be slain unless I also am slain with him." And they ate. And the woman asked them, "Upon what errand come you here?" "We come to seek Olwen for this youth." Then said the woman, "In the name of Heaven, since no one from the castle hath yet seen you, return again whence you came." "Heaven is our witness, that we will not return until we have seen the maiden." Said Kai, "Does she ever come hither, so that she may be seen?" "She comes here every Saturday to wash her head, and in the vessel where she washes, she leaves all her rings, and she never either comes herself or sends any messengers to fetch them." "Will she come here if she is sent to?" "Heaven knows that I will not destroy my soul, nor will I betray those that trust me; unless you will pledge me your faith that you will not harm her, I will not send to her." "We pledge it," said they. So a message was sent, and she came.

The maiden was clothed in a robe of flame-colored silk, and about her neck was a collar of ruddy gold, on which were precious emeralds and rubies. More yellow was her head than the flower of the broom, and her skin was whiter than the foam of the wave, and fairer were her hands and her fingers than the blossoms of the wood anemone amidst the spray of the meadow fountain. The eye of the trained hawk, the glance of the three-mewed falcon was not brighter than hers. Her bosom was more snowy than the breast of the white swan, her cheek was redder than the reddest roses. Whoso beheld her was filled with her love. Four white trefoils sprung up wherever she trod. And therefore was she called Olwen.

She entered the house, and sat beside Kilhwch upon the foremost bench; and as soon as he saw her he knew her. And Kilhwch said unto her, "Ah! maiden, thou art she whom I have loved; come away with me, lest they speak evil of thee and of me. Many a day have I loved thee." "I cannot do this, for I have pledged my faith to my father not to go without his counsel, for his life will last only until the time of my espousals. Whatever is, must be. But I will give thee advice if thou wilt take it. Go, ask me of my father, and that which he shall require of thee, grant it, and thou wilt obtain me; but if thou deny him anything, thou wilt not obtain me, and it will be well for thee if thou escape with thy life." "I promise all this, if occasion offer," said he.

She returned to her chamber, and they all rose up and followed her to the castle. And they slew the nine porters that were at the nine gates in silence. And they slew the nine watch-dogs without one of them barking. And they went forward to the hall.

"The greeting of Heaven and of man be unto thee, Yspaddaden Penkawr," said they. "And you, wherefore come you?" "We come to ask thy daughter Olwen, for Kilhwch the son of Kilydd, the son of Prince Kelyddon." "Where are my pages and my servants? Raise up the forks beneath my two eyebrows which have fallen over my eyes, that I may see the fashion of my son-in-law." And they did so. "Come hither tomorrow, and you shall have an answer."

They rose to go forth, and Yspaddaden Penkawr seized one of the three poisoned darts that lay beside him, and threw it after them. And Bedwyr caught it, and flung it, and pierced Yspaddaden Penkawr grievously with it through the knee. Then he said, "A cursed ungentle son-in-law, truly. I shall ever walk the worse for his rudeness, and shall ever be without a cure. This poisoned iron pains me like the bite of a gadfly. Cursed be the smith who forged it, and the anvil whereon it was wrought! So sharp is it!"

That night also they took up their abode in the house of Custennin the herdsman. The next day with the dawn they arrayed themselves in haste and proceeded to the castle, and entered the hall, and they said, "Yspaddaden Penkawr, give us thy daughter in consideration of her dower and her maiden fee, which we will pay to thee and to her two kinswomen likewise. And unless thou wilt do so, thou shalt meet with thy death on her account." Then he said, "Her four great-grandmothers, and her four great-grandsires are yet alive, it is needful that I take counsel of them." "Be it so," answered they, "we will go to meat." As they rose up, he took the second dart that was beside him, and cast it after them. And Menw the son of Gwaedd caught it, and flung it back at him, and wounded him in the center of the breast, so that it came out at the small of his back. "A cursed ungentle son-in-law, truly," said he, "the hard iron pains me like the bite of a horse-leech. Cursed be the hearth whereon it was heated, and the smith who formed it! So sharp is it! Henceforth, whenever I go up a hill, I shall have a scant in my breath, and a pain in my chest, and I shall often loathe my food." And they went to meat.

And the third day they returned to the palace. And Yspaddaden Penkawr said to them, "Shoot not at me again unless you desire death. Where are my attendants? Lift up the forks of my eyebrows which have fallen over my eyeballs, that I may see the fashion of my son-in-law." Then they arose, and, as they did so, Yspaddaden Penkawr took the third poisoned dart and cast it at them. And Kilhwch caught it and threw it vigorously, and wounded him through the eyeball, so that the dart came out at the back of his head. "A cursed ungentle son-in-law, truly! As long as I remain alive, my eyesight will be the worse. Whenever I go against the wind, my eyes will water; and peradventure my head will burn, and I shall have a giddiness every new moon. Cursed be the fire in which it was forged. Like the bite of a mad dog is the stroke of this poisoned iron." And they went to meat.

And the next day they came again to the palace, and they said, "Shoot not at us any more, unless thou desirest such hurt, and harm, and torture as thou now hast, and even more." "Give me thy daughter, and if thou wilt not give her, thou shalt receive thy death because of her." "Where is he that seeks my daughter? Come hither where I may see thee." And they placed him a chair face to face with him.

Said Yspaddaden Penkawr, "Is it thou that seekest my daughter?" "It is I," answered Kilhwch. "I must have thy pledge that thou wilt not do towards me otherwise than is just, and when I have gotten that which I shall name, my daughter thou shalt have." "I promise thee that willingly," said Kilhwch, "name what thou wilt." "I will do so," said he.

"Seest thou yonder vast hill?" "I see it." "I require that it be rooted up, and that the grubbings be burned for manure on the face of the land, and that it be ploughed and sown in one day, and in one day that the grain ripen. And of that wheat I intend to make food and liquor fit for the wedding of thee and my daughter. And all this I require done in one day."

"It will be easy for me to compass this, although thou mayest think that it will not be easy."

"Though this be easy for thee, there is yet that which will not be so. No husbandman can till or prepare this land, so wild is it, except Amaethon the son of Don, and he will not come with thee by his own free will, and thou wilt not be able to compel him."

"It will be easy for me to compass this, although thou mayest think that it will not be easy."

"Though thou get this, there is yet that which thou wilt not get. Govannon the son of Don to come to the headland to rid the iron, he will do no work of his own good will except for a lawful king, and thou wilt not be able to compel him."

"It will be easy for me to compass this."

"Though thou get this, there is yet that which thou wilt not get; the two dun oxen of Gwlwlyd, both yoked together, to plough the wild land yonder stoutly. He will not give them of his own free will, and thou wilt not be able to compel him."

"It will be easy for me to compass this."

"Though thou get this, there is yet that which thou wilt not get; the yellow and the brindled bull yoked together do I require."

"It will be easy for me to compass this."

"Though thou get this, there is yet that which thou wilt not get; the two horned oxen, one of which is beyond, and the other this side of the peaked mountain, yoked together in the same plough. And these are Nynniaw and Peibaw whom God turned into oxen on account of their sins."

"It will be easy for me to compass this."

"Though thou get this, there is yet that which thou wilt not get. Seest thou yonder red tilled ground?"

"I see it."

"When first I met the mother of this maiden, nine bushels of flax were sown therein, and none has yet sprung up, neither white nor black; and I have the measure by me still. I require to have the flax to sow in the new land yonder, that when it grows up it may make a white wimple for my daughter's head, on the day of thy wedding."

"It will be easy for me to compass this, although thou mayest think that it will not be easy."

"Though thou get this, there is yet that which thou wilt not get. Honey that is nine times sweeter than the honey of the virgin swarm, without scum and bees, do I require to make bragget for the feast."

"It will be easy for me to compass this, although thou mayest think that it will not be easy."

"The vessel of Llwyr the son of Llwyryon, which is of the utmost value. There is no other vessel in the world that can hold this drink. Of his free will thou wilt not get it, and thou canst not compel him."

"It will be easy for me to compass this, although thou mayest think that it will not be easy."

"Though thou get this, there is yet that which thou wilt not get. The basket of Gwyddneu Garanhir, if the whole world should come together, thrice nine men at a time, the meat that each of them desired would be found within it. I require to eat therefrom on the night that my daughter becomes thy bride. He will give it to no one of his own free will, and thou canst not compel him."

"It will be easy for me to compass this, although thou mayest think that it will not be easy."

"Though thou get this, there is yet that which thou wilt not get. The horn of Gwlgawd Gododin to serve us with liquor that night. He will not give it of his own free will, and thou wilt not be able to compel him."

"It will be easy for me to compass this, although thou mayest think that it will not be easy."

"Though thou get this, there is yet that which thou wilt not get. The harp of Teirtu to play to us that night. When a man desires that it should play, it does so of itself, and when he desires that it should cease, it ceases. And this he will not give of his own free will, and thou wilt not be able to compel him."

"It will be easy for me to compass this, although thou mayest think that it will not be easy."

"Though thou get this, there is yet that which thou wilt not get. The cauldron of Diwrnach Wyddel, the steward of Odgar the son of Aedd, king of Ireland, to boil the meat for thy marriage feast."

"It will be easy for me to compass this, although thou mayest think that it will not be easy."

"Though thou get this, there is yet that which thou wilt not get. It is needful for me to wash my head, and shave my beard, and I require the tusk of Yskithyrwyn Penbaedd to shave myself withal, neither shall I profit by its use if it be not plucked alive out of his head."

"It will be easy for me to compass this, although thou mayest think that it will not be easy."

"Though thou get this, there is yet that which thou wilt not get. There is no one in the world that can pluck it out of his head except Odgar the son of Aedd, king of Ireland."

"It will be easy for me to compass this."

"Though thou get this, there is yet that which thou wilt not get. I will not trust any one to keep the tusk except Gado of North Britain. Now the threescore Cantrevs of North Britain are under his sway, and of his own free will he will not come out of his kingdom, and thou wilt not be able to compel him."

"It will be easy for me to compass this, although thou mayest think that it will not be easy."

"Though thou get this, there is yet that which thou wilt not get. I must spread out my hair in order to shave it, and it will never be spread out unless I have the blood of the jet-black sorceress, the daughter of the pure white sorceress, from Pen Nant Govid, on the confines of Hell."

"It will be easy for me to compass this, although thou mayest think that it will not be easy."

"Though thou get this, there is yet that which thou wilt not get. I will not have the blood unless I have it warm, and no vessels will keep warm the liquid that is put therein except the bottles of Gwyddolwyd Gorr, which preserve the heat of the liquor that is put into them in the east, until they arrive at the west. And he will not give them of his own free will, and thou wilt not be able to compel him."

"It will be easy for me to compass this, although thou mayest think that it will not be easy."

"Though thou get this, there is yet that which thou wilt not get. Some will desire fresh milk, and it will not be possible to have fresh milk for all, unless we have the bottles of Rhinnon Rhin Barnawd, wherein no liquor ever turns sour. And he will not give them of his own free will, and thou wilt not be able to compel him."

"It will be easy for me to compass this, although thou mayest think that it will not be easy."

"Though thou get this, there is yet that which thou wilt not get. Throughout the world there is not a comb or scissors with which I can arrange my hair, on account of its rankness, except the comb and scissors that are between the two ears of Twrch Trwyth, the son of Prince Tared. He will not give them of his own free will, and thou wilt not be able to compel him."

"It will be easy for me to compass this, although thou mayest think that it will not be easy."

"Though thou get this, there is yet that which thou wilt not get. It will not be possible to hunt Twrch Trwyth without Drudwyn the whelp of Greid, the son of Eri."

"It will be easy for me to compass this, although thou mayest think that it will not be easy."

"Though thou get this, there is yet that which thou wilt not get. Throughout the world there is not a leash that can hold him, except the leash of Cwrs Cant Ewin."

"It will be easy for me to compass this, although thou mayest think that it will not be easy."

"Though thou get this, there is yet that which thou wilt not get. Throughout the world there is no collar that will hold the leash except the collar of Canhastyr Canllaw."

"It will be easy for me to compass this, although thou mayest think that it will not be easy."

"Though thou get this, there is yet that which thou wilt not get. The chain of Kilydd Canhastyr to fasten the collar to the leash."

"It will be easy for me to compass this, although thou mayest think that it will not be easy."

"Though thou get this, there is yet that which thou wilt not get. Throughout the world there is not a huntsman who can hunt with this dog, except Mabon the son of Modron. He was taken from his mother when three nights old, and it is not known where he now is, nor whether he is living or dead."

"It will be easy for me to compass this, although thou mayest think that it will not be easy."

"Though thou get this, there is yet that which thou wilt not get. Gwynn Mygdwn, the horse of Gweddw, that is as swift as the wave, to carry Mabon the son of Modron to hunt the boar Trwyth. He will not give him of his own free will, and thou wilt not be able to compel him."

"It will be easy for me to compass this, although thou mayest think that it will not be easy."

"Though thou get this, there is yet that which thou wilt not get. Thou wilt not get Mabon, for it is not known where he is, unless thou find Eidoel, his kinsman in blood, the son of Aer. For it would be useless to seek for him. He is his cousin."

"It will be easy for me to compass this, although thou mayest think that it will not be easy."

"Though thou get this, there is yet that which thou wilt not get. Garselit the Gwyddelian is the chief huntsman of Ireland; the Twrch Trwyth can never be hunted without him."

"It will be easy for me to compass this, although thou mayest think that it will not be easy."

"Though thou get this, there is yet that which thou wilt not get. A leash made from the beard of Dillus Varvawc, for that is the only one that can hold those two cubs. And the leash will be of no avail unless it be plucked from his beard while he is alive, and twitched out with wooden tweezers. While he lives he will not suffer this to be done to him, and the leash will be of no use should he be dead, because it will be brittle."

"It will be easy for me to compass this, although thou mayest think that it will not be easy."

"Though thou get this, there is yet that which thou wilt not get. Throughout the world there is no huntsman that can hold those two whelps except Kynedyr Wyllt, the son of Hettwn Glafyrawc; he is nine times more wild than the wildest beast upon the mountains. Him wilt thou never get, neither wilt thou ever get my daughter."

"It will be easy for me to compass this, although thou mayest think that it will not be easy."

"Though thou get this, there is yet that which thou wilt not get. It is not possible to hunt the boar Trwyth without Gwynn the son of Nudd, whom God has placed over the brood of devils in Annwvyn, lest they should destroy the present race. He will never be spared thence."

"It will be easy for me to compass this, although thou mayest think that it will not be easy."

"Though thou get this, there is yet that which thou wilt not get. There is not a horse in the world that can carry Gwynn to hunt the Twrch Trwyth, except Du, the horse of Mor of Oerveddawg."

"It will be easy for me to compass this, although thou mayest think that it will not be easy."

"Though thou get this, there is yet that which thou wilt not get. Until Gilennhin the king of France shall come, the Twrch Trwyth cannot be hunted. It will be unseemly for him to leave his kingdom for thy sake, and he will never come hither."

"It will be easy for me to compass this, although thou mayest think that it will not be easy."

"Though thou get this, there is yet that which thou wilt not get. The Twrch Trwyth can never be hunted without the son of Alun Dyved; he is well skilled in letting loose the dogs."

"It will be easy for me to compass this, although thou mayest think that it will not be easy."

"Though thou get this, there is yet that which thou wilt not get. The Twrch Trwyth cannot be hunted unless thou get Aned and Aethlem. They are as swift as the gale of wind, and they were never let loose upon a beast that they did not kill him."

"It will be easy for me to compass this, although thou mayest think that it will not be easy."

"Though thou get this, there is yet that which thou wilt not get; Arthur and his companions to hunt the Twrch Trwyth. He is a mighty man, and he will not come for thee, neither wilt thou be able to compel him."

"It will be easy for me to compass this, although thou mayest think that it will not be easy."

"Though thou get this, there is yet that which thou wilt not get. The Twrch Trwyth cannot be hunted unless thou get Bwlch, and Kyfwlch [and Sefwlch], the grandsons of Cleddyf Difwlch. Their three shields are three gleaming glitterers. Their three spears are three pointed piercers. Their three swords are three griding gashers, Glas, Glessic, and Clersag. Their three dogs, Call, Cuall, and Cavall. Their three horses, Hwyrdydwg, and Drwgdydwg, and Llwyrdydwg. Their three wives, Och, and Garam, and Diaspad. Their three grandchildren, Lluched, and Vyned, and Eissiwed. Their three daughters, Drwg, and Gwaeth, and Gwaethav Oll. Their three hand-maids [Eheubryd, the daughter of Kyfwlch; Gorasgwrn, the daughter of Nerth; and Gwaedan, the daughter of Kynvelyn]. These three men shall sound the horn, and all the others shall shout, so that all will think that the sky is falling to the earth."

"It will be easy for me to compass this, although thou mayest think that it will not be easy."

"Though thou get this, there is yet that which thou wilt not get. The sword of Gwrnach the Giant; he will never be slain except therewith. Of his own free will he will not give it, either for a price or as a gift, and thou wilt never be able to compel him."

"It will be easy for me to compass this, although thou mayest think that it will not be easy."

"Though thou get this, there is yet that which thou wilt not get. Difficulties shalt thou meet with, and nights without sleep, in seeking this, and if thou obtain it not, neither shalt thou obtain my daughter."

"Horses shall I have, and chivalry; and my lord and kinsman Arthur will obtain for me all these things. And I shall gain thy daughter, and thou shalt lose thy life."

"Go forward. And thou shalt not be chargeable for food or raiment for my daughter while thou art seeking these things; and when thou hast compassed all these marvels, thou shalt have my daughter for thy wife."

All that day they journeyed until the evening, and then they beheld a vast castle, which was the largest in the world. And lo, a black man, huger than three of the men of this world, came out from the castle. And they spoke unto him, "Whence comest thou, O man?" "From the castle which you see yonder." "Whose castle is that?" asked they. "Stupid are ye truly, O men. There is no one in the world that does not know to whom this castle belongs. It is the castle of Gwrnach the Giant." "What treatment is there for guests and strangers that alight in that castle?" "Oh! Chieftain, Heaven protect thee. No guest ever returned thence alive, and no one may enter therein unless he brings with him his craft."

Then they proceeded towards the gate. Said Gwrhyr Gwalstawt Ieithoedd, "Is there a porter?" "There is. And thou, if thy tongue be not mute in thy head, wherefore dost thou call?" "Open the gate." "I will not open it." "Wherefore wilt thou not?" "The knife is in the meat, and the drink is in the horn, and there is revelry in the hall of Gwrnach the Giant, and except for a craftsman who brings his craft, the gate will not be opened tonight." "Verily, porter," then said Kai, "my craft bring I with me." "What is thy craft?" "The best burnisher of swords am I in the world." "I will go and tell this unto Gwrnach the Giant, and I will bring thee an answer."

So the porter went in, and Gwrnach said to him, "Hast thou any news from the gate?" "I have. There is a party at the door of the gate who desire to come in." "Didst thou inquire of them if they possessed any art?" "I did inquire," said he, "and one told me that he was well skilled in the burnishing of swords." "We have need of him then. For some time have I sought for some one to polish my sword, and could find no one. Let this man enter, since he brings with him his craft." The porter thereupon returned and opened the gate. And Kai went in by himself, and he saluted Gwrnach the Giant. And a chair was placed for him opposite to Gwrnach. And Gwrnach said to him, "Oh man! is it true that is reported of thee, that thou knowest how to burnish swords?" "I know full well how to do so," answered Kai. Then was the sword of Gwrnach brought to him. And Kai took a blue whetstone from under his arm, and asked him whether he would have it burnished white or blue. "Do with it as it seems good to thee, and as thou wouldest if it were thine own." Then Kai polished one half of the blade and put it in his hand. "Will this please thee?" asked he. "I would rather than all that is in my dominions that the whole of it were like unto this. It is a marvel to me that such a man as thou should be without a companion." "Oh! noble sir, I have a companion, albeit he is not skilled in this art." "Who may he be?" "Let the porter go forth, and I will tell him whereby he may know him. The head of his lance will leave its shaft, and draw blood from the wind, and will descend upon its shaft again." Then the gate was opened, and Bedwyr entered. And Kai said, "Bedwyr is very skilful, although he knows not this art."

And there was much discourse among those who were without, because that Kai and Bedwyr had gone in. And a young man who was with them, the only son of Custennin the herdsman, got in also. And he caused all his companions to keep close to him as he passed the three wards, and until he came into the midst of the castle. And his companions said unto the son of Custennin, "Thou hast done this! Thou art the best of all men." And thenceforth he was called Goreu, the son of

Custennin. Then they dispersed to their lodgings, that they might slay those who lodged therein, unknown to the Giant.

The sword was now polished, and Kai gave it unto the hand of Gwrnach the Giant, to see if he were pleased with his work. And the Giant said, "The work is good, I am content therewith." Said Kai, "It is thy scabbard that hath rusted thy sword, give it to me that I may take out the wooden sides of it and put in new ones." And he took the scabbard from him, and the sword in the other hand. And he came and stood over against the Giant, as if he would have put the sword into the scabbard; and with it he struck at the head of the Giant, and cut off his head at one blow. Then they despoiled the castle, and took from it what goods and jewels they would. And again on the same day, at the beginning of the year, they came to Arthur's Court, bearing with them the sword of Gwrnach the Giant.

Now, when they told Arthur how they had sped, Arthur said, "Which of these marvels will it be best for us to seek first?" "It will be best," said they, "to seek Mabon the son of Modron; and he will not be found unless we first find Eidoel the son of Aer, his kinsman." Then Arthur rose up, and the warriors of the Islands of Britain with him, to seek for Eidoel; and they proceeded until they came before the Castle of Glivi, where Eidoel was imprisoned. Glivi stood on the summit of his castle, and he said, "Arthur, what requirest thou of me, since nothing remains to me in this fortress, and I have neither joy nor pleasure in it; neither wheat nor oats? Seek not therefore to do me harm." Said Arthur, "Not to injure thee came I hither, but to seek for the prisoner that is with thee." "I will give thee my prisoner, though I had not thought to give him up to any one; and therewith shalt thou have my support and my aid."

His followers said unto Arthur, "Lord, go thou home, thou canst not proceed with thy host in quest of such small adventures as these." Then said Arthur, "It were well for thee, Gwrhyr Gwalstawt Ieithoedd, to go upon this quest, for thou knowest all languages, and art familiar with those of the birds and the beasts. Thou, Eidoel, oughtest likewise to go with my men in search of thy cousin. And as for you, Kai and Bedwyr, I have hope of whatever adventure ye are in quest of, that ye will achieve it. Achieve ye this adventure for me."

They went forward until they came to the Ousel of Cilgwri. And Gwrhyr adjured her for the sake of Heaven, saying, "Tell me if thou knowest aught of Mabon the son of Modron, who was taken when three nights old from between his mother and the wall." And the Ousel answered, "When I first came here, there was a smith's anvil in this place, and I was then a young bird; and from that time no work has been done upon it, save the pecking of my beak every evening, and now there is not so much as the size of a nut remaining thereof; yet the vengeance of Heaven be upon me, if during all that time I have ever heard of the man for whom you inquire. Nevertheless I will do that which is right, and that which it is fitting that I should do for an embassy from Arthur. There is a race of animals who were formed before me, and I will be your guide to them."

So they proceeded to the place where was the Stag of Redynvre. "Stag of Redynvre, behold we are come to thee, an embassy from Arthur, for we have not heard of any animal older than thou. Say, knowest thou aught of Mabon the son of Modron, who was taken from his mother when three nights old?" The Stag said, "When first I came hither, there was a plain all around me, without any trees save one oak sapling, which grew up to be an oak with an hundred branches. And that oak has since perished, so that now nothing remains of it but the withered stump; and from that day to this I have been here, yet have I never heard of the man for whom you inquire. Nevertheless, being an embassy from Arthur, I will be your guide to the place where there is an animal which was formed before I was."

So they proceeded to the place where was the Owl of Cwm Cawlwyd. "Owl of Cwm Cawlwyd, here is an embassy from Arthur; knowest thou aught of Mabon the son of Modron, who was taken after three nights from his mother?" "If I knew I would tell you. When first I came hither, the wide valley you see was a wooded glen. And a race of men came and rooted it up. And there grew there a second wood; and this wood is the third. My wings, are they not withered stumps? Yet all this time, even until today, I have never heard of the man for whom you inquire. Nevertheless, I will be the guide of Arthur's embassy until you come to the place where is the oldest animal in this world, and the one that has traveled most, the Eagle of Gwern Abwy."

Gwrhyr said, "Eagle of Gwern Abwy, we have come to thee an embassy from Arthur, to ask thee if thou knowest aught of Mabon the son of Modron, who was taken from his mother when he was three nights old." The Eagle said, "I have been here for a great space of time, and when I first came hither there was a rock here, from the top of which I pecked at the stars every evening; and now it is not so much as a span high. From that day to this I have been here, and I have never heard of the man for whom you inquire, except once when I went in search of food as far as Llyn Llyw. And when I came there, I struck my talons into a salmon, thinking he would serve me as food for a long time. But he drew me into the deep, and I was scarcely able to escape from him. After that I went with my whole kindred to attack him, and to try to destroy him, but he sent messengers, and made peace with me; and came and besought me to take fifty fish spears out of his back. Unless he know something of him whom you seek, I cannot tell who may. However, I will guide you to the place where he is."

So they went thither; and the Eagle said, "Salmon of Llyn Llyw, I have come to thee with an embassy from Arthur, to ask thee if thou knowest aught concerning Mabon the son of Modron, who was taken away at three nights old from his mother." "As much as I know I will tell thee. With every tide I go along the river upwards, until I come near to the walls of Gloucester, and there have I found such wrong as I never found elsewhere; and to the end that ye may give credence thereto, let one of you go thither upon each of my two shoulders." So Kai and Gwrhyr Gwalstawt Ieithoedd went upon the two shoulders of the salmon, and they proceeded until they came unto the wall of the prison, and they heard a great wailing and lamenting from the dungeon. Said Gwrhyr, "Who is it that laments in this

311

house of stone?" "Alas, there is reason enough for whoever is here to lament. It is Mabon the son of Modron who is here imprisoned; and no imprisonment was ever so grievous as mine, neither that of Llud Llaw Ereint, nor that of Greid the son of Eri." "Hast thou hope of being released for gold or for silver, or for any gifts of wealth, or through battle and fighting?" "By fighting will whatever I may gain be obtained."

Then they went thence, and returned to Arthur, and they told him where Mabon the son of Modron was imprisoned. And Arthur summoned the warriors of the Island, and they journeyed as far as Gloucester, to the place where Mabon was in prison. Kai and Bedwyr went upon the shoulders of the fish, whilst the warriors of Arthur attacked the castle. And Kai broke through the wall into the dungeon, and brought away the prisoner upon his back, whilst the fight was going on between the warriors. And Arthur returned home, and Mabon with him at liberty.

Said Arthur, "Which of the marvels will it be best for us now to seek first?" "It will be best to seek for the two cubs of Gast Rhymhi." "Is it known," asked Arthur, "where she is?" "She is in Aber Deu Cleddyf," said one. Then Arthur went to the house of Tringad, in Aber Cleddyf, and he inquired of him whether he had heard of her there. "In what form may she be?" "She is in the form of a she-wolf," said he; "and with her there are two cubs." "She has often slain my herds, and she is there below in a cave in Aber Cleddyf."

So Arthur went in his ship Prydwen by sea, and the others went by land, to hunt her. And they surrounded her and her two cubs, and God did change them again for Arthur into their own form. And the host of Arthur dispersed themselves into parties of one and two.

On a certain day, as Gwythyr the son of Greidawl was walking over a mountain, he heard a wailing and a grievous cry. And when he heard it, he sprang forward, and went towards it. And when he came there, he drew his sword, and smote off an anthill close to the earth, whereby it escaped being burned in the fire. And the ants said to him, "Receive from us the blessing of Heaven, and that which no man can give we will give thee." Then they fetched the nine bushels of flax-seed which Yspaddaden Penkawr had required of Kilhwch, and they brought the full measure without lacking any, except one flax-seed, and that the lame pismire brought in before night.

As Kai and Bedwyr sat on a beacon carn on the summit of Plinlimmon, in the highest wind that ever was in the world, they looked around them, and saw a great smoke towards the south, afar off, which did not bend with the wind. Then said Kai, "By the hand of my friend, behold, yonder is the fire of a robber!" Then they hastened towards the smoke, and they came so near to it, that they could see Dillus Varvawc scorching a wild boar. "Behold, yonder is the greatest robber that ever fled from Arthur," said Bedwyr unto Kai. "Dost thou know him?" "I do know him," answered Kai, "he is Dillus Varvawc, and no leash in the world will be able to hold

Drudwyn, the cub of Greid the son of Eri, save a leash made from the beard of him thou seest yonder. And even that will be useless, unless his beard be plucked alive with wooden tweezers; for if dead, it will be brittle." "What thinkest thou that we should do concerning this?" said Bedwyr. "Let us suffer him," said Kai, "to eat as much as he will of the meat, and after that he will fall asleep." And during that time they employed themselves in making the wooden tweezers. And when Kai knew certainly that he was asleep, he made a pit under his feet, the largest in the world, and he struck him a violent blow, and squeezed him into the pit. And there they twitched out his beard completely with the wooden tweezers; and after that they slew him altogether.

And from thence they both went to Gelli Wic, in Cornwall, and took the leash made of Dillus Varvawc's beard with them, and they gave it into Arthur's hand. Then Arthur composed this Englyn:

Kai made a leash
Of Dillus son of Eurei's beard.
Were he alive, thy death he'd be.

And thereupon Kai was wroth, so that the warriors of the Island could scarcely make peace between Kai and Arthur. And thenceforth, neither in Arthur's troubles, nor for the slaying of his men, would Kai come forward to his aid for ever after.

Said Arthur, "Which of the marvels is it best for us now to seek?" "It is best for us to seek Drudwyn, the cub of Greid the son of Eri."

A little while before this, Creiddylad the daughter of Lludd Llaw Ereint, and Gwythyr the son of Greidawl, were betrothed. And before she had become his bride, Gwyn ap Nudd came and carried her away by force; and Gwythyr the son of Greidawl gathered his host together, and went to fight with Gwyn ap Nudd. But Gwyn overcame him, and captured Greid the son of Eri, and Glinneu the son of Taran, and Gwrgwst Ledlwm, and Dynvarth his son. And he captured Penn the son of Nethawg, and Nwython, and Kyledyr Wyllt his son. And they slew Nwython, and took out his heart, and constrained Kyledyr to eat the heart of his father. And therefrom Kyledyr became mad. When Arthur heard of this, he went to the North, and summoned Gwyn ap Nudd before him, and set free the nobles whom he had put in prison, and made peace between Gwyn ap Nudd and Gwythyr the son of Griedawl. And this was the peace that was made: —that the maiden should remain in her father's house, without advantage to either of them, and that Gwyn ap Nudd and Gwythyr the son of Greidawl should fight for her every first of May, from thenceforth until the day of doom, and that whichever of them should then be conqueror should have the maiden.

And when Arthur had thus reconciled these chieftains, he obtained Mygdwn, Gweddw's horse, and the leash of Cwrs Cant Ewin.

And after that Arthur went into Armorica, and with him Mabon the son of Mellt, and Gware Gwallt Euryn, to seek the two dogs of Glythmyr Ledewic. And when he had got them, he went to the West of Ireland, in search of Gwrgi Seven; and Odgar the son of Aedd king of Ireland went with him. And thence went Arthur into the North, and captured Kyledyr Wyllt; and he went after Yskithyrwyn Penbaedd. And Mabon the son of Mellt came with the two dogs of Glythmyr Ledewic in his hand, and Drudwyn, the cub of Greid the son of Eri. And Arthur went himself to the chase, leading his own dog Cavall. And Kaw, of North Britain, mounted Arthur's mare Llamrei, and was first in the attack. Then Kaw, of North Britain, wielded a mighty axe, and absolutely daring he came valiantly up to the boar, and clave his head in twain. And Kaw took away the tusk. Now the boar was not slain by the dogs that Yspaddaden had mentioned, but by Cavall, Arthur's own dog.

And after Yskithyrwyn Penbaedd was killed, Arthur and his host departed to Gelli Wic in Cornwall. And thence he sent Menw the son of Teirgwaedd to see if the precious things were between the two ears of Twrch Trwyth, since it were useless to encounter him if they were not there. Albeit it was certain where he was, for he had laid waste the third part of Ireland. And Menw went to seek for him, and he met with him in Ireland, in Esgeir Oervel. And Menw took the form of a bird; and he descended upon the top of his lair, and strove to snatch away one of the precious things from him, but he carried away nothing but one of his bristles. And the boar rose up angrily and shook himself so that some of his venom fell upon Menw, and he was never well from that day forward.

After this Arthur sent an embassy to Odgar, the son of Aedd king of Ireland, to ask for the cauldron of Diwrnach Wyddel, his purveyor. And Odgar commanded him to give it. But Diwrnach said, "Heaven is my witness, if it would avail him anything even to look at it, he should not do so." And the embassy of Arthur returned from Ireland with this denial. And Arthur set forward with a small retinue, and entered into Prydwen, his ship, and went over to Ireland. And they proceeded into the house of Diwrnach Wyddel. And the hosts of Odgar saw their strength. When they had eaten and drunk as much as they desired, Arthur demanded to have the cauldron. And he answered, "If I would have given it to any one, I would have given it at the word of Odgar king of Ireland."

When he had given them this denial, Bedwyr arose and seized hold of the cauldron, and placed it upon the back of Hygwyd, Arthur's servant, who was brother, by the mother's side, to Arthur's servant, Cachamwri. His office was always to carry Arthur's cauldron, and to place fire under it. And Llenlleawg Wyddel seized Caledvwlch, and brandished it. And they slew Diwrnach Wyddel and his company. Then came the Irish and fought with them. And when he had put them to flight, Arthur with his men went forward to the ship, carrying away the cauldron full of Irish money. And he disembarked at the house of Llwydden the son of Kelcoed, at Porth Kerddin in Dyved. And there is the measure of the cauldron.

Then Arthur summoned unto him all the warriors that were in the three Islands of Britain, and in the three Islands adjacent, and all that were in France and in Armorica, in Normandy and in the Summer Country, and all that were chosen footmen and valiant horsemen. And with all these he went into Ireland. And in Ireland there was great fear and terror concerning him. And when Arthur had landed in the country, there came unto him the saints of Ireland and besought his protection. And he granted his protection unto them, and they gave him their blessing. Then the men of Ireland came unto Arthur, and brought him provisions. And Arthur went as far as Esgeir Oervel in Ireland, to the place where the Boar Trwyth was with his seven young pigs. And the dogs were let loose upon him from all sides. That day until evening the Irish fought with him, nevertheless he laid waste the fifth part of Ireland. And on the day following the household of Arthur fought with him, and they were worsted by him, and got no advantage. And the third day Arthur himself encountered him, and he fought with him nine nights and nine days without so much as killing even one little pig. The warriors inquired of Arthur what was the origin of that swine; and he told them that he was once a king, and that God had transformed him into a swine for his sins.

Then Arthur sent Gwrhyr Gwalstawt Ieithoedd, to endeavor to speak with him. And Gwrhyr assumed the form of a bird, and alighted upon the top of the lair, where he was with the seven young pigs. And Gwrhyr Gwalstawt Ieithoedd asked him, "By him who turned you into this form, if you can speak, let some one of you, I beseech you, come and talk with Arthur." Grugyn Gwrych Ereint made answer to him. (Now his bristles were like silver wire, and whether he went through the wood or through the plain, he was to be traced by the glittering of his bristles.) And this was the answer that Grugyn made: "By him who turned us into this form, we will not do so, and we will not speak with Arthur. That we have been transformed thus is enough for us to suffer, without your coming here to fight with us." "I will tell you. Arthur comes but to fight for the comb, and the razor, and the scissors which are between the two ears of Twrch Trwyth." Said Grugyn, "Except he first take his life, he will never have those precious things. And tomorrow morning we will rise up hence, and we will go into Arthur's country, and there will we do all the mischief that we can."

So they set forth through the sea towards Wales. And Arthur and his hosts, and his horses and his dogs, entered Prydwen, that they might encounter them without delay. Twrch Trwyth landed in Porth Cleis in Dyved, and Arthur came to Mynyw. The next day it was told to Arthur that they had gone by, and he overtook them as they were killing the cattle of Kynnwas Kwrr y Vagyl, having slain all that were at Aber Gleddyf, of man and beast, before the coming of Arthur.

Now when Arthur approached, Twrch Trwyth went on as far as Preseleu, and Arthur and his hosts followed him thither, and Arthur sent men to hunt him; Eli and Trachmyr, leading Drudwyn the whelp of Greid the son of Eri, and Gwarthegyd the son of Kaw, in another quarter, with the two dogs of Glythmyr Ledewic, and Bedwyr leading Cavall, Arthur's own dog. And all the warriors ranged themselves

315

around the Nyver. And there came there the three sons of Cleddyf Divwlch, men who had gained much fame at the slaying of Yskithyrwyn Penbaedd; and they went on from Glyn Nyver, and came to Cwm Kerwyn.

And there Twrch Trwyth made a stand, and slew four of Arthur's champions, Gwarthegyd the son of Kaw, and Tarawc of Allt Clwyd, and Rheidwn the son of Eli Atver, and Iscovan Hael. And after he had slain these men, he made a second stand in the same place. And there he slew Gwydre the son of Arthur, and Garselit Wyddel, and Glew the son of Ysgawd, and Iscawyn the son of Panon; and there he himself was wounded.

And the next morning before it was day, some of the men came up with him. And he slew Huandaw, and Gogigwr, and Penpingon, three attendants upon Glewlwyd Gavaelvawr, so that Heaven knows he had not an attendant remaining, excepting only Llaesgevyn, a man from whom no one ever derived any good. And together with these he slew many of the men of that country, and Gwlydyn Saer, Arthur's chief Architect.

Then Arthur overtook him at Pelumyawc, and there he slew Madawc the son of Teithyon, and Gwyn the son of Tringad, the son of Neved, and Eiryawn Penllorau. Thence he went to Aberteivi, where he made another stand, and where he slew Kyflas the son of Kynan, and Gwilenhin king of France. Then he went as far as Glyn Ystu, and there the men and the dogs lost him.

Then Arthur summoned unto him Gwyn ab Nudd, and he asked him if he knew aught of Twrch Trwyth. And he said that he did not.

And all the huntsmen went to hunt the swine as far as Dyffryn Llychwr. And Grugyn Gwallt Ereint and Llwydawg Govynnyad closed with them and killed all the huntsmen, so that there escaped but one man only. And Arthur and his hosts came to the place where Grugyn and Llwydawg were. And there he let loose the whole of the dogs upon them, and with the shout and barking that was set up, Twrch Trwyth came to their assistance.

And from the time that they came across the Irish sea, Arthur had never got sight of him until then. So he set men and dogs upon him, and thereupon he started off and went to Mynydd Amanw. And there one of his young pigs was killed. Then they set upon him life for life, and Twrch Llawin was slain, and then there was slain another of the swine, Gwys was his name. After that he went on to Dyffryn Amanw, and there Banw and Bennwig were killed. Of all his pigs there went with him alive from that place none save Grugyn Gwallt Ereint and Llwydawg Govynnyad.

Thence he went on to Llwch Ewin, and Arthur overtook him there, and he made a stand. And there he slew Echel Forddwytwll, and Garwyli the son of Gwyddawg Gwyr, and many men and dogs likewise. And thence they went to Llwch Tawy. Grugyn Gwrych Ereint parted from them there, and went to Din Tywi. And thence he proceeded to Ceredigiawn, and Eli and Trachmyr with him, and a multitude likewise. Then he came to Garth Gregyn, and there Llwydawg Govynnyad fought in the midst of them, and slew Rhudvyw Rhys and many others with him. Then Llwydawg went thence to Ystrad Yw, and there the men of Armorica met him, and there he slew Hirpeissawg the king of Armorica, and Llygatrudd Emys, and Gwrbothu, Arthur's uncles, his mother's brothers, and there was he himself slain.

Twrch Trwyth went from there to between Tawy and Euyas, and Arthur summoned all Cornwall and Devon unto him, to the estuary of the Severn, and he said to the warriors of this Island, "Twrch Trwyth has slain many of my men, but, by the valor of warriors, while I live he shall not go into Cornwall. And I will not follow him any longer, but I will oppose him life to life. Do ye as ye will." And he resolved that he would send a body of knights, with the dogs of the Island, as far as Euyas, who should return thence to the Severn, and that tried warriors should traverse the Island, and force him into the Severn. And Mabon the son of Modron came up with him at the Severn, upon Gwynn Mygdwn, the horse of Gweddw, and Goreu the son of Custennin, and Menw the son of Teirgwaedd; this was betwixt Llyn Lliwan and Aber Gwy. And Arthur fell upon him together with the champions of Britain. And Osla Kyllellvawr drew near, and Manawyddan the son of Llyr, and Kacmwri the servant of Arthur, and Gwyngelli, and they seized hold of him, catching him first by his feet, and plunged him in the Severn, so that it overwhelmed him. On the one side, Mabon the son of Modron spurred his steed and snatched his razor from him, and Kyledyr Wyllt came up with him on the other side, upon another steed, in the Severn, and took from him the scissors. But before they could obtain the comb, he had regained the ground with his feet, and from the moment that he reached the shore, neither dog, nor man, nor horse could overtake him until he came to Cornwall. If they had had trouble in getting the jewels from him, much more had they in seeking to save the two men from being drowned. Kacmwri, as they drew him forth, was dragged by two millstones into the deep. And as Osla Kyllellvawr was running after the boar, his knife had dropped out of the sheath, and he had lost it, and after that, the sheath became full of water, and its weight drew him down into the deep, as they were drawing him forth.

Then Arthur and his hosts proceeded until they overtook the boar in Cornwall, and the trouble which they had met with before was mere play to what they encountered in seeking the comb. But from one difficulty to another, the comb was at length obtained. And then he was hunted from Cornwall, and driven straight forward into the deep sea. And thenceforth it was never known whither he went; and Aned and Aethlem with him. Then went Arthur to Gelli Wic, in Cornwall, to anoint himself, and to rest from his fatigues.

Said Arthur, "Is there any one of the marvels yet unobtained?" Said one of his men, "There is—the blood of the witch Orddu, the daughter of the witch Orwen, of Pen Nant Govid, on the confines of Hell." Arthur set forth towards the North, and came to the place where was the witch's cave. And Gwyn ab Nudd, and Gwythyr the son of Greidawl, counselled him to send Kacmwri, and Hygwyd his brother, to fight with the witch. And as they entered the cave, the witch seized upon them, and she caught Hygwyd by the hair of his head, and threw him on the floor beneath her. And Kacmwri caught her by the hair of her head, and dragged her to the earth from off Hygwyd, but she turned again upon them both, and drove them both out with kicks and with cuffs.

And Arthur was wroth at seeing his two attendants almost slain, and he sought to enter the cave; but Gwyn and Gwythyr said unto him, "It would not be fitting or seemly for us to see thee squabbling with a hag. Let Hiramreu and Hireidil go to the cave." So they went. But if great was the trouble of the first two that went, much greater was that of these two. And Heaven knows that not one of the four could move from the spot, until they placed them all upon Llamrei, Arthur's mare. And then Arthur rushed to the door of the cave, and at the door he struck at the witch, with Carnwennan his dagger, and clove her in twain, so that she fell in two parts. And Kaw, of North Britain, took the blood of the witch and kept it.

Then Kilhwch set forward, and Goreu the son of Custennin with him, and as many as wished ill to Yspaddaden Penkawr. And they took the marvels with them to his court. And Kaw of North Britain came and shaved his beard, skin, and flesh clean off to the very bone from ear to ear. "Art thou shaved, man?" said Kilhwch. "I am shaved," answered he. "Is thy daughter mine now?" "She is thine," said he, "but therefore needest thou not thank me, but Arthur who hath accomplished this for thee. By my free will thou shouldest never have had her, for with her I lose my life." Then Goreu the son of Custennin seized him by the hair of his head, and dragged him after him to the keep, and cut off his head and placed it on a stake on the citadel. Then they took possession of his castle, and of his treasures.

And that night Olwen became Kilhwch's bride, and she continued to be his wife as long as she lived. And the hosts of Arthur dispersed themselves, each man to his own country. And thus did Kilhwch obtain Olwen, the daughter of Yspaddaden Penkawr.

THE SECOND BATTLE OF MAG TURED (MOYTURA)

translated by Whitley Stokes (1891)

The Tuatha De Dannan lived in the northern isles of the world, learning lore and magic and druidism and wizardry and cunning, until they surpassed the sages of the arts of heathendom. There were four cities in which they learned lore and science and diabolic arts, to wit Falias and Gorias, Murias and Findias. Out of Falias was brought the Stone of Fal, which was in Tara. It used to roar under every king that would take the realm of Ireland. Out of Gorias was brought the Spear that Lug had. No battle was ever won against it or him who held it in his hand. Out of Findias was brought the Sword of Nuada. When it was drawn from its deadly sheath, no one ever escaped from it, and it was irresistible. Out of Murias was brought the Dagda's Cauldron. No company ever went from it unthankful. Four wizards (there were) in those four cities. Morfesa was in Falias: Esras was in Gorias: Uscias was in Findias: Semias was in Murias. Those are the four poets of whom the Tuatha De learnt lore and science.

Now the Tuatha De Danann made an alliance with the Fomorians, and Balor grandson of Net gave his daughter Ethne to Cian son of Diancecht, and she brought forth the gifted child, Lug.

The Tuatha De came with a great fleet to Ireland to take it from the Fir Bolg. They burnt their ships at once on reaching the district of Corcu Belgatan (that is, Connemara today), so that they should not think of retreating to them; and the smoke and the mist that came from the vessels filled the neighboring land and air. Therefore it was conceived that they had arrived in clouds of mist.

The first battle of Moytura was fought between them and the Fir Bolg; and the Fir Bolg were routed and a hundred thousand of them were slain, including their king Eochaid son of Erc.

In that battle, moreover, Nuada's hand was stricken off—it was Sreng son of Sengann that struck it off him—, so Diancecht the leech put on him a hand of silver with the motion of every hand; and Credne the brazier helped the leech.

Now the Tuatha De Danann lost many men in the battle including Edleo son of Alla, and Ernmas and Fiachra and Turill Bicreo.

319

But such of the Fir Bolg as escaped from the battle went in flight to the Fomorians, and settled in Arran and in Islay and in Mann and Rathlin.

A contention as to the sovereignty of the men of Ireland arose between the Tuatha De and their women; because Nuada, after his hand has been stricken off, was disqualified to be king. They said that it would be fitter for them to bestow the kingdom on Bres son of Elotha, on their own adopted son; and that giving the kingdom to him would bind the alliance of the Fomorians to them. For his father, Elotha son of Delbaeth, was king of the Fomorians.

Now the conception of Bres came to pass in this way:

Eri, Delbaeth's daughter, a woman of the Tuatha De, was one day looking at the sea and the land from the house of Maeth Sceni, and she beheld the sea in perfect calm as if it were a level board. And as she was there she saw a vessel of silver on the sea. Its size she deemed great, but its shape was not clear to her. And the stream of the wave bore it to land. Then she saw that in it was a man of fairest form. Golden-yellow hair was on him as far as his two shoulders. A mantle with bands of golden thread was around him. His shirt had trimmings of golden thread. On his breast was a brooch of gold, with the sheen of a precious stone therein. He carried two white silver spears and in them two smooth riveted shafts of bronze. Five circlets of gold adorned his neck, and he was girded with a golden-hilted sword with inlayings of silver and studs of gold.

The man said to her: "Is this the time that our lying with thee will be easy?"

"I have not made a tryst with thee, verily," said the woman. But they stretched themselves down together. The woman wept when the man would rise.

"Why weepest thou?" said he.

"I have two things for which I should lament," said the woman. "Parting from thee now that we have met. And the fair youths of the Tuatha De Danann have been entreating me in vain, and my desire is for thee since thou hast possessed me."

"Thy anxiety from these two things shall be taken away," said he. He drew his golden ring from his middle-finger, and put it into her hand, and told her that she should not part with it, by sale or by gift, save to one whose finger it should fit.

"I have another sorrow," said the woman. "I know not who hath come to me."

"Thou shall not be ignorant of that," said he. "Elotha son of Delbaeth, king of the Fomorians, hath come to thee. And of our meeting thou shalt bear a son, and no name shall be given him save Eochaid Bres, that is Eochaid the beautiful; for every beautiful thing that is seen in Ireland, whether plain or fortress or ale or torch or woman or man or steed, will be judged in comparison with that boy, so that man say of it then 'it is a *bres*.'"

After that the man went back again by the way he had come, and the woman went to her house, and to her was given the famous conception.

She brought forth the boy, and he was named, as Elotha had said, Eochaid Bres. When a week after the woman's lying-in was complete the boy had a fortnight's growth; and he maintained that increase till the end of his first seven years, when he reached a growth of fourteen years. Because of the contest which took place among the Tuatha De the sovereignty of Ireland was given to the boy; and he gave seven hostages to Ireland's champions, that is, to her chiefs, to guarantee the restoring of the sovereignty if his own misdeeds should give cause. His mother afterwards bestowed land upon him, and on the land he had a stronghold built, called Dun Brese; and it was the Dagda that built that fortress.

Now when Bres had assumed the kingship, the Fomorians, —Indech son of Dea Domnann, and Elotha son of Delbaeth, and Tethra, three Fomorian kings, laid tribute upon Ireland so that there was not a smoke from a roof in Ireland that was not under tribute to them. The champions were also reduced to their service; to wit, Ogma had to carry a bundle of firewood, and the Dagda became a rath-builder, and had to dig the trenches about Rath Brese.

The Dagda became weary of the work, and he used to meet in the house an idle blind man named Cridenbel, whose mouth was out of his breast. Cridenbel thought his own ration small and the Dagda's large. Whereupon he said: "O Dagda! Of thy honor let the three best bits of thy ration be given to me!" So the Dagda used to give them to him every night. Large, however, were the lampooner's bits, the size of a good pig. But those three bits were a third of the Dagda's ration. The Dagda's health was the worse for that.

One day, then, as the Dagda was in the trench digging a rath, he saw the Mac Oc coming to him. "That is good, O Dagda," says the Mac Oc.

"Even so," said the Dagda.

"What makes thee look so ill?" said the Mac Oc.

"I have cause for it," said the Dagda, "every evening Cridenbel the lampooner demands the three best bits of my portion."

"I have counsel for thee," said the Mac Oc. He put his hand into his purse, took out three crowns of gold, and gave them to him.

"Put these three gold pieces into the three bits which thou givest at close of day to Crindenbel," said the Mac Oc. "These bits will then be the goodliest on thy dish; and the gold will turn in his belly so that he will die thereof, and the judgment of Bres thereon will be wrong. Men will say to the king; 'The Dagda has killed Cridenbel by means of a deadly herb which he gave him.' Then the king will order thee to be slain. But thou shalt say to him: 'What thou utterest, O king of the warriors of the Fene, is not a prince's truth. For I was watched by Cridenbel when I was at my work, and he used to say to me "Give me, O Dagda, the three best bits of thy portion. Bad is my housekeeping tonight." So I should have perished thereby had not the three gold coins which I found today helped me. I put them in my ration. I then gave it to Cridenbel, for the gold was the best thing that was before me. Hence, then, the gold is inside Cridenbel, and he died of it.'" The Dagda followed this advice, and was called before the king.

"It is clear", said the king. "Let the lampooner's belly be cut open to know if the gold be found therein. If it be not found, thou shalt die. If, however, it be found, thou shalt have life."

After that they cut open the lampooner's belly, and the three coins of gold were found in his stomach, so the Dagda was saved. Then the Dagda went to his work on the following morning, and to him came the Mac Oc and said: "Thou wilt soon finish thy work, but thou shalt not seek reward till the cattle of Ireland are brought to thee, and of them choose a heifer black-maned."

Thereafter the Dada brought his work to an end, and Bres asked him what he would take as a reward for his labor. The Dagda answered: "I charge thee," said he, "to gather the cattle of Ireland into one place." The king did this as the Dagda asked, and the Dagda chose of them the heifer which Mac Oc had told him to choose. That seemed weakness to Bres: he thought that the Dagda would have chosen somewhat more.

Now Nuada was in his sickness, and Diancecht put on him a hand of silver with the motion of every hand therein. That seemed evil to his son Miach. Miach went to the hand which had been replaced by Diancecht, and he said "joint to joint of it and sinew to sinew," and he healed Nuada in thrice three days and nights. The first seventy-two hours he put it against his side, and it became covered with skin. The second seventy-two hours he put it on his breast. . . . That cure seemed evil to Diancecht. He flung a sword on the crown of his son's head and cut the skin down to the flesh. The lad healed the wound by means of his skill. Diancecht smote him again and cut the flesh till he reached the bone. The lad healed this by the same means. He struck him a third blow and came to the membrane of his brain. The lad healed this also by the same means. Then he struck the fourth blow and cut out the brain, so that Miach died, and Diancecht said that the leech himself could not heal him of that blow.

Thereafter Miach was buried by Diancecht and herbs three hundred and sixty-five, according to the number of his joints and sinews, grew through the grave. Then Airmed opened her mantle and separated those herbs according to their properties. But Diancecht came to her, and he confused the herbs, so that no one knows their proper cures unless the Holy Spirit should teach them afterwards. And Diancecht said "If Miach be not, Airmed shall remain."

So Bres held the sovereignty as it had been conferred upon him. But the chiefs of the Tuatha De murmured greatly against him, for their knives were not greased by him, and however often they visited him their breaths did not smell of ale. Moreover, they saw not their poets nor their bards nor their lampooners nor their harpers nor their pipers nor their jugglers nor their fools amusing them in the household. They did not go to the contests of their athletes. They saw not their champions proving their prowess at the king's court, save only one man, Ogma son of Ethliu. This was the duty which he had, to bring fuel to the fortress. He used to carry a bundle every day from Clew Bay islands. And because he was weak from want of food, the sea would sweep away from him two thirds of his bundle. So he could only carry one third, and yet he had to supply the host from day to day. Neither service nor taxes were paid by the tribes, and the treasures of the tribe were not delivered by the act of the whole tribe.

Once upon a time there came a-guesting to Bres's house, Cairbre son of Etain, poet of the Tuatha De. He entered a cabin narrow, black, dark, wherein there was neither fire nor furniture nor bed. Three small cakes, and they dry, were brought to him on a little dish. On the morrow he arose and he was not thankful. As he went across the enclosure, he said:

> Without food quickly on a dish:
> Without a cow's milk whereon a calf grows;
> Without a man's abode in the gloom of night:
> Without paying a company of story-tellers, let that be Bres's condition.
> Let there be no increase in Bres.

Now that was true. Nought save decay was on Bres from that hour. That is the first satire that was ever made in Ireland.

Now after that the Tuatha De went together to have speech with their fosterson, Bres son of Elotha, and demanded of him their sureties. He gave them the restitution of the realm, and he was not well pleased with them for that. He begged to be allowed to remain till the end of seven years. "That shall be granted," said the same assembly; "but thou shalt remain on the same security. Every fruit that comes to thy hand, both house and land and gold and silver, cows and food, and freedom from rent and taxes until then."

"Ye shall have as ye say," said Bres.

This is why they were asked for the delay: that he might gather the champions of the fairy-mound, the Fomorians, to seize the tribes by force. Grievous to him seemed his expulsion from his kingdom.

Then he went to his mother and asked her whence was his race. "I am certain of that," said she; and she went on to the hill hence she had seen the vessel of silver in the sea. She then went down to the strand, and gave him the ring which had been left with her for him, and he put I round his middle-finger, and it fitted him. For the sake of no one had she formerly given it up, either by sale or gift. Until that day there was none whom it suited.

Then they went forward till they reached the land of the Fomorians. They came to a great plain with many assemblies therein. They advanced to the fairest of these assemblies. Tidings were demanded of them there. They replied that they were of the men of Ireland. They were then asked whether they had hounds; for at that time it was the custom, when a body of men went to an assembly, to challenge them to a friendly contest. "We have hounds," said Bres. Then the hounds had a coursing-match, and the hounds of the Tuatha De were swifter than the hounds of the Fomorians. Then they were asked whether they had steeds for a horse-race. They answered, "We have;" and their steeds were swifter than the steeds of the Fomorians. They were then asked whether they had any one who was good at sword-play. None was found save Bres alone. So when he set his hand to the sword, his father recognized the ring on his finger and inquired who was the hero. His mother answered on his behalf and told the king that Bres was as son of his. Then she related to him the whole story even as we have recounted it.

His father was sorrowful over him. Said the father: "What need has brought thee out of the land wherein thou didst rule?"

Bres replied: "Nothing has brought me save my own injustice and arrogance. I stript them of their jewels and treasures and their own food. Neither tribute nor taxes had been taken from them up to that time."

"That is bad," said the father. "Better were their prosperity than their kingship. Better their prayers than their curses. Why hast thou come hither?"

"I have come to ask you for champions," said he. "I would take that land by force."

"Thou shouldst not gain it by injustice if thou didst not gain it by justice," said the father.

"Then what counsel hast thou for me?" said Bres.

Thereafter he sent Bres to the champion, to Balor grandson of Net, the king of the Isles, and to Indech son of Dea Domnann the king of the Fomorians; and these assembled all the troops from Lochlann westwards unto Ireland, to impose their tribute and their rule by force on the Tuatha De, so that they made one bridge of vessels from the Foreigner's Isles to Erin. Never came to Ireland an army more horrible or fearful than that host of the Fomorians. Men from Scythia of Lochlann and men out of the Western Isles were rivals in that expedition.

Now as to the Tuatha De, this is what they were doing. After Bres, Nuada was again in sovereignty over the Tuatha De. At that time he held a mighty feast at Tara for them. Now there was a certain warrior on his way to Tara, whose name was Lug Samildanach. And there were then two doorkeepers at Tara, namely Gamal son of Figal and Camall son of Riagall. When one of these was on duty he saw a strange company coming towards him. A young warrior fair and shapely, with a king's trappings, was in the forefront of that band. They told the doorkeeper to announce their arrival at Tara. The doorkeeper asked: "Who is there?"

"Here there is Lug Lamfada (i.e. Lugh Long-Arm) son of Cian son of Diancecht and of Ethne daughter of Balor. Fosterson, he, of Tailltiu daughter of Magmor king of Spain and of Eochaid the Rough son of Duach."

The doorkeeper asked of Lug Samildanach: "What art dost thou practice?" said he; "for no one without an art enters Tara."

"Question me," said he; "I am a wright."

The doorkeeper answered: "We need thee not. We have a wright already, even Luchta son of Luachaid."

He said: "Question me, O doorkeeper! I am a smith."

The doorkeeper answered him: "We have a smith already, Colum Cualleinech of the three new processes."

He said: "Question me: I am a champion."

The doorkeeper answered: "We need thee not. We have a champion already, Ogma son of Ethliu."

He said again: "Question me: I am a harper."

"We need thee not. We have a harper already, Abcan son of Bicelmos whom the Tuatha De Danann chose in the fairy-mounds."

Said he: "Question me: I am a hero."

The doorkeeper answered: "We need thee not. We have a hero already, even Bresal Etarlam son of Eochaid Baethlam."

Then he said: "Question me, O doorkeeper! I am a poet and I am a historian."

"We need thee not. We have already a poet and historian, even En son of Ethaman."

He said, "Question me: I am a sorcerer."

"We need thee not. We have sorcerers already. Many are our wizards and our folk of might."

He said: "Question me; I am a leech."

"We need thee not. We have for a leech Diancecht."

"Question me," said he; "I am a cupbearer."

"We need thee not. We have cupbearers already, even Delt and Drucht and Daithe, Tae and Talom and Trog, Glei and Glan and Glesi."

He said: "Question me: I am a good brazier."

"We need thee not. We have a brazier already, Credne Cerd."

He said again, "Ask the king," said he, "whether he has a single man who possesses all these arts, and if he has I will not enter Tara."

Then the doorkeeper went into the palace and declared all to the king. "A warrior has come before the enclosure," said he. "His name is Samildanach (many-gifted), and all the arts which thy household practice he himself possesses, so that he is the man of each and every art."

The king said then that the chess-boards of Tara should be taken to Samildanach, and he won all the stakes, so that then he made the *Cro* of Lug. (But if chess was invented at the epoch of the Trojan war, it had not reached Ireland then, for the battle of Moytura and the destruction of Troy occurred at the same time.)

Then that was related to Nuada. "Let him into the enclosure," says he; "for never before has man like him entered this fortress."

Then the doorkeeper let Lug pass him, and he entered the fortress and sat down in the sage's seat, for he was a sage in every art.

Then the great flag-stone, to move which required the effort of four-score yoke of oxen, Ogma hurled through the house, so that it lay on the outside of Tara. This was a challenge to Lug. But Lug cast it back, so that it lay in the center of the palace and made it whole.

"Let a harp be played for us," said the company. So the warrior played a sleep-strain for the hosts and for the king the first night. He cast them into sleep from that hour to the same time on the following day. He played a wail-strain, so that they were crying and lamenting. He played a laugh-strain, so that they were in merriment and joyance.

Now Nuada, when he beheld the warrior's many powers, considered whether Samildanach could put away from them the bondage which they suffered from the Fomorians. So they held a council concerning the warrior. The decision to which Nuada came was to change seats with the warrior. So Samildanach went to the king's seat, and the king rose up before him till thirteen days had ended. Then on the morrow he met with the two brothers, Dagda and Ogma, on Grellach Dollaid. And his brothers Goibniu and Diancecht were summoned to them. A full year were they in that secret converse, wherefore Grellach Dollaid is called Amrun of the Tuatha De Danann.

Thereafter the wizards of Ireland were summoned to them, and their medical men and charioteers and smiths and farmers and lawyers. They held speech with them in secret. Then Nuada inquired of the sorcerer whose name was Mathgen what power he could wield? He answered that through his contrivance he would cast the mountains of Ireland on the Fomorians, and roll their summits against the ground. And he declared to them that the twelve chief mountains of the land of Erin would support the Tuatha De Danann, in battling for them, to wit, Sliab League, and Denna Ulad and the Mourne Mountains, and Bri Ruri and Sliab Bladma and Sliab Snechtai, Sliab Mis and Blai-sliab and Nevin and Sliab Maccu Belgadan and Segais and Cruachan Aigle.

Then he asked the cupbearer what power he could yield. He answered that he would bring the twelve chief lochs of Ireland before the Fomorians, and that they would not find water therein, whatever thirst might seize them. These are those lochs: Dergloch, Loch Luimnigh, Loch Corrib, Loch Ree, Loch Mask, Strangford Loch, Belfast Loch, Loch Neagh, Loch Foyle, Loch Gara, Loch Reag, Marloch. They would betake themselves to the twelve chief rivers of Ireland – Bush, Boyne, Baa, Nem, Lee, Shannon, Moy, Sligo, Erne, Finn, Liffey, Suir; and they will all be hidden from the Fomorians, so that they will not find a drop therein. Drink shall be provided for the men of Ireland, though they bide in the battle to the end of seven years.

Then said Figol son of Mamos, their druid: "I will cause three showers of fire to pour on the faces of the Fomorian host, and I will take out of them two thirds of their valor and their bravery and their strength, and I will bind their urine in their own bodies and in the bodies of their horses. Every breath that the men of Ireland shall exhale will be an increase in valor and bravery and strength to them. Though they bide in the battle till the end of seven years, they will not be weary in any wise."

Said the Dagda: "The power such ye boast I shall wield it all by myself." "It is thou art the Dagda (good hand), with everyone:" wherefore thenceforward the name "Dagda" adhered to him. Then they separated from the council, agreeing to meet again that day three years.

Now when the provision of the battle had been settled, Lug and Dagda and Ogma went to the three Gods of Danu, and these gave Lug the plan of the battle; and for seven years they were preparing for it and making their weapons.

The Dagda had a house in Glenn Etin in the north, and he had to meet a woman in Glenn Etin a year from that day, about Samain (Halloween) before the battle. The river Unius of Connacht roars to the south of it. He beheld the woman in Unius in Corann, washing herself, with one of her two feet at Allod Echae (i.e., Echumech), to the south of the water, and the other at Loscuinn, to the north of the water. Nine loosened tresses were on her head. The Dagda conversed with her, and they made a union. "The Bed of the Couple" is the name of the place thenceforward. The woman that is here mentioned is the Morrigu. Then she told the Dagda that the Fomorians would land at Mag Scetne, and that he should summon Erin's men of art to meet her at the Ford of Unius, and that she would go into Scetne to destroy Indech son of Dea Domnann, the king of the Fomorians, and would deprive him of the blood of his heart and the kidneys of his valor. Afterwards she gave two handfuls of that blood to the hosts that were waiting at the Ford of Unius. "Ford of Destruction" became its name, because of that destruction of the king. Then that was done by the wizards, and they chanted spells on the hosts of the Fomorians.

This was a week before Samain, and each of them separated from the other until all the men of Ireland came together on Samain. Six times thirty hundred was their number, that is, twice thirty hundred in every third.

Then Lug sent the Dagda to spy out the Fomorians and to delay them until the men of Ireland should come to the battle. So the Dagda went to the camp of the Fomorians and asked them for a truce of battle. This was granted to him as he asked. Porridge was then made for him by the Fomorians, and this was done to mock him, for great was his love for porridge. They filled for him the king's cauldron, five fists deep, into which went four-score gallons of new milk and the like quantity of meal and fat. Goats and sheep and swine were put into it, and they were all boiled together with the porridge. The were spilt for him into a hole in the ground, and Indech told him that he would be put to death unless he consumed it all; he should eat his fill so that he might not reproach the Fomorians with inhospitality.

Then the Dagda took his ladle, and it was big enough for a man and woman to lie on the middle of it. These then were the bits that were in it, halves of salted swine and a quarter of lard. "Good food this," said the Dagda. . . .

At the end of the meal he put his curved finger over the bottom of the hole on mold and gravel. Sleep came upon him then after eating his porridge. Bigger than a house-cauldron was his belly, and the Fomorians laughed at it. Then he went away from them to the strand of Eba. Not easy was it for the hero to move along owing to the bigness of his belly. Unseemly was his apparel. A cape to the hollow of his two elbows. A dun tunic around him, as far as the swelling of his rump. It was, moreover, long breasted, with a hole in the peak. Two brogues on him of horse-hide, with the hair outside. Behind him a wheeled fork to carry which required the effort of eight men, so that its track after him was enough for the boundary-ditch of a province. Wherefore it is called "The Track of the Dagda's Club"

Then the Fomorians marched till they reached Scente. The men of Ireland were in Mag Aurfolaig. These two hosts were threatening battle. "The men of Ireland venture to offer battle to us," said Bres son of Elotha to Indech son of Dea Domnann. "I will fight anon," said Indech, "so that their bones will be small unless they pay their tributes."

Because of Lug's knowledge the men of Ireland had made a resolution not to let him go into battle. So his nine fosterers were left to protect him, Tollus-dam and Ech-dam and Eru, Rechtaid the white and Fosad and Fedlimid, Ibor and Scibar and Minn. They feared an early death for the hero owing to the multitude of his arts. Therefore they did not let him forth to the fight.

The chiefs of the Tuatha De Danann were gathered round Lug. And he asked his smith, Goibniu, what power he wielded for them? "Not hard to tell," said he. "Though the men of Erin bide in the battle to the end of seven years, for every spear that parts from its shaft, or sword that shall break therein, I will provide a new weapon in its place. No spear-point which my hand shall forge," said he, "shall make a missing cast. No skin which it pierces shall taste life afterwards. That has not been done by Dolb the smith of the Fomorians."

"And thou, O Diancecht," said Lug, "what power canst thou wield?"

"Not hard to tell, "said he. "Every man who shall be wounded there, unless his head be cut off, or the membrane of his brain or his spinal marrow be severed, I will make quite whole in the battle on the morrow."

"And thou, O Credne," said Lug to his brazier, "what is thy power in the battle?"

"Not hard to tell," said Credne. "Rivets for their spears, and hilts for their swords, and bosses and rims for their shields, I will supply them all."

"And thou, O Luchta," said Lug to his wright, "what service wilt thou render in the battle?"

"Not hard to tell, said Luchta. "All the shields and javelin-shafts they require, I will supply them all."

"And thou, O Ogma," said Lug to his champion, "what is thy power in the battle?"

"Not hard to tell," said he. "I will repel the king and three enneads of his friends, and capture up to a third of his men." . . .

"And ye, O sorcerers," said Lug, "what power will you wield?"

"Not hard to tell," said the sorcerers. "We shall fill them with fear when they have been overthrown by our craft, till their heroes are slain, and deprive them of two thirds of their might, with constraint on their urine."

"And ye, O cupbearers," said Lug, "what power?"

"Not hard to tell, "said the cupbearers. "We will bring a strong thirst upon them, and they shall not find drink to quench it."

"And ye, O druids," said Lug, "what power?"

"Not hard to tell," said the druids. "We will bring showers of fire on the faces of the Fomorians, so that they cannot look upwards, and so that the warriors who are contending with them may slay them by their might."

"And thou, O Cairbre son of Etain," said Lug to his poet, "what power canst thou wield in the battle?"

"Not hard to tell," said Cairbre. "I will make a satire on them. And I will satirize them and shame them, so that through the spell of my art they will not resist warriors."

"And ye, O Be-culle and O Dianann," said Lug to his two witches, "what power can ye wield in the battle?"

"Not hard to tell," said they. "We will enchant the trees and the stones and the sods of the earth, so that they shall become a host under arms against them, and shall rout them in flight with horror and trembling."

"And thou, O Dagda," said Lug, "what power canst thou wield on the Fomorian host in the battle?"

"Not hard to tell," said the Dagda. "I will take the side of the men of Erin both in mutual smiting and destruction and wizardry. Under my club the bones of the Fomorians will be as many as hailstones under the feet of herds of horses where you meet on the battlefield of Moytura."

So thus Lug spoke with every one of them in turn; and he strengthened and addressed his army, so that each man of them had the spirit of a king or a mighty lord. Now everyday a battle was fought between the tribe of the Fomorians and the Tuatha De, save only that kings or princes were not delivering it, but only keen and haughty folk.

Now the Fomorians marveled at a certain thing which was revealed to them in the battle. Their spears and their swords were blunted and broken and such of their men as were slain did not return on the morrow. But it was not so with the Tuatha De. For though their weapons were blunted and broken today, they were renewed on the morrow, because Goibniu he smith was in the forge making swords and spears and javelins. For he would make those weapons by three turns. Then Luchta the wright would make the spearshafts by three chippings, and the third chipping was a finish and would set them in the ring of the spear. When the spearheads were stuck in the side of the forge he would throw the rings with the shafts, and it was needless to set them again. Then Credne the brazier would make the rivets by three turns, and would cast the rings of the spears to them; and thus they used to cleave together.

This then is what used to put fire into the warriors who were slain, so that they were swifter on the morrow. Because Diancecht and his two sons, Octriuil and Miach, and his daughter Airmed sang spells over the well named Slane. Now their mortally wounded men were cast into it as soon as they were slain. They were alive when they came out. Their mortally wounded became whole through the might of the incantation of the four leeches who were about the well. Now that was harmful to the Fomorians, so they sent a man of them to spy out the battle and the actions of the Tuatha De, namely Ruadan son of Bres and of Brig the Dagda's daughter. For he was a son and a grandson of the Tuatha De. Then he related to the Fomorians the work of the smith and the wright and the brazier and the four leeches who were around the well. He was sent again to kill one of the artisans, that is Goibniu. From him he begged a spear, its rivets from the brazier and its shaft from the wright. So all was given to him as he asked. There was a woman there grinding the weapons, Cron mother of Fianlug; she it is that ground Ruadan's spear. Now the spear was given to Ruadan by a chief, wherefore the name "a chief's spear" is still given to weavers' beams in Erin.

Now after the spear had been given to him, Ruadan turned and wounded Goibniu. But Goibnui plucked out the spear and cast it at Ruadan, so that it went through him, and he died in the presence of his father in the assembly of the Fomorians. The Brig came and bewailed her son. She shrieked at first, she cried at last. So that then for the first time crying and shrieking were heard in Erin. Now it was that Brig who invented a whistle for signalling at night.

Then Goibniu into the well, and he became whole. There was a warrior with the Fomorians, Octriallach son of Indech son of Dea Domnann, son of the Fomorian king. He told the Fomorians that each man of them should bring a stone of the stones of Drowes to cast into the well of Slane in Achad Abla to the west of Moytura, to the east of Loch Arboch. So they went, and a stone for each man was cast into the well. Wherefore the cairn thus made is called Octriallach's Cairn. But another name for that well is Loch Luibe, for Diancecht put into it one of every herb (*lub*) that grew in Erin.

Now when the great battle came, the Fomorians marched out of their camp, and formed themselves into strong battalions. Not a chief nor man of prowess of them was without a hauberk against his skin, a helmet on his head, a broad spear in his right hand, a heavy sharp sword on his belt, a firm shield on his shoulder. To attack the Fomorian host on that day was "striking a head against a cliff," was " a hand in a serpent's nest," was "a face up to fire." These were the kings and chiefs that were heartening the host of the Fomorians, namely, Balor son of Dot son of Net, Bres son of Elotha, Tuiri Tortbuillech son of Lobos, Goll and Irgoll Loscennlomm son of Lommglunech, Indech son of Dea Domnann the king of the Fomorians, Octriallach son of Indech, Omna and Bagna, Elotha son of Delbaeth.

On the other side the Tuatha De Danann arose and left their nine comrades keeping Lug, and they marched to the battle. When the battle began, Lug escaped from his guardians with his charioteer, so that it was he who was in front of the hosts of the Tuatha De. Then a keen and cruel battle was fought between the tribe of the Fomorians and the men of Ireland. Lug was heartening the men of Ireland that they should fight the battle fervently, so that they should not be any longer in bondage. For it was better for them to find death in protecting their fatherland than to bide under bondage and tribute as they had been. . . .

The hosts uttered a great shout as they entered the battle. Then they came together and each of them began to smite the other. Many fine men fell there. Great the slaughter and the grave-lying that was there. Pride and shame were there side by side. There was anger and indignation. Abundant was the stream of blood there over the white skin of young warriors mangled by the hands of eager men. Harsh was the noise of the heroes and the champions mutually fending their spears and their shields and their bodies when the others were smiting them with spears and with swords. Harsh, moreover, was the thunder that was there throughout the battle, the shouting of the warriors and the clashing of the shields, the flashing and whistling of the glaives and the ivory-hilted swords, the rattling and jingling of the quivers, the sound and winging of the darts and the javelins, and the crashing of the weapons. The ends of their fingers and of their feet almost met in the mutual blows, and owing to the slipperiness of the blood under the feet of the soldiers, they would fall from their upright posture and beat their heads together as they sat. The battle was a gory, ghastly melee, and the river Unsenn rushed with corpses.

Then Nuada Silver-Hand and Macha, daughter of Ernmass, fell by Balor grandson of Net. And Cassmael fell by Octriallach son of Indech. Lug and Balor of the Piercing Eye met in the battle. An evil eye had Balor the Fomorian. That eye was never opened save only on a battlefield. Four men used to lift up the lid of the eye with a polished handle which passed through its lid. If an army looked at the eye, though they were many thousands in number they could not resist a few warriors. It had a poisonous power. Once when his father's druids were concocting charms, he came and looked out of the window, and the fume of the concoction came under it, so that the poison of the concoction afterwards penetrated the eye that looked. He and Lug met. "Lift up mine eyelid, my lad," said Balor, "that I may see the babbler who is conversing with me."

The lid was raised from Balor's eye. Then Lug cast a sling-stone at him, which carried the eye through his head while his own army looked on. And the sling-stone fell on the host of the Fomorians, and thrice nine of them died beside it, so that the crowns of their heads came against the breast of Indech son of Dea Domnann, and a gush of blood sprang over his lips. Said Indech: "Let Loch Half-green my poet be summoned to me!" Half-green was he from the ground to the crown of his head.

Loch went to the king. "Make known to me," said Indech, "who has flung this cast on me."

Then the Morrigu, daughter of Ernmass, came, and heartened the Tuatha De to fight the battle fiercely and fervently. Thereafter the battle became a rout, and the Fomorians were beaten back to the sea. The champion Ogma son of Ethliu, and Indech son of Dea Domnann the king of the Fomorians, fell in single combat. Loch Half-green besought Lug for quarter. "Give me my three wishes," said Lug.

"Thou shalt have them," said Loch. "Till Doom I will ward off from Ireland all plundering by the Fomorians, and, at the end of the world, every ailment." So Loch was spared. Then he sang to the Gael the "decree of fastening."

Loch said that he would bestow names on Lug's nine chariots because of the quarter that had been given him. So Lug told him to name them.

"What is the number of the slain?" said Lug to Loch.

"I know not the number of peasants and rabble. As to the number of Fomorian lords and nobles and champions and kings' sons and overkings I know, even five thousand three score and three men: two thousand and three fifties: four score thousand and nine times five: eight score and eight: four score and seven: four score and six: eight score and eight: four score and seven: four score and six: eight score and five: two and forty including Net's grandson. That is the number of the slain of the Fomorian overkings and high nobles who fell in the battle. Howbeit, as to the number of peasants and common people and rabble, and folk of every art besides who came in company with the great army – for every champion and every high chieftain and every overking of the Fomorians came with his host to the battle, so that all fell there, both his freemen and his slaves – we reckon only a few of the servants of the overkings. This then is the number that I have reckoned of these as I beheld: seven hundred, seven score and seven men . . . together with Sab Uanchennach son of Cairbre Colc, son was he of a servant of Indech son of Dea Domnann, that is a son of a servant of the Fomorian king. As to what fell besides of "half men" and of those who reached not the heart of the battle, these are in no wise numbered till we number stars of heaven, sand of sea, flakes of snow, dew on lawn, hailstones, grass under feet of herds, and Manannan mac Lir's horses (waves) in a sea storm."

Thereafter Lug and his comrades found Bres son of Elotha unguarded. He said: "It is better to give me quarter than to slay me."

"What then will follow from that?" said Lug

"If I be spared," says Bres, "the cows of Erin will always be in milk."

"I will set this forth to our wise men," said Lug.

So Lug went to Maeltne Mor-brethach , and said to him: "Shall Bres have quarter for giving constant milk to the cows of Erin?"

"He shall not have quarter," said Maeltne; "he has no power over their age or their offspring, though he can milk them so long as they are alive."

Lug said to Bres: "That does not save thee: thou hast no power over their age and their offspring, though thou canst milk them. Is there aught else that will save thee, O Bres?" said Lug.

"There is in truth. Tell thy lawyer that for sparing me the men of Ireland shall reap a harvest in every quarter of the year."

Said Lug to Maeltne: "Shall Bres be spared for giving the men of Ireland a harvest of corn every quarter?"

"This has suited us," said Maeltne: "the spring for ploughing and sowing, and the beginning of summer for the end of the strength of corn, and the beginning of autumn for the end of the ripeness of corn and for reaping it. Winter for consuming it."

"That does not rescue thee," said Lug to Bres; "but less than that rescues thee."

"What?" said Bres.

"How shall the men of Ireland plough? How shall they sow? How shall they reap? After making known these three things thou wilt be spared."

"Tell them," said Bres, "that their ploughing be on a Tuesday, their casting seed into the field be on a Tuesday, their reaping on a Tuesday." So through that stratagem Bres was let go free.

In that fight, then, Ogma the champion found Orna the sword of Tethra, a king of the Fomorians. Ogma unsheathed the sword and cleansed it. Then the sword related whatsoever had been done by it; for it was the custom of swords at that time, when unsheathed, to set forth the deeds that had been done by them. And therefore swords are entitled to the tribute of cleansing them after they have been unsheathed. Hence, also, charms are preserved in swords thenceforward. Now the reason why demons used to speak from weapons at that time was because weapons were worshipped by human beings at that epoch, and the weapons were among the safeguards of that time. . . .

Now Lug and the Dagda and Ogma pursued the Fomorians, for they had carried off the Dagda's harper, whose name was Uaitne. Then they reached the banqueting-house in which were Bres son of Elotha and Elotha son of Delbaeth. There hung the harp on the wall. That is the harp in which the Dagda had bound the melodies so that they sounded not until by his call he summoned them forth; when he said this below:

> Come Daurdabla!
> Come Coir-cethar-chuir!
> Come summer, Come winter!
> Mouths of harps and bags and pipes!

Now that harp had two names, Daur-da-bla "Oak of two greens" and Coir-cethar-chuir "Four-angled music."

Then the harp went forth from the wall, and killed nine men, and came to the Dagda. And he played for them the three things whereby harpers are distinguished, to wit, sleep-strain and smile-strain and wail-strain. He played wail-strain to them, so that their tearful women wept. He played smile-strain to them, so their women and children laughed. He played sleep-strain to them, and the company fell asleep. Through that sleep the three of them escaped unhurt from the Fomorians though these desired to slay them.

Then the Dagda brought with him the heifer which had been given to him for his labor. For when she called her calf all the cattle of Ireland which the Fomorians had taken as their tribute, grazed.

Now after the battle has won and corpses cleared away, the Morrigu, daughter of Ernmas, proceeded to proclaim that battle and the mighty victory which had taken place, to the royal heights of Ireland and to its fairy hosts and its chief waters and its river mouths. And hence it is that Badb (i.e., the Morrigu) also describes high deeds. "Hast thou any tale?" said everyone to her then. And she replied:

> Peace up to heaven
> Heaven down to earth,
> Earth under heaven,
> Strength in every one, etc.

Then, moreover, she was prophesying the end of the world, and foretelling every evil that would be therein, and every disease and every vengeance. Wherefore then she sang this lay below:

> I shall not see a world that will be dear to me.
> Summer without flowers,
> Kine will be without milk,
> Women without modesty,
> Men without valor,
> Captures without a king. . . .
> Woods without mast,
> Sea without produce. . . .
> Wrong judgments of old men,
> False precedents of lawyers,
> Every man a betrayer,
> Every boy a reaver.
> Son will enter his fathers bed,
> Father will enter his son's bed,
> Every one will be his brother's brother in law. . . .
> An evil time!
> Son will deceive his father,
> Daughter will deceive her mother.

5. FINNISH

Kalevala is now regarded as the Finnish national folk epic. The stories that make up what we know as *Kalevala* were collected from oral traditions and compiled into an epic poem by Dr. Elias Lönnrot. The first edition was published in Finnish in 1835 and an expanded edition, nearly twice as long, was issued in 1849. *Kalevala* was first translated into English by John Martin Crawford in 1888. A new translation was made by W. F. Kirby in 1907 for the Everyman series.

According to Humphrey Carpenter, Tolkien discovered *Kalevala*, in the Kirby translation, around 1911. A few years later, at Exeter College, he discovered a Finnish grammar, and the Finnish language was a strong influence on the language he began developing at this time. It would come to be known as Quenya, one form of Elvish. Tolkien soon afterwards read a paper to a college society on *Kalevala*, commenting that "these mythological ballads are full of that very primitive undergrowth that the literature of Europe has on the whole been steadily cutting and reducing for many centuries . . . I would that we had more of it left—something of the same sort that belonged to the English." (Carpenter, *Tolkien: A Biography*, p. 59.)

Around the same time Tolkien began to work on his first verse and prose epic, "The Story of Kullervo," retelling one story from *Kalevala*. He never finished it, but parts of the story of Kullervo, who unknowingly commits incest and kills himself on his own sword after he discovers what he has done, were soon to become the foundation of Tolkien's own story of Túrin Turambar, which began as part of his *Book of Lost Tales* ("Turambar and the Foalókë" in *The Book of Lost Tales, Part Two*) and evolved in various forms, including an abandoned alliterative poem, "The Lay of the Children of Húrin" (in *The Lays of Beleriand*), and the more extensive prose version

"Narn i Hîn Húrin: The Tale of the Children of Húrin" (in *Unfinished Tales*). The whole Túrin story is told in briefer form in chapter 21 ("Of Túrin Turambar") in *The Silmarillion*.

W. F. Kirby's translation of *Kalevala* follows the expanded 1849 edition, and contains fifty runos (or song sections). "The Story of Kullervo" (as selected here) is told in runos 31 through 36. Kirby's translation has been widely reprinted. Other recommended editions of the full work include the prose translation by Francis Peabody Magoun, Jr., which appeared in 1963 under the title *The Kalevala, or Poems of the Kaleva District*. More recently, a new verse translation by Keith Bosley was published, as *The Kalevala*, by Oxford University Press in 1989.

THE STORY OF KULLERVO

from *Kalevala: The Land of Heroes*, translated by W. F. Kirby (1907)

Untamo and Kullervo (Runo XXXI)

[Argument: Untamo wages war against his brother Kalervo, overthrows Kalervo and his army, sparing only a single pregnant woman of the whole clan. She is carried away to Untamo's people, and gives birth to her son Kullervo. Kullervo resolves in his cradle to take revenge on Untamo, and Untamo attempts several times to put him to death, but without success. When Kullervo grows up, he spoils all his work, and therefore Untamo sells him as a slave to Ilmarinen.]

'Twas a mother reared her chickens,
Large the flock of swans she nurtured;
By the hedge she placed the chickens,
Sent the swans into the river,
And an eagle came and scared them,
And a hawk that came dispersed them,
And a flying bird dispersed them.
One he carried to Carelia,
Into Russia bore the second,
In its home he left the third one.

 Whom the bird to Russia carried
Soon grew up into a merchant;
Whom he carried to Carelia,
Kalervo was called by others,
While the third at home remaining,
Bore the name of Untamoinen,
For his father's lifelong anguish,
And his mother's deep affliction.

 Untamoinen laid his netting
Down in Kalervo's fish-waters:
Kalervoinen saw the netting,

337

In his bag he put the fishes.
Untamo of hasty temper
Then became both vexed and angry,
And his fingers turned to battle,
With his open palms he urged it,
Making strife for fishes' entrails,
And for perch-fry made a quarrel
    Thus they fought and thus contended,
Neither overcame the other,
And though one might smite the other,
He himself again was smitten.
    At another time it happened,
On the next and third day after,
Kalervoinen oats was sowing,
Back of Untamoinen's dwelling.
    Sheep of Untamo most reckless
Browsed the oats of Kalervoinen,
Whereupon his dog ferocious
Tore the sheep of Untamoinen.
    Untamo began to threaten
Kalervo, his very brother;
Kalervo's race vowed to slaughter,
Smite the great, and smite the little,
And to fall on all the people,
And their houses burn to ashes.
    Men with swords in belt he mustered,
Weapons for their hands provided,
Little boys with spears in girdle,
Handsome youths who shouldered axes,
And he marched to furious battle,
Thus to fight his very brother.
    Kalervoinen's son's fair consort
Then was sitting near the window,
And she looked from out the window,
And she spoke the words which follow:
"Is it smoke I see arising,
Or a gloomy cloud that rises,
On the borders of the cornfields,
Just beyond the new-made pathway?"
    But no dark cloud there was rising,
Nor was smoke ascending thickly,
But 'twas Untamo's assemblage
Marching onward to the battle.

On came Untamo's assemblage,
In their belts their swords were hanging,
Kalervo's folk overwhelming,
And his mighty race they slaughtered,
And they burned his house to ashes,
Like a level field they made it.
    Left of Kalervo's folk only
But one girl, and she was pregnant;
Then did Untamo's assemblage
Lead her homeward on their journey,
That she there might sweep the chamber,
And the floor might sweep from litter.
    But a little time passed over,
When a little boy was born her,
From a most unhappy mother,
So by what name should they call him?
Kullervo his mother called him,
Untamo, the Battle-hero.
    Then the little boy they swaddled,
And the orphan child they rested
In the cradle made for rocking,
That it might be rocked to lull him.
    So they rocked the child in cradle,
Rocked it till his hair was tossing,
Rocked him for one day, a second,
Rocked him on the third day likewise,
When the boy began his kicking,
And he kicked and pushed about him,
Tore his swaddling clothes to pieces,
Freed himself from all his clothing,
Then he broke the lime-wood cradle,
All his rags he tore from off him.
    And it seemed that he would prosper,
And become a man of mettle.
Untamola thought already
That when he was grown to manhood,
He would grow both wise and mighty,
And become a famous hero,
As a servant worth a hundred;
Equal to a thousand servants.
Thus he grew for two and three months,
But already in the third month,
When a boy no more than knee-high,

He began to speak in thiswise:
"Presently when I am bigger,
And my body shall be stronger,
I'll avenge my father's slaughter,
And my mother's tears atone for."
    This was heard by Untamoinen,
And he spoke the words which follow:
"He will bring my race to ruin,
Kalervo reborn is in him."
Thereupon the heroes pondered
And the old crones all considered
How to bring the boy to ruin,
So that death might come upon him.
    Then they put him in a barrel,
In a barrel did they thrust him,
And they pushed it to the water,
Pushed it out upon the billows.
    Then they went, to look about them,
After two nights, after three nights,
If the boy had sunk in water,
Or had perished in the barrel.
    In the waves he was not sunken,
Nor had perished in the barrel,
He had 'scaped from out the barrel,
And upon the waves was sitting,
In his hand a rod of copper,
At the end a line all silken,
And for lake-fish he was fishing,
As he floated on the water.
There was water in the lakelet,
Which perchance might fill two ladles,
Or if more exactly measured,
Partly was a third filled also.
    Untamo again reflected,
"How can we o'ercome the infant,
That destruction come upon him,
And that death may overtake him?"
    Then he bade his servants gather
First a large supply of birch-trees,
Pine-trees with their hundred needles,
Trees from which the pitch was oozing,
For the burning of the infant,
And for Kullervo's destruction.

So they gathered and collected
First a large supply of birch-trees,
Pine-trees with their hundred needles,
Trees from which the pitch was oozing,
And of bark a thousand sledgefuls,
Ash-trees, long a hundred fathoms.
Fire beneath the wood they kindled,
And the pyre began to crackle,
And the boy they cast upon it,
'Mid the glowing fire they cast him.
Burned the fire a day, a second,
Burning likewise on the third day,
When they went to look about them.
Knee-deep sat the boy in ashes,
In the embers to his elbows.
In his hand he held the coal-rake,
And was stirring up the fire,
And he raked the coals together.
Not a hair was singed upon him,
Not a lock was even tangled.
    Then did Untamo grow angry.
"Where then can I place the infant,
That we bring him to destruction,
And that death may overtake him?"
So upon a tree they hanged him,
Strung him up upon an oak-tree.
    Two nights and a third passed over,
And upon the dawn thereafter,
Untamo again reflected:
"Time it is to look around us,
Whether Kullervo has fallen,
Or is dead upon the gallows."
    Then he sent a servant forward,
Back he came, and thus reported:
"Kullervo not yet has perished,
Nor has died upon the gallows.
Pictures on the tree he's carving,
In his hands he holds a graver.
All the tree is filled with pictures,
All the oak-tree filled with carvings;
Here are men, and here are sword-blades,
And the spears are leaning by them."
    Where should Untamo seek aidance,

'Gainst this boy, the most unhappy?
Whatsoever deaths he planned him,
Or he planned for his destruction,
In the jaws of death he fell not,
Nor could he be brought to ruin.
  And at length he grew full weary
Of his efforts to destroy him,
So he reared up Kullervoinen
As a slave beneath his orders.
  Thereupon said Untamoinen,
And he spoke the words which follow:
"If you live as it is fitting,
Always acting as is proper,
In my house I will retain you,
And the work of servants give you.
I will pay you wages for it,
As I think that you deserve it,
For your waist a pretty girdle,
Or upon your ear a buffet."
  So when Kullervo was taller,
And had grown about a span-length,
Then he found some work to give him,
That he should prepare to labor.
'Twas to rock a little infant,
Rock a child with little fingers.
"Watch with every care the infant,
Give it food, and eat some also,
Wash his napkins in the river,
Wash his little clothes and cleanse them."
  So he watched one day, a second,
Broke his hands, and gouged his eyes out,
And at length upon the third day,
Let the infant die of sickness,
Cast the napkins in the river,
And he burned the baby's cradle.
  Untamo thereon reflected,
"Such a one is quite unfitted
To attend to little children,
Rock the babes with little fingers.
Now I know not where to send him,
Nor what work I ought to give him.
Perhaps he ought to clear the forest?"
So he went to clear the forest.

Kullervo, Kalervo's offspring,
Answered in the words which follow:
"Now I first a man can deem me,
When my hands the axe are wielding.
I am handsomer to gaze on,
Far more noble than aforetime,
Five men's strength I feel within me
And I equal six in valor."
Then he went into the smithy,
And he spoke the words which follow:
"O thou smith, my dearest brother,
Forge me now a little hatchet,
Such an axe as fits a hero,
Iron tool for skilful workman,
For I go to clear the forest,
And to fell the slender birch-trees."
So the smith forged what he needed,
And an axe he forged him quickly;
Such an axe as fits a hero,
Iron tool for skilful workman.
Kullervo, Kalervo's offspring,
Set to work the axe to sharpen,
And he ground it in the daytime,
And at evening made a handle.
Then he went into the forest,
High upon the wooded mountains,
There to seek the best of planking,
And to seek the best of timber.
With his axe he smote the tree-trunks,
With the blade of steel he felled them,
At a stroke the best he severed,
And the bad ones at a half-stroke.
Five large, trees at length had fallen,
Eight in all he felled before him,
And he spoke the words which follow,
And in words like these expressed him:
"Lempo may the work accomplish,
Hiisi now may shape the timber!"
In a stump he struck his axe-blade,
And began to shout full loudly,
And he piped, and then he whistled,
And he said the words which follow:
"Let the wood be felled around me,

Overthrown the slender birch-trees,
Far as sounds my voice resounding,
Far as I can send my whistle.
   "Let no sapling here be growing, ·
Let no blade of grass be standing,
Never while the earth endureth,
Or the golden moon is shining,
Here in Kalervo's son's forest,
Here upon the good man's clearing.
   "If the seed on earth has fallen,
And the young corn should shoot upward,
If the sprout should be developed,
And the stalk should form upon it,
May it never come to earing,
Or the stalk-end be developed."
   Then the mighty Untamoinen,
Wandered forth to gaze about him,
Learn how Kalervo's son cleared it,
And the new slave made a clearing.
But he found not any clearing,
And the young man had not cleared it.
   Untamo thereon reflected,
"For such labor he's unsuited,
He has spoiled the best of timber,
And has felled the best for planking.
Now I know not where to send him,
Nor what work I ought to give him.
Should I let him make a fencing?"
So he went to make a fencing.
   Kullervo, Kalervo's offspring,
Set himself to make a fencing,
And for this he took whole pine-trees,
And he used them for the fence-stakes,
Took whole fir-trees from the forest,
Wattled them to make the fencing,
Bound the branches fast together
With the largest mountain-ashtrees;
But he made the fence continuous,
And he made no gateway through it,
And he spoke the words which follow,
And in words like these expressed him:
"He who cannot raise him birdlike,
Nor upon two wings can hover,

344

Never may he pass across it,
Over Kalervo's son's fencing!"
    Then did Untamo determine
Forth to go and gaze around him,
Viewing Kalervo's son's fencing
By the slave of war constructed.
    Stood the fence without an opening
Neither gap nor crevice through it,
On the solid earth it rested,
Up among the clouds it towered.
    Then he spoke the words which follow:
"For such labor he's unsuited.
Here's the fence without an opening,
And without a gateway through it.
Up to heaven the fence is builded,
To the very clouds uprising;
None can ever pass across it,
Pass within through any opening.
Now I know not where to send him,
Nor what work I ought to give him.
There is rye for threshing ready."
So he sent him to the threshing.
    Kullervo, Kalervo's offspring,
Set himself to do the threshing,
And the rye to chaff he pounded,
Into very chaff he threshed it.
Soon thereafter came the master,
Strolling forth to gaze around him,
See how Kalervo's son threshed it,
And how Kullervoinen pounded.
All the rye to chaff was pounded,
Into very chaff he'd threshed it.
    Untamoinen then was angry.
"As a laborer he is useless.
Whatsoever work I give him,
All his work he spoils from malice.
Shall I take him into Russia,
Shall I sell him in Carelia,
To the smith named Ilmarinen,
That he there may wield the hammer?"
    Kalervo's son took he with him,
And he sold him in Carelia,
To the smith named Ilmarinen,

Skilful wielder of the hammer.
What then gave the smith in payment?
Great the payment that he made him;
For he gave two worn-out kettles,
And three halves of hooks he gave him,
And five worn-out scythes he gave him,
And six worn-out rakes he gave him,
For a man the most unskillful,
For a slave completely worthless.

Kullervo and the Wife of Ilmarinen   (Runo XXXII)

[Argument: The wife of Ilmarinen makes Kullervo her herdsman and mali-
ciously bakes him a stone in his lunch. She then sends him out with the cattle, after
using the usual prayers and charms for their protection from bears in the pastures.]

Kullervo, Kalervo's offspring,
Old man's son, with blue-dyed stockings,
Finest locks of yellow color,
And with shoes of best of leather,
To the smith's house went directly,
Asked for work that very evening,
Asked the master in the evening,
And the mistress in the morning:
"Give me something now to work at,
Give me work that 1 may do it,
Set me something now to work at,
Give some work to me the wretched!"
Then the wife of Ilmarinen,
Pondered deeply on the matter,
What the new slave could accomplish,
What the new-bought wretch could work at,
And she took him as her herdsman,
Who should herd her flocks extensive.
Then the most malicious mistress,
She, the smith's wife, old and jeering,
Baked a loaf to give the herdsman,
And a great cake did she bake him,
Oats below and wheat above it,
And between, a stone inserted.
Then she spread the cake with butter,
And upon the crust laid bacon,
Gave it as the slave's allowance,

As provision for the herdsman.
She herself the slave instructed,
And she spoke the words which follow:
"Do not eat the food I give you,
Till in wood-the herd is driven."
    Then did Ilmarinen's housewife
Send the herd away to pasture,
And she spoke the words which follow,
And in words like these expressed her:
"Send the cows among the bushes,
And the milkers in the meadow,
Those with wide horns to the aspens,
Those with curved horns to the birches,
That they thus may fatten on them,
And may load themselves with tallow,
There upon the open meadows,
And among the wide-spread borders,
From the lofty birchen forest,
And the lower growing aspens,
From among the golden fir-woods,
From among the silver woodlands.
    "Watch them, Jumala most gracious,
Guard them, O thou kind Creator,
Guard from harm upon the pathway,
And protect them from all evil,
That they come not into danger,
Nor may fall in any evil.
    "As beneath the roof-tree watch them,
Keep them under thy protection,
Watch them also in the open,
When beyond the fold protect them,
That the herd may grow more handsome,
And the mistress' cattle prosper,
To the wish of our well-wishers,
'Gainst the wish of our ill-wishers.
    "If my herdsman is a bad one,
Or the herd-girls should be timid,
Make the willow then a herdsman,
Let the alder watch the cattle,
Let the mountain-ash protect them,
And the cherry lead them homeward,
That the mistress need not seek them,
Nor need other folks be anxious.

"If the willow will not herd them,
Nor the mountain-ash protect them,
Nor the alder watch the cattle,
Nor the cherry lead them homeward,
Send thou then thy better servants,
Send the Daughters of Creation,
That they may protect my cattle,
And the whole herd may look after.
Very many are thy maidens,
Hundreds are beneath thy orders,
Dwelling underneath the heavens,
Noble Daughters of Creation.
　　"Suvetar, the best of women,
Etelätär, Nature's old one,
Hongatar, the noble mistress,
Katajatar, maiden fairest,
Pihlajatar, little damsel,
Tuometar, of Tapio daughter,
Mielikki, the wood's step-daughter,
Tellervo, the maid of Tapio,
May ye all protect my cattle,
And protect the best among them,
Through the beauty of the summer,
In the pleasant time of leafage,
While the leaves on trees are moving,
Grass upon the ground is waving.
　　"Suvetar, the best of women,
Etelätär, Nature's old one,
Spread thou out thy robe of softness,
And do thou spread out thy apron,
As a covering for my cattle,
For the hiding of the small ones,
That no ill winds blow upon them,
Nor an evil rain fall on them.
　　"Do thou guard my flock from evil,
Guard from harm upon the pathways,
And upon the quaking marshes,
Where the surface all is shifting,
Where the marsh is always moving,
And the depths below are shaking,
That they come not into danger,
Nor may fall in any evil,
That no hoof in swamp is twisted,

Nor may slip among the marshes,
Save when Jumala perceives it,
'Gainst the will of him, the Holy.
    "Fetch the cow-horn from a distance,
Fetch it from the midst of heaven,
Bring the mead-horn down from heaven,
Let the honey-horn be sounded.
Blow into the horn then strongly,
And repeat the tunes resounding,
Blow then flowers upon the hummocks,
Blow then fair the heathland's borders,
Make the meadow's borders lovely,
And the forest borders charming,
Borders of the marshes fertile,
Of the springs the borders rolling.
    "Then give fodder to my cattle,
Give the cattle food sufficient,
Give them food of honey-sweetness,
Give them drink as sweet as honey,
Feed them now with hay all golden,
And the heads of silvery grasses,
From the springs of all the sweetest,
From the streams that flow most swiftly,
From the swiftly-rushing torrents,
From the swiftly-running rivers,
From the hills all golden-shining,
And from out the silvery meadows.
    "Dig them also wells all golden
Upon both sides of the pastures,
That the herd may drink the water,
And the sweet juice then may trickle
Down into their teeming udders,
Down into their swelling udders,
That the veins may all be moving,
And the milk may flow in rivers,
And the streams of milk be loosened,
And may foam the milky torrents,
And the milk-streams may be silent,
And the milk-streams may be swollen,
And the milk be always flowing,
And the stream be always dropping,
Down upon the greenest haycocks,
And no evil fingers guide it;

That no milk may flow to Mana,
Nor upon the ground be wasted.
　"There are many who are wicked,
And who send the milk to Mana,
And upon the ground who waste it,
Give the cattle's yield to others.
They are few, but they are skilful
Who can bring the milk from Mana,
Sourest milk from village storage,
And when new from other quarters.
　"Never has indeed my mother
Sought for counsel in the village,
Brought it from another household;
But she fetched her milk from Mana,
Sour milk brought from those who stored it,
And fresh milk obtained from others;
Had the milk from distance carried,
Had it fetched from distant regions,
Fetched the milk from realms of Tuoni,
'Neath the earth in Mana's kingdom.
Secretly at night they brought it,
And in murky places hid it,
That the wicked should not hear it,
Nor the worthless ones should know it,
Nor bad hay should fall into it,
And it should be saved from spoiling.
　"Thus my mother always told me
In the very words which follow:
'Where has gone the yield of cattle,
Whither has the milk now vanished?
Has it been conveyed to strangers,
Carried to the village storehouse,
In the laps of beggar-wenches,
In the arms of those who envy,
Or among the trees been carried,
And been lost amid the forest,
And been scattered in the woodlands,
Or been lost upon the heathlands?
　"'But no milk shall go to Mana,
Nor the yield of cows to strangers,
In the laps of beggar-wenches,
In the arms of those who envy,
Nor among the trees be carried,

Nor be lost amid the forest,
Nor be scattered in the woodlands
Nor be lost upon the heathlands.
In the house the milk is useful,
And at all times it is needed;
In the house there waits the mistress,
In her hand the wooden milk-pail.'
　"Suvetar, the best of women,
Etelätär, Nature's old one,
Go and fodder my Syötikki,
Give thou drink to my Juotikki,
Milk confer upon Hermikki,
And fresh fodder give Tuorikki,
Give thou milk unto Mairikki,
Put fresh milk into the cowhouse,
From the heads of brightest herbage,
And the reeds of all the forest,
From the lovely earth up-springing,
From the hillocks rich in honey,
From the sweetest meadow-grasses,
And the berry-bearing regions,
From the goddess of the heather,
And the nymph who tends the grasses,
And the milkmaid of the cloudlets,
And the maid in midst of heaven.
Give the cows their milk-filled udders
Always filled to overflowing,
To be milked by dwarfish women,
That a little girl may milk them.
　"Rise, O virgin, from the valley,
From the spring, in gorgeous raiment,
From the spring, O maiden, rise thou,
From the ooze arise, O fairest.
From the spring take thou some water,
Sprinkle thou my cattle with it,
That the cattle may be finer,
And the mistress' cattle prosper,
Ere the coming of the mistress,
Ere the herd-girl look upon them,
She, the most unskillful mistress,
And the very timid herd-girl.
　"Mielikki, the forest's mistress,
Of the herds the bounteous mother,

Send the tallest of thy handmaids,
And the best among thy servants,
That they may protect my cattle,
And my herd be watched and tended
Through the finest of the summer,
In the good Creator's summer,
Under Jumala's protection,
And protected by his favor.
    "Tellervo, O maid of Tapio,
Little daughter of the forest,
Clad in soft and beauteous garments,
With thy yellow hair so lovely,
Be the guardian of the cattle,
Do thou guard the mistress' cattle
All through Metsola so lovely,
And through Tapiola's bright regions
Do thou guard the herd securely,
Do thou watch the herd unsleeping.
    "With thy lovely hands protect them,
With thy slender fingers stroke them,
Rub them with the skins of lynxes,
Comb them with the fins of fishes,
Like the hue of the lake creatures,
Like the wool of ewe of meadow.
Come at evening and night's darkness,
When the twilight round is closing,
Then do thou lead home my cattle,
Lead them to their noble mistress,
On their backs the water pouring,
Lakes of milk upon their cruppers.
    "When the sun to rest has sunken,
And the bird of eve is singing,
Then I say unto my cattle,
Speak unto my horned creatures.
    "'Come ye home, ye curve-horned cattle.
Milk-dispensers to the household,
In the house 'tis very pleasant,
Where the floor is nice for resting.
On the waste 'tis bad to wander,
Or upon the shore to bellow,
Therefore you should hasten homeward,
And the women fire will kindle,
In the field of honeyed grasses,

On the ground o'ergrown with berries.'
   "Nyyrikki, O son of Tapio,
Blue-coat offspring of the forest!
Take the stumps of tallest pine-trees,
And the lofty crowns of fir-trees,
For a bridge in miry places,
Where the ground is bad for walking,
Deep morass, and swampy moorland,
And the treacherous pools of water.
Let the curve-horned cattle wander,
And the split-hoofed cattle gallop,
Unto where the smoke is rising,
Free from harm, and free from danger,
Sinking not into the marshes,
Nor embogged in miry places.
   "If the cattle pay no heeding,
Nor will home return at nightfall,
Pihlajatar, little damsel,
Katajatar, fairest maiden,
Quickly cut a branch of birch-tree,
Take a rod from out the bushes,
Likewise take a whip of cherry,
And of juniper to scourge them,
From the back of Tapio's castle,
From among the slopes of alder.
Drive the herd towards the household,
At the time for bathroom-heating;
Homeward drive the household cattle,
Cows from Metsola's great forest.
   "Otso, apple of the forest,
With thy honey-paws so curving,
Let us make a peace between us,
Haste to make a peace between us,
So that always and for ever
In the days that we are living,
Thou wilt fell no hoofèd cattle,
Nor wilt overthrow the milch-kine,
Through the finest of the summer,
In the good Creator's summer.
   "When thou hear'st the cow-bells ringing,
Or thou hear'st the cow-horn sounding,
Cast thee down among the hillocks,
Sleep thou there upon the meadow,

Thrust thine ears into the stubble,
Hide thy head among the hillocks,
Or conceal thee in the thickets,
To thy mossy lair retreat thou,
Go thou forth to other districts,
Flee away to other hillocks,
That thou mayst not hear the cow-bells,
Nor the talking of the herdsmen.
    "O my Otso, O my darling,
Handsome one, with paws of honey,
I forbid thee to approach them,
Or molest the herd of cattle,
Neither with thy tongue to touch them,
Nor with ugly mouth to seize them,
With thy teeth to tear to pieces,
Neither with thy claws to scratch them.
    "Go thou slouching through the meadow,
Go in secret through the pasture,
Slinking off when bells are ringing,
Shun the talking of the shepherds.
If the herd is on the heathland,
Then into the swamps retreat thou,
If the herd is in the marshes,
Then conceal thee in the thickets,
If the herd should climb the mountain,
Quickly then descend the mountain,
If the herd should wander downward,
Wander then along the mountain,
If they wander in the bushes,
To the thicker woods retreat thou,
If the thicker wood they enter,
Wander then into the bushes,
Wander like the golden cuckoo,
Like the dove of silver color,
Move aside as moves the powan,
Glide away like fish in water,
As a flock of wool drifts sideways,
Or a roll of flax the lightest,
In thy fur thy claws conceal thou,
In thy gums thy teeth conceal thou,
That the herd thou dost not frighten,
Nor the little calves be injured.
    "Let the cattle rest in quiet,

Leave in peace the hooféd cattle,
Let the herd securely wander,
Let them march in perfect order
Through the swamps and through the open,
Through the tangle of the forest,
Never do thou dare to touch them,
Nor to wickedly molest them.
    "Keep the former oath thou sworest,
There by Tuonela's deep river,
By the raging fall of water,
At the knees of the Creator.
Thou hast been indeed permitted,
Three times in the course of summer,
To approach the bells when ringing,
And the tinkling of the cow-bells,
But 'tis not permitted to thee,
Nor permission has been given,
To commence a work of evil,
Or a deed of shame accomplish.
    "Should thy frenzy come upon thee,
And thy teeth be seized with longing,
Cast thy frenzy in the bushes,
On the heath thy evil longing,
Then attack the trees all rotten,
Overthrow the rotten birch-trees,
Turn to trees in water standing,
Growl in berry-bearing districts.
    "If the need for food should seize thee,
Or for food the wish thou feelest,
Eat the fungi in the forest,
And do thou break down the ant-hills,
And the red roots do thou delve for;
These are Metsola's sweet dainties.
Eat no grass reserved for fodder,
Neither do thou hurt my pasture.
    "When in Metsola the honey
Is fermenting and is working,
On the hills of golden color,
And upon the plains of silver,
There is food for those who hunger,
There is drink for all the thirsty,
There is food to eat that fails not,
There is drink that never lessens.

"Let us make a league eternal,
Make an endless peace between us,
That we live in perfect quiet
And in comfort all the summer,
And to us the lands are common,
And our provender delicious.
    "If thou dost desire a combat,
And wouldst live in hopes of battle,
Let us combat in the winter,
And contend in time of snowfall.
When the marshes thaw in summer,
And the pools are all unfrozen,
Never venture to approach thou,
Where the golden herd is living.
    "When thou comest to this country,
And thou movest in this forest,
We at any time will shoot you,
Though the gunners should be absent.
There are very skilful women,
All of them accomplished housewives,
And they will destroy your pathway,
On your journey bring destruction,
Lest you might work any evil,
Or indulge in any mischief,
Ill by Jumala not sanctioned,
And against his blessed orders.
    "Ukko, thou, of Gods the highest,
Shouldst thou hear that he is coming,
Then do thou transform my cattle,
Suddenly transform my cattle,
Into stones convert my own ones,
Change my fair ones into tree-trunks,
When the monster roams the district,
And the big one wanders through it.
    "If I were myself a Bruin,
Roamed about a honey-pawed one,
Never would I dare to venture
To the feet of aged women.
There are many other regions,
There are many other penfolds,
Where a man may go to wander,
Roaming aimless at his pleasure.
Therefore move thy paws across them,

Do thou move thy paws across them,
In the blue wood's deep recesses,
In the depths of murmuring forest.
    "On the heath o'er pine-cones wander,
Tramp thou through the sandy districts,
Go thou where the way is level,
Do thou bound along the lakeshore,
To the furthest bounds of Pohja,
To the distant plains of Lapland.
There indeed mayst thou be happy,
Good it is for thee to dwell there,
Wandering shoeless in the summer,
Wandering sockless in the autumn,
Through the wide expanse of marshland,
And across the wide morasses.
    "But if thou should not go thither,
If thou canst not find the pathway,
Hasten then to distant regions,
Do thou wander, on thy pathway
Unto Tuonela's great forest,
Or across the heaths of Kalma.
There are marshes to be traversed,
There are heaths that thou mayst traverse,
There is Kirjos, there is Karjos,
There are many other cattle,
Fitted with their iron neck-chains,
Ten among them altogether;
There the lean kine quickly fatten,
And their bones are soon flesh-covered.
    "Be propitious, wood and forest,
Be thou gracious, O thou blue wood,
Give thou peace unto the cattle,
And protection to the hoofed ones,
Through the whole length of the summer,
Of the Lord the loveliest season.
    "Kuippana, thou king of woodland,
Active graybeard of the forest,
Hold thy dogs in careful keeping,
Watch thou well thy dogs and guard them;
Thrust some fungus in one nostril,
In the other thrust an apple,
That they may not smell the cattle,
And they may not scent their odor.

Bind their eyes with silken ribands,
Likewise bind their ears with linen,
That they may not hear them moving,
And they may not see them walking.
    "If this is not yet sufficient,
And they do not much regard it,
Then do thou forbid thy children,
Do thou drive away thy offspring.
Lead them forth from out this forest,
From this lakeshore do thou drive them,
From the lands where roam the cattle,
From among the spreading willows,
Do thou hide thy dogs in caverns,
Nor neglect to bind them firmly,
Bind them with the golden fetters,
With the slender silver fetters,
That they may commit no evil,
And be guilty of no outrage.
    "If this is not yet sufficient,
And they do not much regard it,
Ukko, then, O golden monarch,
Ukko, O thou silver guardian,
Hearken to my words so golden,
Listen to my lovely sayings!
Take a snaffle made of rowan,
Fix it on their stumpy muzzles,
Or if rowan will not hold them,
Cast thou then a copper muzzle,
If too weak is found the copper,
Forge thou then an iron muzzle,
If they break the iron muzzle,
And it should itself be shattered,
Drive thou then a stake all golden,
Through the chin and through the jawbone,
Do thou close their jaws securely,
Fix them that they cannot move them,
That they cannot move their jawbones,
And their teeth can scarcely open,
If the iron is not opened,
If the steel should not be loosened,
If with knife it is not severed,
If with hatchet 'tis not broken."
    Then did Ilmarinen's housewife,

Of the smith the wife so artful,
Drive from out their stalls the cattle,
Send the cattle forth to pasture,
After them she sent the shepherd,
That the slave should drive the cattle.

The Death of Ilmarinen's Wife (Runo XXXIII)

[Argument: While Kullervo is in the pasture in the afternoon he tries to cut the cake with his knife which he completely spoils, and this goes to his heart the more because the knife was the only remembrance left to him of his family. To revenge himself on the mistress, he drives the cattle into the marshes to be devoured by beasts of the forest, and gathers together a herd of wolves and bears, which he drives home in the evening. When the mistress goes to milk them she is torn to pieces by the wild beasts.]

Kullervo, Kalervo's offspring,
Put his lunch into his wallet,
Drove the cows along the marshes,
While across the heath he wandered,
And he spoke as he was going,
And repeated on his journey,
"Woe to me, a youth unhappy,
And a youth of wretched fortune!
Wheresoe'er I turn my footsteps,
Nought but idleness awaits me;
I must watch the tails of oxen,
And must watch the calves I follow,
Always tramping through the marshes,
Through the worst of level country."
      Then upon the ground he rested,
On a sunny slope he sat him,
And he then composed these verses,
And expressed himself in singing:
"Sun of Jumala, O shine thou,
Of the Lord, thou wheel, shine warmly,
On the warder of the smith's herd,
And upon the wretched shepherd,
Not on Ilmarinen's household,
Least of all upon the mistress,
For the mistress lives luxurious,
And the wheaten-bread she slices,
And the finest cakes devours,

And she spreads them o'er with butter,
Gives the wretched shepherd dry bread,
Dry crusts only for his chewing,
Only oaten-cake she gives me,
Even this with chaff she mixes,
Even straw she scatters through it,
Gives for food the bark of fir-tree,
Water in a birch-bark bucket,
Upscooped 'mid the grassy hillocks.
March, O sun, and wheat, O wander,
Sink in Jumala's own season,
Hasten, sun, among the pine-trees,
Wander, wheat, into the bushes,
'Mid the junipers, O hasten,
Fly thou to the plains of alder,
Lead thou then the herdsman homeward,
Give him butter from the barrel,
Let him eat the freshest butter,
Over all the cakes extending."
      But the wife of Ilmarinen
While the shepherd was lamenting,
And while Kullervo was singing,
Ate the butter from the barrel,
And she ate the freshest butter,
And upon the cakes she spread it,
And hot soup had she made ready,
But for Kullervo cold cabbage,
Whence the dog the fat had eaten,
And the black dog made a meal from,
And the spotted dog been sated,
And the brown dog had sufficient.
      From the branch there sang a birdling,
Sang a small bird from the bushes,
"Time 'tis for the servant's supper,
O thou orphan boy, 'tis evening."
      Kullervo, Kalervo's offspring,
Looked, and saw the sun was sinking,
And he said the words which follow:
"Now the time has come for eating,
Yes, the time has come for eating,
Time it is to take refreshment."
      So to rest he drove the cattle,
On the heath he drove the cattle,

360

And he sat him on a hillock,
And upon a green hill sat him.
From his back he took his wallet,
Took the cake from out the wallet,
And he turned it round and eyed it,
And he spoke the words which follow:
"Many a cake is outside handsome,
And the crust looks smooth from outside,
But within is only fir-bark,
Only chaff beneath the surface."
From the sheath he took his knife out,
And to cut the cake attempted.
On the stone the knife struck sharply,
And against the stone was broken.
From the knife the point was broken;
And the knife itself was broken.
Kullervo, Kalervo's offspring,
Looked, and saw the knife was broken,
And at length he burst out weeping,
And he said the words which follow:
"Save this knife I'd no companion,
Nought to love except this iron,
'Twas an heirloom from my father,
And the aged man had used it.
Now against a stone 'tis broken,
'Gainst a piece of rock 'tis shattered
In the cake of that vile mistress,
Baked there by that wicked woman.
"How shall I for this reward her,
Woman's prank, and damsel's mockery,
And destroy the base old woman,
And that wicked wench, the bakeress?"
Then a crow cawed from the bushes,
Cawed the crow, and croaked the raven.
"O thou wretched golden buckle,
Kalervo's surviving offspring,
Wherefore art thou so unhappy,
Wherefore is thy heart so troubled?
Take a switch from out the bushes,
And a birch from forest-valley,
Drive the foul beasts in the marshes,
Chase the cows to the morasses,
Half to largest wolves deliver,

Half to bears amid the forest.
"Call thou all the wolves together,
All the bears do thou assemble,
Change the wolves to little cattle,
Make the bears the larger cattle,
Lead them then like cattle homeward,
Lead them home like brindled cattle;
Thus repay the woman's jesting,
And the wicked woman's insult."
    Kullervo, Kalervo's offspring,
Uttered then the words which follow:
"Wait thou, wait thou, whore of Hiisi,
For my father's knife I'm weeping,
Soon wilt thou thyself be weeping,
And be weeping for thy milchkine."
    From the bush a switch he gathered,
Juniper as whip for cattle,
Drove the cows into the marshes,
And the oxen in the thickets,
Half of these the wolves devoured,
To the bears he gave the others,
And he sang the wolves to cattle,
And he changed the bears to oxen,
Made the first the little cattle,
Made the last the larger cattle.
    In the south the sun was sinking,
In the west the sun descended,
Bending down towards the pine-trees
At the time of cattle-milking.
Then the dusty wicked herd-boy,
Kullervo, Kalervo's offspring,
Homeward drove the bears before him,
And the wolf-flock to the farmyard,
And the bears he thus commanded,
And the wolves he thus instructed:
"Tear the mistress' thighs asunder,
See that through her calves you bite her,
When she comes to look around her,
And she bends her down to milk you."
    Then he made a pipe of cow-bone,
And a whistle made of ox-horn,
From Tuomikki's leg a cow-horn,
And a flute from heel of Kirjo,

Then upon the horn blew loudly,
And upon his pipe made music.
Thrice upon the hill he blew it,
Six times at the pathway's opening.
    Then did Ilmarinen's housewife,
Wife of smith, an active woman,
Who for milk had long been waiting,
And expecting summer butter,
Hear the music on the marshes,
And upon the heath the cattle,
And she spoke the words which follow,
And expressed herself in thiswise:
"Praise to Jumala be given,
Sounds the pipe, the herd is coming,
Whence obtained the slave the cow-horn,
That he made a horn to blow on?
Wherefore does he thus come playing,
Blowing tunes upon the cow-horn,
Blowing till he bursts the eardrums,
And he gives me quite a headache?"
    Kullervo, Kalervo's offspring,
Answered in the words which follow:
"In the swamp the horn was lying,
From the sand I brought the cow-horn,
To the lane I brought your cattle,
In the shed the cows are standing;
Come you forth to smoke the cattle,
And come out to milk the cattle."
    Then did Ilmarinen's housewife
Bid the mother milk the cattle.
"Mother, go and milk the cattle,
Do thou go to tend the cattle,
For I think I cannot finish
Kneading dough as I would have it."
    Kullervo, Kalervo's offspring,
Answered in the words which follow:
"Ever do the thrifty housewives,
Ever do the careful housewives
Go the first to milk the cattle,
Set themselves to milk the cattle."
    Then did Ilmarinen's housewife
Hasten forth to smoke the cattle,
And she went to milk the cattle,

And surveyed the herd before her,
Gazed upon the horned cattle,
And she spoke the words which follow:
"Beauteous is the herd to gaze on,
Very sleek the horned cattle,
They have all been rubbed with lynx-skin
And the wool of sheep of forest,
Well-filled, too, are all their udders,
And expanded with their fullness."
　　So she stooped her down to milk them,
And she sat her down for milking,
Pulled a first time and a second,
And attempted it a third time,
And the wolf sprang fiercely at her,
And the bear came fiercely after.
At her mouth the wolf was tearing,
And the bear tore through her tendons,
Halfway through her calves they bit her,
And they broke across her shinbones.
　　Kullervo, Kalervo's offspring
Thus repaid the damsel's jesting,
Damsel's jesting, woman's mocking,
Thus repaid the wicked woman.
　　Ilmarinen's wife illustrious
Then herself was brought to weeping,
And she spoke the words which follow:
"Ill thou dost, O wicked herdsman,
Driving bears unto the homestead,
To the yard these wolves gigantic."
　　Kullervo, Kalervo's offspring
Heard, and thus he made her answer:
"Ill I did, a wicked herd-boy,
Not so great as wicked mistress.
In my cake a stone she-baked me,
Baked a lump of rock within it,
On the stone my knife struck sharply,
'Gainst the rock my knife was shattered;
'Twas the knife of mine own father,
Of our race a cherished heirloom."
　　Then said Ilmarinen's housewife,
"O thou herd-boy, dearest herd-boy,
Wilt thou alter thy intention,
And recall thy words of magic,

And release me from the wolf's jaws,
From the bear's claws now release me?
Better shirts will I then give you,
And will give you handsome aprons,
Give you wheaten-bread, and butter,
And the sweetest milk for drinking,
For a year no work will give you,
Give you light work in the second.
    "If you haste not to release me,
Come not quickly to my rescue,
Death will quickly fall upon me,
And to earth shall I be altered."
    Kullervo, Kalervo's offspring,
Answered in the words which follow:
"If you die, so may you perish,
If you perish, may you perish!
Room there is in earth to hold you,
Room in Kalma's home for lost ones,
For the mightiest there to slumber,
For the proudest to repose them."
    Then said Ilmarinen's housewife,
"Ukko, thou, of Gods the highest,
Haste to bend thy mighty crossbow,
Of thy bows the best select thou,
Take thou then a bolt of copper,
And adjust it to the crossbow,
Shoot thou then a flaming arrow,
Shoot thou forth the bolt of copper,
Shoot it quickly through the arm-pits,
Shoot it that it split the shoulders.
Thus let Kalervo's son perish,
Shoot thou dead this wicked creature,
Shoot him with the steel-tipped arrow,
Shoot him with thy bolt of copper."
    Kullervo, Kalervo's offspring,
Uttered then the words which follow:
"Ukko, thou, of Gods the highest,
Shoot me not as she has prayed thee,
Shoot the wife of Ilmarinen,
Do thou kill this wicked woman,
Ere from off this spot she riseth,
Or can move herself from off it."
    Then did Ilmarinen's housewife,

Wife of that most skilful craftsman,
On the spot at once fall dying,
Fell, as falls the soot from kettle,
In the yard before her homestead,
In the narrow yard she perished.
    Thus it was the young wife perished,
Thus the fairest housewife perished,
Whom the smith so long had yearned for,
And for six long years was sought for,
As the joy of Ilmarinen,
Pride of him, the smith so famous.

Kullervo and His Parents (Runo XXXIV)

[Argument: Kullervo escapes from the homestead of Ilmarinen, and wanders sorrowfully through the forest, where he meets with the Old Woman of the Forest, who informs him that his father, mother, brothers and sisters are still living. Following her directions he finds them on the borders of Lapland. His mother tells him that she had long supposed him to be dead, and also that her elder daughter had been lost when gathering berries.]

Kullervo, Kalervo's offspring,
He, the youth with blue-dyed stockings.
And with yellow hair the finest,
And with shoes of finest leather,
Hurried quickly on his journey
From the home of Ilmarinen,
Ere report could reach the master
Of the death his wife had suffered,
And might harm him in his anger,
And he might at once destroy him.
    From the smith he hurried piping,
Joyful left the lands of Ilma,
On the heath his horn blew loudly,
Shouted loudly in the clearing,
And he dashed through plains and marshes,
While the heath re-echoed loudly,
And his horn kept loudly blowing,
And made horrible rejoicing.
    In the smithy did they hear it,
At the forge the smith was standing,
To the lane he went to listen,
To the yard to look around him,

Who was playing in the forest,
And upon the heath was piping.
  Then he saw what just had happened,
Saw the truth without deception,
There he saw his wife was resting,
Saw the fair one who had perished,
Where she in the yard had fallen,
On the grass where she had fallen.
  Even while the smith was standing,
All his heart was dark with sorrow;
Many nights he spent in weeping,
Many weeks his tears were flowing,
And his soul like tar was darkened,
And his heart than soot no lighter.
  Kullervo still wandered onwards,
Aimlessly he hurried forward,
For a day through thickest forest,
Through the timber-grounds of Hiisi,
And at evening, when it darkened,
Down upon the ground he threw him.
  There the orphan boy was sitting,
And the friendless one reflected:
"Wherefore have I been created,
Who has made me, and has doomed me,
Thus 'neath moon and sun to wander
'Neath the open sky for ever?

  "Others to their homes may journey,
And may travel to their dwellings,
But my home is in the forest,
And upon the heath my homestead.
In the wind I find my fire-place,
In the rain I find my bathroom.
  "Never, Jumala most gracious,
Never in the course of ages,
Form a child thus mis-created,
Doomed to be for ever friendless,
Fatherless beneath the heavens,
From the first without a mother,
As thou, Jumala, hast made me,
And hast formed me to be wretched,
Formed me like a wandering seagull,
Like a seagull on the lake-cliffs.
Shines the sun upon the swallow,

Brightly shines upon the sparrow,
In the air the birds are joyous,
I myself am never happy,
On my life the sun shines never,
And my life is always joyless.
    "Now I know not who has nursed me,
And I know not who has borne me,
For, as water-hens are used to,
Or as ducks among the marshes,
Like the teal on shore she left me,
Or in hollow stone, merganser.
    "I was small, and lost my father,
I was weak, and lost my mother,
Dead is father, dead is mother,
All my mighty race has perished,
Shoes of ice to wear they left me,
Filled with snow they left my stockings,
On the ice they left me lying,
Rolling on the platform left me,
Thus I fell into the marshes,
And amid the mud was swallowed
    "But in all my life I never,
Never in my life I hastened,
Through the swamp to make a platform,
Or a bridge in marshy places;
But I sank not in the marshes,
For I had two hands to help me,
And I had five nimble fingers,
And ten nails to lift me from it."
    Then into his mind it entered
In his brain he fixed the notion
Unto Untamo to journey,
There his father's wrongs avenging,
Father's wrongs, and tears of mother,
And the wrongs himself had suffered.
    Then he spoke the words which follow:
"Wait thou, wait thou, Untamoinen,
Watch thou, of my race destroyer!
If I seek thee out in battle,
I will quickly burn thy dwelling,
And thy farms to flame deliver."
    Then an old dame came to meet him,
Blue-robed Lady of the Forest,

And she spoke the words which follow,
And in words like these expressed her:
"Whither goeth Kullervoinen,
Where will Kalervo's son hasten?"

Kullervo, Kalervo's offspring,
Answered in the words which follow:
"In my mind the thought has entered,
In my brain has fixed the notion
Hence to other lands to wander,
Unto Untamo's own village,
There my father's death avenging,
Father's wrongs, and tears of mother,
There with fire to burn the houses,
And to burn them up completely."

But the old wife made him answer,
And she spoke the words which follow:
"No, your race has not yet perished,
Nor has Kalervo been murdered;
For your father still is living,
And on earth in health your mother."

"O my dearest of old women,
Tell me, O my dear old woman,
Where I yet may find my father,
Where the fair one who has borne me?"

"Thither is thy father living,
There the fair one who has borne thee,
Far away on Lapland's borders,
On the borders of a fishpond."

"O my dearest of old women,
Tell me, O my dear old woman,
How I best can journey to them,
And the road I may discover?"

"Easy 'tis for thee to journey,
Though to thee unknown the pathway.
Through the forest must thou journey,
By the river thou must travel,
Thou must march one day, a second,
And must march upon the third day,
Then must turn thee to the north-west,
Till you reach a wooded mountain,
Then march on beneath the mountain,
Go the left side of the mountain,
Till thou comest to a river,

(On the right side thou wilt find it,)
By the riverside go further,
Till three waterfalls rush foaming,
When thou comest to a headland,
With a narrow tongue projecting,
And a house at point of headland,
And beyond a hut for fishing.
There thy father still is living,
There the fair one who has borne thee,
There thou'lt also find thy sisters,
Two among the fairest maidens."
　　　Kullervo, Kalervo's offspring,
Started then upon his journey,
And he marched, one day, a second,
Likewise marched upon the third day,
Then he turned him to the north-west,
Till he reached a wooded mountain,
Then he marched halfway below it,
Turning westward from the mountain,
Till at length he found the river,
And he marched along the river,
On the west bank of the river,
Past three water-falls he journeyed,
Till at length he reached a headland
With a narrow tongue projecting,
And a house at point of headland,
And beyond, a hut for fishing.
　　　Thereupon the house he entered,
In the room they did not know him.
"From what lake has come the stranger,
From what country is the wanderer?"
　　　"Is your son then all forgotten,
Know you not your child, your offspring.
Who by Untamo's marauders,
With them to their home was carried,
Greater not than span of father,
Longer not than mother's spindle?"
　　　Then his mother interrupted,
And exclaimed the aged woman,
"O my son, my son unhappy,
O my golden brooch so wretched,
Hast thou then, with eyes yet living,
Wandered through these countries hither,

When as dead I long had mourned thee,
Long had wept for thy destruction?
    "I had two sons in the past days,
And two daughters of the fairest,
And among them two have vanished,
Two are lost among the elder,
First my son in furious battle,
Then my daughter, how I know not.
Though my son has reached the homestead,
Never has returned my daughter."
    Kullervo, Kalervo's offspring,
In his turn began to question.
"How then has your daughter vanished,
What has happened to my sister?"
    Then his mother made him answer,
And she spoke the words which follow:
"Thus has disappeared my daughter,
Thus it happened to your sister.
To the wood she went for berries,
Sought for raspberries 'neath the mountain,
There it is the dove has vanished,
There it is the bird has perished,
Thus she died without our knowledge,
How she died we cannot tell you.
    "Who is longing for the maiden?
Save her mother, no one missed her.
First her mother went to seek her,
And her mother sought, who missed her,
Forth I went, unhappy mother,
Forth I went to seek my daughter,
Through the wood like bear I hurried,
Speeding through the wastes like otter,
Thus I sought one day, a second,
Sought her also on the third day.
When the third day had passed over,
For a long time yet I wandered,
Till I reached a mighty mountain,
And a peak of all the highest,
Calling ever on my daughter,
Ever grieving for the lost one.
    "'Where is now my dearest daughter?
O my daughter, come thou homeward!'
    "Thus I shouted to my daughter,

Grieving ever for the lost one,
And the mountains made me answer,
And the heaths again re-echoed,
'Call no more upon thy daughter,
Call no more, and shout no longer,
Never will she come back living,
Nor return unto her household,
Never to her mother's dwelling,
To her aged father's boathouse.'"

Kullervo and His Sister (Runo XXXV)

[Argument: Kullervo attempts to do different kinds of work for his parents, but only succeeds in spoiling everything, so his father sends him to pay the land-dues. On his way home he meets his sister who was lost gathering berries, whom he drags into his sledge. Afterwards, when his sister learns who he is, she throws herself into a torrent, but Kullervo hurries home, relates his sister's terrible fate to his mother, and proposes to put an end to his own life. His mother dissuades him from suicide; and advises him to retire to some retreat where he may be able to recover from his remorse. But Kullervo resolves before all things to avenge himself on Untamo.]

Kullervo, Kalervo's offspring,
With the very bluest stockings,
After this continued living,
In the shelter of his parents,
But he comprehended nothing,
Nor attained to manly wisdom,
For his rearing had been crooked,
And the child was rocked all wrongly,
By perversest foster-father,
And a foolish foster-mother.
    Then to work the boy attempted,
Many things he tried his hand at,
And he went the fish to capture,
And to lay the largest drag-net,
And he spoke the words which follow,
Pondered as he grasped the oar:
"Shall I pull with all my efforts,
Row, exerting all my vigor;
Shall I row with common efforts,
Row no stronger than is needful?"
    And the steersman made him answer,
And he spoke the words which follow:

"Pull away with all your efforts,
Row, exerting all your vigor,
Row the boat in twain you cannot,
Neither break it into fragments."
　　Kullervo, Kalervo's offspring,
Pulled thereat with all his efforts,
Rowed, exerting all his vigor,
Rowed in twain the wooden rowlocks,
Ribs of juniper he shattered,
And he smashed the boat of aspen.
　　Kalervo came forth to see it,
And he spoke the words which follow:
"No, you understand not rowing,
You have split the wooden rowlocks,
Ribs of juniper have shattered,
Shattered quite the boat of aspen.
Thresh the fish into the drag-net,
Perhaps you'll thresh the water better."
　　Kullervo, Kalervo's offspring,
Then went forth to thresh the water,
And as he the pole was lifting,
Uttered he the words which follow:
"Shall I thresh with all my efforts,
Putting forth my manly efforts;
Shall I thresh with common efforts,
As the threshing-pole is able?"
　　Answered thereupon the net-man,
"Would you call it proper threshing,
If with all your strength you threshed not,
Putting forth your manly efforts?"
　　Kullervo, Kalervo's offspring,
Threshed away with all his efforts,
Putting forth his manly efforts.
Into soup he churned the water,
Into tow he threshed the drag-net,
Into slime he crushed the fishes.
　　Kalervo came forth to see it,
And he spoke the words which follow:
"No, you understand not threshing,
Into tow is threshed the drag-net,
And the floats to chaff are beaten,
And the meshes torn to fragments,
Therefore go and pay the taxes,

Therefore go and pay the land-dues.
Best it is for you to travel,
Learning wisdom on the journey."
    Kullervo, Kalervo's offspring,
With the very bluest stockings,
And with yellow hair the finest,
And with shoes of finest leather,
Went his way to pay the taxes,
And he went to pay the land-dues.
    When he now had paid the taxes,
And had also paid the land-dues,
In his sledge he quickly bounded,
And upon the sledge he mounted,
And began to journey homeward,
And to travel to his country.
    And he drove, and rattled onward,
And he traveled on his journey,
Traversing the heath of Väino,
And his clearing made aforetime.
    And by chance a maiden met him,
With her yellow hair all flowing,
There upon the heath of Vajno,
On his clearing made aforetime.
    Kullervo, Kalervo's offspring,
Checked the sledge upon the instant,
And began a conversation,
And began to talk and wheedle:
"Come into my sledge, O maiden,
Rest upon the furs within it."
    From her snowshoes said the maiden,
And she answered, as she skated,
"In thy sledge may Death now enter,
On thy furs be Sickness seated."
    Kullervo, Kalervo's offspring,
With the very bluest stockings,
With his whip then struck his courser,
With his beaded whip he lashed him.
Sprang the horse upon the journey,
Rocked the sledge, the road was traversed,
And he drove and rattled onward,
And he traveled on his journey,
On the lake's extended surface,
And across the open water,

And by chance a maiden met him,
Walking on, with shoes of leather,
O'er the lake's extended surface,
And across the open water.
    Kullervo, Kalervo's offspring,
Checked his horse upon the instant,
And his mouth at once he opened,
And began to speak as follows:
"Come into my sledge, O fair one,
Pride of earth, and journey with me."
    But the maiden gave him answer,
And the well-shod maiden answered:
"In thy sledge may Tuoni seek thee,
Manalainen journey with thee."
    Kullervo, Kalervo's offspring,
With the very bluest stockings,
With the whip then struck his courser,
With his beaded whip he lashed him.
Sprang the horse upon his journey,
Rocked the sledge, the way was shortened,
And he rattled on his journey,
And he sped upon his pathway,
Straight across the heaths of Pohja,
And the borders wide of Lapland.
    And by chance a maiden met him,
Wearing a tin brooch, and singing,
Out upon the heaths of Pohja,
And the borders wide of Lapland.
    Kullervo, Kalervo's offspring,
Checked his horse upon the instant,
And his mouth at once he opened,
And began to speak as follows:
"Come into my sledge, O maiden,
Underneath my rug, my dearest,
And you there shall eat my apples,
And shall crack my nuts in comfort."
    But the maiden made him answer,
And the tin-adorned one shouted:
"At your sledge I spit, O villain,
Even at your sledge, O scoundrel!
Underneath your rug is coldness,
And within your sledge is darkness."
    Kullervo, Kalervo's offspring,

With the very bluest stockings,
Dragged into his sledge the maiden,
And into the sledge he pulled her,
And upon the furs he laid her,
Underneath the rug he pushed her.
    And the maiden spoke unto him,
Thus outspoke the tin-adorned one:
"From the sledge at once release me,
Leave the child in perfect freedom,
That I hear of nothing evil,
Neither foul nor filthy language,
Or upon the ground I'll throw me,
And will break the sledge to splinters,
And will smash your sledge to atoms,
Break the wretched sledge to pieces."
    Kullervo, Kalervo's offspring,
With the very bluest stockings,
Opened then his hide-bound coffer,
Clanging raised the pictured cover,
And he showed her all his silver,
Out he spread the choicest fabrics,
Stockings too, all gold-embroidered,
Girdles all adorned with silver.
    Soon the fabrics turned her dizzy,
To a bride the money changed her,
And the silver it destroyed her,
And the shining gold deluded.
    Kullervo, Kalervo's offspring,
With the very bluest stockings,
Thereupon the maiden flattered,
And he wheedled and caressed her,
With one hand the horse controlling,
On the maiden's breast the other.
    Then he sported with the maiden,
Wearied out the tin-adorned one,
'Neath the rug all copper-tinseled,
And upon the furs all spotted.
Then when Jumala brought morning,
On the second day thereafter,
Then the damsel spoke unto him,
And she asked, and spoke as follows:
"Tell me now of your relations,
What the brave race that you spring from,

From a mighty race it seems me,
Offspring of a mighty father."
    Kullervo, Kalervo's offspring,
Answered in the words which follow:
"No, my race is not a great one,
Not a great one, not a small one,
I am just of middle station,
Kalervo's unhappy offspring,
Stupid boy, and very foolish,
Worthless child, and good for nothing.
Tell me now about your people,
And the brave race that you spring from,
Perhaps from mighty race descended,
Offspring of a mighty father."
    And the girl made answer quickly,
And she spoke the words which follow:
"No, my race is not a great one,
Not a great one, not a small one,
I am just of middle station,
Kalervo's unhappy daughter,
Stupid girl, and very foolish,
Worthless child, and good for nothing.
    "When I was a little infant,
Living with my tender mother,
To the wood I went for berries,
'Neath the mountain sought for raspberries.
On the plains I gathered strawberries,
Underneath the mountain, raspberries,
Plucked by day, at night I rested,
Plucked for one day and a second,
And upon the third day likewise,
But the pathway home I found not,
In the woods the pathways led me,
And the footpath to the forest.
    "There I stood, and burst out weeping,
Wept for one day and a second,
And at length upon the third day,
Then I climbed a mighty mountain,
To the peak of all the highest.
On the peak I called and shouted,
And the woods made answer to me,
While the heaths re-echoed likewise:
'Do not call, O girl so senseless,

Shout not, void of understanding!
There is no one who can hear you,
None at home to hear your shouting.'
　"Then upon the third and fourth days,
Lastly on the fifth and sixth days,
I to take my life attempted,
Tried to hurl me to destruction,
But by no means did I perish,
Nor could I, the wretched, perish.
　"Would that I, poor wretch, had perished,
Hapless one, had met destruction,
That the second year thereafter,
Or the third among the summers,
I had shone forth as a grass-blade,
As a lovely flower existed,
On the ground a beauteous berry,
Even as a scarlet cranberry,
Then I had not heard these horrors,
Would not now have known these terrors."
　Soon as she had finished speaking,
And her speech had scarce completed,
Quickly from the sledge she darted,
And she rushed into the river,
In the furious foaming cataract,
And amid the raging whirlpool,
There she found the death she sought for,
There at length did death o'ertake her,
Found in Tuonela a refuge,
In the waves she found compassion.
　Kullervo, Kalervo's offspring,
From his sledge at once descended,
And began to weep full loudly,
With a piteous lamentation.
"Woe my day, O me unhappy,
Woe to me, and all my household,
For indeed my very sister,
I my mother's child have outraged!
Woe my father, woe my mother,
Woe to you, my aged parents,
To what purpose have you reared me,
Reared me up to be so wretched!
Far more happy were my fortune,
Had I ne'er been born or nurtured,

Never in the air been strengthened,
Never in this world had entered.
Wrongly I by death was treated,
Nor disease has acted wisely,
That they did not fall upon me,
And when two nights old destroy me."
    With his knife he loosed the collar,
From the sledge the chains he severed,
On the horse's back he vaulted,
On the whitefront steed he galloped,
But a little way he galloped,
But a little course had traversed,
When he reached his father's dwelling,
Reached the grass-plot of his father.
    In the yard he found his mother,
"O my mother who hast borne me,
O that thou, my dearest mother,
E'en as soon as thou hadst borne me,
In the bath-room smoke hadst laid me,
And the bath-house doors had bolted,
That amid the smoke I smothered,
And when two nights old had perished,
Smothered me among the blankets,
With the curtain thou hadst choked me,
Thrust the cradle in the fire,
Pushed it in the burning embers.
    "If the village folk had asked thee,
'Why is in the room no cradle?
Wherefore have you locked the bath-house?'
Then might this have been the answer:
'In the fire I burned the cradle,
Where on hearth the fire is glowing,
While I made the malt in bath-house,
While the malt was fully sweetened.'"
    Then his mother asked him quickly,
Asked him thus, the aged woman:
"O my son, what happened to thee,
What the dreadful news thou bringest?
Seems from Tuonela thou comest;
As from Manala thou comest."
    Kullervo, Kalervo's offspring,
Answered in the words which follow:
"Horrors now must be reported,

And most horrible misfortunes.
I have wronged my very sister,
And my mother's child dishonored.
    "First I went and paid the taxes,
And I also paid the land-dues,
And by chance there came a maiden,
And I sported with the maiden,
And she was my very sister,
And the child of mine own mother.
    "Thereupon to death she cast her,
Plunged herself into destruction,
In the furious foaming cataract,
And amid the raging whirlpool.
But I cannot now determine
Not decide and not imagine
How myself to death should cast me,
I the hapless one, should slay me,
In the mouths of wolves all howling,
In the throats of bears all growling,
In the whale's vast belly perish,
Or between the teeth of lake-pike."
    But his mother made him answer:
"Do not go, my son, my dearest,
To the mouths of wolves all howling,
Nor to throats of bears all growling,
Neither to the whale's vast belly,
Neither to the teeth of lake-pike.
Large enough the Cape of Suomi,
Wide enough are Savo's borders,
For a man to hide from evil,
And a criminal conceal him.
Hide thee there for five years, six years,
There for nine long years conceal thee,
Till a time of peace has reached thee,
And the years have calmed thine anguish."
    Kullervo, Kalervo's offspring,
Answered in the words which follow:
"Nay, I will not go in hiding,
Fly not forth, a wicked outcast,
To the mouth of Death I wander,
To the gate of Kalma's courtyard,
To the place of furious fighting,
To the battle-field of heroes.

Upright still is standing Unto,
And the wicked man unfallen,
Unavenged my father's sufferings,
Unavenged my mother's tear-drops,
Counting not my bitter sufferings,
Wrongs that I myself have suffered."

The Death of Kullervo (Runo XXXVI)

[Argument: Kullervo prepares for war and leaves home joyfully, for no one but his mother is sorry that he is going to his death. He comes to Untamola, lays waste the whole district, and burns the homestead. On returning home he finds his home deserted, and no living thing about the place but an old black dog, with which he goes into the forest to shoot game for food. While traversing the forest he arrives at the place where he met his sister, and ends his remorse by killing himself with his own sword.]

Kullervo, Kalervo's offspring,
With the very bluest stockings,
Now prepared himself for battle,
And prepared himself for warfare.
For an hour his sword he sharpened,
Sharpened spear-points for another.
    Then his mother spoke unto him,
"Do not go, my son unhappy,
Go not to this mighty battle,
Go not where the swords are clashing!
He who goes for nought to battle,
He who willful seeks the combat,
In the fight shall find his death-wound,
And shall perish in the conflict,
By the sword-blades shall he perish,
Thus shall fall, and thus shall perish.
    "If against a goat thou fightest,
And wouldst meet in fight a he-goat,
Then the goat will overcome thee,
In the mud the he-goat cast thee,
That like dog thou home returnest,
Like a frog returnest homeward."
    Kullervo, Kalervo's offspring,
Answered in the words which follow:
"In the swamps I shall not sink me,
Nor upon the heath will stumble,

In the dwelling-place of ravens,
In the fields where crows are croaking.
If I perish in the battle,
Sinking on the field of battle,
Noble 'tis to fill in battle,
Fine 'mid clash of swords to perish,
Exquisite the battle-fever,
Quickly hence a youth it hurries,
Takes him quickly forth from evil,
There he falls no more to hunger."
    Then his mother spoke and answered,
"If you perish in the battle,
Who shall cater for your father,
And shall tend the old man daily?"
    Kullervo, Kalervo's offspring,
Answered in the words that follow:
"Let him perish on the dust-heap,
Leave him in the yard to perish."
    "Who shall cater for your mother,
And shall tend the old dame daily?"
    "Let her die upon a haycock,
In the cowshed let her stifle."
    "Who shall cater for thy brother,
Tend him day by day in future?"
    "Let him perish in the forest,
Let him faint upon the meadow."
    "Who shall cater for thy sister,
Tend her day by day in future? "
    "Let her fall in well, and perish,
Let her fall into the wash-tub."
    Kullervo, Kalervo's offspring,
Just as he his home was leaving,
Spoke these words unto his father:
"Now farewell, O noble father!
Shall you perhaps be weeping sorely,
If you hear that I have perished,
And have vanished from the people,
And have perished in the battle?"
    Then his father gave him answer:
"Not for thee shall I be weeping,
If I hear that you have perished,
For another son I'll rear me,
And a better son will rear me,

And a son by far more clever."
    Kullervo, Kalervo's offspring,
Answered in the words which follow:
"Nor for you shall I be weeping,
If I hear that you have perished.
I will make me such a father,
Mouth of clay, and head of stonework,
Eyes of cranberries from the marshes,
And a beard of withered stubble,
Legs of willow-twigs will make him,
Flesh of rotten trees will make him."
    Then he spoke unto his brother:
"Now farewell, my dearest brother.
Shall you weep for my destruction,
If you hear that I have perished,
And have vanished from the people,
And have fallen in the battle?"
    But his brother gave him answer,
"Not for you shall I be weeping,
If I hear that you have perished.
I will find myself a brother,
Better brother far than thou art,
And a brother twice as handsome."
    Kullervo, Kalervo's offspring,
Answered in the words which follow:
"Nor for you shall I be weeping,
If I hear that you have perished.
I will make me such a brother,
Head of stone, and mouth of sallow,
Eyes of cranberries I will make him,
Make him hair of withered stubble,
Legs of willow-twigs will make him,
Flesh of rotten trees will make him."
    Then he spoke unto his sister,
"Now farewell, my dearest sister.
Shall you weep for my destruction,
If you hear that I have perished,
And have vanished from the people,
And have perished in the battle?"
    But his sister gave him answer:
"Not for you shall I be weeping,
If I hear that you have perished.
I will find myself a brother,

Better brother far than thou art,
And a brother far more clever."
    Kullervo, Kalervo's offspring,
Answered in the words which follow:
"Nor for you shall I be weeping,
If I hear that you have perished.
I will make me such a sister,
Head of stone and mouth of sallow,
Eyes of cranberries I will make her,
Make her hair of withered stubble,
Ears of water-lily make her,
And of maple make her body."
    Then he said unto his mother,
"O my mother, O my dearest,
Thou the fair one who hast borne me,
Thou the golden one who nursed me,
Shalt thou weep for my destruction,
Shouldst thou hear that I have perished,
And have vanished from the people,
And have perished in the battle?"
    Then his mother gave him answer,
And she spoke the words which follow:
"Not thou knowest a mother's feelings,
Nor a mother's heart esteemest.
I shall weep for thy destruction,
If I hear that thou hast perished,
And from out the people vanished,
And have perished in the battle;
Weep until the house is flooded,
Weep until the floor is swimming,
Weep until the paths are hidden,
And with tears the cowsheds weighted,
Weep until the snows are slippery,
Till the ground is bare and slippery,
Lands unfrozen teem with verdure,
And my tears flow through the greenness.
    "If I cannot keep on weeping,
And no strength is left for grieving,
Weeping in the people's presence,
I will weep in bath-room hidden,
Till the seats with tears are flowing,
And the flooring all is flooded."

Kullervo, Kalervo's offspring,
With the very bluest stockings,
Went with music forth to battle,
Joyfully he sought the conflict,
Playing tunes through plains and marshes,
Shouting over all the heathland,
Crashing onwards through the meadows,
Trampling down the fields of stubble.
And a messenger o'ertook him,
In his ear these words he whispered:
"At thy home has died thy father,
And thy aged parent perished.
Now return to gaze upon him,
And arrange for his interment."
Kullervo, Kalervo's offspring,
Made him answer on the instant:
"Is he dead, so let him perish.
In the house there is a gelding,
Which unto the grave can drag him,
And can sink him down to Kalma."
Played he, as he passed the marshes,
And he shouted in the clearings,
And a messenger o'ertook him,
In his ear these words he whispered:
"At thy home has died thy brother,
And thy parent's child has perished.
Now return to gaze upon him,
And arrange for his interment."
Kullervo, Kalervo's offspring,
Made him answer on the instant:
"Is he dead, so let him perish.
In the house there is a stallion,
Which unto the grave can drag him,
And can sink him down to Kalma."
Through the marshes passed he, playing,
Blew his horn amidst the fir-woods,
And a messenger o'ertook him,
In his ear these words he whispered:
"At thy home has died thy sister,
And thy parent's child has perished.
Now return to gaze upon her,
And arrange for her interment."

Kullervo, Kalervo's offspring,
Made him answer on the instant:
"Is she dead, so let her perish.
In the house a mare is waiting,
Which unto the grave can drag her,
And can sink her down to Kalma."
    Through the meadows marched he shouting,
In the grassfields he was shouting,
And a messenger o'ertook him,
In his ear these words he whispered:
"Now has died thy tender mother,
And thy darling mother perished.
Now return to gaze upon her,
And arrange for her interment"
    Kullervo, Kalervo's offspring,
Answered in the words which follow:
"Woe to me, a youth unhappy,
For my mother now has perished,
Wearied as she made the curtains,
And the counterpane embroidered.
With her long spool she was working,
As she turned around her spindle.
I was not at her departure,
Near her when her soul was parting.
Perhaps the cold was great and killed her,
Or perchance was bread too scanty.
    "In the house with care, O wash her,
With the Saxon soap, the finest,
Wind her then in silken wrappings,
Wrap her in the finest linen,
Thus unto the grave convey her,
Sink her gently down to Kalma,
Then upraise the songs of mourning,
Let resound the songs of mourning,
For not yet can I turn homeward,
Untamo is still unfallen,
Yet unfelled the man of evil,
Undestroyed is yet the villain."
    Forth he went to battle, playing,
Went to Untola rejoicing,
And he said the words which follow:
"Ukko, thou, of Gods the highest,
Give me now a sword befitting,

Give me now a sword most splendid,
Which were worth an army to me,
Though a hundred came against me."
    Then the sword he asked was granted,
And a sword of all most splendid,
And he slaughtered all the people,
Untamo's whole tribe he slaughtered,
Burned the houses all to ashes,
And with flame completely burned them,
Leaving nothing but the hearthstones,
Nought but in each yard the rowan.
    Kullervo, Kalervo's offspring,
Then to his own home retired,
To his father's former dwelling,
To the home-fields of his parents.
Empty did he find the homestead,
Desolate the open places;
No one forward came to greet him,
No one came his hand to offer.
    To the hearth he stretched his hand out,
On the hearth the coals were frozen,
And he knew on his arrival,
That his mother was not living.
    To the stove he stretched his hand out,
At the stove the stones were frozen,
And he knew on his arrival,
That his father was not living.
    On the floor his eyes then casting,
All he noticed in confusion,
And he knew on his arrival,
That his sister was not living.
    To the mooring-place he hastened,
But no boats were at their moorings,
And he knew on his arrival,
That his brother was not living.
    Thereupon he broke out weeping,
And he wept one day, a second,
And he spoke the words which follow:
"O my mother, O my dearest,
Hast thou left me nought behind thee,
When thou livedst in this country?
    "But thou hearest not, O mother,
Even though my eyes are sobbing,

387

And my temples are lamenting,
And my head is all complaining."
    In the grave his mother wakened,
And beneath the mould made answer:
"Still there lives the black dog, Musti,
Go with him into the forest,
At thy side let him attend thee,
Take him to the wooded country,
Where the forest rises thickest,
Where reside the forest-maidens,
Where the Blue Maids have their dwelling,
And the birds frequent the pine-trees,
There to seek for their assistance,
And to seek to win their favor."
    Kullervo, Kalervo's offspring,
At his side the black dog taking,
Tracked his path through trees of forest,
Where the forest rose the thickest.
But a short way had he wandered,
But a little way walked onward,
When he reached the stretch of forest,
Recognized the spot before him,
Where he had seduced the maiden,
And his mother's child dishonored.
    There the tender grass was weeping,
And the lovely spot lamenting,
And the young grass was deploring,
And the flowers of heath were grieving,
For the ruin of the maiden,
For the mother's child's destruction.
Neither was the young grass sprouting,
Nor the flowers of heath expanding,
Nor the spot had covered over,
Where the evil thing had happened,
Where he had seduced the maiden,
And his mother's child dishonored.
    Kullervo, Kalervo's offspring,
Grasped the sharpened sword he carried,
Looked upon the sword and turned it,
And he questioned it and asked it,
And he asked the sword's opinion,
If it was disposed to slay him,
To devour his guilty body,

And his evil blood to swallow.
  Understood the sword his meaning,
Understood the hero's question,
And it answered him as follows:
"Wherefore at thy heart's desire
Should I not thy flesh devour,
And drink up thy blood so evil?
I who guiltless flesh have eaten,
Drank the blood of those who sinned not?'
  Kullervo, Kalervo's offspring,
With the very bluest stockings,
On the ground the haft set firmly,
On the heath the hilt pressed tightly,
Turned the point against his bosom,
And upon the point he threw him,
Thus he found the death he sought for,
Cast himself into destruction.
  Even so the young man perished,
Thus died Kullervo the hero,
Thus the hero's life was ended,
Perished thus the hapless hero.
  Then the aged Väinämöinen,
When he heard that he had perished,
And that Kullervo had fallen,
Spoke his mind in words that follow:
"Never, people, in the future,
Rear a child in crooked fashion,
Rocking them in stupid fashion,
Soothing them to sleep like strangers.
Children reared in crooked fashion,
Boys thus rocked in stupid fashion,
Grow not up with understanding,
Nor attain to man's discretion,
Though they live till they are aged,
And in body well-developed."

BIBLIOGRAPHY

Translation Sources

Old English:
"Beowulf" and "The Finnesburg Fragment." Translated by John R. Clark Hall. *Beowulf and The Finnsburg Fragment: A Translation into Modern English Prose.* London: Swan Sonnenschein & Company, 1911.

"The Wanderer" and "The Seafarer." Translated by N. Kershaw [Nora Kershaw Chadwick]. *Anglo-Saxon and Norse Poems.* Cambridge: At the University Press, 1922.

"The Battle of Maldon." Translated by Cosette Faust and Stith Thompson. *Old English Poems Translated into the Original Meter Together with Short Selections from Old English Prose.* Chicago: Scott, Foresman and Company, 1918.

Middle English:
"Sir Gawain and the Green Knight." Translated by Jessie L. Weston. *Sir Gawain and the Green Knight: A Middle-English Arthurian Romance.* London: David Nutt, 1898. Second edition, 1900.

"Pearl." Translated by Charles G. Osgood, Jr. *Pearl: An Anonymous English Poem of the Fourteenth Century.* Princeton: Published by the Translator, 1907.

"The Reeve's Tale," "The Nun's Priest's Tale" and "The Franklin's Tale." Translated by John S. P. Tatlock and Percy MacKaye. *The Complete Poetical Works of Geoffrey Chaucer Now First Put into Modern English.* New York: Macmillan, 1912.

"How Alexander Came to the Trees of the Sun and the Moon." Retold by Robert Steele. *The Story of Alexander*. London: David Nutt, 1894.

Old Norse:
"Prologue" and "Gylfaginning." Translated by Arthur Gilchrist Brodeur. *The Prose Edda* by Snorri Sturluson. New York: The American-Scandinavian Foundation, 1916.

"The Saga of King Heidrek the Wise." Translated by N. Kershaw [Nora Kershaw Chadwick]. *Stories and Ballads of the Far Past*. Cambridge: At the University Press, 1921.

Celtic:
   Welsh: "The Four Branches of the Mabinogion" (I. "Pwyll Prince of Dyved;" II. "Branwen the Daughter of Llyr;" III. "Manawyddan the Son of Llyr;" IV. "Math the Son of Mathonwy."); "Kilhwch and Olwen." Translated by Lady Charlotte Guest. *The Mabinogion: from the Llyfr Coch o Hergest and Other Ancient Welsh Manuscripts*. London: Longman, Brown, Green and Longman; Llandovery: William Rees, 1849. 3 volumes. Second edition, retitled: *The Mabinogion: From the Welsh of the Llyfr Coch o Hergest (The Red Book of Hergest) in the Library of Jesus College, Oxford*. London: Bernard Quaritch, 1877.

   Irish: "The Second Battle of Mag Tured (Moytura)." Translated by Whitley Stokes, *Review Celtique*, v. 12 (1891). Reprinted in *Ancient Irish Tales*, edited by Tom Peete Cross and Clark Harris Slover. New York: Henry Holt, 1936.

Finnish:
"The Story of Kullervo." Translated by W. F. Kirby. *Kalevala, The Land of Heroes*. London: Dent, 1907. 2 vols.

General Bibliography

Anderson, Douglas A., ed. *The Annotated Hobbit: Revised and Expanded Edition*. Boston: Houghton Mifflin, 2002.

——. *Tales Before Tolkien: The Roots of Modern Fantasy.* New York: Ballantine Books, 2003.

Bates, Brian. *The Real Middle-earth: Magic and Mystery in the Dark Ages.* London: Sidgwick & Jackson, 2002.

Carpenter, Humphrey, ed., with the assistance of Christopher Tolkien. *The Letters of J. R. R. Tolkien.* Boston: Houghton Mifflin, 1981.

Carpenter, Humphrey. *Tolkien: A Biography.* Boston: Houghton Mifflin, 1977.

Challis, Erica, ed. *The People's Guide to J. R. R. Tolkien.* Cold Spring Harbor, New York: Cold Spring Press, 2003.

Chance, Jane, ed. *Tolkien the Medievalist.* London and New York: Routledge, 2003.

Chance, Jane. *Tolkien's Art: A Mythology for England: Revised Edition.* Lexington: University Press of Kentucky, 2001.

Gordon, E. V., ed. *Pearl.* Oxford: At the Clarendon Press, 1953.

Hammond, Wayne G., with the assistance of Douglas A. Anderson. *J. R. R. Tolkien: A Descriptive Bibliography.* Winchester: St. Paul's Bibliographies, 1993.

Shippey, Tom. *J. R. R. Tolkien: Author of the Century.* Boston: Houghton Mifflin, 2001.

——. *The Road to Middle-earth: Revised and Expanded Edition.* Boston: Houghton Mifflin, 2003.

Sisam, Kenneth, ed. *Fourteenth Century Verse & Prose.* Oxford: At the Clarendon Press, 1921. Reprint, 1925, including Tolkien's *A Middle English Vocabulary.*

Tolkien, J. R. R. *Ancrene Wisse: The English Text of the Ancrene Riwle.* London: Published for the Early English Text Society by the Oxford University Press, 1962.

——. *Beowulf and the Critics.* Edited by Michael D. C. Drout. Tempe, Arizona: Arizona Center for Medieval and Renaissance Studies, 2002.

——. "Beowulf: The Monsters and the Critics," in *Proceedings of the British Academy*, v. 22. London: Oxford University Press, 1936, pp. 245-295.

——. "Chaucer as a Philologist: *The Reeve's Tale*," in *Transactions of the Philological Society 1934*. London: Published for the Society by David Nutt, 1934, pp. 1-70.

——. "English and Welsh," in *Angles and Britons: O'Donnell Lectures.* Cardiff: University of Wales Press, 1963, pp. 1-41.

——. *Finn and Hengest: The Fragment and the Episode.* Edited by Alan Bliss. London: George Allen & Unwin, 1982.

——. "The History of Middle-earth" series. Edited by Christopher Tolkien:
Volume 1: *The Book of Lost Tales, Part One.* Boston: Houghton Mifflin, 1984.
Volume 2: *The Book of Lost Tales, Part Two.* Boston: Houghton Mifflin, 1984.
Volume 3: *The Lays of Beleriand.* Boston: Houghton Mifflin, 1985.
Volume 4: *The Shaping of Middle-earth.* Boston: Houghton Mifflin, 1986.
Volume 5: *The Lost Road and Other Writings.* Boston: Houghton Mifflin, 1987.
Volume 6: *The Return of the Shadow.* Boston: Houghton Mifflin, 1988.
Volume 7: *The Treason of Isengard.* Boston: Houghton Mifflin, 1989.
Volume 8: *The War of the Ring.* Boston: Houghton Mifflin, 1990.
Volume 9: *Sauron Defeated.* Boston: Houghton Mifflin, 1992.
Volume 10: *Morgoth's Ring.* Boston: Houghton Mifflin, 1993.

Volume 11: *The War of the Jewels*. Boston: Houghton Mifflin, 1994.
Volume 12: *The Peoples of Middle-earth*. Boston: Houghton Mifflin, 1996.

———. "The Homecoming of Beorhtnoth Beorhthelm's Son," in *Essays and Studies 1953*, edited by Geoffrey Bullough. London: John Murray, 1953, pp. 1-18.

———. "The Lay of Aotrou and Itroun," *The Welsh Review*, v. 4 no. 4 (December 1945), pp. 254-266.

———. *The Lord of the Rings*. Boston: Houghton Mifflin, 2002.

———. *A Middle English Vocabulary*. Oxford: At the Clarendon Press, 1922.

———. *The Monsters and the Critics and Other Essays*. Edited by Christopher Tolkien. London: George Allen & Unwin, 1983

———. *The Old English Exodus: Text, Translation, and Commentary*. Edited by Joan Turville-Petre. Oxford: At the Clarendon Press, 1981.

———. "Prefatory Remarks on Prose Translation of *Beowulf*," in *Beowulf and the Finnesburg Fragment*, translated by John R. Clark Hall, revised by C. L. Wrenn. London: George Allen & Unwin, 1940, pp. viii-xli.

———. *The Reeve's Tale: Version Prepared for Recitation at the 'Summer Diversions'*. Oxford: [no publisher], 1939.

———. *The Silmarillion*. Edited by Christopher Tolkien. Boston: Houghton Mifflin, 1977.

———. *Sir Gawain and the Green Knight*. Edited by J. R. R. Tolkien and E. V. Gordon. Oxford: At the Clarendon Press, 1925.

———. *Sir Gawain and the Green Knight, Pearl, and Sir Orfeo*. Edited by Christopher Tolkien. Boston: Houghton Mifflin, 1975.

———. *Sir Orfeo*. Oxford: Academic Copying Office, 1944.

———. *The Tolkien Reader*. New York: Ballantine Books, 1966.

———. *Unfinished Tales*. Edited by Christopher Tolkien. Boston: Houghton Mifflin, 1980.

TheOneRing®.net

FORGED BY AND FOR FANS OF JRR TOLKIEN

Serving Middle-earth Since the First Age

Since its publication, J.R.R. Tolkien's *The Lord of the Rings* has become one of the best-selling books of all time. In 1999 Peter Jackson and New Line Cinema began the momentous task of bringing Tolkien's epic to the big screen.

TheOneRing.net (TORn) was forged by the combined vision of the four founding members to meet the groundswell of interest in the film adaptation of the book. Since May of 1999, TORn has become something scarcely imagined at its inception. With 45 staff members living in 15 countries and readers from over 150 countries, TORn must be thought of as a culmination of worldwide Tolkien fandom.

About TheOneRing.net:

• #1 internet source of up-to-date *Lord of the Rings* news and information.

• Front Page News updated at least three times daily.

• One of the original and most trusted Tolkien movie websites.

• Features more than 10 different sections with over 800 pages.

• Contains extensive information about Tolkien's books and film adaptations.

• Offers up-to-date news and information about the cast and creators of *The Lord of the Rings*.